Huntington Library Publications

Fields

OF

The Atlantic Monthly

LETTERS TO AN EDITOR
1861-1870

---

by James C. Austin

The Huntington Library
SAN MARINO, CALIFORNIA
1953

COPYRIGHT 1953
BY HENRY E. HUNTINGTON LIBRARY & ART GALLERY

* * *

COPYRIGHT 1953
BY JOHN MEAD HOWELLS AND MILDRED HOWELLS, LITERARY EXECUTORS OF WILLIAM DEAN HOWELLS: ALL LETTERS FROM WILLIAM DEAN HOWELLS IN THE JAMES T. FIELDS COLLECTION OF THE HUNTINGTON LIBRARY WHICH ARE HEREIN PUBLISHED FOR THE FIRST TIME.

LIBRARY OF CONGRESS CATALOG CARD NUMBER: 53-12551

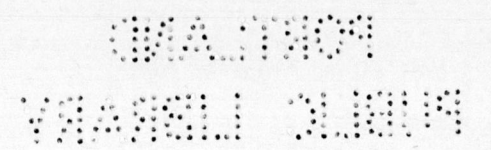

PRINTED BY
ANDERSON, RITCHIE & SIMON : LOS ANGELES
DESIGN BY JOSEPH SIMON

TABLE OF CONTENTS

PREFACE ... vii

Part One: *The Man at the Desk*

FOREWORD TO PART ONE ... 3
I. PUBLISHER-POET ... 7
II. EDITOR-ESSAYIST ... 26

Part Two: *From the Hub*

FOREWORD TO PART TWO ... 43
III. JAMES RUSSELL LOWELL ... 45
IV. OLIVER WENDELL HOLMES ... 70
V. HENRY WADSWORTH LONGFELLOW ... 84
VI. JULIA WARD HOWE ... 99
VII. EDWARD EVERETT HALE ... 115
VIII. JOHN TOWNSEND TROWBRIDGE ... 128
IX. WILLIAM DEAN HOWELLS ... 139
X. THE OTHER BOSTONIANS ... 164

Part Three: *From the Rim*

FOREWORD TO PART THREE ... 183
XI. JOHN GREENLEAF WHITTIER ... 185
XII. NATHANIEL HAWTHORNE ... 208
XIII. THOMAS WENTWORTH HIGGINSON ... 244
XIV. DAVID ATWOOD WASSON ... 249
XV. HARRIET BEECHER STOWE ... 266
XVI. THE TRANSCENDENTALISTS ... 300
XVII. LADIES, MILITANTS, AND DILETTANTES ... 309

Part Four: *From the Hinterland*

FOREWORD TO PART FOUR	325
XVIII. BAYARD TAYLOR	327
XIX. JAMES PARTON	340
XX. NEW YORK TO SAN FRANCISCO	358

Part Five: *From Our Old Home*

FOREWORD TO PART FIVE	375
XXI. CHARLES DICKENS AND CHARLES READE	379
XXII. TENNYSON AND BROWNING, AND SHADES OF KEATS	395
XXIII. ELIZABETH SHEPPARD, HARRIET MARTINEAU, GEORGE ELIOT	406

Part Six: *Away from the Desk*

FOREWORD TO PART SIX	421
XXIV. LATTER DAYS	423
XXV. YESTERDAYS	429
WORKS OF FIELDS	437
INDEX	441

PREFACE

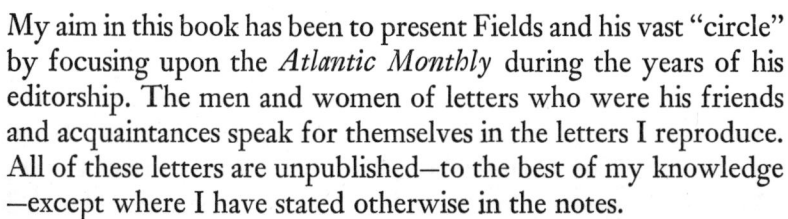

My aim in this book has been to present Fields and his vast "circle" by focusing upon the *Atlantic Monthly* during the years of his editorship. The men and women of letters who were his friends and acquaintances speak for themselves in the letters I reproduce. All of these letters are unpublished—to the best of my knowledge—except where I have stated otherwise in the notes.

I have reproduced in full as many of the letters as I could, so that sometimes there is more in a letter than I care to discuss in the text. But on the other hand the reader may be assured that the whole statement of the letter writer is before him. A small amount of standardization was necessary in transcribing the letters, but I have tried to change them as little as possible. Apostrophes have been added in ordinary possessives and contractions when the writer left them out. Periods have been added after abbreviations and at ends of sentences. Superscript word endings like 18th or recd have been placed on the line, and where desirable a period has been added to show that they are abbreviated forms. Where punctuation or spelling was doubtful because of equivocal handwriting or any other reason, normal usage has been imposed. Spacing has been standardized throughout, but the writer's intentions have been respected wherever they could be determined.

I am indebted in this work to Mr. Mark Antony De Wolfe Howe's excellent and delightful biographies which have not only supplied me with a great deal of information but have served as something of a model of style and good humor. Professor William Charvat's publications on Fields, though brief, have been quite valuable, and his and Professor Tryon's *Cost Books of Ticknor and Fields* has been very useful. In general I have given the complete bibliographical data on each source at its first occurrence in each chapter, but I have used the following sources so often that I have made exceptions of them and have used shortened forms wherever they occur after their initial appearance in the book: *The Cost Books of Ticknor and Fields*, ed. Warren S. Tryon and William Charvat (New York: Bibliographical Society of America, 1949); Annie Adams Fields, *Authors and Friends* (Boston: Houghton, Mifflin and Company, 1897); Annie Adams Fields, *James T. Fields, Biographical Notes and Personal Sketches* (Boston: Houghton, Mifflin and Company, 1881); James T. Fields, *Yesterdays with Authors* (Boston: J. R. Osgood and Company, 1872); Mark Antony De Wolfe Howe, *Memories of a Hostess* (Boston: The Atlantic Monthly Press, 1922); Frank Luther Mott, *A History of American Magazines* (Cambridge: Harvard University Press, 1938); Horace Elisha Scudder, *James Russell Lowell: A Biography* (Boston: Houghton, Mifflin and Company, 1901).

Most of the Fields letters are in the Huntington Library, the Library of Harvard University, the Longfellow House, and the private collection of Mrs. Z. B. Adams, the widow of Annie Fields's nephew. By far the largest number is in the Huntington Library, which has catalogued some five thousand letters from and to Fields, and has also a great deal of uncatalogued material, including Fields's letters to Annie, his lecture notes and manuscripts, and miscellaneous notes. I am truly grateful for the kindnesses I received from the Huntington staff, but especially to Mr. Herbert C. Schulz, Curator of Manuscripts, and to Miss Phyllis Rigney, who went to a great deal of trouble to prepare for microfilming the vast number of manuscripts I wished to use. In the following pages all of the letters that are not marked otherwise are from the Fields manuscripts collection in the Huntington Library.

At the Longfellow House, which contains nearly all of Fields's numerous letters to Longfellow and copies of Longfellow's to Fields, I received the generous assistance of the late Professor Henry Wadsworth Longfellow Dana and of Mr. Henry De Valcourt, the succeeding Librarian. Miss Caroline Jakeman of the Houghton Library at Harvard kindly gave me a list of Harvard's Fields material, which consists of two volumes of letters to Fields from various well-known writers, copies of Hawthorne's letters

Preface

to Fields, and some miscellaneous material; and I am indebted to her and to Dr. William A. Jackson, Librarian of the Houghton Library, for the use of material in the Harvard libraries. To Mrs. Z. B. Adams of Boston and her daughter Mrs. B. P. Bole of Cleveland, Ohio, I am grateful for the use of a five-volume edition of Fields's *Yesterdays with Authors* containing a collection of manuscript letters to Fields and his wife that have been almost wholly overlooked heretofore.

I also wish to acknowledge the services of the following libraries and their staffs, who without exception gave me assistance beyond what was required of them:

>American Antiquarian Society
>Dartmouth College Library
>The Davis Library of Phillips Exeter Academy
>Henry W. and Albert A. Berg Collection of
>   The New York Public Library
>The Historical Society of Pennsylvania
>The Library of Congress
>Library of The Essex Institute
>Massachusetts Historical Society
>Portsmouth (New Hampshire) Public Library
>The Public Library of the City of Boston

Each of these libraries has some Fields material, especially the Berg Collection of New York, which contains several manuscript letters to Fields from various correspondents; the Essex Institute of Salem, which has many of Whittier's original letters to Fields in its Oak Knoll Collection; and the Massachusetts Historical Society, which holds Annie Fields's diary and letters to her relatives.

My work was greatly facilitated by the aid of Miss Marcia Kanevsky and Mr. Kenneth Kostiha, who helped read proof, by the supplementary researches of some of my students, by the assistance of the Ohio University Fund, and by the cooperation of the librarians at Western Reserve University, Waynesburg College, Ohio Wesleyan University, Ohio University, Washington and Jefferson College, and the Cleveland Public Library. And I am grateful for the assistance of my parents and my wife's parents while the work was in progress.

I cannot imagine a better counsellor than Professor Lyon N. Richardson of Western Reserve University, who criticized patiently and meticulously my all-too-rough draft and my later copy. He was always there with encouragement (and also with healthy sarcasm) when I really needed it. His aid extended far beyond the immediate ends of this book.

And most of all, thanks are due to my wife, who has a major share in this work. She not only discussed the material with me most perceptively, but examined and abstracted thousands of manuscript letters, went through dozens of volumes of magazines to find references to Fields or the *Atlantic* or the *Atlantic* contributors, copied letters from microfilm, aided in proofreading, and typed the final copy.

For permission to publish the otherwise unpublished manuscripts in their possession, I am indebted to the libraries and collectors already mentioned. The following individuals also most kindly gave me their consent to publish the previously unpublished material in this book: Mr. Julian Burroughs; Mrs. Robert A. Burns; Miss Sibyl Eyre Crowe; Mr. George W. Curtis; Mr. Ralph Morton Diaz; Mr. Henry C. Dickens; Mrs. Samuel A. Eliot; Messrs. Fisher, Dowson, and Wasbrough and the Trustees of the Will of Hallam Lord Tennyson; Mrs. Vinton Freedley; Mr. Conrad G. Goddard; Mr. Francis C. Gray; Mr. Edward E. Hale; Mr. Manning Hawthorne; Mr. Clarence L. Hay; Miss Mildred Howells; Mr. William S. Jackson; Mr. Walter N. Landor; Mrs. S. W. Macdonough; Sir John Murray; Mr. James Parton; Mr. Greenleaf W. Pickard; Mr. Frederic Wolsey Pratt; Mr. John Richards; Miss Rosalind Richards; Mr. Lyman Beecher Stowe; Mrs. Eleanor Talbot: Mr. Arthur T. Trowbridge. To Professors Robert E. Butler and Donald R. Tuttle, I am grateful for permission to quote from their unpublished dissertations on Howells and Aldrich respectively. Thanks are due also to the Duke University Press and Professor Milton E. Flower for permission to quote from Flower's *James Parton, the Father of Modern Biography*; to Mr. Joseph F.

Preface

Henry, to quote from the *Letters and Journals of Thomas Wentworth Higginson*; to the Houghton Mifflin Company, to quote from Horace E. Scudder's *James Russell Lowell: A Biography* and John T. Trowbridge's *My Own Story*; to Mr. M. A. De Wolfe Howe, to quote from his *Memories of a Hostess* and *New Letters of James Russell Lowell*; to the J. B. Lippincott Company, to quote from Forrest Wilson's *Crusader in Crinoline*; and to the *New England Quarterly*, to quote from my article therein. I have been delighted and greatly aided by the correspondence I have received from descendants, heirs, collectors, and scholars of the authors I have studied.

Finally I wish to acknowledge the assistance of the Publications Committee of the Huntington Library, who made the publication of this book possible.

JAMES C. AUSTIN

Athens, Ohio
July, 1953

PART ONE

THE MAN AT THE DESK

FOREWORD TO PART ONE

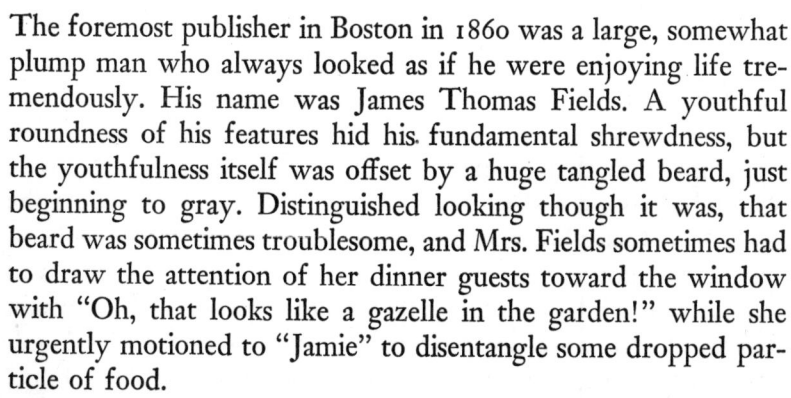

The foremost publisher in Boston in 1860 was a large, somewhat plump man who always looked as if he were enjoying life tremendously. His name was James Thomas Fields. A youthful roundness of his features hid his fundamental shrewdness, but the youthfulness itself was offset by a huge tangled beard, just beginning to gray. Distinguished looking though it was, that beard was sometimes troublesome, and Mrs. Fields sometimes had to draw the attention of her dinner guests toward the window with "Oh, that looks like a gazelle in the garden!" while she urgently motioned to "Jamie" to disentangle some dropped particle of food.

Fields's reputation for geniality was due partly to his wife's charm and competence as a hostess, but also to the jovial sparkle in his eyes and his deferential manner in conversation. His talk seemed a "triumph of meekness and animal spirits without noise or abruptness,—full of enjoyment, and perfectly unconscious."[1] Though ready with puns and anecdotes when the occasion prompted, he was not a witty speaker like Holmes or Lowell, but he was easier to talk to. In fact he was a better listener than speaker, and his conversation was designed to make his interlocutor pleased with himself. His manner derived from a former shyness, and was rather deliberately cultivated.

He was known as one who could say "no" most gently,[2] and his diplomacy with writers was almost unmatched. Even Gail Hamilton, whose quarrel with Fields was notorious, had to confess that she feared to meet her publisher face to face because his persuasiveness invariably overcame her arguments. She appreci-

---

[1] Mary Russell Mitford to an anonymous correspondent about 1852, in James T. Fields, "Mary Russell Mitford," *Some Noted Princes, Authors, and Statesmen of Our Time*, ed. James Parton (New York, 1885), pp. 144-45.

[2] Fitz-Greene Halleck to Fields, April 22, 1867.

ated his charm but was suspiciously aware of his shrewdness: "I had been familiar for several years with Mr. [Fields's] gifts and graces, and know that, though they were charming for social intercourse, they were not easily reducible to two and a half, still less to three and one-third per cent."[3]

Fields's house on Charles Street in Boston was the scene of many a meeting with distinguished men of letters. Originally number 37, it was changed in 1866 to 148; the site today is occupied by a garage. It was one of a row of two- and three-story brick buildings with their backs toward the Charles River. Nearby, at number 164, was the home of Oliver Wendell Holmes. At the rear of the Fields house was a pleasant garden which yet remains. Inside, the house was crammed with portraits, paintings, and *objets d'art,* and one of the best collections of rare books in Boston. There were books from the libraries of Charles Lamb and Leigh Hunt; rare editions and manuscripts of Milton, Pope, Gray; and dozens of autographed copies of contemporary works. The Fieldses were justly proud of their not unread library.

Fields's contemporary fame was great. The friend and publisher of Dickens, De Quincey, Tennyson, and Thackeray, of Hawthorne, Longfellow, Lowell, Holmes, and Stowe, he was considered almost as one of them. William Dean Howells described the Fields of the sixties from the point of view of the rising young author:

I stood as much in awe of him as his jovial soul would let me; and if I might I should like to suggest to the literary youth of this day some notion of the importance of his name to the literary youth of my day. He gave aesthetic character to the house of Ticknor & Fields, but he was by no means a silent partner on the economic side. No one can forecast the fortune of a new book, but he knew as well as any publisher can know not only whether a book was good, but whether the reader would think so; and I suppose that his house made as few bad guesses, along with their good ones, as any house that ever tried the uncertain temper of the public with its ventures. In the minds of all who loved the plain brown cloth and tasteful print of its issues

---

[3]Mary Abigail Dodge (pseud. Gail Hamilton), *A Battle of the Books* (New York, 1870), p. 68.

Foreword to Part One

he was more or less intimately associated with their literature; and those who were not mistaken in thinking De Quincey one of the delightfulest authors in the world, were especially grateful to the man who first edited his writings in book form, and proud that this edition was the effect of American sympathy with them. At that day, I believed authorship the noblest calling in the world, and I should still be at a loss to name any nobler. The great authors I had met were to me the sum of greatness, and if I could not rank their publisher with them by virtue of equal achievement, I handsomely brevetted him worthy of their friendship, and honored him in the visible measure of it.[4]

[4]William Dean Howells, *Literary Friends and Acquaintance* (New York, 1901), pp. 40-41.

Chapter I:
Publisher-Poet

JAMES T. FIELDS was born December 31, probably in 1817,[1] in Portsmouth, New Hampshire. It is said that the family name was Field, but he "added the other letter because he liked to curl the s, and later he couldn't change back."[2] He was the son of Michael Field, who married Margaret Beck on March 6, 1816.[3] Michael was the captain of the brig *Siren*, transporting merchandise to and from Europe and along the American coast. His last voyage according to the Portsmouth newspaper began on December 20, 1819, when he sailed for Baltimore. He was lost at sea when James was three or four years old. The family that remained consisted of James, his brother George A. Fields, who became a bookbinder in Boston, and his mother, who died in 1848 and was buried in Cambridge, Massachusetts.

James's strict Unitarian up-bringing had its effects on his later life: he was always honest, tolerant, and very "moral," though

---

[1] Fields's birth date is not at all certain. His wife, Annie Adams Fields, in *James T. Fields, Biographical Notes and Personal Sketches* (Boston, 1881), recorded it as December 31, 1816, but her book is frequently unreliable. The reliable Mark Antony De Wolfe Howe concurred in "James Thomas Fields," *Early Years of the Saturday Club*, ed. Edward Emerson (Boston, 1918), pp. 376-87, but his information probably came directly from Mrs. Fields, his personal friend. The best evidence, however, favors the 1817 date, which is the one reported by Claude M. Fuess in the *Dictionary of American Biography*. Genealogical notes in the Portsmouth Public Library give this date, and *The New England Historic and Genealogical Register* records his death in April 1881 "aged 63 years." The birth is not registered in the Portsmouth public records.

[2] J. W. Field (of no recognized relationship) to Dr. Thwing, February 14, 1922, in the Thwing Collection, Western Reserve University Library.

[3] The Records of the South Parish, Portsmouth, in which the marriage is recorded, list Michael's surname as Fields, but the Portsmouth newspaper consistently calls him Field. For all my information from Portsmouth, I am indebted to Miss Dorothy M. Vaughan, Librarian, Portsmouth Public Library.

an individualist. While he had the ordinary boy's interest in games and sports, he early showed a more-than-ordinary desire for learning, for he pursued his taste for literature beyond the requirements of his teachers. One of his letters written in 1872 records his lasting appreciation of a friend "whose 'Virgil' I borrowed when a lad at the High School."[4] As early as the thirties Fields was known among his friends for his library of two or three hundred volumes, which grew to impressive proportions—in terms of first editions, autographed and annotated copies, rare books, and manuscripts—before he died. But in his youth the family finances were not such that he could continue his schooling beyond his graduation from the Portsmouth High School in 1831 or buy many books in Portsmouth. This explains the exaggerated respect which he—like many another self-made man—had for culture and cultured people. His attitude is particularly noticeable in his early high-flown attempts at verse.

In 1831, when he was only thirteen (or fourteen), Fields was sent to Boston to take a job as clerk—and probably errand boy—for Carter and Hendee, owners of the "Old Corner Bookstore." He took an immediate liking to the work and rapidly built up a remarkable knowledge of books and bookselling. In 1832 the Old Corner Bookstore became the property of Allen and Ticknor, and Fields began his long and successful relationship with William D. Ticknor, who in 1834 became sole owner of the firm, upon Allen's withdrawal.

Meanwhile Fields did not neglect his future. In 1837 he became a member of the Boston Mercantile Library Association, a club devoted to the encouragement of literary pursuits among businessmen. He made many useful friends in the Association, most important of them being Edwin Percy Whipple, the critic. Whipple, two years his junior, has recorded Fields's youthful shyness among strangers, which contrasts exceedingly with his widely acknowledged exuberance among his friends.[5] The thirties were formative

---

[4]Fields to Mr. Hackett, July 15, 1872.
[5]Edwin Percy Whipple, "Recollections of James T. Fields," *Atlantic Monthly*, XLVIII (August 1881), 254.

8

years for Fields, and he developed his literary understanding among such men as Whipple, of whom Poe—always a delicious antidote to New England complacence—said: "He has been infected with that unmeaning and transparent heresy—the cant of critical Boswellism—by dint of which we are to shut our eyes tightly to all autorial blemishes, and open them, like owls, to all autorial merits."[6] Poe's comment would apply equally well to much of Fields's critical writing, though as an editor and publisher he was eminently capable of sifting the good from the bad.

On September 13, 1838, Fields was given the honor of composing and delivering the Mercantile Library Association's *Anniversary Poem*, which was accorded such appreciation that the Association requested that it be put in print. It was privately printed by William D. Ticknor in 1838. It reveals a good deal of its author, not only as a writer but as a man. In highly stilted heroic couplets, the poem presumes to glorify the American businessman. It is full of bombast, chauvinism, and sentimentality, and recommends that the merchant live for more than the mere "hope of gain and wealth beyond the seas."

By the time he was twenty-three, Fields was already acquiring a reputation as a writer and a man of influence in the book business. He was well enough known that his friend Rufus Griswold asked him to contribute and to help secure other contributors to his *New Yorker* magazine.[7] Later he was not only represented by three poems in Griswold's *Poets and Poetry of America* (1842), but he was consulted by the editor in preparing the volume. He was famous enough to gain a public hearing of his reading of a poem at the Boston Lyceum in 1841.[8] He began—though at a respectful distance—a lifelong correspondence with Longfellow.[9]

---

[6] Edgar Allan Poe, *The Literati*.

[7] R. W. Griswold to Fields, April 26?, 1840?. See the further correspondence with Griswold in the Huntington Library and the Public Library of the City of Boston (hereafter referred to as Boston Public Library).

[8] Fields to Griswold, September 15, 1841, MS in Boston Public Library.

[9] Fields to Longfellow, January 1, 1840, MS in the Longfellow House, Cambridge, Mass.

And he became in 1843 a junior partner of the publishing firm, which changed its name from William D. Ticknor to William D. Ticknor and Company.

He published his first collected *Poems* in March 1849. In spite of his reputation among bookmen, the book was printed in the relatively small lot of a thousand copies, and sales did not warrant a second edition. In contrast, Longfellow's *Kavanagh* was published two months later in a first edition of five thousand copies, four thousand of which were sold the first week; but Longfellow was the firm's top seller, far outranking all others, and Fields's edition of one thousand was not bad for a beginner.[10] The book contained "Commerce," an abridged version of the 1838 *Anniversary Poem*, and another poem which Fields had read before the Mercantile Library Association in 1848, "The Post of Honor." Besides these two long poems there were twenty-seven short ones. Fields was not a prolific writer; in view of his feverish business activity, it is remarkable he turned out as much as he did. His thoroughly conventional verses were appreciated by his friends; it flattered his ego to be able to tell Griswold that Whittier, Longfellow, and Holmes had praised "The Ballad of the Tempest" and "The Antlers," two of the poems in the collection.[11]

His second volume of *Poems* was printed in 1854 in a small private edition of five hundred copies, most of which were presented to friends.[12] It is rather amusing to notice Fields's economy in compiling the volume. Twenty-five of the fifty-two short poems are identical, or nearly so, with ones in the 1849 volume. Of the remaining twenty-seven several are short excerpts, dressed up with new titles, from "Commerce" and "The Post of Honor." The new verses are relatively few and not very different from the earlier ones—a little neater, a little more generalized and noncommittal, and not so pretentious. By this time Fields realized that the place for his poetry was in small gift volumes.

[10]Warren S. Tryon and William Charvat (eds.), *The Cost Books of Ticknor and Fields* (New York, 1949), pp. 136-38.

[11]Fields to Griswold, February 28, 1849, MS in Boston Public Library.

[12]Tryon and Charvat, pp. 274-75.

Fields was more outstanding as an editor. In addition to his aid to Rufus Griswold in the editing of *Poets and Poetry of America*, he contributed similar counsel to Griswold's *Prose Writers of America* (1846) and *Female Poets of America* (1848). *The Boston Book* (1849 but dated 1850), one of a series of anthologies containing writings by Bostonians, was Fields's own production. He collected and edited the first complete works of De Quincey (beginning in 1850), a tremendous task because of the writer's characteristic whimsicality and disorder. And in 1861 he edited *Favorite Authors*, a popular collection of prose and poetry that ran through several editions.

It was not surprising that S. Austin Allibone should solicit Fields's help in compiling his valuable *Dictionary of English Literature and British and American Authors*. The correspondence probably began in 1855:

Phila. August 30. 1855

Dear Sir:

I had the pleasure this morning of receiving through Mr. Owen a copy of some of your poems, for which please accept my thanks. May I add a notice of this volume to the article under your name?

Allow me, dear sir, to express my gratification at the interest you take in my arduous undertaking. The approbation and friendly co-operation of those who can appreciate labours of this character is truly encouraging.

I am, dear sir, your obliged & obedient,   S. Austin Allibone

In 1856 Allibone asked Fields to suggest additions to the dictionary:

Phila. March 10. 1856

My dear Mr. Fields:

I am this morning in receipt of kind favour of 7th inst. for which you have my warm Ack'ts. You are the very man to strengthen a weary traveller:—sometimes weary, but full of nerve, if he may say so of himself. We are stereotyping *Gibbon, Edward*: so that any name beyond that—if sent within a day or two—can be inserted in my MS.; and I shall be indebted to you for any additions.

I am, in great haste, and with equal regard, very truly yours.

S. Austin Allibone

Did you see my life of Edward Everett, pub. in one of our papers?

Fields was prompt to compliment Allibone upon the completion of Volume I in 1858:

Boston. Dec. 22d

My dear Allibone. All Hail! Welcome! I have as "great a pleasure" in accepting it. It looks grand and glorious. What a superb article on Byron—the only one I have had the time to read—and how finely Everett and Ticknor talk in your pages! More anon. Best wishes— Ever Yours—& your wife's—

J. T. Fields.

Fields was also becoming known as a lecturer. So far as his letters reveal, his first series of lectures was delivered as early as the winter of 1850-51. His correspondence with Richard Storrs Willis, brother of N. P. Willis, not only mentions this event but relates an instance of Fields's aid to young writers. Willis wrote, November 7, 1850:

So you lecture this winter? You ought of course to keep your hand in with the rhymes, your proportion of the great lectures generally taking that form. I have had, meself, invitations [to lecture] from Troy and various places.... I mention this subject because you rather brought me out as a lecturer you know, and most vastly assumed the responsibility of this part of my career.

Fields delivered several lectures during the fifties, although he had little time for a prepared series. In 1853 he read a poem of his own, "Eloquence," before the Phi Beta Kappa Society at Harvard. On February 9, 1854, he delivered a lecture in Brooklyn, and on July 26 he read a poem at Dartmouth College.[13]

By 1845 Fields was sufficiently established to consider marriage with Mary Willard, of Boston. He was a man ill fated in love during this period, however; Mary died of consumption while they were still engaged. Later the same disease killed her sister Eliza, whom Fields courted and married in 1850, only to lose her the next year. Her death was one of the saddest experiences in Fields's life. Letters of sympathy arrived from many sides. One from R. C. Winthrop, candidate for Governor of Massachusetts,

---

[13]Fields to Griswold, January 30, 1854, and July 21, 1854, MSS in Boston Public Library.

reads in part: "I tell you how much you were missed yesterday, and how sincerely your brethren of the P[hi] B[eta] K[appa] Society sympathized with you in your affliction."[14] Another from the writer "Grace Greenwood" contains some description of Eliza:

New Brighton July 25 1851

My dear friend—
  When most I would, I hardly dare approach you—restrained, thrown back as I feel myself by that awe which the presence of a great grief ever imposes.—I never so miserably feel how unskilled am I in the pharmacy of sorrow as when I would apply some healing balsam of sympathy and consolation to "hurt minds"—I never so feel this insufficiency of language as when I would stanch with words the bleeding of a wounded heart.—I never seem so far away from my most familiar friends, from those for whom I have the truest affection as when they stand in the dread isolation—rayed about by the holiness of sorrow.
  We are all too like those friends of Jesus, who in his hour of extremest agony "stood gazing from afar off." I will no longer draw back from the fear that word of mine will come discordantly through your sad silence—that any hand when laid lightest, will fall harshly on the heart-strings yet vibrating from the touch of the angel of death—I will come to you thus, and say that I give you my most sorrowful sympathy in this your great affliction—that many are the thoughts I give to you and to *her*, called so suddenly away from all the happiness and hopes of her young life—Yet is it not well for her to know only the brightness and the sweetness of the morning—being spared the noon-tide weariness and the chill and shadow of the night? Taking such rich unwasted affections with her, as she goes to possess the loves of heaven—what a double inheritance!—If you are of any spiritual philosophy, you will not think your Eliza *dead*—not even beyond the circle of your arms, but only *unseen*—and your utmost grief will be not that her quiet sympathy, her love are lost to you, but that you will "see *her face no more*." I believe that for you, man could as well tread out her memory under the grave-sod, as Heaven itself bury under its divinest joys the tender memory of her mortal love.
  Since she has gone, my dear friend, I have felt much regret that I did not know her better. It was seldom that I had the happiness of seeing her, and then for only a few moments at a time. I *felt* rather than knew her to be a gentle and amiable being—a sweet household

[14]R. C. Winthrop to Fields, July 18, 1851.

spirit—not striking and captivating at first, by a brilliant manner, but quietly winning on one's regard by her soft and most unassuming ways—not demonstrative of affection, but bearing about with her an atmosphere of love like a light perfume of home-flowers.

It was thus she impressed me by her half-timid, half-dignified manner—by the expression of her face, by all she said, and by her silence as well.

I hope that your health has not entirely given way under the oppression of anxiety and grief. May God who has seen fit so heavily to afflict you—strengthen and bless you.
Ever truly your friend
Sara J. Clarke

Probably Fields's bereavements were one reason for the large amount of "graveyard poetry" he wrote, although his verses are impersonal and in a strain that was far from unusual at the time. Recurring themes in his early poems are the deaths of children or maidens, visits to the graves of loved ones, and elegies on lost friends.

At the age of thirty-seven Fields was married a second time, to Annie Adams, a cousin of Mary and Eliza Willard. He described her to his English friend, Mary Russell Mitford, on October 27, 1854, shortly before the marriage:

My Very Dear Friend.—Have you room in your heart for one more American? I began a note to you some days ago and had proceeded but a few lines on my way to Swallowfield when it occurred to me to wait till a little affair then on the tapis had been consummated so that I might communicate the news. It is now all settled and I am happy. Let us shake hands across the Atlantic and you will please to congratulate me that after an engagement of a few weeks I am, on the 7th or 10th of next month to go to church with one of the best Yankee girls of my acquaintance. Indeed she is the best in any body's acquaintance. Just the girl you wd. choose for me. She has never written books altho' she is capable of doing that some; never held an argument on Woman's Rights or Wrongs in her whole life, and so full of goodness of heart and beauty that you would say at once "that is the maid of all others for my friend Fields." Her name is Annie Adams, and I have known her from her childhood and have held her on my knee many and many a time. Her father (and this must recommend her to your favor) is one of our leading Physicians & a great admirer of Miss Mitford, as well as his daughter. In short

Annie is a girl after your own heart and she told me to give her love to you and ask you to love her, and so I have promised both her requests shall be granted.

Only twenty at the time of her marriage, Annie came to be almost as prominent as her husband. A writer of many books in her own right—for example, *Under the Olive* (1880), *James T. Fields: Biographical Notes and Personal Sketches* (1881), *Authors and Friends* (1893), *A Shelf of Old Books* (1894), and biographies of Harriet Beecher Stowe and Nathaniel Hawthorne—she was also the central figure in M. A. De Wolfe Howe's *Memories of a Hostess* (1922). She belonged to an established Boston family—President John Adams was one of her ancestors—and her social poise counterbalanced Fields's slight shyness. Under her influence the Fields home on Charles Street became the most delightful gathering place for literary people in Boston. "I shall not feel that I have seen Boston until I have seen you!" wrote Anne Douglas Sedgwick to Annie,[15] and her attitude was not unusual. Annie's conscientious womanliness made her many warm friends, such as Harriet Beecher Stowe, Celia Thaxter, Sarah Orne Jewett, among the women, while her youth and beauty as well as her adulation appealed to the men. A jocular letter from Walter Savage Landor, received while the Fieldses were in Europe, illustrates the male attitude. Landor was eighty-five when he wrote:

My dear Madame,
    Your letter very much flatters and delights me. We men, you know, always are delighted when they are flattered by the ladies. Some even are pleased with it from men. My ribs are not to be tickled from that quarter. Do not forget your promise to visit me again at Florence, but be sure to bring your husband with you for I would not on any account make him jealous. I wish I could persuade myself that I shall not be so. I *have* been, heretofore, and my ears have been pulled for it. After confession the penitent folds his arms, which I will do the moment I have said how proud I am to have the privilege of calling myself your obliged and obedient,   W. S. Landor
Feb. 26. Florence, Via Nunciatina 2671[16]

---

[15]Anne Douglas Sedgwick to Annie Fields, no date, MS in Harvard University Library.   [16]MS in Harvard University Library.

William D. Ticknor and Company began its rise to greatness in the forties. The publication of Longfellow's *Evangeline* in 1847 upon terms very generous to the author[17] marked the commencement of the firm's relations not only with Longfellow but with other great New England writers. In 1849 Whittier and Lowell and in 1850 Hawthorne followed Longfellow's lead. Holmes had published medical works with Ticknor as early as 1842, and in 1848 he arranged to have the firm issue a volume of his poems. These writers, like most of the others, thereafter remained faithful to the firm, at least as long as Fields was in it. His policies of unpretentious friendliness and generosity as well as fairness to authors were calculated to keep them with him. By the middle fifties the firm's reputation was such that writers might even take lower royalties in order to secure the prestige of the famous imprint on the title page.

In 1849 the firm became Ticknor, Reed and Fields, but there was no change in the organization. Reed had come into the company as a junior partner along with Fields, and he evidently had merely a financial interest. Ticknor, because of his original investment, was still the senior partner. He was also Fields's senior in years. It is perhaps too easy to underrate Ticknor's importance in the combination. His part was less spectacular but no less indispensable than Fields's. It was his investment and his unfailing financial wisdom that kept the firm steady.

The famous title of Ticknor and Fields became official on June 6, 1854, upon Reed's withdrawal from the company. The partners contributed equally in buying out Reed, but Ticknor continued as senior partner until his death in 1864.[18]

During the forties and fifties the book-publishing business in America underwent a considerable revolution, partly through the efforts of Fields himself. In his position as junior partner he was "responsible for the literary and social contacts of the firm"—which meant public relations, advertising, and promotion.[19] One

[17] Tryon and Charvat, p. 111.   [18] Ibid., pp. xvii-xxi.
[19] Most of the material in this and the following paragraph is from William Charvat, "James T. Fields and the Beginnings of Book Promotion, 1840-1855," *Huntington Library Quarterly*, VIII (November, 1944), 75-94.

reason for his success was his acquaintanceship with reviewers and critics like Whipple, Griswold, Park Benjamin, and H. T. Tuckerman. Because of the book-promoting methods of the time, such acquaintanceships were of the first importance.

Book reviewing in the mid-nineteenth century actually amounted to large-scale advertising; the press reception of a book often resulted from its backers' influence and had little connection with the quality of the book or the public approval accorded it. Book publishers bought a good deal of advertising in newspapers, and the size of the publishers' accounts influenced the quantity and quality of reviews. The publishers in the fifties used several techniques to control reviews: the distribution of complimentary copies as bribes to reviewers and editors, the preparation of notices by the publisher, which were sent along with editorial copies to save editors "the trouble" of writing their own reviews, and the employment of paid publicity men who wrote reviews and influenced other reviewers. Besides these methods, which he fully exploited, Fields developed some of his own. He advanced his firm's book sales to an unprecedented degree in the South and West by making influential friends among editors, reviewers, and booksellers in those sections. In addition he won the friendship of young men who later became famous as critics: G. W. Curtis, Henry Alden, Thomas Bailey Aldrich, and William Dean Howells were conspicuous examples. Such tactics as Fields employed were generally accepted among the initiated, and he was only more successful than the others because of his geniality and tact. It was his promoting talents that enabled the firm to sell on a national scale and hence to make Boston the chief center for the publication of literary works in the United States. Harpers in New York and Carey-Lea-Blanchard in Philadelphia were in the early days the only publishers who could challenge the position of Ticknor and Fields on a more than local scale. It is hardly possible to exaggerate Fields's importance in creating an economic foundation for New England literary development.

He was almost as successful in his relations with England. Literary piracy was notoriously prevalent because of the lack of an international copyright law, but Fields was one of the first to pay English writers for permission to print their works in America simultaneously with the English publication. Although writers did not receive an amount comparable to what they get under present-day copyright laws, they were grateful for anything at all. Among his English clients were such men as Thackeray, De Quincey, Arnold, Browning, and Tennyson. Fields also arranged with English publishers to print the books of his American writers at the same time that these books appeared in America or shortly before. Longfellow and Hawthorne, to mention only two among many, received through Fields's bargaining what they considered generous allowances from English publishers for the rights of simultaneous publication of some of their works.

Fields forwarded his business in England as he did in America by personal contacts with writers and publishers. On his first trip abroad in 1847 he was little more than a likable autograph-hunter, but he made important acquaintances. His reverence for England and English writers was almost unbounded. Hawthorne once suspected him of feeling as Hawthorne himself felt, "that America is a country to boast of, and to get out of."[20] At any rate he was willing to confess to Hawthorne after a tour of the continent, "Here we are once more in old England (how much better as a place to arrive in than any other on the world's stranger soil) and we feel at home once more."[21]

Fields described his early pilgrimage to Griswold:

Steamer Britannica. off Halifax. Friday. Sept. 11, 1847
Dear Rufus.

I promised to write you from Europe but my rapid flight gave me no leisure for correspondence. What I have seen we will talk over some fine day at Jones' or elsewhere, but at present "I cannot enlarge," as the alderman said to the Mayor. I have visited many spots of great historical & literary interest,—shrines to which my feet made no unwilling pilgrimages I assure you. I have sailed on the Rhine from Cologne to Mayence; stood at the tombs of great warriors from Richard Coeur de Leon to Napoleon; walked over Waterloo and

[20]Hawthorne to Fields, February 3, 1859.
[21]Fields to Hawthorne, April 25, 1860.

Runnymede; loitered à Pere la Chaise; mused at Abbotsford & Newstead; talked at Rydal with Wordsworth; at Our Village with Miss Mitford; in his sanctum with Christopher North, who by the way mentioned your Poets of America as a Book on his shelves & one which he loved to read;—You will see by these enumerations from my catalogue that I was not idle during my sojourn in distant lands. I have escaped by the good blessing of God a death at sea; the account of our disaster you will read in the papers. It was a slight thread to hang a ship's company's lives upon, but the time had not come for us to make our departure from the lower world. It is a terrible experience, that of seeing two hundred souls fearfully looking out upon a rocky shore uncertain of the issue.

   I write this hasty line that you may see I have not forgotten you. We shall no doubt meet before long either in Phila. or Boston when we will talk these things over. I come home with every wish gratified as far as relates to those countries I have visited, and with a firm conviction that where our lives are cast there blessings most abound. America is the world's picked garden & I thank Heaven I am one of her sons & your old friend, always most truly,

James T. Fields[22]

Shipwreck was not the greatest of Fields's worries. He had a tendency to seasickness, which he thought he inherited from his mother[23] and which hounded him on all his many ocean voyages. Sometimes the illness would last for days after he had landed. Once in 1854 it forced him to give up a trip after he had already begun it, and turn back when the ship reached Nova Scotia. There is no doubt but that he would have gone more frequently to England, especially during his later years, had it not been for the certainty of an unpleasant passage.

   In 1851, after the death of Eliza, Fields made his second trip to Europe. In doing so he had a chance to refresh his acquaintance with the elderly Miss Mitford, who, despite the fact that they saw each other only during Fields's two brief sojourns in England, was one of the publisher's dearest friends. Because of her ill health she did not expect to see him a third time, and their parting was painful. She wrote:

[22]MS in Boston Public Library.
[23]Fields to Alexander Ireland, May 11, 1871.

Perhaps you are right dearest Mr. Fields—a formal parting would be only a great sorrow. For my own part I do not think that I would have loved a son better than I do you—& I believe, that, although those who have natural ties which I have not must of course give you a more divided affection, yet I do firmly believe that my feelings are shared by many whom you will leave behind you. I believe too that the consciousness of this and the warm heart which has produced this attachment in others will bring you back to England—whether you will find your poor old friend must be doubtful—but it will be something to live for.[24]

Fields's respect for Miss Mitford's literary judgment was such that it affected his own taste. "Few letters in the English language," he said, "are superior to hers, and I think they will come to be regarded as among the choicest specimens of epistolary literature" —and this in a volume containing letters from Hawthorne and Dickens! "I am inclined to think," he continued, "that her correspondence, so full of point in allusions, so full of anecdote and recollections, will be considered among her finest writings. Her criticisms, not always the wisest, were always piquant and readable."[25] His reliance on her discrimination and his own critical limitations are disclosed in a letter written to her on August 23, 1852, while he was still in England: "Today I am to dine with Mr. Thackeray whose books I have never read. What do you think of them? They look at a glance sour and unfeeling but they are widely popular and must be full of *something* or the public wd. not read them."[26]

Fields was soon to know Thackeray much better. Although he failed to understand Thackeray's writing at this time, he was willing to aid him in planning a lecture tour in the United States. By October it was decided that the popular writer would arrive in America the following month, and his agent, E. E. Crowe, wrote to Fields in Boston for assistance in arranging the tour:

[24]Mary Russell Mitford to Fields, August 22?, 1852?.

[25]James T. Fields, *Yesterdays with Authors* (Boston, 1886), p. 275.

[26]Fields to Mitford, August 23, 1852. This was written well after the publication of *The Book of Snobs, Vanity Fair*, and *Pendennis*.

Publisher-Poet

13. Young St. Kensington Oct. 1st/52.

Sir,

At Mr. Thackeray's request I write to announce that he proposes sailing for Boston by the *Canada* on the 30th of this month. It has been arranged that I shall accompany Mr. Thackeray on his journey & that all business connected with the delivery of his Lectures shall be conducted through me. I have the pleasure, in consequence, of writing to you in his name & behalf.

We hope to reach Boston by the 11th or 12th, & to remain there till the end of the month. And as Mr. Thackeray is desirous of commencing his Lectures as soon as possible after his arrival, he begs you to have the kindness to make all necessary arrangements with regard to place & publicity, in pursuance of the promise you were so good as to make him, when on your visit to this country.

Should there be any places in the neighbourhood of Boston, where, according to your opinion, Mr. T.'s Lectures would be favourably received, he would feel very thankful, if you would make the arrangements necessary for his appearance; & he will gladly abide by any agreements wh. you may think proper to make in his name, & for the month of November. There will be plenty of time for an answer addressed to Mr. T. 13. Young St. Kensington, between now & the proposed period of our embarkation, & in case you have any communications to make, perhaps you will be so good as to address him or me there.

Believe me, Sir, your very faithful servant
E. Crowe. Junr.

By December Thackeray was in the United States, and Fields and Crowe were arranging the details for his lectures in Boston:

Dec. 2nd '52 Clarendon. N. Y.

My dear Mr. Fields

Mr. Thackeray wishes me to ask you whether it would not be advisable to fix the figure of single-tickets at Boston, at the same price as that wh. was commanded here; namely 75 cents. He, however, gladly leaves the matter in your hands, knowing that whatever you determine on will be for the best.

Believe me yours very truly
Eyre Crowe

Thackeray's American trip was such a success that another was planned for 1855-1856. It was during the second tour that he suddenly became homesick and boarded the first ship for England.

An interesting letter to Fields from G. W. Curtis predicted the event:

> Thack. is here and there are endless dinners. He gave one on Sunday to Wallack which was roystering. It was the drollest dinner of which I was ever part.
>
> He will give us the slip suddenly. May is always too much for him. He remembers how beautiful England is.—Who does not, that has ever seen it then?[27]

Before long the prediction came true. Fields related the anecdote in *Yesterdays with Authors*:

> He was to have visited various cities in the Middle and Western States; but he took up a newspaper one night, in his hotel in New York, before retiring, saw a steamer advertised to sail the next morning for England, was seized with a sudden fit of homesickness, rang the bell for his servant, who packed up his luggage that night, and the next day he sailed. The first intimation I had of his departure was a card which he sent by the pilot of the steamer, with these words upon it: "Good by, Fields; good by, Mrs. Fields; God bless everybody, says W. M. T."[28]

In the fall of 1859 Fields, this time accompanied by Annie, once more visited his English friends. Hawthorne, also in England, remarked on the number of these friends: "Your friends here, whenever I see any of them speak of Mrs. Fields and yourself with great enthusiasm of regard; the gentlemen esteeming you the most fortunate husband in the world, and the ladies (I believe) equally envying her as a wife. If I were you, I would not leave a country where your merits are so adequately recognized."[29] In a letter to Cyrus Bartol, shortly before embarking for home, Fields described his tour. He left England as planned on June 16, 1860, in the company of the Hawthorne family and Harriet Beecher Stowe:

>   Chatsunth June 5, 1860
>
> Dear Shepherd.
>   Your most kind and most welcome slip of paper came sailing across the Atlantic to gladden our hearts the morning we left London. Thank

[27] George William Curtis to Fields, April 16, 1856.
[28] Fields, *Yesterdays*, pp. 23-24.
[29] Hawthorne to Fields, February 11, 1860, copy in Harvard University Library.

you very much. To day we sit at our cottage window looking toward the Duke's park. The deer are nibbling musically among the grass. We take out our writing materials having just returned from Haddon Hall. "Waiter, have lunch prepared in fifteen minutes, as we leave in the 2.20 train for York." "Yes Sir," and now as Annie has packed our carpet bag and as we have enjoyed to the top of our bent the June glories of England's greenest of all the world's green lanes, here goes a short "howd'ye do" to No. 17 Chestnut St. just to say how we gladden always at the sight of your friendly hand shaken over the ink stand to us your roaming sheep. On the 16th of this month in the "Europa" we intend to set sail for Charles Street. I hope we shall reach there before July, and find that little breakfast room where we shook hands, in the body, that morning we walked away down the steps with grieving lips to find Europe and live in it for a whole year. What we have seen and enjoyed, if our lives are spared, we intend to get you all into a snug corner some day and pour into your ears. Have a large tunnel ready, for the quantity is not small. Now we are bound to the North; to Edinburgh and Abbotsford, and Melrose. Then to the English lakes, rambling over the Westmoreland hills, peeping into the homes where once lived Wordsworth & Southey & dear old De Quincey, now dead and buried from my mortal sight who was so eloquent and affectionate when I saw Lasswade a few years ago. Glorious as London is, we were not sorry to get away and rest from our labours. Incessant "dinners" spoil the appetite, and I am hungry for a plain pick at a Yankee chicken, or a pull at a dish of chowder! I hate to eat with a flunkey in full livery rustling behind my chair, and prefer to sit at meat without a white neck cloth round my jugular. Our kindest love to you and your girls, mother and daughter. We long to see you all round the old fireside once more. God bless you. Ever yours

James T. Fields

By the time he returned from this trip to Europe, Fields was already a prominent man. His literary judgment was undisputed among the worthiest. "I have the highest confidence in your taste and judgment," wrote George Henry Boker, "and I shall take all such suggestions kindly."[30] American authors clamored for the privilege of printing with Ticknor and Fields, and more and more

---

[30] Boker to Fields, December 12, 1855. See Longfellow's opinion of Fields's criticism in James C. Austin, "J. T. Fields and the Revision of Longfellow's Poems: Unpublished Correspondence," *New England Quarterly*, XXIV (June 1951), 239-50.

English writers were being recruited. A single sour note was to be heard occasionally among the applause: the firm's bookkeeping was rather haphazard and informal, and an occasional protest was sounded because of the vagueness of a contract. For example, Boker had written whimsically a few years before:

My dear Fields,   Philadelphia, Nov. 27th 1856.

When we first entered upon our literary arrangement, you promised to send me a note containing the terms of the agreement between the house of Ticknor & Fields and your humble servant. As you have done nothing of the kind, and continue to do it most strenuously, permit me to stir you up vigorously on this point. The want of written agreements has been the cause of so many blunders and misunderstandings in my few business transactions, that I have sworn an oath, as high as heaven and as deep as hell, never to enter on any future arrangement without having the terms of the contract clearly set forth in writing. Therefore, O my Fields, do drop me a formal official note, containing your understanding of the matter, or I shall be forsworn, and the guilt will all be yours. I will reply, in due form, and my note shall be enrolled among the archives of your illustrious house. Neglect your business, neglect your friends and family, get drunk, go to the devil generally, even write poetry, but do not neglect this, in Heaven's sweet name! dear, dear, dear Fields!

How does the book go on?—or, rather, how does the book go off? I am doing all that I can, modestly, with my friends here, for our common interest. People speak well of the poems to me, but with their lips closed, in that infernal Philadelphia manner which leaves one in doubt as to their meaning; and, whether you understand them or not, their manner is perfectly odious to a man with a heart in his breast. Yesterday, the "North American" newspaper called me "promising," for the five hundredth time. I wish Bayard were here to laugh over that with me. It is a favorite joke of his. That newspaper will call me "promising" till I go down with sorrow and white hairs to the grave; and then, doubtless, say that I am a "promising young man" to go into a better world—woe is me!

Don't forget the agreement, don't!

Yours sincerely,
Geo. H. Boker

P. S. Send me such "notices" as may be uttered in Boston and the neighbourhood.   G. H. B.

But bookkeeping was not what it is today, and Ticknor and Fields were perhaps no more lax than their rivals.

Back in 1848 Fields had said to Bayard Taylor, then a rising young author: "I stand at a desk where I can gauge a man's depth in the public-reading-estimation."[31] If the remark was true then, it was even more so in 1860. Fields had effectively demonstrated his understanding of the public tastes in reading, and his opinion of a writer's potentialities was one of the most valued in the country. It remained for him to prove his skill in his crowning achievement, the editorship of the *Atlantic Monthly*.

---

[31]Fields to Taylor, December 26, 1848.

Chapter II:
Editor-Essayist

As EARLY AS 1853, Francis H. Underwood, a young abolitionist with literary ambitions, discussed with James Russell Lowell the possibility of starting a literary magazine to represent New England. John P. Jewett and Company, the publishing house that was to back the venture, withdrew at the last minute, and their plans came to nothing until 1857, when Underwood again approached Lowell with his idea. The two men, upon investigating, found they could rely on contributions from Longfellow, Emerson, Holmes, and Whittier, and it only remained to persuade a publisher to undertake the risk. They decided to approach Moses Dresser Phillips, senior partner of the firm of Phillips, Sampson and Company, for whom Underwood was then working. William Lee, the junior partner (Mr. Sampson having died some time before), was easily persuaded, and with a little tact Underwood managed to get the approval also of Phillips, who was gratified with the opportunity of contact with the New England literary men. Phillips, Sampson and Company were mildly successful publishers of cheap reprints of standard literary works; they had also printed two of Harriet Beecher Stowe's remunerative books. They were therefore in a position to make the new venture.

On the fifth of May 1857, Phillips gave a dinner at the Parker House in Boston for the members and contributors of the new organization. Present were Phillips, Underwood, Lowell, Holmes, Emerson, Longfellow, John Lothrop Motley, and J. Elliot Cabot. This was the first meeting of what became the Atlantic Club, which later merged, virtually if not nominally, with the Saturday Club. E. P. Whipple and Mrs. Stowe were soon added to the list of original contributors, and Holmes named the magazine the *Atlantic Monthly*.

Besides representing New England literature, which it earnestly did, the purpose of the *Atlantic* was manifold. In literature, politics, and art, the founders intended that the magazine should lead in the expression of free and unbiased opinion. It was not to avoid taking sides when the occasion called for it; in fact, one of Underwood's main objectives, as shown by his patronage of Lowell, Whittier, and Stowe, was to produce a high-class antislavery magazine. Always the writers were to keep within the bounds of dignity and moral straitness, which were to characterize the *Atlantic* among its rivals, and the appointment of Lowell as editor insured that such would be the case. In subject matter the magazine was not expected to appeal to the general public, but was to contain enough light literature and timely commentary to make it pay as a monthly. *Harper's New Monthly Magazine*, begun in 1850, had achieved the same sort of thing, but the *Atlantic* was to outdo even *Harper's* in dignity and seriousness of purpose.

As it turned out, the *Atlantic* also outdid *Harper's* in its reliance upon American contributors, for a large percentage of the literature in *Harper's* was pirated from English magazines or printed by agreement with the British author at the same time that it appeared in England. According to the original plan, the *Atlantic* was to secure and pay for contributions from all over the United States and from England as well. Though intended as an organ for the New England literati, it was to avoid provincialism by a selection of some of the best literature from abroad for its pages. Actually, however, nearly all the early contributions were written within a very short distance of Boston.

The first number of the magazine was that of November 1857. It appeared in October, the regular practice being to release each issue on the twentieth of the month preceding the date on the cover. Most issues during the first dozen years contained exactly 127 pages, excluding advertising, though occasionally a few more were added; after Fields's retirement the length was increased slightly. Not until the February 1860 number, shortly after Ticknor and Fields purchased it, did the *Atlantic* accept advertising. It was the first of the literary magazines to do so. An average of seven pages in the back of each issue was thereafter devoted to advertisements for books, sewing machines, pianos, organs, and patent medicines. Publishers' advertisements were by far the most frequent, especially those of Ticknor and Fields.[1] The *Atlantic* contained no illustrations, although line drawings were introduced on rare occasions when the subject matter of an article demanded them. The practice of adding the author's name to each contribution was not begun until 1870, but beginning with the July 1862 issue the semi-annual index contained most of the names. Even in 1857, however, the list of contributors was an open secret. The *Atlantic* originally sold for three dollars a year, the same as *Harper's*, but the price was raised to four dollars during the Civil War. In the middle of Fields's editorship, a single copy cost thirty-five cents.

From the first the magazine prospered. Although it never had or hoped to have the circulation of the more popular magazines, it operated at a profit despite the Panic of 1857 which was in progress at its birth. When Phillips, Sampson and Company collapsed in 1859, following the death of Phillips, the magazine was in no way responsible.[2]

Phillips died in August 1859 and within a few weeks the firm passed into the hands of assignees, Harvey Jewell and Alexander H. Rice, who published the October number of the magazine. Meanwhile the fate of the *Atlantic* was uncertain. It was rumored that the Harper brothers might absorb it; a Philadelphia concern was interested in buying it; and there were feeble efforts by some members of the old firm to take it over. Lowell rejected a plan to buy it himself with the aid of a few friends who had suggested the idea.[3]

---

[1]For a study of the advertising in the *Atlantic* I am indebted to one of my students, John Fries Portmann.

[2]Lowell to Charles Eliot Norton in Horace Elisha Scudder, *James Russell Lowell: A Biography* (Boston, 1901), I, 450.

[3]Ibid., pp. 450-51. Scudder's version contradicts that in the "Contributor's Club" related in the next paragraph. Scudder says "there was a lively competition among publishers to secure the publication," while the other version states that

Editor-Essayist

It was finally bought by Ticknor and Fields. The story of the transaction was related by an anonymous writer in the "Contributor's Club" of the Fiftieth Anniversary Number of the *Atlantic*. Rice set out to obtain bids for the purchase of the magazine, but with no success. The day of the deadline having arrived and no bids having been received, he walked over to the Old Corner Bookstore and attempted to persuade Ticknor to make an offer. Fields was abroad at the time. Ticknor refused but was finally persuaded, without knowing that he was the only bidder, to write out a nominal offer of ten thousand dollars. Rice left and returned later with the news that the *Atlantic* belonged to Ticknor and Fields. Ticknor was shocked, fearing he had made a blunder.

Though Fields had nothing to do with the purchase and was probably more shocked than Ticknor,[4] he almost immediately took charge of the magazine, still permitting Lowell the full powers of editorship. But just one year after Fields's return from Europe, Lowell was out. The replacement of Lowell by Fields himself involved a saving in salary, which in this period of economic decline was important, and Fields had ideas for the future of the magazine—more young contributors, wider circulation, a broader popular appeal. The July 1861 issue of the *Atlantic* was Fields's. At least one of the contributors, T. W. Higginson, considered the change "a great thing for the magazine." The new editor, he said, had "the promptness and business qualities which Lowell signally wanted.... Fields's taste is very good and far less crotchety than Lowell's, who strained at gnats and swallowed camels, and Fields is always casting about for good things, while Lowell is rather disposed to sit still and let them come. It was a torment

---

there were no bidders. Perhaps the "lively competition" was merely rumored to enhance the magazine's value, as Scudder's vague examples suggest. The facts that both Jewell and Rice were assignees and that a price of ten thousand dollars was paid for the magazine are verified in a facsimile of the receipt, printed in M. A. De Wolfe Howe, *The Atlantic Monthly and Its Makers* (Boston, 1919), p. 36.

[4] See John Townsend Trowbridge, *My Own Story* (Boston, 1903), pp. 257-58.

to deal with Lowell and it is a real pleasure with Fields."[5] Being both editor and publisher, Fields was able to manage the payments for contributions as he pleased. He introduced the practice of paying for articles when they were accepted instead of waiting until they were printed. He was one of the first editors to advance money for articles to be written. And he not infrequently increased a writer's rate of pay voluntarily when he thought the increase was deserved. His policy of generosity was designed to keep his writers with him, and he hated to permit any of his regular contributors to write for other magazines.

But the changes in the *Atlantic* that the new editorship brought were hardly noticeable to the reader. Lowell had established the magazine's reputation for dignity and integrity, and Fields was careful not to undermine it. The new editor's "popularization" consisted largely in reducing the number of scholarly literary and historical articles—like "American Antiquity," "The Dramatic Element in the Bible," or "Original Memories of Mrs. Piozzi," which had appeared in Lowell's time—and replacing them with light fiction by Hale, Trowbridge, Harriet Prescott, and others. Lowell had conscientiously resisted Fields's efforts in this direction, even going out of his way to reject fiction that other editors jumped at.[6] Fields, on the other hand, was constantly seeking new fiction writers and new fiction by old writers.

His search for material that would lighten the magazine was

---

[5] Thomas Wentworth Higginson, *Letters and Journals of Thomas Wentworth Higginson*, ed. Mary Thacher Higginson (Boston, 1921), pp. 111-12. See the same writer's *Cheerful Yesterdays* (Boston, 1898), pp. 184-85.

The complete editorial succession of the *Atlantic* to the present day is as follows: 1857-1861, Lowell; 1861-1870, Fields; 1871-1881, William Dean Howells; 1881-1890, Thomas Bailey Aldrich; 1890-1898, Horace Scudder; 1898-1899, Walter Hines Page; 1899-1909, Bliss Perry; 1909-1938, Ellery Sedgwick; 1938–, Edward A. Weeks.

[6] See John Townsend Trowbridge, "An Early Contributor's Recollections," *Atlantic Monthly*, C (November 1907), 582-93. An interesting sidelight on the subject of the *Atlantic*'s refinement of tone is to be found in Frederick L. Allen, "One Hundred Years of *Harper's*," *Harper's Magazine*, CCI (October 1950), 30. The present editor of *Harper's* in his summary of the hundred years of publication of that magazine mentions the *Atlantic* only once, and the omissions are conspicuous: "In that golden age [the late 1800's] of what we now think of as the old-fashioned family magazine, illustrated with exquisite line

his biggest editorial problem. He urged Bayard Taylor to send him "*short* storyish papers that have fun as an element in them." He talked the subject over with Howells, shortly after the latter's appointment as assistant editor, as one of their first jobs. When James Parton submitted another author's article on horse racing to Fields, the main selling point was that it would serve as a relief from the "Emersonian and Whippletonian articles" and keep the New Yorkers from saying the *Atlantic* was too literary.[7]

Fields wanted light articles because he wanted to broaden the circulation of the magazine, for magazines did not rely upon advertising to keep them afloat in those days. With his publishing connections throughout the country and his wide acquaintance both at home and abroad, he was eminently qualified for the job. The *Atlantic* had the services of Nicholas Trübner, who acted as Ticknor and Fields's London agent, to distribute the magazine in England. That it was read in England is evidenced by many letters that Fields received from his friends there. The editor received some valuable publicity in California from his friend Thomas Starr King when King gave public readings of poems by Longfellow, Holmes, Lowell, Whittier, and Fields himself, prior to their appearance in the magazine.[8] Bret Harte's interest in the *Atlantic* was an indication of its reputation in California by the end of Fields's editorship. Advertisers from as far away as Texas were able to reach their local customers through its pages. But the South was practically ruled out from the beginning as a source of subscribers because of the magazine's stand for abolition. The total circulation rose from 32,000 subscriptions in 1863 to 50,000 in 1870 under Fields's care.[9]

---

engravings, *Harper's* was rivaled for preeminence only by the younger *Century* and the still younger *Scribner's*—with the *Atlantic Monthly* as a somewhat more austere competitor for place on the library tables of the solid and respectable citizenry from coast to coast."

[7] Fields to Taylor, March 31, 1864; William Dean Howells to Annie Fields, about 1866 (MS 2409); James Parton to Fields, September 27, 1867.

[8] Thomas Starr King to Fields, October 29, 1862, and February 10, 1863.

[9] Annie Fields, *James T. Fields*, p. 84. Frank Luther Mott, *A History of American Magazines* (Cambridge, 1938), II, 505-506. Circulation fell back in 1870, largely because of Harriet Beecher Stowe's article on Byron. See chapter on Stowe, below.

In spite of Fields's personal apathy toward politics in contrast to Lowell's ardor, the number of political articles in the *Atlantic* increased slightly under Fields.[10] There were those, such as T. W. Higginson, who thought that this was not enough,[11] but it is true that the magazine's political stand was made unquestionably clear to any perceptive reader. President Lincoln respected the *Atlantic*'s unique position in American thought. In July 1864 James Roberts Gilmore, an ardent Methodist who wrote under the name of "Edmund Kirke," and the Methodist Colonel James F. Jaquess of the Preachers' Regiment, the Seventy-third Illinois Volunteers, paid a visit through the battle lines to Jefferson Davis. With Lincoln's secret approval they hoped to find out whether there was a chance for a settlement of the war. They returned to report to Lincoln that Davis was still determined to fight, not for slavery, but for independence. The President was eager to get the report to the public because of its significance to Northern morale. "Can't you get it into the *Atlantic Monthly*?" he asked. "It would have a less partisan look there." Because of the necessity for speed, a brief notice of Davis' words was printed in one of the Boston newspapers upon the suggestion of Senator Sumner, and the full report, "Our Visit to Richmond in 1864," was printed in the *Atlantic* for September and December 1864. "God's hand is in it," Lincoln had said to Gilmore at the close of their interview. "This may be worth as much to us as half a dozen battles. Get the thing out as soon as you can; but don't forget to send me the proof of what you write for the Atlantic."[12]

The magazine's stand was pretty consistently Republican. After the war, articles such as Whipple's "The President and His Accomplices" (November 1866), Boutwell's "The Usurpation" (October 1866), and an anonymous writer's "The Causes for Which a President Can Be Impeached" (January 1867) denounced

---

[10]For a rough numerical classification of the subjects discussed in *Atlantic* articles during representative years of the editorships of Lowell, Fields, and Howells, I am indebted to one of my students, James Klingensmith.

[11]Higginson to Fields, January 1862, in Higginson, *Letters*, pp. 113-14.

[12]Ellery Sedgwick (ed.), *Atlantic Harvest* (Boston, 1947), pp. 239-41.

President Johnson's unfortunate administration.[13] Naturally the *Atlantic* favored the Grant administration, as indicated by "The Intellectual Character of President Grant" (May 1869) and C. G. Crane's "Our New President" (March 1869). It also favored the Republican policy toward the resumption of specie payments. James Parton's articles in 1869 aligned the *Atlantic* against Washington lobbying. As early as April 1867 Bayard Taylor registered his anti-trust sentiments in "Travel in the United States," and James K. Medbery followed with "The Great Erie Imbroglio" in July 1868. There were also articles on the bettering of conditions in the South, especially those of the Negro, and on government control of immigration.

The subjects covered in the *Atlantic* during Fields's years were, in approximate diminishing order according to the number of items in each class: literary notices, poems, fiction, biography, science, politics, unclassified articles, American places, art, history, religion, and music. The amount of poetry was markedly less than it was in either the editorship preceding or that following Fields's—for which he deserves credit, as the number of poor poems he had to reject was phenomenal. The amount of fiction was at its lowest during the Civil War, for writers felt fiction-writing to be futile at such a time, and Fields had not yet fully mobilized his campaign for more stories.

Because of Fields's personal magnetism and because of the reputation the *Atlantic* had gained, there was never any difficulty in getting an abundance of contributions. From the beginning, the editor's job had been mostly to select the best of what he already had. The pay was not the least of the attractions offered by the *Atlantic*. It paid roughly from five to ten dollars a page for prose during the early years,[14] and the rates for poetry were considerably higher, fifty dollars being a standard price for a short poem

---

[13] I am indebted to Robert E. Butler, "William Dean Howells as Editor of The Atlantic Monthly" (unpublished doctoral dissertation at Rutgers University, 1950), pp. 200-206, for an excellent summary of the political articles in the *Atlantic* after 1866.

[14] Mott, II, 20-21.

by a famous writer. In special cases a prose writer or poet might receive a great deal more. Dickens' "George Silverman's Explanation" brought a thousand dollars for thirty-eight pages, and George Eliot's eight-and-a-half page poem "Agatha" brought three hundred pounds in 1869. Longfellow's poetry, when it could be had, was highly remunerative to the author. Prices rose during the decade of Fields's editorship; while ten dollars a page was considered very good pay before the war, this amount became ordinary for most established writers during the late sixties. The pay scale of the *Atlantic* was notably higher than that of most of its contemporaries.

Because of his publishing duties, Fields did not have time to do as much writing as the editors before and after him did. Virtually his total output during the period was ten contributions to the magazine: five poems, one review, and four essays. Nevertheless, it was while he was editor that he developed what talent he had for writing to the highest degree it ever reached. The training in criticizing the works of other writers made him aware of his own shortcomings. Never again did he attempt anything beyond his powers of attainment, or succumb to the sentimentality and banality that had made up the work of his youth.

The poetry is the least commendable of his work, but there were many worse poems in the *Atlantic*. "A Soldier's Ancestry" (August 1861) and "The Sleeping Sentinel" (January 1863) are epigrammatic verses based on ancient historical anecdotes, and timely because of their references to the honor and severity of war. "The Stormy Petrel" (November 1861) is an imitation of Whittier. Before printing the poem, Fields had submitted it to Longfellow, who replied that "the theme is striking, and you have treated it with Wordsworthian simplicity, which is the right way, if not the only way, for such a theme."[15] The opening verses are some of Fields's best:

---

[15]Longfellow to Fields, September 25, 1861, in James C. Austin, "J. T. Fields and the Revision of Longfellow's Poems: Unpublished Correspondence," *New England Quarterly*, XXIV (June 1951), 244. That Longfellow referred to this poem is surmised from the dates.

> Where the gray crags beat back the northern main,
> And all around, the ever restless waves,
> Like white sea-wolves, howl on the lonely sands,
> Clings a low roof, close by the sounding surge.

"The White Throated Sparrow" (August 1863) is also imitative, this time of Shelley's "To a Skylark," with traces of Keats's "Ode to a Nightingale." It is difficult to choose the best of the poem's lines, for it has the merit of consistency in both tone and quality. However, the following verses are representative:

> Up in yon tremulous mist where morning wakes
> Illimitable shadows from their dark abodes,
> Or in this woodland glade tumultuous grown
> With all the murmurous language of the trees,
> No blither presence fills the vocal space.
> The wandering rivulets dancing through the grass,
> The gambols, low or loud, of insect-life,
> The cheerful call of cattle in the vales,
> Sweet natural sounds of the contented hours,—
> All seem less jubilant when thy song begins.

Fields's only acknowledged book review during his editorship concerns *A Book about Doctors* by J. Cordy Jeaffreson (April 1862). Fields is startlingly frank about his dislike of the author's previous works, though he approves of the present volume:

> Mr. Jeaffreson is not usually either a brilliant or a sensible man with pen in hand, albeit he dates from "Rolls Chambers, Chancery Lane." He is apt to select slow coaches, whenever he attempts a ride. His "Novels and Novelists" is a sad move in the "deadly lively" direction, and his "Crewe Rise" has not risen to much distinction among the reading crew. In those volumes of departed rubbish he sinks very low, whenever he essays to mount; but his dulness is innoxious, for few there be who can say, "We have read him." His "Book about Doctors" is the best literary venture he has yet made. It is not a dull volume. The anecdotes so industriously collected keep attention alert, and one feels inclined to applaud Mr. Jeaffreson as the leaves of his book are turned.

Such humor and such hostility are not frequent in *Atlantic* reviews of the mid-nineteenth century. The lively essay continues with humorous anecdotes and quotations.

Fields's proper medium was the informal essay, and he wrote some of his best essays during the sixties. He had already written four for the *Atlantic*, besides one review, while Lowell was editor. "My Friend's Library" (October 1861), the first to appear after the change of editorship, is probably Fields's best literary production apart from his reminiscences. He revealed his fondness for books when he described what was actually his own library in Charles Street:

> I scarcely know a greater pleasure than to be allowed for a whole day to spend the hours unmolested in my friend A's library. So much *privilege* abounds there, I call it *Urbanity Hall*. It is a plain, modestly appointed apartment, overlooking a broad sheet of water; and I can see, from where I sit and read, the sail-boats go tilting by, and glancing across the bay. Sometimes, when a rainy day sets in, I run down to my friend's house, and ask leave to browse about the library,—not so much for the sake of reading, as for the intense enjoyment I have in turning over the books that have a personal history attached. Many of them once belonged to authors whose libraries have been dispersed. My friend has enriched her editions with autographic notes of those fine spirits who wrote the books which illumine her shelves, so that one is constantly coming upon some fresh treasure in the way of a literary curiosity. I am apt to discover something new every time I take down a folio or a miniature volume. As I ramble on from shelf to shelf,
>
> > "Straight mine eye hath caught new pleasures,"
>
> and the hours often slip by into the afternoon, and glide noiselessly into twilight, before dinner-time is remembered.

One can find in the library a translation of Boccaccio that had belonged to Leigh Hunt, a first edition of *Paradise Lost*, a volume of Richard Baxter owned by Wordsworth, a copy of Wordsworth's 1815 *Poetical Works* personally annotated by the author, autograph letters of Samuel Johnson and Walter Scott, and so on. "My Friend's Library" appeared in 1877 in Fields's collection of essays, *Underbrush*, as did all his other essays contributed to the *Atlantic* during his editorship, with the exception of the last, "Some Memories of Charles Dickens."

Of the other essays, the next was "How to Rough It" (December 1861), an enthusiastic discussion of hiking, with appropriate literary anecdotes. Fields was no novice on this subject, for when Dickens visited Boston in 1867, Fields was the only one of his friends able to keep up with him on his regular morning excursions. "The Pettibone Lineage" (April 1865) is a short narrative about the vanity of pride of family. Fields had reason for frequent embarrassment upon this subject, for like the hero of his story he had no noble pedigree. The last essay he did while he was still full-time editor was "Some Memories of Charles Dickens" (August 1870), written upon the death of the English novelist. It was the only literary reminiscence Fields wrote during the period but it was the earliest of the essays that were to appear in *Yesterdays with Authors*, his major work, written mostly after his retirement. Hastily composed as this essay is, it contains personal details about Dickens not be to found elsewhere.

Besides acting as editor and essayist, Fields did not neglect his publishing duties. The firm's sale of books was at a peak during the sixties. Publishing was rapidly becoming a big business, and it required almost superhuman management to supply the increasing demand for good books throughout the country. By the 1870's the business of a publishing house had become almost too much for one or two men to handle,[16] as Fields's successor, James R. Osgood, found out to his sorrow. An example of the new kind of problems Fields was encountering was the printers' strike which he settled singlehandedly in 1869. It took place at the plant of Welch, Bigelow and Company, exclusive printers for the firm, and Annie Fields wrote of it in her diary for February 21:

By the way, there was a strike yesterday in the Cambridge University Printing office of Welsh[*sic*] & Bigelow. Mr. Welsh came to Mr. Fields with the figures. Jamie looked at them dispassionately & decided that the printers were right and at the present rates they would be unable to live. It will probably make a difference of $15,000 a year to the firm's receipts but Jamie prefers to have it so. Mr. Welsh must have felt much easier in his mind when they parted.[17]

[16] William Charvat, "James T. Fields and the Beginnings of Book Promotion, 1840-1855," *Huntington Library Quarterly*, VIII (November, 1944), 94.
[17] MS in the Massachusetts Historical Society.

In 1864 the firm bought the *North American Review*, a quarterly with Lowell and Charles Eliot Norton as editors; in 1865 commenced *Our Young Folks*, a juvenile magazine edited by Howard M. Ticknor, Gail Hamilton, Lucy Larcom, and J. T. Trowbridge; in 1866 the weekly eclectic magazine *Every Saturday* was started, with Thomas Bailey Aldrich as editor; and in 1867 the first annual volume of the *Atlantic Almanac* was published under the editorship of Holmes and D. G. Mitchell. Thus Ticknor and Fields were the publishers of five periodicals in the sixties, and although Fields was directly responsible for only one of them, he had more than a casual interest in their welfare and was often called upon for aid by both editors and contributors.

The title "Ticknor and Fields" lasted until 1868, although Howard M. Ticknor had replaced his father, William D. Ticknor, upon the death of the latter in 1864. Howard proved incompatible and was forced out of the company in October 1868, whereupon the reorganized company became Fields, Osgood and Company with Fields as senior partner and James R. Osgood and John S. Clark as junior partners. Osgood had been a clerk in the firm since 1858 and became head of the new James R. Osgood and Company in 1871, upon Fields's retirement. Meanwhile the business had outgrown the Old Corner Bookstore, and in 1865 the offices were moved to 124 Tremont Street, at the corner of Hamilton Place, which also became the headquarters of the *Atlantic*.

In addition to his business activities, Fields was continually taking part in public and private charities, often but not always at the instigation of his wife. He helped Reverend C. A. Bartol in a campaign for aid to needy people in Kansas. He collected and published writings of various authors for the great Boston Fair of 1864. He aided in the charities for the freedmen after the Emancipation. He was an active member of the International Copyright Society that strove to establish juster laws for authors. And he helped organize a series of readings for the aid of Southern schools. He was constantly aiding and giving advice to individuals. Parke Godwin, writer and editorial assistant on the

Editor-Essayist

New York *Evening Post,* asked his counsel in choosing a school for his son. A. D. White, president of Cornell University, asked him for a recommendation of a certain Cambridge man for a professorship. And Senator Charles Sumner received his help in attempting to get the Senator's speeches published by subscription.[18] He was more active than ever socially. In addition to entertaining visiting celebrities like Trollope and Dickens, he constantly played host to American writers and friends. He was a member of the Phi Beta Kappa Society and became a member of the Saturday Club, though his club affiliations were not numerous considering his position. Finally, from April to November 1869, he turned over his editorial duties to assistant editor Howells and vacationed with Annie in Europe, but there his social activity was intensified and life was a continual round of parties, dinners, breakfasts, and visits.

It was no wonder that his health began to fail in the sixties. In 1863 he suffered a distressing attack of neuralgia,[19] and though previously very healthy, he began to complain of colds and other disturbances. It was partly because of his health that he retired from business December 31, 1870.

---

[18] C. A. Bartol to Fields, February 13, 1861; W. H. Furness to Fields, June 24, 1864; Lydia Child to Fields, February 25, 1865; James Parton to Fields, March 29, 1868; Parke Godwin to Fields, September 25, 1867; A. D. White to Fields, November 7, 1867. MSS in Harvard University Library: Fields to Sumner, January 2, 1868, and January 14, 1869. Oak Knoll Collection, Essex Institute: Annie Fields to Whittier, September 3, 1868 (EW 625).

[19] Fields to Hawthorne, November 9, 1863.

PART TWO

FROM THE HUB

FOREWORD TO PART TWO

The center of the *Atlantic* (as of the universe) was Boston. The magazine was edited, printed, and published there; most of its contributors lived in the vicinity; New England subjects were frequent in its pages; and above all its whole character, from the editorial policy to the actual prose style of some of the most remote contributors, was largely dictated by the prevailing tastes in the Hub.

Professor Mott has calculated that thirty-five out of fifty-four contributors to the first volume (November 1857 to December 1858) were New Englanders.[1] The percentage decreased slightly during Fields's editorship. According to the present writer's rough estimate, forty per cent of the more important contributors under both Lowell and Fields made their homes in Boston, Cambridge, or suburbs, during most of the time they contributed; and another twenty per cent lived in New England. These figures merely suggest the true picture, however, for only three of those from outside New England contributed more than a dozen times before 1871. Hence, the total amount of the magazine written in Boston and New England was overwhelming.

As for the content of the *Atlantic*, when it was not sectional in itself—as was the work of Holmes, Whittier, or Rose Terry Cooke—it was usually tinged with the sectional attitude. Thus, the magazine's outlook on matters of scholarship was that of Harvard College, as represented by Asa Gray and Louis Agassiz in science, Lowell and Ticknor in language, and President Eliot in education. Parkman, Prescott, and Motley, all Bostonians, were the leading writers on history, and the Boston ministers James Freeman Clarke and Cyrus Bartol, the leading writers on religion. Besides the political articles by Lowell, there were some by Sumner. In literary criticism Lowell also had a place, and later Howells,

[1] Mott, II, 496.

and in addition there was the Boston critic E. P. Whipple. Poetry was represented not only by Longfellow, Lowell, and Holmes, but also by Julia Ward Howe, T. W. Parsons, C. P. Cranch, and James and Annie Fields. And in fiction were Holmes, Edward Everett Hale, and Henry James, not to mention the Bostonians by adoption, Howells, T. B. Aldrich, and J. T. Trowbridge. All these writers lived in or about Boston, and were pacemakers in their respective fields. And they were the core of the *Atlantic*.

Their significance in American literature was estimated by T. W. Higginson at the end of the century:

> There has been endless discussion as to the true worth of the literary movement of which the circle of "Atlantic" writers was the source. ... Time alone can decide the precise award; the essential fact is that in this movement American literature was born, or, if not born,—for certainly Irving and Cooper had preceded, was at least set on its feet. Whether it could not have been better born is a profitless question.... this group of writers was doubtless a local product; but so is every new variety of plum or pear which the gardener finds in his garden. He does not quarrel with it for having made its appearance in some inconvenient corner instead of in the centre, nor does he think it unpardonable that it did not show itself everywhere at once; the thing of importance is that it has arrived.[2]

Though the *Atlantic* writers were in many ways provincial, they marked an era in which American literature had at last achieved a full-blown, independent existence.

---

[2] Thomas Wentworth Higginson, *Cheerful Yesterdays* (Boston, 1898), pp. 187-88.

Chapter III:
James Russell Lowell

JAMES RUSSELL LOWELL'S success as editor of the *Atlantic* and his establishment of certain precedents that have survived in the magazine even to this day are unquestioned. But he had troubles enough during his editorship, some of them arising from the temper of the times and the conditions under which he worked, some from his own character and shortcomings. There were difficulties to be expected in establishing a new periodical—setting its tone so as to fix a place for it among the reading public, gathering writers who would meet and uphold standards, initiating a scale of pay for contributors—but Lowell managed these almost flawlessly. There were other difficulties that are to be found in any editor's job—the handling of valuable writers so as to keep them contributing, the rejecting of poor and inappropriate material, the equitable handling of payments to writers—these Lowell managed at least satisfactorily. But many details combine to show that, whereas Lowell was the ideal person to begin the directorship of the *Atlantic*, he was less successful in the long run. His ultimate displacement by Fields was the result of the accumulation of his failings, unimportant as each of them was and many of them unpreventable.

One of Lowell's obstacles was the moral censorship required by certain segments of the reading public. Especially explosive, of course, were references to religious unorthodoxy and suggestions of sensuality. The situation is illustrated by what happened when Lowell donated an editorial copy of Whitman to the Harvard College Library. The repercussion did not come until two years after his retirement from the *Atlantic*, when, happening upon the book in the library, Reverend W. L. Gage registered his disapproval with the donor. Lowell explained that while editor he had sent all his editorial copies of books to the library, and that *Leaves of Grass* was "a book I never looked into farther than to satisfy myself that it was a solemn humbug. Still, I think the business of a library is to have *every* book in it." However, he thanked his correspondent "for calling my attention to a part of this book of which I knew nothing, and I will take care to keep it out of the way of the students."[1]

Lowell was more cautious about public opinion than Fields was later, for the magazine's prestige had yet to be earned and a false step might alienate readers. Also, he lacked Fields's gift, natural to all great editors, of intuitive sympathy with his readers. Lowell was painfully conscientious in matters of public taste. So much as a suggestive word or phrase would receive his careful consideration, and he felt that censorship was an appreciable part of his job. For example, he wrote to T. W. Higginson on December 9, 1858:

I like your article ["Ought Women to Learn the Alphabet?"] so much that it is already in press as leader of next number. You misunderstood me. I want no change except the insertion of a qualifying "perhaps" where you speak of the natural equality of the sexes, and that as much on your own account as mine—because I think it not yet *demonstrated*. Even in this, if you prefer it, have your own way.

I only look upon my duty as a vicarious one for Phillips & Sampson, that nothing may go in (before we are firm on our feet) that helps the "religious" press in their warfare on us. Presently we shall be even with them, and have a *free* magazine in its true sense. I never allow any personal notion of mine to interfere, except in cases of obvious obscurity, bad taste, or bad grammar.[2]

In speaking of the warfare of the "religious" press, Lowell had in mind the attacks on Holmes's *The Autocrat of the Breakfast-Table*. In the case of Holmes, Lowell stoutly upheld the author's right to speak his mind. Thoreau was not treated so well. By the

---

[1] James Russell Lowell, *New Letters of James Russell Lowell*, ed. M. A. De Wolfe Howe (New York, 1932), pp. 115-16.

[2] James Russell Lowell, *Letters of James Russell Lowell*, ed. Charles Eliot Norton (New York, 1893), I, 287.

unauthorized deletion of a passage in "Chesuncook," which appeared in the *Atlantic* in 1858, Lowell made an enemy of the author.[3] What may have happened is that Lowell, thinking the passage might be interpreted as non-Christian, canceled it tentatively with the intention of asking Thoreau's permission before the final printing, and then, becoming swamped with manuscripts and other business, forgot to write to him. Such was Lowell's manner of working. At any rate, the action was hardly excusable, and Thoreau did not contribute again to the *Atlantic* until Fields became editor.

Politically, too, Lowell was cautious. In the days before the war, people were extremely touchy about their prejudices, and though the *Altantic* was avowedly a political magazine, it could easily have been squashed in the collision of opposing factions. At least once Lowell suppressed his own convictions in the interest of the *Atlantic*'s increasing circulation, for "I think it would be unwise," he explained, "to let the magazine take a losing side unless clear justice required it. Am I not right?"[4] From a commercial point of view he probably was right. In several instances he confessed to a fear of certain controversial subjects. "Editorially," he wrote to Higginson, "I am a little afraid of Brown [presumably John Brown of Osawatomie] and Ticknor would be more so."[5] One can hardly help feeling sorry for the poor editor, beset by a prying public on one side, a self-righteous contributor on the other, and a timid publisher behind.

As a matter of fact, Lowell was much more politically conscious than his employers, Ticknor and Fields. His articles on the slavery question and on the administrations of Buchanan and Lincoln were as courageous as anything that appeared in the pages of the *Atlantic* during Fields's editorship. Although the *Atlantic* policy was neither timid nor reactionary under Fields, it was nearly always on the side of the majority—at least in New Eng-

---

[3]See Richmond Croom Beatty, *James Russell Lowell* (Nashville, 1942), pp. 146-47.
[4]Scudder, I, 424-25.
[5]Lowell to Thomas Wentworth Higginson, October 24, 1859.

land—but Lowell anticipated the majority opinion in some cases. Indeed Lowell's own *Biglow Papers*, Second Series, perhaps the most effective political propaganda of the decade, appeared in the magazine under Fields's editorship; but violent as these papers sometimes were, they were generally aimed at dissenting minorities rather than the majority.[6]

Another of Lowell's difficulties was that he thought he was overworked, and when one considers that he read all the manuscripts submitted to him—all in longhand!—one is inclined to agree. Of course, other editors at that time had the same problems and survived, but Lowell was extremely fastidious in choosing his articles, and was temperamentally unsuited to the drudgery. Furthermore, although his writing habits customarily depended upon his moods, he felt bound as editor of the *Atlantic* to make his own contributions to its pages. He continually complained of all this to his friends.[7]

It was because of this constant bustle that Lowell's handling of manuscripts was rather slipshod, and that some were lost or overlooked. He refers to one of them in a letter to Higginson:

My dear Higginson,   Cambridge 27th Aug. 1860.

Your article on Parker is by this time in type for the October number. I should have printed it before had I known that it was in my possession. As ill-luck would have it, it was the bottom one of a bundle of Mss. which I was working down through with no notion that it contained anything but anonymous matter. I wondered you had not sent it, & kept the Fayal back that I might have room for it when it came. Fayal is also in type & is capital, though our foreman at the printing-office (who is a native) thinks you are hard on them. I can't see it, for the impression I got was a remarkably pleasant one.

I like your Parker very much—though I question the epithet "*noble frankness*" which you apply to his treatment of the dead—who couldn't answer. But I think you have treated the subject with great judgment & discretion. Your *twenty* languages is a good many.

                              Cordially yours
                              J. R. Lowell.

[6] See Arthur Voss, "Backgrounds of Lowell's Satire in 'The Biglow Papers,'" *New England Quarterly*, XXIII (March 1950), 47-64.

[7] See, for example, his letter to C. E. Norton in Lowell, *Letters*, I, 303-304.

Higginson's "Theodore Parker" did appear in the October and "Fayal and the Portuguese" in the November number.[8] But Lowell was still finding manuscripts in his study as late as March 1862, almost a year after his editorship had ended.[9]

Another shortcoming of Lowell's, and one that had something to do with his being replaced, was that he made little effort to search out new contributors.[10] The array of writers he and Underwood collected at the start served well enough throughout his editorship. Such writers as Emerson, Holmes, Whittier, Stowe, and Higginson were attractions enough for any magazine, and of course there were many unsolicited contributions from writers who were delighted to have their names appear along with these. But this was not looking to the future, nor was it taking advantage of possibilities outside New England.

The thing that contributed most to the change in editorship of the *Atlantic* was that Lowell took his literature too seriously. Matters of taste were vital to him; he was more concerned with raising and upholding the literary standards of his magazine and its public than in catering to readers' desires. But his publishers had an eye toward circulation, and although they wanted an elegant magazine, they were willing to mitigate their ideals. "There is a constant pressure on me," wrote Lowell, "to 'popularize' the magazine, which I resist with clamor."[11] At least part of this pressure originated with Fields. In a most revealing letter to the publisher in December 1860, Lowell answered the accusation of heaviness in the *Atlantic* and outlined his editorial principles:

My dear Fields, Cambridge, St. Headache. 1860
 I shall try to get into town after my recitations today, & shall hope to see you. If not—then please say to Mr. Clarke that his last course was *fish*, & that he need not see the article (which is already printing) in order to put a tail on it. I think it would be well if he would say

---

[8] See Thomas Wentworth Higginson, *Old Cambridge* (New York, 1899), pp. 179-80.
[9] Lowell, *Letters*, I, 319-20.
[10] Scudder, I, 427.
[11] Ibid., p. 424.

a word (in the present aspect of matters) about the interests which unite the East & West &c—carefully avoiding to call the railways "the iron bands that" &c for the eighteen thousandth time.

The sonnet I think better than common—but it may be partiality for Miss Loring.

Mr. Nichols [George Nichols of Metcalf and Company, printers for Ticknor and Fields] tells me that you sighed a little over *heavy* articles & instanced that on Roger Bacon [by Charles Eliot Norton]. All Ham Connexion is at a discount in these secession days—but I think you are wrong—not merely about that article which seemed to me as interesting as it was thorough—but on the general question. I hope I need not say that I never let any personal feeling influence me consciously in editing the magazine—so do not think it is Norton I am defending. I stick to the principle. If we make our Magazine merely entertaining how are we better than those Scribes & Pharisees the Harpers? We want to make it interesting to as many *classes* of people as we can, especially to such as give tone to public opinion in literacy, if there be any such in America.

I forgot to speak to you about your article ["Getting Home Again"] which I liked so well as to wish it had been longer. They spell Coli*s*eum Colo*ss*eum nowadays.

In great haste   truly yours
              J. R. Lowell[12]

As early as 1859, when Ticknor and Fields bought the *Atlantic*, Lowell had foreseen the possibility of Fields's taking his place.

As friend to friend, I may say that I think it [the new ownership] just the best arrangement possible, though I did not like to say so beforehand too plainly.... Whether T[icknor] will want *me* or not, is another question. I suppose that he will think that Fields will make a good editor, beside saving the salary, and F. may think so too. In certain respects he would, as the dining editor for example, to look after authors when they came to Boston and the like. I shall be quite satisfied, anyhow,—though the salary is a convenience, for I have done nothing to advance my own private interest in the matter.[13]

In addition, then, to Fields's greater promotional ability and his preference for lighter reading matter, there was a financial reason for the change. Not that the magazine was not paying—but the

---

[12]MS in the Henry W. and Albert A. Berg Collection, New York Public Library. Part printed in Lowell, *New Letters*, pp. 99-100.
[13]Letter to Norton, no date, in Scudder, I, 451.

effects of the Panic of 1857 had not yet passed, and most businessmen were thinking in terms of economy. If Fields took over the editorial position, the company could eliminate the expense of paying someone else.

The transfer of editorship was effected without hard feelings. There is no trace of bitterness in any of the correspondence between Fields and Lowell during these years; in fact Lowell's magnanimity even surpassed Fields's—a trait for which the latter was famous. In May 1861, having completed the June number of the magazine, the old editor turned over the remaining manuscripts to the new one:

Elmwood. 23rd May. 1861.
My dear Fields,

I send you a number of communications which I have for some time intended to offer for the "Atlantic Monthly"—I meant to say—your valuable & instructive periodical. Lights of the age (as you will doubtless find them to be) I hunted about till I could find a candlebox to pack them in—a fitting mummy-case. I have never tried whether they would *burn*, for which want of scientific curiosity you will perhaps not thank me.

I wish you all joy of your worm! You will find it no bad apprenticeship or prelude for that warmer & more congenial world to which all successful booksellers are believed by devout authors to go. I was going to say I was glad to be rid of my old man of the sea. But I don't believe I am. I doubt if we see the finger of Providence so readily in the stoppage of a salary as in its beginning or increment. A bore, moreover, that is periodical gets a friendly face at last & we miss it on the whole. Even the gout men don't like to have stop *too* suddenly, lest it may have struck to the stomach.

Well, goodbye delusive royalty! I abdicate with what grace I may. I lay aside my paper crown & feather sceptre. I have been at least no Bourbon—if I have not learned much, I have forgotten a great deal.

Whatever I can do for the A. M. I shall be glad to do. How much I can write I don't know, & it is not of much consequence. My head is not so strong as it used to be, & I want to rest. But I would rather write on these terms—to be paid at the end of the year if matters prosper with you—if not, to say no more about it. I think T. & F. deserve some gratitude from authors—at least I for one acknowledge my debt in that kind & would like to pay it. You have treated me well in every way & I am not too proud to say I am grateful for it.

Among the Mss you will find two by Norton. One of them a notice of De Tocqueville—very timely now. Let me have so much favor with the new ministry as to get them printed soon. Mr. Flagg's article on trees I have paid for—perhaps too much—but he says he will write more, if that is the case, & make all square. I have paid him either $45. or $50—I think $50. but he will know.

I wish to say in black & white that I am perfectly satisfied with the arrangement you have made. You will be surprised before long to find how easily you get on without me, & wonder that you ever thought me a necessity. It is amazing how quietly the waters close over one. He carries down with him the memory of his splash & struggle & fancies it still going on when the last bubble even has burst long ago. Good bye. Nature is equable. I have lost the Atlantic but my cow has calved as if nothing had happened.

           Cordially yours
           J. R. L.

P. S. Always glad to see you at Elmwood. We have the finest dandelions you ever saw—every blossom as big as the sun on a tavernsign.[14]

It was such a relief to be free from the editorship that Lowell did not write anything immediately. But by September he was contributing to the *Atlantic* again. While editor, he had averaged two or three contributions per month. He did not keep this up, but he did send something about every two months—everything he wrote—until he became editor of the *North American Review*, which naturally took a large portion of his efforts. Now a much larger share of his work was poetry. While editor, he had felt it necessary, for the magazine's sake, to write political articles and book reviews, but now that he had more time to pamper his moods, his inclination to versify returned.

His interest in the *Atlantic* did not wane, and from time to time he would send Fields contributions from other writers or suggestions for book reviews, as well as work of his own. On October 8, 1861, for example, he sent three pieces by Walt Whitman, but they were not accepted. In the letter accompanying these, he wrote of his own efforts: "I set about a poem last night —*à propos* of the times and hope to finish it tomorrow, and if it

---

[14]Part printed in Lowell, *Letters*, I, 310-11.

turn out to be good for anything, I will send it at once and you can print or no as you like. I will go at a proser for December if you like. I have a tolerable theme."[15] Probably Lowell never finished the poem he had in progress. The "proser" was "Self-Possession *vs.* Preposession," which was put into the December number. It is Lowell's last essay for the *Atlantic* on the Civil War, and it argues that no great leader has yet appeared for the North, but that the time is ripe for one.

In January 1862 Lowell began his second series of *The Biglow Papers*, the first having appeared in the *Boston Courier* and the *National Anti-Slavery Standard* in 1846-48. Along with the second number in the new series Lowell sent the following letter:

My dear Fields,   Elmwood, 1st Jany., 1862.

I sent Number Two to Mr. Nichols this morning. If I am *not* mistaken, it will *take*. 'Tis about Mason & Slidell, & I have ended it with a little ballad with a refrain that I hope has a kind of *tang* to it. I put so much work into Number One that I thought I ought to have more for it, as Mr. Biglow seems the only one of our firm that produces very marketable wares. But I have felt like a Jew ever since, & if I overrated their popularity & they *don't* take as well as I hoped, I shall refund the money. Mind that. One can't help being a fool, but he needn't be a knave if he take pains enough. I can't feel easy if I think I have been paid more than I'm worth. It would worry my life out. So that is the understanding—if the things don't have a run, all you pay me over fifty dollars a number is a loan & this writing is my note for it.

I enclose a note just received from Mr. George Walker of Springfield. Will you attend to it?

Do you want any more literary notices? I have some Calderon translations I should like to say a few words about.

I wish you & Ticknor a happy New Year & remain
                              truly yours
                              J. R. Lowell.[16]

---

[15]Lowell, *New Letters*, pp. 101-102. M. A. De Wolfe Howe conjectured that the poem Lowell was writing was "The Washers of the Shroud," the war poem in the November 1861 issue. If that were the case, however, the presses must have been stopped to insert it, for the November issue was probably being printed by October 8.

[16]Part printed in Lowell, *New Letters*, p. 102.

The protestations in the first paragraph illustrate Lowell's attitude throughout his correspondence with Fields. Hawthorne was the only other major contributor to the *Atlantic* who worried about being overpaid.

The new Biglow series did not flow easily from Lowell's pen, and several of his letters indicate the mental difficulties he had to overcome. "It's no use," he wrote to Fields on June 5, 1862:

> I reverse the gospel difficulty, and while the flesh is willing enough, the spirit is weak. My brain must lie fallow a spell—there is no superphosphate for those worn-out fields. Better no crop than small potatoes. I want to have the *passion* of the thing on me again and beget lusty Biglows. I am all the more dejected because you have treated me so well.[17]

The chief cause of his despondency was the war. The Union cause meant much to him, and the unfortunate progress of McClellan's Peninsular Campaign left him unable to compose, even satirically. Bitter as they were, the several parts of *The Biglow Papers* were not written during Lowell's lowest moments.

In the February 1863 number of the *Atlantic* Lowell published the last of the papers to appear until almost the end of the war. In March he wrote that he needed a rest. The letter refers evidently to a request by Fields for a review of Charles Godfrey Leland's *Sunshine in Thought*, in which the author advocated an excessively optimistic philosophy of life and literature. Fields had stipulated a review of half a page, and Lowell took this up as a subject for jest:

20th March, 1863.

My dear Fields,
> You are very clever in rapping your contributors over the knuckles. You think I am too longwinded, eh, Gil Blas? Well I won't wish you better taste, for I had come to pretty much the same conclusion myself & made up my mind not to write anything more till my brains got settled, or whatever it is they want. So I take myself off your hands. I have read Leland's book. The first part is very clever & sensible, but the last two thirds seem to me of dangerous tendency, though he doesn't mean it. To notice it fitly would ask some thought,

---

[17]Scudder, II, 42.

& should, I fancy, be allowed more space not on account of the book altogether, but of the subject. But I cannot do it, long or short.

I hope your *"Roba di Roma"* came back safely. I did not get them till Thursday & so, as I make it a point to read what I notice, could not send the article sooner.

Very truly yours
J. R. Lowell.

Leland's book was eventually reviewed by E. P. Whipple. Lowell's review of William Wetmore Story's *Roba di Roma* was accepted and printed in the April number. For seven months Lowell published nothing while his "brains got settled," but his letter had alarmed Fields, who feared that the banter had a serious intent. Lowell's next letter assured him that it was merely banter, and suggested that the author's "weakness of spirit" had a physical basis:

My dear Fields,   Elmwood, 26th March, 1863

    the[18] late Revd. Dr. Parkman used to divide mankind into two classes: the fools & the d——d fools. Now, having my choice, I should rank myself with the former rather than the latter. Do you suppose, if my vanity had been wounded, I should have deliberately written you a note to tell you so? Not a bit of it. What I wrote was simply true, that I had at last made up my mind to take care of my health—to which end I have been sedulously devoting myself for the last three weeks—& do you think, when I have almost given up tobacco that I would continue to indulge in writing? If I were anxious to write, I could find plenty of chances—indeed, I have just declined an editorship—but it is not that. I am tired & want rest, my brains are muddled & need to settle & clarify. That is all. In my note I merely assumed by way of badinage that what you said about the half page was meant as a hint. If I had seriously taken it so, I should not have been in the least offended. Criticism can't very well vex me till I find a critic more exacting than myself—& for that I shall wait a good while.

    The "Atlantic" & you have always treated me as well as any man could wish. I am as far as possible from having any complaint to make, & if ever I have, I shall not make it sideways, you may be sure, but straightforward. So far from it, I had meant to ask to have two books left over for me to notice when I felt bright enough, Clough's Poems & Fisher's book on the Constitution.

---

[18] Lowell frequently began with a lower-case letter after the salutation.

Begging you therefore to believe that when I feel wronged, I shall say so & that you need not fancy it till I do,

I remain as ever truly yours
J. R. Lowell.

Lowell did not write the reviews of Clough and Fisher.

His reiteration of his gratitude to Ticknor and Fields makes it clear how Fields secured the loyalty of his writers; he did it in the best possible way: by treating them well. Lowell wrote of it again in August:

Elmwood, 26th Aug. 1863.

My dear Fields,

When I say a thing, I mean it, & I have told you before, & always shall tell you, that T. & F. have not only treated me well but generously. As for making new terms, my only dissatisfaction with the old has been that I felt as if I could do nothing to justify them. I think you rate me above my value,—certainly above any value I set upon myself as far as popularity goes. Of course, I should blush & be pleased, if what I wrote could justify you in paying me twice what you do, but when I make a fool of myself 'tis from heat of blood, never with malice prepense. As Saadi might have written in his solemn way—"The fish always wants water & the poet gold: But neither knows how much he wants of either till he is out of it. Yet this difference I note between poet & fish, that the former is always, the latter only sometimes, out."

The moral of which is that if you will send me your check for this poem when you get it, & not wait till it is printed, the "terms" will satisfy. Of course, if you think it worth a thousand dollars, draw your check accordingly.

I call it a "poem" coolly enough not knowing yet what it is—for I have written it & copied it since ten this morning & it is now barely one o'clock. So instead of a song "it may turn out a sermon"—& a dull one.

It was not because I was cross that I have not written—but because nothing would *write me*, & I long ago made up my mind that if a poet lose fire by growing older, he at least gains the wisdom not deliberately to *water* his reputation (*extend*, I think is the technical term) as too many younkers & prodigals do.

Cordially yours
J. R. Lowell.

P. S. You see the modern application? Is it *too* close & direct? I meant not so to have it. But I have another copy of verses if you don't like these. But "Thay have said: quhat say thay? Let tham say?"

The poem Lowell sent was the first part of "Two Scenes from the Life of Blondel." The "modern application" is the representation of Abraham Lincoln in the ideal king of the poem. In a sense, the poem is a response to the essay of the year before, "Self-Possession *vs.* Prepossession." Lowell had found the leader he was looking for.

Fields's reply to Lowell's letter must have been gracious, for Lowell wrote again on August 31: "I really do not know what to say. You give me altogether too much and lay me under an obligation which I shall have confidence enough in your friendliness to rest under for the present, because the money will be of use to me. But I shall consider myself as owing you more verses than you debit me with."[19]

A few days later Lowell wrote that he had composed a second part for the poem—a cavalier counterpart to the first. Both parts appeared in the November *Atlantic* under the single title, "Two Scenes from the Life of Blondel."

Elmwood, 8th Septr. 1863.

My dear Fields,

I have written a Palinode to "Blondel" & so made two poems of it. The latter half is half-humorous &, I think will help the effect. You see how dangerous it is to pay a poet handsomely beforehand. I don't know where I shall stop. I shall be sending an epic presently.

But what I write about is *Piatt*. Can't you publish his book? I have read over his Mss. & marked what I liked best, advising him to make a small volume & have it choice. I think there is real & great merit in some of them & think you would do well to secure him, for if he lives he will make his mark. (He knows nothing of this.)

Also. Professor Peirce's son Charles has been writing on the Pronunciation of English in Shakspeare's time. His essays would make three or four short articles & would do credit to the "Atlantic." I spoke about them to you once before. I asked him to do nothing about them till I had spoken to you. I think you want some articles of the kind. You had better take them on my recommendation. I have read them & am sure they are well & scholarly done.

Pray write me your decision at your convenience. I should like your notion also, of the second part of Blondel, which (in the first

---

[19] Lowell, *Letters*, I, 328.

relief of incubation) I am inclined to think clever. But there was nothing wiser than Horace's ninth year—only it overwhelms us like a ninth wave (*that's* Wendell's, *tenth* the Latins said, but I wanted nine) & if we kept our verses so long we should print none of 'em. A strong argument for monthly magazines you see.

Cordially yours
J. R. Lowell.

Lowell still had a fatherly interest in the *Atlantic*. His recommendations of new writers and articles and his criticism of those that appeared in the magazine were generally good; and, whether Fields followed it or not, he respected Lowell's advice. The praise of John James Piatt, who thus far had published only *Poems of Two Friends* in collaboration with Howells, shows that Lowell was not wholly blind to new names in literature. But Fields did not publish Piatt's new book, *The Nests at Washington, and Other Poems*, written in collaboration with Sarah Morgan Piatt, the poet's wife. Nor did he publish any other of Piatt's books. Peirce's articles were not printed in the *Atlantic*, though Lowell had the author write on Shakespearean pronunciation for the *North American Review* the following year.

Another letter of Lowell's accompanying the manuscript of "Memoriae Positum R. G. S.," the elegy on the Civil War hero Robert Gould Shaw, praises the work of Edward Everett Hale, whose "The Man without a Country" had just appeared in the *Atlantic*: "Get more of him. He has that lightness of touch & ease of narration that are worth everything. . . . I confess I am rather weary of the highpressure style."[20] By this time, November 30, 1863, Lowell was coming around to Fields's opinion in favor of light literature. Hale immediately became a frequent contributor to the *Atlantic*. As for the poem on Shaw, which appeared in the January 1864 number, Lowell insisted upon not being paid for it—if the undated letter which follows is rightly assigned to this period:

In my lecture-room—Friday.

My dear Fields, the account must stand as it did. I forgot what I was sending you till I saw it again. I can't take money for this—'twould

[20]Printed in ibid., 333-34.

be like selling a lock of sacred hair. We will make it even some other way.

I am glad you like it. I ought to say that *I* cut it down myself after writing my note to you.

"Master of Elmwood!" quotha! it has nearly mastered me with repairs & hasn't half done tumbling down, & unpainting itself & otherwise delapidating yet.

Yrs. Ever
J. R. L. [FI 3051]

In spite of his chivalrous attitude, however, Lowell was a little pinched for money, and when he was offered the editorship of the *North American Review*, he accepted, with the condition that Charles Eliot Norton be co-editor. Only a few months before, he had refused a similar offer, but now his need got the better of his indolence and he submitted once again to the old drudgery—now quarterly, however, instead of monthly. In January 1864 the new editors published their first number, and Lowell's contributions to the *Atlantic* became correspondingly fewer. In October Ticknor and Fields bought the *North American Review*, and Lowell was once again working for them. He wrote to Fields on October 18: "It's a great compliment you pay me that, whenever I have fairly begun to edit a journal you should buy it." The letter continues with the usual complaints about the lack of inspiration; a Biglow paper in progress had gone wrong. As a matter of fact, the author contributed only two more Biglow papers, Numbers X and XI, in the April 1865 and May 1866 issues of the *Atlantic*. Meanwhile Fields had suggested that Lowell try his hand at a serialized novel, but the idea was rejected: "In the first place I can't write one nor conceive how any one else can; & in the next—I would sooner be hanged than begin to print anything before I had wholly finished it. Moreover, what can a man do who is in a treadmill?"[21] The novel remained something to talk about[22] but was never begun. Still Lowell did not forget Fields; he continued to contribute three or four pieces a year,

---

[21] Printed in ibid., 341-43.
[22] See Scudder, II, 57-58. See also Beatty, pp. 198-99.

mostly poetry but occasionally a story or article, until Fields retired.

In addition, he wrote two pieces for the Ticknor and Fields juvenile magazine, *Our Young Folks*: a poem, "Hob Gobbling's Song," which appeared in the January issue, and a fairy tale, "Uncle Cobus's Story," in the July issue of 1867. He wrote Fields in October of the preceding year:

Elmwood: Tuesday. 23rd Octr. '66.

My dear Fields,

First, I very heartily thank you & (to encourage you) let you know that I sent it [a book?] to Child, who has read it & says it is &c &c. I mean to work ahead as fast as I can with the rest.

Next, you asked me once for a Fairy-story &, I suppose, never expected to hear of it again. But it is not safe to cast bread on *my* waters. I invented a kind of one at once, & yesterday & the day before contrived to write it, partly to spite an infernal pain I was suffering & which got me under at last. I think I have told it simply enough, & was surprised to find how easy it was to write in words mostly of one syllable. I think there are some pleasant humors in it, but it may have suffered from my being in such a wretched condition while I wrote it. Please read it yourself, & show it to no one. To tell the honest truth I have never read O. Y. F. & so do not know whether it is suitable or not. Perhaps I could write it over again—but that might spoil it, for I might not be able to fancy myself so vividly telling it again as I did before.

Also: I have a jolly little poem that should do for a Xmas number called "Hob Gobbling's Song" written years ago for my nephews now all dead. Just think of it! & three of the four in battle. Who *could* have dreamed it twenty years ago?

You will think I am mad to bombard you thus, but no, I am only beginning to feel the sort of spring-impulse of my college-freedom. I mean to work off old scores this winter if I can.

Will you let me know whether T. & F. have sent me a check on account of N. A. R.? They commonly send it earlier. I am in no want of it, having lightened one of the Firm of his purse the other day— but we have a postboy now & I never have any faith in newfangled things—so I began to fear it might have miscarried.

Goodbye, my dear Maecenas, & be sure that I shall never forget your uniform liberality to my poor Muse.   Cordially yours
J. R. Lowell.[23]

[23]Part printed in Scudder, II, 105-106.

In 1868 Lowell received a journal of a tour through New England in 1834, written by John B. Minor of Virginia, and he offered to make selections from it for the *Atlantic*:

Elmwood, 12th July, 1868. ¼ to 9 a. m. Wind W. & by N., therm. 88°.
My dear Fields,
as I swelter here, it is some consolation for me that you are roasting in that Yankee-baker which we call the W[hi]te Mts. That repercussion of the sun's heat from so many angles at once (the focus being the tourist) always struck me as one of the sublimest examples of the unvarying operation of natural laws. I wish you & Mrs. Fields might be made exceptions, but it can hardly be helped. Give my best regards to her.

What I write about is this. There has been put into my hands to dispose of the Journal of a Virginia Gentleman during a short tour in N. E. partly on foot. The date 1834—which is now ages ago. There is not a great deal of it, but I found it truly entertaining. I think I could make selections from it that would run through four or five numbers of the "Atlantic." It comes from his widow, who is left very poor (I suspect) with four children. Now do you want it? And if so, what do you think it would be worth? When I say it is entertaining I do not mean for fanatics like me, who would cradle I know not how many tons of common earth for a grain of the gold of human nature, but for folks in general. It is not only interesting but valuable, & the character of the author, as it blinks out continually, most engaging. It seems to me remarkable that there is positively not an illnatured word from the first page to the last. Now you know that I have once or twice pressed Sybilline* books upon you which you wouldn't take. Don't let this one slip through your fingers. I think it might be published afterwards in a small volume with advantage, but of its adaptation to the "Atlantic" I have no doubt.

Now a word for myself. I want Mr. Nichols back again. W[elch] & B[igelow] have no sufficient reader (this is confidential) now that B's eyes have failed, & we have to do an amount of proofreading ourselves which is quite beyond my toleration. It wastes my time & above all my eyes, which are getting tender. I know the N. A. doesn't pay, but I would rather give it up altogether than go on as at present. Mr. Nichols *was entirely right* in every respect as to this matter, & was very moderate in all his conduct about it. His terms are certainly not unreasonable—$100. a quarter—of which it was no more than fair that W. & B. should pay half. Pray let me know your decision. I had to give five solid hours to the last proofs (they were not my own) that I read.

What an overwhelmingly pleasant time Longfellow is having in England! It must be a bore—yet of the pleasantest kind. Well, he deserves it all, & therefore, I trust, enjoys it.

I hope you have been having a good time—for me it is always coming as that *cuss* of a Mackay says.

With best remembrances to Mrs. Fields,

Yours ever
J. R. L.[24]

(*Sybilline, i/y/ G. N.[George Nichols])

The proposal of the journal was accepted, and Lowell began editing it with an introduction for the *Atlantic*. It began in the August 1870 number under the title *A Virginian in New England Thirty-five Years Ago*. A rather commonplace journal in itself, it was almost the only writing by a Southerner to appear in the magazine while Fields was editor.

Regardless of his friendliness, Lowell had to be treated carefully, and Fields was the person to do it. Fields visited him once, after a brief absence from town, to find that Lowell "had become quite morbid because, while J. was away, a smaller sum than usual was sent him for his last poem. He thought it a delicate way of saying they wished to drop him." So wrote Mrs. Fields in her diary for July 25, 1868; she continued: "Lowell is a man deeply pervaded with fine discontents. I do not believe the most favorable circumstances would improve him. Success, of which he has a very small share considering his deserts (for his books have a narrow circulation), would make him gayer and happier; whether so wise a man, I cannot but doubt."[25]

Besides writing for the three Ticknor and Fields publications, *Our Young Folks*, the *Atlantic Monthly*, and the *North American Review*, Lowell added his share to the *Atlantic Almanac*. His two contributions, "My Garden Acquaintance" and "A Good Word for Winter," appeared in the 1869 and 1870 numbers re-

---

[24] Part printed in Scudder, II, 135-36.
[25] Mark Antony De Wolfe Howe, *Memories of a Hostess* (Boston, 1922), p. 109.

spectively. He wrote to Fields after receiving his check for the former.

Elmwood, 7th Septr. 1868.

My dear Fields,

    I ought long ago to have acknowledged your note enclosing a check for my contribution to the "Atlantic Almanac." I was almost ashamed to take it, for the article was not worth the money, but 'twould be a violation both of principle & decency to return anything in such cases, so I shall hope to make it up one of these days by writing something worth more than its price & so bring the balance even. I should have written before, but I have been going about the earth as diligently as a certain personage mentioned in Scripture, & who is spoken of as a lion—a beast for which I am also sometimes mistaken in out of the way places where they don't see many of the species. My last adventure was to Shelter Island where I spent a very pleasant week, & saw the place where Kidd *really* buried something—more by token it was afterwards dug up in presence of commissioners from Massachusetts sent by Governor Bellamont. I think there is a certain pleasure in seeing even where treasure *has been*—unless it be one's own pockets. I envied them their climate down there, where I saw box trees as thick almost as my thigh & fifteen feet tall. They had been growing, it was thought ever since the house was built, a hundred & thirty one years ago! One plants to some purpose on such conditions.

    I am sorry Mr. Bigelow disappoints us, for I am afraid we shall have but a dull number of the N. A. this time. I have pressed Stephen into the service, & he is up stairs now doing us something on English politics. I am trying to drive the coach myself so that Gurney may enjoy his new-moon as he ought, but my hand is so out that I fear landing in the ditch. However, if I only arrive *some*where, though even in the mud, it will be better than nothing. Let us hope for the best & that the mud will be soft.

    Pray who wrote the article on Hawthorne in the last "Atlantic"? A woman, I think. [The article was by Elizabeth Peabody.] I found it very interesting, & on the whole the most adequate thing about H. I have seen, though a little clumsy here & there. But it was *good*, & I love to see him praised as he deserves. I don't think people have any kind of true notion yet what a Master he was, God rest his soul! Shakspeare, I am sure, was glad to see him on the other side.

    I wish I could do what you ask for the "Atlantic." Your offer is generous, but what could I do? My brain is a disenchanted Fortunatus purse which I turn upside down & shake in vain. I am getting fat &

dull. I thank you all the same, but I find fairy-money no longer. Sometimes I think I *might*, but who knows? We are all so conceited!

Give my kind regards to Mrs. Fields &
I am always cordially yours
J. R. L.

[Written in at head of letter:] Will you give me Mr. Bigelow's address?[26]

Lowell was increasingly flighty and irritable, and more reluctant to promise contributions in advance. Fields often proposed plans for regular articles, but in vain. A poem or article from Lowell remained a pleasant surprise. In fact, aside from the Biglow papers which were usually unpredictable as to both subject and time of appearance, he seldom wrote a page for Fields by request.

The *North American Review* was one cause of his peevishness at this time. Like any regular duty, for Lowell it had become a bore. In September 1868 he whimsically tendered his resignation from the editorship. But a few days later he changed his mind and wrote to Fields: "The fact is I was cross, and did not quite like being brought up with such a round turn at my time of life.... I am as touchy as if I were even poorer than I am."[27] Also the *North American* was not a paying enterprise, and that added to Lowell's discouragement.

In spite of their familiarity, Fields was rather awed by Lowell. Unlike most of the old-school New England writers—Longfellow, Hawthorne, Emerson, Holmes—Lowell was slightly Fields's junior, but he had a certain forbidding dignity as well as his confessed touchiness. Fields seldom ventured to correct or revise any of his work, and when he did, it was only in minor matters. This was unlike the editor's treatment of other writers, even the world-

[26] Part printed in Lowell, *Letters*, I, 404-405.

[27] Scudder, II, 125. See Lowell to Fields, September 24?, 1868, and September 30, 1868, printed in part in Scudder, II, 119, 122-25. By March 12, 1869, Fields was persuaded that the quarterly was not worth continuing, and wrote to Norton in Europe: "We have determined, as the North America Review is an out-of-the-pocket, certainly of five or six thousand a year, to let it die with the October number of this year. Let us mourn over it together when we meet in London." (MS in Harvard University Library.) Perhaps Norton influenced the publisher's decision to hold on, for the *North American* survived for many decades. See also Beatty, pp. 199-200.

wide favorite Longfellow, whom Fields frequently advised, often to the poet's advantage. However, in the case of Lowell's "The Flying Dutchman," a poem on old-fashionedness written for the January 1869 issue of the *Atlantic*, Fields did criticize—or so Lowell's letter would indicate:

> The trouble with the "Flying Dutchman" is not in what I left out, but in what I couldn't get in. Let us be honest with each other, my dear Lorenzo de' Medici, if we can't be with anybody else. The conception of the verses is good; the verses are bad. I ought not to have taken your check, but I should not have been true to my guild else.... But there is a month yet. Let me forget it, and perhaps I can do it again better. If not, I have the germ of a little prose essay in my head, which I think will more than take its place if all goes well.[28]

The essay in Lowell's head was "On a Certain Condescension in Foreigners," a denunciation of the European attitude, especially the English, toward America. In his next letter the author indicated that he had finished the first draft and taken it to the printer, Welch, Bigelow and Company, in Cambridge. Meanwhile Fields had suggested some revisions of another of Lowell's works, evidently the prefatory note to *Under the Willows, and Other Poems*, published by Fields, Osgood and Company late in 1868 and dated 1869:

> Elmwood, 29th Octr. 1868
>
> Mr. Lowell presents his compliments to Mr. Fields & I am much obliged to you for the corrections he has kindly suggested in his prefatory note.
>
> You see, my dear Fields, that I *can* ride two horses at once with perfect steadiness when I try. But the I is so strong in human nature that it will peep out through the mask of the third person. Will you give our best thanks to Mrs. Fields for the tickets to Mrs. Carey's concert? Unhappily they came too late. They were mailed in Cambridgeport which is farther (by post) from Cambridge than Boston is—because they go back to Boston for a fresh start.—The essay I spoke of is nearly finished & I think will be entertaining. It is entitled "On a certain Condescension in foreigners." I left word at the "University Press" to have plate proofs struck-off. Bigelow was not there.
>
> Yours always
> J. R. L.

---

[28]Lowell, *Letters*, I, 397-98.

Both "The Flying Dutchman" and "On a Certain Condescension in Foreigners" were in the January *Atlantic*.

In 1869 Lowell was already looking around for a foreign ministry and had his friends alerted to help him. In the hope of using his influence on Lowell's behalf, Fields wrote to Charles Sumner on January 14, 1869, and after a discussion of the publication of one of the Senator's speeches, asked him to see what could be done for Lowell.

> I wish to say one word about another matter. James Russell Lowell, I happen to know, would not be unwilling to go abroad for three or four years. Has he not earned the right, by all the capital work he has done for the country, to be sent to Europe by the Grant Government. Of course Italy would suit him best, but we have Marsh there, the right man in the right place, perhaps. Lowell has every qualification for a foreign minister, as you know, and his friends here are very much in earnest, for an appointment, that will both honor the man and his country.

The letter failed in its effect, but it is a credit to Fields, for he stood to lose by such an appointment not only a valued contributor but also an able editor of the *North American*.

He showed his friendship for Lowell in another way that year. It was the year of Fields's last European tour, and he and Annie decided to invite Lowell's daughter, Mabel, to go with them. Meanwhile the *Atlantic* was to be left in the hands of William Dean Howells. Young and relatively new with the company, Howells was competent, but he might need occasional advice. Furthermore, Fields himself had found it comfortable to have a second editor to share the responsibility of rejecting manuscripts, and Lowell could fill this place for Howells quite well. Fields tactfully mentioned his desire for Lowell to watch over the magazine with the proposal to take Mabel to Europe. Lowell answered:

[29]MS in Harvard University Library.

James Russell Lowell

My dear Fields,   Elmwood, 19th Jany. 1869.

   I have been thinking over your very kind invitation to Mabel, &, after turning it in every possible way, I have come to the conclusion that the only way to treat a generous offer is to be generous enough to accept it. My pride stood a little in the way, but my Commonsense whispered me that I had no right to feed my pride at my daughter's expense. And moreover, my dear Fields, you left a most delicate loophole for my pride to creep out of in conferring on me a kind of militia-generalship of the A. M. while you were away. Now if you will let me make it something real—that is, if you will let me read the proofsheets, I can be of some service in preventing Dr. Bowditch (for example, merely) from writing such awful English, & mayhap in some other cases, as a consulting physician. Moreover, I should like to translate for "Every Saturday" something now & then—as for instance the article on *Déak*, & the dramatic sketch of Octave Feuillet lately published in the *Révue de Deux Mondes*. May I? And, moreover, you will let me repay you if ever I can? I wish you to understand that I am profoundly sensible of your kindness & that therefore the less I say about it the better. But I *am* so. I don't think the child will detract from the pleasure of your journey & so I say "God bless you, Yes!" I will see you in a day or two & talk it over.

   Do you see that H. T. Tuckerman is to commence his autobiography in Putnam's Magazine? At least, I take it for granted from the title—"The Ass in Life & Literature." If sincerely done, it will be interesting. I see that the "Saturday Review" speaks kindly of "Under the Willows," which is as good as another edition on this side the pond. With kind regards to Mrs. Fields,

gratefully yours
J. R. L.[30]

The extent of Lowell's "militia-generalship" is not made wholly clear by the correspondence, but in at least one case the acting editor consulted him on a slightly questionable poem by Bayard Taylor,[31] and if Howells had followed his advice to suppress Harriet Beecher Stowe's article on Lady Byron, the magazine might not have lost fifteen thousand subscribers in 1870.[32] Thus the first

---

[30] Part printed in Scudder, II, 137-38.
[31] William Dean Howells to Fields, August 24, 1869.
[32] See Lowell, *New Letters*, pp. 146-47; William Dean Howells, *Life in Letters of William Dean Howells*, ed. Mildred Howells (Garden City, 1928), I, 149; and Mott, II, 505-506.

editor of the *Atlantic Monthly* found himself once again overseeing the progress of his magazine. In reality he had stood by as a kind of unpaid consulting editor ever since 1861: Fields had profited by his advice and suggestions and had always been ready to accept whatever Lowell wished to contribute.

Upon Fields's return from abroad, Lowell, wishing to show his appreciation of a friendship which had been genuine as well as lucrative for both, decided to dedicate a volume to the publisher. In his letter of November 23, 1869, he gave Fields the choice of either *The Cathedral* or *Among My Books.* "Will you accept the dedication yourself? You know I meant to inscribe my Essays to you, but I foresee that they will not be out—I was going to say before Xmas, but as I wrote the word 'out' came a proofsheet, and since then I have been at the Pr[inting] O[ffice] and Bigelow says they *will*. So now which will you have?"[33] *The Cathedral* was settled upon, and Lowell wrote to Fields after the dedication had been sent to the printer. At the same time he was concerned with repaying Fields for Mabel's traveling expenses.

Elmwood: 17th Decr. 1869.

My dear Fields,
    Mabel tells me that she compared her account with that of Mrs. Fields just before leaving England, & found that they agreed. The amount was just three dollars less than I had reckoned it would be. I had put it, by guess, at $750. I am exceedingly annoyed that it has not already been paid. Within a day or two it shall be. The moment I got your first note I went into Boston & made an arrangement for the money, but for some unaccountable reason it has not yet been sent me. I hope to get it this morning.
    You must allow me also to clear off the rest, which I put at $2500, as soon as I can. There is no earthly reason why I shouldn't & a great many why I should. I hate any kind of money obligations between friends. When I have paid this off, the kindness will be left & the obligation gone. I shall be able to manage it before long. I never could see any reason why poets should claim an immunity beyond other folks. It is not wholesome for them.
    I hope people will like the "Cathedral" well enough to make the

---

[33] Lowell, *New Letters*, pp. 151-52.

dedication worth having. But I have arrived at the desponding stage which always follows production.

With kindest regards to Mrs. Fields,

Yours always
J. R. Lowell.

The Cathedral had been originally written for the *Atlantic* of January 1870. Fields had suggested that it be also printed as a book, and the book publication took place at about the same time as the magazine publication. Lowell's dedication reads as follows:

To
Mr. James T. Fields

My dear Fields:

Dr. Johnson's sturdy self-respect led him to invent the Bookseller as a substitute for the Patron. My relations with you have enabled me to discover how pleasantly the Friend may replace the Bookseller. Let me record my sense of many thoughtful services by associating your name with a poem which owes its appearance in this form to your partiality.

Cordially yours,
J. R. Lowell

Cambridge, *November 29, 1869.*

The year after the publication of *The Cathedral*, Fields gave up his editorship to Howells, a staunch friend of Lowell. But regardless of their friendship, Lowell's contributions became fewer under the new regime.

Chapter IV:
Oliver Wendell Holmes

OLIVER WENDELL HOLMES had more to do with the initial success of the *Atlantic* than any other contributor except Lowell. It was he who proposed the magazine's title, and it was *The Autocrat of the Breakfast-Table* that captivated the reading public. Lowell, upon being named editor, declared that Holmes would have been a better choice: "Depend upon it," he said, "Doctor Holmes will be our most effective writer. He is to do something that will be felt. He will be a new power in letters." Underwood, then the assistant editor, later acknowledged the magazine's debt to Holmes: "That it survived those early perils and became established as the representative of the matured thought, the literary conscience and the growing art of New England, is due to Doctor Holmes more than to any other man."[1]

The Autocrat of the Breakfast-Table began in the first issue in 1857 and continued through 1858. It excited comment: "Some cried out that [Holmes] was undignified; others would have it that he was nothing more than an 'inordinate egotist'; another didn't think that his puns were very good; another was offended at his use of slang; and some one suggested that the poems, which were scattered among the pages, though brilliant, 'showed as ill as diamonds among the spangles of the court fool.' "[2] But whether their criticisms praised or condemned, people talked about the Autocrat and his reputation spread. Fields, not yet connected with the *Atlantic Monthly*, was one of his well-wishers. The pub-

[1] Francis H. Underwood, "Oliver Wendell Holmes," *Scribner's Illustrated Magazine*, XVIII (May 1879), 121. (The quotation of Lowell, above, is from the same source.)

[2] John T. Morse, Jr., *Life and Letters of Oliver Wendell Holmes* (Boston, 1896), I, 207.

lisher wrote to Bayard Taylor of the new magazine and its dazzling contributor:

> I often wonder if you see the good things that appear in our new Boston monthly "The Atlantic." A series of papers by Holmes called the "Autocrat of the Breakfast Table" are among the great literary "strikes" of our time. They are as wise, as witty, and golden opinions from all sorts of people are showered upon him.[3]

In addition to the Autocrat series, Holmes contributed sixteen pieces to the magazine during the three years and eight months of Lowell's editorship. Among his contributions were *The Professor at the Breakfast-Table* and *The Professor's Story*, afterwards called *Elsie Venner*. Like the *Autocrat* they called forth a great deal of protest, but they were nonetheless popular. So mild and pious a man as Whittier said of the novel: "Holmes is doing a great thing with his story in the Atlantic."[4]

Not only was Holmes a great thing for the *Atlantic*, but it was a great thing for him. It was through his contributions to the magazine that his reputation spread beyond Boston and his fame became national and international. In 1861, having completed the monthly installments of *The Professor's Story*, he wrote to Motley in Europe of his success:

> The magazine which you helped to give a start to has prospered, since its transfer to Ticknor & Fields. . . . I suppose I have made more money and reputation out of it than anybody else, on the whole. I have written more than anybody else, at any rate.

But he added a complaint about the abuse he had received from critics:

> But, oh! such a belaboring as I have had from the so-called "evangelical" press, for the last two or three years, almost without intermission! There must be a great deal of weakness and rottenness, when such extreme bitterness is called out by such a good-natured person as I can claim to be in print. It is a new experience to me, but is made up for by a great amount of sympathy from men and women, old and young, and such confidences and such sentimental *épanchements*,

---

[3]Fields to Bayard Taylor, August 30, 1858.
[4]John Greenleaf Whittier to Fields, July 15, 1860.

that, if my private correspondence is ever aired, I shall pass for a more questionable personage than my domestic record can show me to have been.[5]

The attacks by the religious press actually stimulated the success of Holmes's prose.

Success made the writer—never over-humble—look to his purse; and Lowell discovered about this time that the doctor was displeased with his pay from the *Atlantic*. Lowell wrote to Fields, who now held the purse strings as publisher of the magazine:

Cambridge, 1st March 1861.

My dear Fields,
    do see Dr. Holmes at once and assure him how essential he is to the "Atlantic." He is worth all the rest of us together and has been nettled a little by not being paid so much as he thought right for his "Asylum for decayed Punsters." Nettled, perhaps, is not the right word—but he has conceived that he could carry his wares to a better market. I assured him that he was altogether mistaken—that there was probably some mistake, and that I knew he was valued as he should be by T. & F. &c. &c.
    Now you know what ought to be done and I am sure will do it. An essay from him is as good as a chapter. He needs only a word said to him by you to set all right.
Cordially yours
J. R. Lowell.

Presumably the affair was arranged satisfactorily, for we hear nothing about it again. It was the only ripple in Holmes's smooth relations with the magazine during the editorships of both Lowell and Fields. So far as the correspondence reveals, everything he submitted was accepted and the remuneration was always adequate.

When Ticknor and Fields purchased the *Atlantic* in 1859, Holmes had already been associated with the firm for seventeen years. His *Homeopathy, and Its Kindred Delusions*, published in 1842, was the first book by one of the famous New England writers to receive the Ticknor imprint. He had also been a friend of Fields for many years, and depended upon Fields's literary coun-

---

[5]Holmes to John Lothrop Motley, February 16, 1861, in Morse, II, 156.

sel. "I have been all lost since you have been away," he wrote in 1852 when the publisher was in Europe, "in all that relates to literary matters, to say nothing of the almost daily aid, comfort, and refreshment I imbibed from your luminous presence."[6] In 1858 Holmes became Fields's neighbor at 21—later 164—Charles Street, where he lived until 1870. He looked upon Fields as a familiar friend when the latter became editor as well as publisher of the *Atlantic* in 1861.

There was a notable change in Holmes's contributions to the magazine in 1861, not because of the new editor but rather because of the Civil War. There were no more novels and no more Breakfast Table essays. Holmes is often accused of a lack of political and social conscience, but from the time Fort Sumter was fired upon, the great majority of his contributions to the *Atlantic* were on the war. If they were not profound, they were the kind of thing that had a powerful effect on readers; for example, "Brother Jonathan's Lament for Sister Caroline," "The Wormwood Cordial of History," "The Flower of Liberty," "My Hunt after 'The Captain,'" and "God Save the Flag." The list includes some of the best war pieces to appear in the *Atlantic*.

In writing for the magazine Holmes was fastidious about details. Although he was very pleasant and patient with proofreaders and editors and was not one of those writers who delight in making last-minute changes, the corrections he made in his writings were often minute. One correction involved two words:

> Many thanks for the enclosure; the very fault of which is its profligate punctuality.
> I have corrected two words to avoid repetition.
>
> Yours always
> O. W. H.

Jan. 11. [FI 2207]

Another time, he apologized for revising a slight historical inaccuracy in the poem "Shakespeare":

---

[6]Annie Fields, *Authors and Friends* (Boston, 1897), p. 120.

I am ashamed to be troubled by so slight a thing when battles are raging about us; but I have written:—

> Where Genoa's deckless caravels were blown.

Now Columbus sailed from Palos, and I must change the verse before it is too late.[7]

In the June 1864 *Atlantic* the revised line read: "Where Genoa's roving mariner was blown."

As a contributor to the magazine and because of his influence with Fields and his recognized generosity, Holmes was troubled by people with manuscripts to publish or books they wanted puffed. He usually did his best for them. In 1865 he asked Fields to secure a notice of James Edward Murdoch's *Patriotism in Poetry and Prose*:

My dear Mr. Fields,
 Can't you get me out of this scrape?
 Murdoch came to me last evening with Woodman to get me to say something for his book (sent herewith, to be returned to me) in the At. Mon.—Told him I was busy with poem for class-meeting, which was true. Said I thought you would say a few words for it through one of your critical contributors.
 I think you can, safely and advantageously. Murdoch has made some sixty or seventy (—O! O! O! got my paper wrong—all of my sprained wrist) some sixty or seventy thousand dollars for the Sanitary Commission by speaking these pieces. Some of them are good as you know, and the whole idea of the thing is so patriotic and generous that he is entitled as I think to a few genial words from the fame-dispensing Organ. Why should not you give him a paragraph yourself? or get one of our friends to do it? It would be graceful and make friends.
Yours always
O. W. H.   [FI 2184]

A notice of Murdoch's book appeared in the February 1865 *Atlantic*. More than once Holmes sought notices of Dr. Jacob Bigelow's writings; for example in December 1865 he wrote:

[7]Ibid., p. 126.

My dear Mr. Fields,
 Dr. Bigelow's address ought to have a good critical notice in the Atlantic.
 I think that Dr. *George Putnam* will do it for you (don't tell him I suggested it) and do it in the right way.
 Can't you "fix" it?
Yours always
O. W. H.

Dec. 6

Bigelow's *An Address on the Limits of Education* was reviewed in the February 1866 number.

By this time the war was over and Holmes was setting to work on the most pretentious of his thirty-five contributions to the *Atlantic* during Fields's editorship. Long before, Ticknor and Fields had urged him to undertake an "American" novel, but he had declined:

June 17th 1864

Mess. Ticknor and Fields,
Gentlemen,
 I ought to have made a formal reply before this time to your proposals to me respecting the writing of an American Story.
 The terms seem to me liberal and the offer is tempting.
 There are two reasons which principally induce me to excuse myself from the task at present;—at some future time you may wish to make new proposals and I to accept them. These two reasons are
  1. I want to be free to devote a great part of my time to my professorship, which is now very interesting to me and a source of a good deal of income.
  2. I have no particular need of money, more than I can command, and am willing to wait until the stimulus is a little stronger than at present.
 Your proposition will however serve to give a direction to my thoughts by which it is among the possibilities that we may please needs profit each other at some future time.
 With many thanks for your kindness, I am Gentlemen
Yours very truly
O. W. Holmes.

By 1866, however, Holmes had pondered the proposal and was hard at work on *The Guardian Angel*. He called Fields to his house in September to hear him read it. Annie Fields, in her diary, described Fields's over-enthusiastic reception of it: "Jamie returned in two hours perfectly enchanted. The novel exceeded his hopes. No diminishing of power is to be seen; on the contrary it seems the perfect fruit of a life." Holmes pronounced it the best thing he had done, although he was "very nervous indeed about his work and read it with great reluctance, yet desired to do so. He had read it to no one as yet until Mr. Fields should hear it."[8]

But both Fields and Holmes were wrong about the value of the novel and the reception that awaited it. Fields paid $250 apiece—a very high price—for the twelve installments of the story,[9] which began each issue of the *Atlantic* from January to December 1867. By May the author was already the object of all kinds of abuse for his opinions. His denunciation of incompetent ministers was construed as an attack on the ministerial profession, and his rebellion against Puritan predestination and his suggestion that psychological frailties were not always the fault of their possessor were shocking to orthodox minds. H. H. Brownell commented on Holmes's attackers in a letter to Fields:

Bristol, R. I. May 21st 67

My dear Fields,

I am truly sorry that I cannot be with you next Saturday. Hope to be in Boston Wednesday or Thursday of next week, and to have the pleasure of seeing some of you before I sail. Give my best regards to your wife and to the Doctor. His story is a grand one, and constantly improves on acquaintance. So far, his "G. A." seems to be our Friend Gridley. I expect this latter will fall in love with the young lady next, and there will be the deuce to pay!

As for the petty attacks on him, he has given us so many good similes about the nature of them, that there are none left for me— and he knows well enough that whenever a man goes about to save "the youth of Athens," somebody conservatively sings out that he is corrupting 'em. I think he is likely to survive all I've seen against

---

[8] Annie Fields's diary, September 12, 1866, in Howe, *Memories of a Hostess*, p. 30.
[9] Eleanor M. Tilton, *Amiable Autocrat* (New York, 1947), p. 284.

him so far. Spite and ill-temper, no matter in whom, don't hurt a man like him. The only difficulty in writing on things spiritual is that no amount of human imagination can surpass the bald and naked facts, when sufficiently evidenced, no matter how weak or rough the language describing them. But I am criticizing, which I believe you reserve to yourself or your deputies—

always yours most truly
H. H. B.

The character & emotions of Revd. G. B. S. are as clearly drawn and delicately shaded as anything I ever saw—and there is a deep element of the tragic underlying all. His (Holmes', not Stoker's) women are all admirably truthful—the poor wife *"making an errand"* to the study, and the note of Miss Myrtle, alluding to Miss Posey. The revd. gentleman, perhaps could not relieve his mind as we profane are apt to do, when taken badly aback, by muttering "Hell and damnation!" but doubtless had a good time in improving the cited next day. B.

Holmes himself spoke scornfully of his attackers, but they irritated him. He wrote the following letter to Fields in June. Probably the paper he mentioned was his contribution to the *Atlantic Almanac* for 1868, and the Preface was for the bound edition of *The Guardian Angel*, which was published late in 1867.

Boston June 23d 1867

It shall be done, O most irresistible of men!

On the 20th of July D. V. you shall have your paper. Our *Preface* we will not write until we have got along a little further. We may get suggestions. What a precious crop of carnal rogues has grown up among us since I preached my sermon to ministers through the story of the Rev. Bellamy S! *2 or 3* Ministers, 1 Sunday school teacher, 1 Organist,* and now 1 Sexton** all giving cause for scandal since our mild story pointed out a possible danger!

I have had some extraordinary revelations made to me about another nest of unclean birds, not in this immediate vicinity but still in New England.

It is absurd to pretend that the warning to young people and their parents was uncalled for, taking only the notorious instances as ground for the sermon I preached. I think the good clergymen knew it all quite as well as I do, and will go with me as far as their *esprit du corps* will let them.

I may write my papers on my own model?
Yours always
O. W. Holmes

I hope you and Mrs. Fields are enjoying yourselves to your heart's content.

Advent[?] *I heard of this within a day or two—I don't know how recent. **Sexton of Dr. Gauntts[?] Church.[10]

Howells revealed many years later that the unorthodox tone of *The Guardian Angel* injured the circulation of the *Atlantic* considerably. Nevertheless, in book form the story reached twenty-three editions by 1887.[11]

In the finished volume of *The Guardian Angel*, Fields received one more tribute among many from the writers he worked with, for Holmes dedicated the book to him. Holmes wrote to him for his acceptance;[12] Fields accepted, of course, and the dedication read: "To/James T. Fields/a Token of Kind Regard/From One of Many Writers/Who Have Found Him/a Wise, Faithful/ and Generous Friend."

One reason Holmes appreciated Fields so much was that the publisher was always eager to print anything he wrote. Whenever he wrote occasional poems, Fields was ready to snap them up for the *Atlantic*, but sometimes Holmes refused to let them be printed because of their evanescence. For instance, he once explained to the editor:

Dear Mr. Fields,

I shan't print my little after dinner poem at all. It was only a china cracker, and it has gone off.
Yours always
O. W. H.

July 19th [FI 2228]

In the same vein he wrote:

[10]MS in possession of Mrs. Z. B. Adams.
[11]William Dean Howells, *Literary Friends and Acquaintance* (New York, 1901), p. 153. Alexander Cowie, *The Rise of the American Novel* (New York, 1948), pp. 497-98. [12]No date, FI 2223.

Dear Mr. Fields,   21 Charles St. July 25

I am glad you like any lines I write, but both the copies of verses were like the bouquets of the evening, for use on that occasion only. I do not mean to print either of them and only sent them to answer an idle moment. I think the φ B K verses on the other hand are well worth saving and am delighted to let them off through the Atlantic.

                         Yours always
                         O. W. H.   [FI 2202]

The Phi Beta Kappa poem was probably the macaronic "Chanson without Music," a more finished production than the others, and of course it was printed in the November 1867 number.

The same year Fields had printed another occasional piece, "All Here, 1829-1867," one of the numerous poems for the Harvard "Class of '29." It appeared in the March *Atlantic*. Holmes's letter about the poem is interesting because of the corrections he made.

Dear Mr. Fields,
    Please correct as follows:
       The old Triennial list remembers
       ———

      Too late for change! no graceless hand
        Shall stretch its cords in vain endeavor

Also please *order for* me to complete my set N. A. Rev. for July '65.
    Also please send Paul Hayne—Box 260 P. O. Augusta, Georgia, The Atlantic for the year 1867, charging do. to me, mildly.

                         Yours always
Jan. 20.   O. W. H.

In the *Atlantic* the line first mentioned, occurring in the third stanza, was corrected as Holmes wished, except that the *t* in *triennial* was not capitalized. The other two lines, in the next-to-last stanza, were not quite as Holmes indicated:

      Too late! too late!—no graceless hand
        Shall stretch its cords in vain endeavor.

The year 1867 was a busy one for the Autocrat. Besides publishing *The Guardian Angel* and the two occasional poems in the *Atlantic*, he took upon himself the co-editorship of the *Altantic*

Almanac along with Donald Grant Mitchell. The first issue of the *Almanac* was that for 1868 and contained essays by G. W. Curtis, Hawthorne, Emerson, Mrs. Louis Agassiz, Dickens, Henry Ward Beecher, Gail Hamilton, and Edward Everett Hale. Mitchell wrote an essay on each of the seasons and Holmes himself wrote an introductory essay entitled "The Seasons." The poetry was by Lowell, Robert Leighton, T. B. Aldrich, Whittier, Tennyson, Elizabeth Akers Allen, Alice Cary, Owen Meredith, Bryant, Thackeray, and Thomas Hood. Some of the contributions were new and some were reprints of older writings. There were also many illustrations by leading artists. The *Almanac*, which appeared in time for the Chirstmas season of 1867, was successful enough to warrant its yearly continuation.

As a man whose editorial judgment could be relied upon, Holmes was more important to Fields than any mere contributor to the *Atlantic*. When the editor went to Europe in 1869, leaving Howells in charge of the magazine, he knew that the young assistant editor would have the advice of Lowell in editorial matters; but Holmes was as influential as Lowell. It was Holmes who was responsible for the publication of Mrs. Stowe's exposé of Lord Byron, in spite of Lowell's admonition; for upon Holmes's insistence Howells accepted it without even seeing it till it was in type.[13] Nor was Fields ignorant of the progress of the magazine during his absence, for besides receiving reports from Howells and Lowell, he got at least one from Holmes, on July 10, 1869:

I have been in correspondence with Mrs. Stowe about her Byron article coming out in the September Atlantic. She asked me to look over her proofs which I did very diligently and made various lesser suggestions which she received very kindly and adopted. It will be more widely read, of course, than any paper which has been written for a long time.—Howells has given up his Witchcraft article and Mr. Upham is going to fight his own battle in the Historical Magazine.[14]

---

[13] Robert E. Butler, "William Dean Howells as Editor of The Atlantic Monthly" (unpublished doctoral dissertation, Rutgers University, May 1950), pp. 47-48.

[14] Part printed in Morse, II, 294-95.

Holmes spoke in the same letter of a "new venture" that he was working upon, but he did not come forth with anything extensive for more than a year. Through Fields's urging, *The Poet at the Breakfast-Table* finally appeared in 1872 after the editor had retired. On February 7, 1870, however, Holmes was still vague about it: "I do not *at this moment* wish to undertake any new continuous labor, but my ambitions are not quite extinguished, and I love to cherish the idea that I may at some future time—not very remote, of course—make one or two more literary ventures."[15] By August 18 Holmes was ready to work, but first he must call in Fields for a consultation: "Won't you come in any evening it suits you, and talk me into a fine frenzy of ambition and composition?"[16] In *Literary Friends and Acquaintance* (page 157), Howells credits himself, along with Osgood, with having elicited *The Poet at the Breakfast-Table*; but as the letters indicate Fields had been encouraging Holmes to write for some time.

Meanwhile Holmes submitted a poem for the January 1871 *Atlantic*, "Dorothy Q., a Family Portrait," perhaps his best statement of the mystery of heredity that he had been pondering for several years. The doctor promised it to Fields in November, if the following letter is correctly assigned to the year 1870:

My dear Mr. Fields,
    I will try to have something for your January number if you will tell me the *very latest* time when it will do to send it in.
Always yours
O. W. H.

Nov. 16th. [FI 2212]

Also beginning in the January 1871 number of the *Atlantic* were Fields's own reminiscences, entitled *The Whispering Gallery* and afterwards published in *Yesterdays with Authors*. In preparing the work Fields went to Holmes for advice. The doctor's comments on both style and content were exceedingly valuable to Fields in the latter's most important work. The respect the two

---

[15] Ibid., I, 219-20.
[16] Ibid., I, 220.

men had for each other appears in their letters at this time. In a footnote in the 1882 edition of *The Autocrat of the Breakfast-Table*, Holmes said of Fields: "Mr. James T. Fields [has left his monument] in the pleasant volumes full of precious recollections; but twenty or thirty years from now old men will tell their boys that... the chief of our literary reminiscents, whose ideal portrait gallery reached from Wordsworth to Swinburne, left us when [he] bowed his head and 'fell on sleep', no longer to delight the guests whom his hospitality gathered around him with the pictures to which his lips gave life and action."[17]

Upon Fields's retirement from business in December 1870, his friendship with Holmes remained undiminished. Each thought of the other when he wanted advice: Fields sought Holmes's opinion on matters of writing, and Holmes sought Fields's on public relations. In 1877, for example, when the doctor was named an honorary member of a new society, Fields was the man to consult on the propriety of accepting:

296 Beacon St. May 11th 1877.

Dear Mr. Fields

Do you know anything about the "Empire City Amateur Pun Association" which hails from 138 5th Avenue New York and has chosen me an honorary member?

I don't like to accept the honor without knowing something about the concern. I was proposed by somebody whose name seems to be

Charles C. Hemnan

and the note is signed thus

Geo. H. Watkyns.
Sec.

Do give me your paternal- or grandpaternal-counsel as of old about this matter and eternally oblige

Yours always
O. W. H.

Here is a poem to pay you for your trouble.

Long after Fields's retirement Holmes's loyalty to the *Atlantic* continued. In 1879 he was still a distinguished contributor; and

[17]Oliver Wendell Holmes, *The Autocrat of the Breakfast-Table* (Boston, 1891), p. 21.

H. O. Houghton, the publisher of the magazine, and Howells, the editor, gave him a breakfast in honor of his seventieth birthday. Fields was among the one hundred guests. The event took place on December 3 and lasted until six in the evening; the *Boston Daily Advertiser* devoted seven columns the next day to the speeches and poems in honor of the Autocrat.[18] In 1885 Holmes, still an *Atlantic* contributor, wrote to Lowell on behalf of Houghton to try to get Lowell to rejoin the ranks of the magazine's writers. And in 1890 the doctor sought a new five-year contract with Houghton to take care of his future writings.

When Fields died in 1881, Holmes was one of the most sympathetic friends of Mrs. Fields, and when she arranged the biography of her husband the same year, she found in the Autocrat a generous counselor. He not only went over all the proof but also advised on the propriety of including and omitting certain portions. It was for him, he said, a "labor of love."[19]

The doctor best expressed his debt to his editor and publisher back in 1867:

By the way, Mr. Fields, do you appreciate the position you hold in our time? There was never anything like it. Why, I was nothing but a roaring kangaroo when you took me in hand, and I thought it was the right thing to stand up on my hind legs, but you combed me down and put me in proper shape.[20]

---

[18]Mark Antony De Wolfe Howe, *Holmes of the Breakfast-Table* (New York, 1939), pp. 141-43.

[19]Holmes to Annie Fields, September 10, 1881.

[20]From Annie Fields's diary, February 28, 1867, in Howe, *Memories of a Hostess*, pp. 34-35.

Chapter V:
Henry Wadsworth Longfellow

LONGFELLOW's acquaintance with Fields began at least as early as 1840, and with the publisher's aid he was earning unheard-of royalties for his books by the 1850's.[1] Hence the magazine was not for him the godsend that it was for Holmes. He would have had no trouble publishing his poems anywhere, though he might not have obtained any more for them. At the same time that he and Fields were skillfully managing his book publications so as to get the most out of them, he was receiving the maximal rate of pay as an *Atlantic* contributor. And it was convenient to have an outlet close to home and controlled by a trusted friend.

Longfellow was among the contributors to the first issue of the *Atlantic*. As early as April 28, 1857, according to his diary, Lowell asked him to contribute:

29th. Lowell was here last evening to interest me in a new Magazine, to be started in Boston by Phillips and Sampson. I told him I would write for it if I wrote for any Magazine.

And on May 20 he "dined in town with the new Magazine Club; discussing title, etc., with no result."[2] His bit in the first number (November 1857) was "Santa Filomena," a poem on Florence Nightingale. Although all contributions were unsigned, the generally known fact of Longfellow's participation was bound to have its effect upon circulation. Longfellow was a major attraction in the magazine for the rest of his life, even though his output

---

[1]Fields to Longfellow, January 1, 1840, MS in the Longfellow House. William Charvat, "Longfellow's Income from His Writings, 1840-50," *Papers of the Bibliographical Society of America*, XXXVIII, 9-21.

[2]Samuel Longfellow, *Life of Henry Wadsworth Longfellow* (Boston, 1893), II, 331-33.

during the sixties was low. Whittier, Lowell, Holmes, and others contributed more often, but Longfellow was the most popular poet, and it was he whom both editor and contributors looked to as a guiding spirit in the poetry of the *Atlantic*. He printed only twenty-three poems under Fields.

Even before Fields became editor, however, Longfellow began submitting his contributions to him instead of to Lowell. One of these, "The Children's Hour," was submitted in July 1860. Fields predicted its singular success:

August 1. 1860

My dear Longfellow.
"The Children's Hour" I think is a charming lyric, & in it goes. Mark my prophetic words. It will be widely popular. The parental public will like it hugely.

Many thanks for the copy of "The Rainy Day" which you are to send to me for Lady Harrington, and which, by some accident, has not yet arrived from Nahant! I trust you are well.
Very truly
J. T. F.[3]

"The Children's Hour" was put into the magazine at once so that it would appear in the September issue. Before it appeared Fields again complimented the author. His constant praise of Longfellow sounds like flattery, but it was sincerely meant.

The Atlantic for Sept. is a goodly No. albeit I am one of the contributors. Read a little poem called "The Children's Hour." To my way of thinking it is a heart-warmer, and will be held close by all your readers. Do send another of the same just as soon as you are moved.[4]

On August 27 Longfellow received fifty dollars for "The Children's Hour."[5] This was the price paid for a poem by Lowell or Holmes, and was standard for major contributors.

The next contribution, "Paul Revere's Ride," was submitted to Fields, though Lowell was still editor, in November 1860. Fields suggested some changes in the final lines which had a great deal to do with the dramatic effect of the poem. He wrote to Longfellow:

[3]MS in the Longfellow House.
[4]Fields to Longfellow, August 12, 1860, MS in the Longfellow House.
[5]Ticknor and Fields to Longfellow, MS in the Longfellow House.

Dear Longfellow.
 Don't you think it better to end Paul Revere's Ride on this line,

> In the hour of darkness and peril and need,
> The People will waken and listen to hear
> The hurrying hoof-beat of his steed,
> And the midnight message of Paul Revere.

It seems to me the last line as it stands above is stronger than the end as it now remains in the proof.
 What do you say?
Yours truly
J. T. Fields

Nov. 23, 1860[6]

Fields's suggestion was adopted with only minor changes. When the magazine was already in print but not yet on sale, Longfellow discovered he had omitted a few lines in the copy of the poem he had sent to the *Atlantic*. He wrote to Fields, but it was too late to do anything about the oversight. Fields replied six days before the magazine was to appear:

Friday morning. Dec. 14 1860

Dear Longfellow.
 The lines are omitted in the magazine, so that you must have left them out of the copy you sent. How unfortunate, as they are so excellent as to rank with the best in the poem, which is saying much for them. It is a fine piece of poetry and painting.
 To day I intended to go to Cambridge and inquire for your health, but alas! I am tied by both legs to my inkstand.
Yours always
J. T. F.[7]

The magazine version of "Paul Revere's Ride" which appeared in the January 1861 *Atlantic* did not contain the following stanza, which presumably was the part Longfellow overlooked:

[6]James C. Austin, "J. T. Fields and the Revision of Longfellow's Poems: Unpublished Correspondence," *New England Quarterly*, XXIV (June 1951), 243. Longfellow's original ending to the poem read:
> In the hour of peril men will hear
> The midnight message of Paul Revere,
> And the hurrying hoof-beat of his steed.

[7]MS in the Longfellow House.

> He has left the village and mounted the steep,
> And beneath him, tranquil and broad and deep,
> Is the Mystic, meeting the ocean tides;
> And under the alders that skirt its edge,
> Now soft on the sand, now loud on the ledge,
> Is heard the tramp of his steed as he rides.

No new poem was forthcoming for several months, and Fields wrote to Longfellow in May 1861 (the dating is uncertain) for a contribution to his July issue:

Dear Longfellow
 I am much in need of a poem from you for the July No. Pray send me one today.
                            Yours Truly
Monday[8]   J. T. F.

But Fields received no contribution, nor did he for another year and a half.

Longfellow's silence was lengthened by the tragic death of his wife on July 9, 1861. But while it rendered him powerless to write for the *Atlantic*, the catastrophe brought him closer to his editor. Fields did everything he could for the poet. He sent gifts, took care of some of Longfellow's correspondence, suggested a tour in the mountains. Toward the end of July he wrote:

                            Tuesday morning.
My Dear Longfellow.
 I send you today Smith's "Edwin of Deira," which holds many fine patches. Yesterday went out "Tannhauser" & the only vol. of Miss Procter I own, or can get, the 2d. one not having as yet been reprinted. I also send a few grapes which look well & I hope they may taste better. Do let me know if I can attend to any matter for you. You know how gladly I would go about any thing you wished done.
 God bless you. I think of many things I do not speak or write, but no body loves you more than I do.
                            J. T. F.
 I wrote to Miss Procter & Freiligrath yesterday.[9]

---

[8]MS in the Longfellow House. The letter is dated [1861?] by someone other than Fields, probably one of Longfellow's descendants.

[9]MS in the Longfellow House.

Longfellow appreciated the sympathy. In September he was still feeling his loss, of course, and he wrote simply in his diary of a visit from Fields: "14th. Fields came out and passed an hour with me. He is very sympathetic."[10]

Throughout the war years Longfellow wrote very little on the Civil War, though his diary shows it to have been often on his mind. To be sure, he could have sold any writing of the kind to the *Atlantic* without the least trouble, for war pieces by less popular writers appeared in every issue. But the death of his wife halted Longfellow's writing almost completely for a while, and then he deliberately buried himself in his translation of Dante as a sort of escape. He wrote one war poem, however, of definite importance because of its popularity—"The Cumberland." The first draft of the poem was written in May 1862. By July Fields knew of it and wanted it: "Why don't you send me the Cumberland poem? Don't consider me an old Cumberland beggar, but I really wish to read the lyric and you said I should do so."[11] But Longfellow was dissatisfied with it and did not send it immediately. Instead he wrote on July 16: "I began copying 'The Cumberland' for you the other day; but gave it up in disgust at the end of the second stanza."[12] A month later he still had not sent it, and Fields wrote in the margin of his letter of August 22 the solitary interrogation " 'Cumberland'?"[13] Within the next few weeks the manuscript was finally sent, but Fields's alert eye caught an error in it: "The 'Cumberland' was *not* a '74', only a frigate altered from a 'Sloop of War'. The rhyme must therefore be 'razeed'."[14] The second line, which originally read, "On board of the Cumberland, seventy-four," was changed to "On board of the Cumberland, sloop-of-war," when it appeared in the December 1862 number of the *Atlantic*.

Fields was usually unsuccessful in getting Longfellow to write

[10] Longfellow, II, 422.
[11] Fields to Longfellow, July 7, 1862, MS in the Longfellow House.
[12] Longfellow, III, 15.
[13] MS in the Longfellow House.
[14] Austin, p. 244.

anything by request. Such was the case when he asked him that same year to write a review of P. M. Irving's *Life and Letters of Washington Irving* for the *Atlantic*. Longfellow would have been an appropriate reviewer, having been a long-time admirer of Irving and having written a sketch of him for the Massachusetts Historical Society in 1859. Fields wrote:

My dear Longfellow.

    I wish very much a loving notice of Irving's Life, say about a page in the "Atlantic." Do you feel like putting your pen to this service? You knew him so well, it occurred to me it might not be an uncongenial task, so I make bold to ask you.

Yours Ever
J. T. F.

Sept. 24.[15]

One year later, when a notice of one of Longfellow's books was needed, Fields succeeded in getting a full-length article on the poet by G. W. Curtis. The occasion was the publication of *Tales of a Wayside Inn* on November 25, 1863, and the article, "Longfellow," appeared five days earlier in the December *Atlantic*. As the book was a Ticknor and Fields publication, the release of Curtis's article was designed to provoke sales. This was typical of Fields's promotional tactics, which he employed to the full in publicizing Longfellow, and it reveals the advantage to the firm in publishing the magazine, regardless of the income from circulation; for the *Atlantic* was an excellent advertising medium for Ticknor and Fields books. Having received an early copy of the article, Longfellow wrote a letter of thanks to Curtis on November 19: "I have just been reading your very generous, and more than generous, article in the Atlantic. If it were not written about myself I should say it is beautifully done. As it is I must say nothing of the kind, but only think it."[16] The following month Whittier, understanding what had taken place, asked Fields: "Is

---

[15] MS in the Longfellow House. Longfellow did not comply with the request, and Fields had to get G. S. Hillard to write the review for the November 1862 number.

[16] Longfellow, III, 23.

there no use to do for me, in a moderate and qualified degree what Curtis has done for Longfellow in the *Atlantic*?"[17]

From 1863 to 1864 was Longfellow's most productive period for the *Atlantic*: he published eleven poems in the magazine during that time. One of these was his poem on Hawthorne. When Hawthorne died on May 19, 1864, Longfellow, having been his closest friend among the New England writers, was one of the first to be notified by the Fieldses. On the twenty-third he attended the funeral and was so much struck by the serenity of the day that he wrote a poem on it, originally called "Concord, May 23, 1864" and later merely "Hawthorne."

> How beautiful it was, that one bright day
> In the long week of rain!
> Though all its splendor could not chase away
> The omnipresent pain.

On June 23 he sent it to Fields for the *Atlantic*: "I have only tried to describe the state of mind I was in on that day. Did you not feel so likewise?"[18] Fields replied with praise: "I am rejoiced that you were in the mood to give expression to your own and all our feelings in such a perfect lyric."[19] The poem was printed in the August issue, and Fields wrote to tell Longfellow how popular it was:

Boston July 24 1864

My Dear Longfellow.
 I was just thinking of sending off a line to you to say how much your Concord poem was admired when yours of yesterday arrived. Haskell told me this morning (he printed the poem in the Transcript) that so many people had been in & spoken of its exquisite beauty and tenderness he could not help coming in to tell me of the great interest it excited in his office. I hear of it today wherever I go & I sincerely think you have never printed a poem that will be more universally

---

[17]John Greenleaf Whittier to Fields, December 25, 1863. Whittier got his article—by D. A. Wasson in the *Atlantic* for March 1864—following the publication of *In War Time*.

[18]Longfellow, III, 38.

[19]See below, Chapter XII.

welcomed. I have read it aloud to every body of taste who comes in since we got home and all say it is perfect. Depend upon it I am right in my estimate of its supreme excellence. Just now I am called away. Come in Tuesday & if you have other poems for the A. M. don't fail to bring them. You have never given me more welcome pieces than of late.

Yours Ever
J. T. F.

Longfellow's response to the request for more poems came in September, when he sent the poem "Wind over the Chimney." Fields set it aside for his January number, always the most impressive number of the year and calculated to attract new subscribers:

Boston Sept. 30. 1864.

My Dear Longfellow.

I am husbanding The Wind poem for my January No. because you may not find another piece for me at present. I must have you in that No. of course & so like a wise steward I keep something ahead in the locker. But don't omit sending me another and another & another if you can before the new year comes in.

Poet Wyman I can't make up my mind to recognize & so I send him back with all his bitter tears.

Hope you will be in today.

Yours always
J. T. F.

Despite Fields's fears, he obtained another contribution before January. Longfellow had written a sonnet which he intended to prefix to one of the books of his Dante translation, but when Fields saw it, he wanted it for the *Atlantic*. Longfellow wrote in his diary for October 6, 1864: "Go down to the printer's with a sonnet, 'On translating Dante.' Meet Fields. He wants it for the Atlantic."[20] The sonnet, beginning "Oft have I seen at some cathedral door," was printed in the December 1864 issue and afterwards served to introduce the first part, "Inferno," of *The Divine Comedy*.

By 1866 Longfellow had written two more sonnets "On Translating the Divina Commedia." Subtitled "Second Sonnet" and

---

[20]Longfellow, III, 47.

"Third Sonnet" in the *Atlantic*, they were introductions to the "Purgatorio" and the "Paradiso" respectively. Again Fields sought them for the magazine as soon as he saw them. He wrote on January 22:

My dear Longfellow.

Your two sonnets have made my day beautiful. They are exquisite, and I must print them in the *Atlantic*. Will you give me the heading to each, and let me put them into an early number. I know of nothing more perfect. Dante himself will rejoice over them in Paradise.

Yours Ever

Saturday night.[21]   J. T. F.

Payment of fifty dollars apiece for the second and third sonnets was sent on January 24, 1866, but they were printed in the July and September issues. A fourth, "How strange the sculptures that adorn these towers!" appeared in the December *Atlantic*, and eventually constituted the second introductory sonnet to the "Inferno." A fifth and sixth sonnet were later written for the "Purgatorio" and the "Paradiso" but were never in the *Atlantic*.

Meanwhile Longfellow was trying to get Fields to print some Dante letters edited and translated by George W. Greene. They were something Longfellow had been thinking of for several months, having suggested the idea to his friend Greene on September 20, 1865: "It came into my mind that a translation of Dante's letters would make a good paper for the Atlantic, and that yours is the pen to do it. . . . I have this morning written to Fields about it."[22] Actually his letter to Fields was written the following day. "There are still extant four or five letters of Dante," he explained, "which have never been translated entire. They would make a capital article for the Atlantic, and Greene is the man to do it."[23] On September 24 Fields had suggested that he and Longfellow talk over the matter when they met. Four months later when the article had been written and handed to

---

[21] MS in the Longfellow House.
[22] Longfellow, III, 60.
[23] Ibid., p. 61. See Fields to Longfellow, September 24, 1865.

Longfellow, Fields wrote the letter of January 24 with which he enclosed the payment for Longfellow's second and third Dante sonnets. He asked to see Greene's mansucript so as to judge how much space it would require in the *Atlantic*:

Boston January 24. 1866.

My dear Longfellow.

 Enclosed I hand you the slip for $100 for the two lovely sonnets.

 Please send me the whole of Greene's Mss. touching the Dante letters & I will then decide about the number of pages I can spare. Friday I hope to be with the Tuscans around your fire. Thank you for asking me to be there [the Dante Club meeting]. Do you ever come to Boston these days? It seems several years since I heard your knock at my door.

Yours Ever
J. T. F.

There was some question as to the appropriateness of Greene's article for the *Atlantic*. Fields feared it would be too heavy, but he wanted to print it for Longfellow's sake. In the end his fears were confirmed; the article was meticulously done but too scholarly and much too long. Fields wrote to Longfellow that it would have to be rejected:

Boston Feb. 5. 1866.

My dear Longfellow.

 I cannot possibly manage all the Dante matter Greene has sent for the Atlantic. What he has prepared will make 30 or 40 pages, & I told him *one* number was all I could devote to the letters. I must therefore bring the mss to you tomorrow-night, as it wd. be folly for me to attempt such a cataract on the heads of our readers. I shd. be torn to pieces.

Yours always
J. T. F.

Longfellow had not given up, however, when he wrote to Greene four days later:

 I wish all things would go on smoothly in this world. Now, here is our good Fields frightened at the length of the Dante letters. But at the last Dante Club, Lowell and Norton, as well as myself, were so positive that they ought to go into the Magazine, that he seemed to take heart. I confess it is a quality of food not adapted to the great mass of Magazine readers. But I trust the Atlantic has some judicious readers who like to have some timber in the building, and not all clapboards.[24]

But the letters were never printed in the *Atlantic*. The incident illustrates Longfellow's earnest efforts to help his friends. It also shows a disagreeable aspect of Fields's job as editor, having to reject material that was admittedly good but too scholarly for a magazine whose existence depended on the number of its readers.

From the beginning of 1867 to the middle of 1870 Longfellow contributed nothing to the *Atlantic*. At first he was busy with the publication of the Dante translation; then he left for a European tour. But he did contribute to *Our Young Folks*. Fields had asked him to take part in the first number, for January 1865:

Boston Oct. 27. 1864.

Dear Longfellow
  It will be a great thing for us in the new Illustrated Magazine if we can print a few verses from your pen. If you cannot find a new one in Craigie House with those jolly little sunny heads about your knee, who can? Do try. May I consider you loyal to the enterprize, and one of the speakers to our growing youth?
Yours always
J. T. F.

Longfellow's first contribution, "Christmas Bells," did not appear until the February number. But he gave the magazine his support by contributing occasionally throughout its existence. Fields also asked him to write for the *Atlantic Almanac*, and on July 13, 1867, when the first one was about to be made up, he wrote: "Has the muse visited you in behalf of our Almanac?" But again Longfellow neglected the first number; nor did he contribute to any of the succeeding ones.

In May 1868 Longfellow sailed for Europe. His letters to Fields were frequent, but one from Dickens to Fields briefly relates the joyous reception the English gave the poet: "Nothing can surpass the respect paid to Longfellow here, from the Queen downward. He is everywhere received and courted, and finds (as I told him

[24]Ibid., p. 72.

he would, when we talked of it in Boston) the workingmen at least as well acquainted with his books as the classes socially above them."[25] In April 1869 the Fieldses too were in Europe, and hoping to meet Longfellow there. The meeting was finally arranged for July; Annie Fields wrote:

Torquay. July 14th 1869.
Dear Mr. Longfellow.
 We were delighted this morning by hearing through my sister that you were to be in London Thursday.
 We shall be there, we hope, on Saturday and Jamie asks me to say with his love that he shall come to see you Sunday, at the Langham hotel.
 It has given added zest to our pleasure today in this lovely place that we are to see you again so soon.
 Believe me (and I write for both as you know) affectionately yours
Annie Fields.

Though Longfellow contributed little to the *Atlantic* in these days, he was still loyal to it. When Fields spoke of retiring, however, Longfellow too thought it best to leave the magazine. He wrote to Fields July 7, 1871:

I come back to my old wish and intention of leaving the Magazine when you do. This is the wisest course, as I could easily persuade you, if I had you alone here by the seaside. But I do not like to write about it, for you see how the paper blots and the ink spreads with the damp.[26]

But Longfellow not only failed to persuade Fields, he continued to contribute to the magazine.
 He still sought Fields's advice in publishing matters. In 1875, for example, Fields advised him to space his contributions to the *Atlantic* so as not to sate his readers' appetites:

Feb. 23.
My dear Longfellow.
 I would not let Howells have the poem at present. And for this reason: he has already printed three pieces in the A. M. lately, &, with

---

[25] Charles Dickens to Fields, July 7, 1868, in Fields, *Yesterdays*, p. 190.
[26] Longfellow, III, 177.

little judgment, put *two* pieces into one number. I would never let him do that again. It weakens the impression of each poem to have two in one number. I would now hold off for a few months. Don't quote me, please, but it seems like squandering your golden thought to appear in any magazine oftener than need be. I would print the "Three Friends of Mine" in the July No. and not before. The last poem you printed in the A. M. has not done its full mission yet. It is constantly reprinted in the papers, and if another comes out so close upon it, the effect is disturbed. I am sure of it.

Ever Yours
J. T. F.

Excuse paper. I write in slippers.

Longfellow did not follow the advice very closely. He did not print "Three Friends of Mine," a series of sonnets, in the *Atlantic* at all, but in the May issue (not July) his "Amalfi" appeared there. Then followed two years of no contributions. Once later he allowed Howells to print more than one contribution in an issue; the March 1878 number contained not only a poem but also a series of sonnets.

When Longfellow wrote a class poem to be delivered at Bowdoin College on July 8, 1875, he again received Fields's counsel. A little anxious about reading the poem before the public, he composed the first draft more than six months ahead of time and sent it to Fields in February. Fields hailed it as a "triumph in poetry" when he replied on March 1: "Depend upon it, you have achieved a marked success, an occasional poem that will be permanent."[27] Fields arranged with his friend Henry Mills Alden, managing editor of *Harper's New Monthly Magazine*, to print the poem, entitled "Morituri Salutamus." The transaction was handled confidentially, and on July 1, Fields wrote to Longfellow: "Please don't say *I* had anything to do about the Harper negotiation."[28] The author received a thousand dollars for the poem.[29]

[27] Austin, p. 249.

[28] MS in the Longfellow House. See Alden to Fields, June 21, 1875.

[29] Longfellow, III, 441. This was not the highest price paid for a single Longfellow poem; "The Hanging of the Crane" brought three thousand dollars from Bonner of the *New York Ledger*, through the agency of Samuel Ward. Ibid.

It was read at Bowdoin on July 7 and printed in the August number of *Harper's Monthly*. Fields sent congratulations a few days later from his summer cottage in Manchester, Massachusetts:

July 12. 1875

My dear Longfellow.

 Congratulations no doubt pour like rain upon you, and so I will only send my little sprinkle from Manchester. I knew it would be all right. The papers far and wide copy your poem & all join in the universal acclamation. I enclose a slip from my Tribune of yesterday which you may not have seen.

 When will you come here and stay under our cottage roof? Do send a line to say what day I am to meet you at the Manchester station.

 My wife sends kindest regards & begs you will be here soon to bless our new abode.

Ever Yours,
J. T. F.

Fields frequently managed the sale of Longfellow's magazine contributions. In 1877 he submitted one for Longfellow to the *Youth's Companion*. "I sent the poem at once (and a lovely poem it is) to the 'Companion,'" he wrote on January 21, "& you will no doubt have a wind, and no blow, from the Editor today."[30]

Another of Longfellow's poems got into print through Fields's agency quite accidentally. When Fields was lecturing in 1877, he asked Longfellow for a new poem to adorn his talk. Longfellow complied with the sonnet "Holidays," which concerned the keeping of special days for the sake of personal memories. It had a special meaning for Longfellow, and he did not want it published. He wrote, "When you played your first card, I was in Portland, and could not send you the Sonnet. Your second finds me here; and as it is a trump, it takes the Sonnet, which you will find enclosed."[31] But someone recorded the sonnet from the lecture and it leaked into print. Fields explained to the author:

August 14. 1877.

My dear Longfellow.

 It is a wicked world! Who could have been so base I know not, especially as I said in my lecture the sonnet was unpublished and must remain so at present. I particularly warned off reporters.

[30] MS in the Longfellow House.   [31] Longfellow, III, 276.

Are not you & I going to Portsmouth this month or next to explore with Mrs. Bartlett the Pepperell Mansion & grounds? Do let us keep in mind that expedition. "Kittery Point" must be visited this summer by you, and I will be your "guide, philosopher, and friend" on that occasion.

Ever Yours
J. T. F.[32]

The friendship of the publisher and the poet continued until Fields's death. Their correspondence suggests that Longfellow was perhaps Fields's closest friend; certainly Fields admired no man more than him. And Longfellow had undying respect for the publisher's business sense as well as love for the man himself. Because of their long intimacy, Fields's death in 1881 was a blow to Longfellow. He wrote in his diary in April:

> 29th. A sorrowful and distracted week. Fields died on Sunday, the 24th, and was buried on Tuesday. Dr. Palfrey died on Tuesday, and will be buried to-day. Two old and intimate friends in one week![33]

And it was Longfellow's poem "Auf Wiedersehen" that was the outstanding tribute among many to the deceased publisher:

> Until we meet again! That is the meaning
> Of the familiar words, that men repeat
>   At parting on the street.
> Ah yes, till then! but when death intervening
> Rends us asunder, with what ceaseless pain
>   We wait for thee again!

---

[32]MS in the Longfellow House.
[33]Longfellow, III, 315.

Chapter VI:
Julia Ward Howe

Julia ward howe's relationship with Fields is important because it presents neglected aspects of both their lives. She was one of the few writers who retired from his aegis in dissatisfaction. But her early business relations with him were as pleasant as those of the many other authors he dealt with. She once expressed her approval of the publisher-editor in verse:

>The Manuscript
>
>Behind the green curtain which shadeth
>A nook, in the Bookseller's shop,
>What pleading of woman persuadeth
>The poet's adviser to stop?
>
>(Lest no one should find himself wiser
>*This* time, for the word that I write,
>Let me state that the Poets' adviser
>Is Fields, and the Muses' Delight.)
>
>Without, brow of Ticknor grows darker—
>Time presses, again and again;
>Holmes, Bigelow, Parsons and Parker
>Are waiting, and waiting in vain.
>
>The pretty girls pause in commanding,
>Unsatisfied, even if served;
>Fields having with them that high standing
>Which painfuller men have deserved.
>
>Within, through the lapse of the morning
>A lady continues to read,
>Encouraged by ill-suppressed yawning,
>And: "ah! very fine—fine indeed!"

Fields of the Atlantic Monthly

Secure in her arm-chair she burrows,
With authorship's gratified smiles,
While wearily gathered in furrows
The brow of our Fields is, the while.

At length, after projects uncertain
And varying plans of escape,
Fields wildly springs thro' the green curtain,
Regardless of rivet or tape;

Glares round him, then seizes a letter
Whose contents he perfectly knows,
Kept sealed for occasions, the better
Some summons of haste to disclose.

"Dear Madam, this note has pursued me
Requiring my presence at once."
"Dear Sir, thinking thus to elude me,
You take me indeed for a dunce.

"Not even the country's salvation,
The Commonwealth's glory and pride
Should call, when a new reputation
May suffer, by what you decide."

Poor Fields, sinking down in the corner
Grows plaintively patient and civil,
A woman, he knows, if you scorn her
(See Byron)'s the veriest devil.

The right of precedence admitting
Which courtesy yields to the sex,
He nods, through a very long sitting,
To measure and rhymes multiplex.

"Now here, do you fathom my meaning,
Or seems the expression obscure?"
"Nay Madam, the thought's overweening,
The line plain as prose, I am sure."

He listens, till thoughts and things mingle,
Till all he perceives of the strain
Is one indiscriminate jingle
That drowsily quiets the brain.

Julia Ward Howe

> Then he smiles from his seat, almost liking
> To catch at the words as they pass,
> Till sudden, the trusty clock's striking
> Has dealt him the real "coup de grace."
>
> He rises, and shows on the dial
> Th' inviolate hour of two;
> Here ends the mild sufferer's trial:
> "Thank God! people dine—even you."
>
> But can she no recompense make him,
> That Lady who thinks herself clever?
> For her publisher now shall she take him?
> For her critic and friend, & forever.   [FI 2611]

In 1853 when Mrs. Howe was thirty-four, Ticknor, Reed and Fields had published her first book, *Passion Flowers*. It had been very successful for a first effort, but had had its detractors. When a writer for the *New York Evening Post* attacked the book, Mrs. Howe was not the kind to take it lying down. Yet despite her usual self-reliance, she was Victorian enough to solicit Fields's sympathy for the weaker sex in asking him to quell the assailant:

Have you seen the Article in the Post? It is vulgar and disgraceful. Will no chivalrous hand strike a blow for me? It ought to be answered —"sensual-minded" is too insulting a term to submit to.[1]

Regardless of such criticism, three thousand copies of the book were printed by February 20, 1854.[2] Mrs. Howe revealed another of her characteristics when she wrote to Fields on March 14 regarding the third edition of a thousand copies: "Pray let me know if the third edition of *Our* Book sells. I am bent on making a thousand dollars within the year. See that it is done." She was constantly watchful of her financial interests, and expected Fields to do his best for her. When she had to wait for her pay, it rankled her, though she jokingly put the blame on "the black Ticknor."[3]

Mrs. Howe was never a major contributor to the *Atlantic*,

---

[1] Howe to Fields, January 21, 1854.
[2] Tryon and Charvat, pp. 267, 277.
[3] Howe to Fields, July 15, 1854.

though her "Battle Hymn of the Republic" was of major importance. Our concern with her is in showing Fields's handling of a minor and somewhat refractory writer. Before Ticknor and Fields bought the magazine, she had contributed two poems, "Hamlet at the Boston" and "The Last Bird," and her popular travel sketch, "A Trip to Cuba." After that she did not appear until Fields became editor, but he immediately gave her top billing. The leader in his first number, July 1861, was Mrs. Howe's poem "Our Orders." It is a rousing call to colors that symbolizes the magazine's spirit during the years of the Civil War:

> Weave no more silks, ye Lyons looms,
>   To deck our girls for gay delights!
> The crimson flower of battle blooms,
>   And solemn marches fill the nights.

And more specifically the author delineates the duty of writers:

> And ye that wage the war of words
>   With mystic fame and subtle power,
> Go, chatter to the idle birds,
>   Or teach the lesson of the hour!
>
> Ye Sibyl Arts, in one stern knot
>   Be all your offices combined!
> Stand close, while Courage draws the lot
>   The destiny of humankind!

The October *Atlantic* contained two of Mrs. Howe's poems, "Our Country" and "Crawford's Statues at Richmond." The former is another war cry—though less successful than "Our Orders"—in which the country is urged to "link thy ways to those of God." "Crawford's Statues at Richmond" is an elegy upon the author's late brother-in-law, Thomas Crawford, sculptor of the equestrian statue of Washington in Richmond, Virginia. Fields had offered some revisions of it including corrections of the punctuation, at which Mrs. Howe was generally inexpert; but she had not been eager to accept them:

Dear Fields,

    I can't mend the lame line—think you find such lines in all long measures. It is like the liberty of spondaic or dactylic lines in hexameters. I think you have over punctuated the line—not like me to pause & grieve. But you know best. Other punctuations all right. In greatest haste

Yr's ever
J. W. H.

P. S. When does the George Sand come out? I might write about Elizabeth Browning but shall do nothing unless I hear from you.

[FI 2587]

Fields retained his own punctuation of the line "Others come to gaze and wonder,—not, like me, to pause and grieve," which may well be considered over-punctuated. The "lame line" might have been any of three lines in the published poem which lacked a syllable.

    Mrs. Howe's third contribution to Fields, "George Sand," is the only prose the editor accepted from her. It begins as a notice of the autobiography of the great individualist across the ocean, whom Mrs. Howe warmly admired as a sister spirit, but it develops into a full-length article of twenty-two pages. Regarding the questionable details of George Sand's life, the article passes over them: "To the world's triumph they belong not, and we honor the decency and self-respect which consign them to oblivion. Nor shall we endeavor to lift the veil which she [Sand] has thus thrown over the most intimate portion of her private life." By September 16 Mrs. Howe had corrected the proof of the article and sent it to Fields from her summer residence near Newport, Rhode Island:

Sept. 16th/61 Lawton's Valley.

Dear Fields,

    Enclosed please find proofs, with many thanks. Your proof reader is too ambitious of correcting style, and to correct him has cost me some trouble. Please see to it that things are printed my way, and not his. I have never had so many liberties taken with any thing of mine, and cannot write, if I am thus to be called to account. I am glad you think well of the article, but I could not write another at the same price, or anything like it. The Tribune pays much better. Hoping soon to seen you, I remain

Your very sincere friend
Julia W. Howe.

The article was printed in the November *Atlantic*. The author's commercial attitude, as exhibited in her letter, was partly responsible for the rather ill-treatment of her later contributions.

Early in December Mrs. Howe submitted undramatically her masterpiece, the "Battle Hymn of the Republic":

Fields!
 Do you want this, and do you like it, and have you any room for it in January number? I recd. your invitation to meet the Trollope's[sic] just five minutes before my departure for Washington, so could only leave a verbal answer, hope you got it.

I am sad and spleeny, and begin to have fears that I may not be, after all, the greatest woman alive. Isn't this a melancholy view of things? but it is a vale, you know. When will the world come to end?
 In haste

sincerely your's[sic]

J. W. H.

S. Boston Dec. 2nd[4] [FI 2641]

Her gloom was not to be dispelled by her check for the contribution—only four dollars.[5] But she became heartened as she grew more and more aware of the poem's increasing popularity. She wrote in her *Reminiscences* of its reception upon its appearance in the February (not January) 1862 issue of the *Atlantic*: "It was somewhat praised on its appearance, but the vicissitudes of the war so engrossed public attention that small heed was taken of literary matters. I knew, and was content to know, that the poem soon found its way to the camps, as I heard from time to time of its being sung in chorus by the soldiers."[6] At any rate, the "Battle Hymn of the Republic" soon spread throughout the North and was reprinted in newspapers and broadsides. The author recorded the comment of one of her friends: "Mrs. Howe ought to die now, for she has done the best that she will ever do."[7] From a literary point of view, the statement contains some truth; the

---

[4]Mrs. Howe's use of the apostrophe is insupportable; it will henceforth be recorded but not marked with [sic].

[5]"Julia Ward Howe," *Dictionary of American Biography*.

[6]Julia Ward Howe, *Reminiscences, 1819-1899* (Boston, 1899), pp. 275-76.

[7]Ibid., p. 276.

"Battle Hymn" is "the one piece by its author that posterity has cared to recall."[8] And it constitutes a landmark in the history of the *Atlantic Monthly*. But after her one great success, Mrs. Howe the writer rather faded from public notice, and her later fame rested upon her lectures and her social services.

Her confidence in her literary ability was increasing in 1862, however. It was given a boost in February, just after the publication of the "Battle Hymn," when the *Continental Monthly* sought her as a contributor on her own terms. She did not like Fields's customary demand that his writers contribute to the *Atlantic* exclusively, but she notified him of the proposal from the *Continental* before taking any steps:

> Wednesday Feb. 12th
>
> My dear Fields,
> The Continental has sent to me, desiring me to name my own terms for contributions to their Magazine, in prose and in verse. I think it would be advantageous for me to make an engagement with them, as I am anxious to earn money, and the Tribune and I have parted amicably. Your *staff* is already made up without me, and I cannot consider myself as regularly under employment by your Monthly. The adoption of what I might furnish you would only be contingent, not by any means certain. Yet I am not willing to enter into new engagements without previous communication with you, as when we last spoke of these matters, more in jest than in earnest, you told me not to write for the Continental. Please therefore to let me hear from you as soon as convenient on the subject. I do not see any incompatibility between writing for you and writing for them—if such an incompatibility exists, you must tell we where it lies. I will also frankly say that in any engagement with them, I should set a higher price upon my poems than that hitherto fixed by the Atlantic. In great haste believe me
>
> Your's ever
> Julia W. Howe   [FI 2617]

Fields's reply was encouraging. According to Mrs. Howe's later statement, he offered to accept for the *Atlantic* all her forthcoming prose as well as a series of poems she was preparing, if she would

---

[8]George F. Whicher, "Literature and Conflict," *Literary History of the United States*, ed. Robert E. Spiller et al. (New York, 1948), p. 568.

remain an exclusive contributor. She declined the *Continental*'s offer.

The series of poems, *Lyrics of the Street*, she sent to Fields on February 20:

My dear Fields,
    I send you my Lyrics of the Street, to look over. Please let me know if you like any or all of them. I have one or two more which I could put in the place of any which may not please you. If you will send for me, I will come and go over them with you. I cannot speak of prices until I know whether you wish to have them, and how many of them.

Your's sincerely
Julia W. Howe

Thursday 20th   [FI 2604]

Not receiving a reply for more than a week, Mrs. Howe commented in a note to the editor's wife: "Please tell Mr. Fields that I am waiting to hear from him about the poems I sent him."[9] On March 5 she saw Fields and received his general approval of the series, but not until the following day did she mention remuneration. Her standards had risen in the preceding months; her poetry was now worth twenty-five dollars per poem, she thought:

My dear Fields,
    I ought perhaps to have told you last evening that I had wished to receive $200. for the poems in your hands. Should you publish as many of them as ten, I think they would be worth as much as that to you. I have offered to send you one or two more to consider in the place of such as may not please you.
    I think I ought not to have less than twenty five dollars for a single poem of any length and *mark*—I mean, out of a series. You may pay me, if you like, $150. for the choice of the poems, and $50. more if you should print more than eight of them. Is not that fair? I think it is. Excuse my clumsiness, and believe me

cordially your's
Julia W. Howe

Thursday 6th   [FI 2591]

[9]Howe to Annie Fields, March 3, 1862.

That evening,[10] Mrs. Howe met her editor at dinner, and he suggested altering the title of *Lyrics of the Street*. When she wrote to him on the following Monday, however, she had determined to retain it:

Excellence!

    I think, "Lyrics of the Street," expresses it best. You can have the Flag whenever you like. I enjoyed the dinner on Thursday particularly.

Your's always
Julia W. Howe

Monday 9th S. Boston   [FI 2590]

"The Flag," perhaps the most chauvinistic of all Mrs. Howe's contributions, and one of the most popular, was not printed until a year later, much to Mrs. Howe's discomfiture. The *Lyrics of the Street* began in the May 1862 issue of the *Atlantic* with the poem "The Telegrams." At irregular intervals during the following months appeared "The Wedding," "The Charitable Visitor," "The Fine Lady," "The Darkened House," and "Play." They were poems on everyday occurrences—deaths, marriages, lost fortunes, poverty—and they always contained a moral. "The Telegrams" sets the tone of the series; it is a rapid succession of messages meaning happiness or despair to their recipients. Interesting is the pair of poems "The Charitable Visitor" and "The Fine Lady." The former describes a lady of social position who is blessed because she visits the poor in the slums, in contrast to the "fine lady," whose "heart is set on folly." "Play," a favorite of Mrs. Howe, was a condemnation of gambling, written in almost a stream-of-consciousness style.

"The Wedding," the second poem from *Lyrics of the Street*, was not published until the July issue. When she returned the corrected proof at the end of May, Mrs. Howe first mentioned the grievance that was to cause her ultimate withdrawal from the

---

[10] My calculation that it was the same evening is based upon the assumption that the following letter is incorrectly dated "Monday 9th" instead of "Monday 10th." The only Monday that fell on the ninth in 1862 was in June, after the title *Lyrics of the Street*, which is questioned in the letter, had already appeared in the magazine.

Atlantic. She had expected the poems to appear consecutively and was annoyed that Fields should permit a month to elapse between the first and second of the series. She had consulted her friend Frederick Hedge, who had concurred with her view:

Dear Fields,
    Is "sphered about" better than "veiled about" in verse 2nd line 2nd?
    Should not midnight and Angel, verse 5th line 4th both have capitals? at least, angel should.
    Verse 6th "*Can* enrich a selfish heart" seems to carry on the meaning better to the next line. Should not dead in the last lines of verse 1rst and last verse have a capital D.?
    Won't you please to send me back the "Sculptor" poem? I want it, and at the present rate of getting on, you have poetry enough of mine for at least eighteen months to come.
    Hedge deplores the interruption of the Lyrics—he says it is a decided mistake. So does every one who speaks of it.
    In haste
                                     Your's always
                                     Julia W. Howe.
Saturday 31rst

Please look over this proof carefully, with a view to the corrections I propose. If you wish, I will come & see you about it, but am very busy.[11]   [FI 2613]

Fields did not return the manuscript of "A New Sculptor," though Mrs. Howe repeatedly reminded him of it. Instead, after a few months' procrastination, he printed the poem in the September 1862 number of the *Atlantic*. Not a part of *Lyrics of the Street*, it concerned the destruction of past ideals by modern ones. Its awkward metrical scheme and its abundance of "poetic diction" make it dull reading.

Meanwhile Mrs. Howe was preparing further contributions. Besides "The Flag" and "A New Sculptor" she submitted in June something called "Dealings with the Devil":

---

[11] In "The Wedding" the expression "veiled about" was retained, "Midnight" and "Angel" both got capital letters, the line "Can enrich a selfish heart" was adopted, and "dead" was spelled without capitals in both instances.

Dear Editor,

I send you my "Dealings with the Devil." I want fifty dollars for it, and want to see it printed in the August number of the Magazine, instead of the Article on Parker I promised you, which I will prepare later, if you still wish for it. You can look over this in the course of the present week. If you should conclude not to want it, please return it when you have made up your mind.

I think I cannot come tonight—it may be possible, but I fear not.
In haste   Your's always
                                          J. W. Howe.
Monday 9th   [FI 2596]

In spite of Fields's generous offers at the beginning of the year, he rejected this piece and it never appeared in the magazine. Mrs. Howe wrote late in June, having just received the rejection:

My dear Fields,

I left town immediately after sending you my MSS, and continued about for some time. On my return, I received it with your note. The good opinion of Alger and Whipple, who heard a part of the paper read, makes me think that you undervalue its' merits. I write now to beg that you would return to me the poem you took from me after the reading at Bartol's. I have forgotten whether it was called "Life Sculpture," or "A new Sculptor," but you will easily remember it. I wish very much to have it again.

By a singular coincidence, Leland publishes in the August Knickerbocker a Conversation with the Devil, written by himself.

Believe me   Your's sincerely
                                          Julia W. Howe.
Friday 27th S. Boston.   [FI 2599]

The third installment of *Lyrics of the Street* was detained until the December 1862 number of the *Atlantic*. Mrs. Howe had been sorely disappointed by the omission from the magazine of "The Funeral," a companion poem to "The Wedding," and she complained of this when she wrote Fields about corrections in her December poem, "The Charitable Visitor":

                                          Springfield Oct. 28th
My dear Fields,

I never, of course, received the proof you sent five weeks since. It must have miscarried strangely. What you sent me yesterday I was unable to correct, through a press of business of immediate necessity which left no moment for doing it. Leaving town this morning, for a three day's journey, the proof was left in my bureau, but I have ordered it sent to me at Greenfield, Mass. at once. In case you should not be able to wait for my correction, I will mention the only two features I remember, which are "mauldin" for maudlin, & "forward" for "froward." I shall return on Thursday evening, in any case, and will attend to it at once, if it be not too late.

I am surprised and sorry that you did not put in "The funeral" which properly follows "The Wedding." The two divided are very like two halves of scissors.   Your's in haste
Julia W. Howe   [FI 2639]

She was more successful in persuading Fields to print "The Fine Lady," which was designed to accompany "The Charitable Visitor." Fields published it the following month, January 1863, as a result of Mrs. Howe's "particular and personal request" of the preceding November:

My dear Fields,

I make it a particular and personal request that you would publish "The Fine Lady" in the next number of the Atlantic. It goes necessarily with "The Charitable Visitor," and should, in my order, have preceded it. If it is not included in the eight poems originally paid for by you, and of which the selection was to be left to yourself, you can include it without extra payment, as I consider it necessary to the expression of my idea, which was one of contrast, the two poems being in my view complementary to each other.

I beg that you would complete the selection as soon as convenient, and return me the balance of the MSS. I should be glad also to receive "The Flag" back again, the time for its' best publication being almost past.

I have heard but one vote on the way in which you have published the "Lyrics." Every body is displeased with it, I am asked again and again why they appear at such long intervals, and the reasons you gave are not more convincing to other people than they were to me. You spoke to me the other day of one or two prose articles, but I cannot help wishing to see justice done to what you have already in your possession, before I undertake any further literary service for the Atlantic.

Believe me, always   Your's sincerely
Julia W. Howe.

Nov. 22nd 13 Chestnut St.   [FI 2640]

When "The Darkened House" was printed in the March 1863 number and no other poem from the series appeared for several months, Mrs. Howe's dissatisfaction mounted. Fields's opinion of her work was obviously low, and he was using the poems merely to fill the unused space in the magazine. The poems may hardly have merited better treatment, but by taking them Fields had kept the author from accepting the attractive offer of the *Continental*, and he might have been expected to display them at their best. When July arrived and nothing of Mrs. Howe's but "The Flag"—not of the series—had appeared, she decided it was time to take action. Fields had finally sent her the proof of another lyric, which never appeared, and when she returned the corrected proof, she informed him that she would contribute nothing more after the completion of the *Lyrics of the Street*:

Thursday July 9th

My dear Fields,

This proof reaches me at Lawton's Valley, settled for the summer. I think the 1rst line of the 2nd verse stands best as it is. For line 3rd verse 4th you can put:

    for guerdon of the right.
  or
    guerdoning the right.

But I do not think it better than recompense, wh. is more simple and direct. Three more of those Lyrics belong to you by our original agreement. I hope that you will choose for two of these "Play," and "Outside the Party." These are two of the most vigorous. The present one seems to me one of the least interesting. I hope too that you will do your best to finish up the series at once. How little satisfied I have been with the manner in which it has been published is well known to you. Your whole treatment of me in this matter has been food, not for anger, but for sad disappointment. It has been most disadvantageous, and compels me to seek literary employment else where.

You have not appreciated these poems, nor any recent productions of mine. It is not for me to praise them, but I receive far echoes of them which tell me that they touch some hearts. Print the remaining three with selection as to their merit, not their shortness, and then let us make *tabula rasa* of all engagements. I may not have worded this letter very carefully, and should be sorry to say anything to you that should not be far within the borders of good manners and good feeling. But this really expresses my state of mind relatively to these matters, and is better said, perhaps, than left to be inferred from ungracious silences.

  With entire regard and goodwill, believe me Your's sincerely
                    Julia W. Howe.
P. S. Should there not be a comma after "day by day" verse 2nd line 2nd.   [FI 2631]

The letter brought an unexpected reaction; Fields suggested the immediate suspension of all her contributions including the *Lyrics of the Street*, though he had published only five of the eight poems he had paid for. Of course, this was unsatisfactory to Mrs. Howe, for although the poems were not appearing at regular intervals, she did want the series in one magazine. She hastened to reply to Fields, in measured tones, reviewing the whole case:

                   Boston July 16th/63
My dear Fields,
  I suppose that neither of us desires a prolonged correspondence in the matter of the Lyrics. Still, I cannot be content to leave the matter as it stands. You had certainly the power to return them to me unpublished, but I do not conceive that anything in my action has given you the right to do so. You certainly promised to publish them, and my complaining of the tardiness with which this promise has, so far, been fulfilled, does not, as I see, absolve you from that promise. This, however, only with regard to the *morale* of the question, since in the actual, I have neither power nor will to do anything. My principal anxiety since receiving your letter has been to satisfy myself that mine gave you no cause of personal offense. In order to satisfy you of this, I must ask you to recall what I wrote, in its' simple construction, and also the circumstances which preceded my writing. But first, as to the charge of ingratitude which your words imply. You have certainly been disposed to treat me with kindness and consideration in the past, and I have done all in my power to reciprocate your kind offices. My dissatisfaction dates from the time of publication of the Lyrics. At that time, I received overtures from the Continental Monthly, which you urgently desired me to decline. You promised, if I would do so, to print any new prose articles at my own price, "all your prose," you said, and made the purchase of the Lyrics. Since that time, you have rejected two prose contributions, in my best manner, without suggesting any work to take their place. In parting with the Lyrics, I did not stipulate as to the time of publication. I

supposed that they would appear without interruption, and was disappointed to find that they did not. You allowed the intervals between them to become so long as, I think, to injure or even destroy their interest as a series. People asked me every where: "why don't your Lyrics appear regularly, once a month?" When I repeated the reasons you gave, people laughed, or shook their heads, and said: "it is a mistake." Unwilling to proceed upon mere personal feeling, I asked various literary men, such as Hedge, Tuckerman, Whipple, Alger and others their opinion. The reply was invariably in accordance with my own perception of the case. You have latterly seemed to forget them altogether, and on being appealed to, chose the shortest, and, I think, the least interesting, which, between two such intervals as would precede and follow it, would make a feeble link of continuity. I begged you to finish this slow work as soon, and as well as possible. This was the substance and the motive of my letter. I thought that the relinquishment of all further engagements upon this basis would be most welcome to you, and indeed, I still think so, and therefore limited my claims upon you to the completion of this work, which cannot so well be finished elsewhere. So much for the *tabula rasa*, which I have supposed, not without reason, to be desired by you. Now for the want of appreciation. You have spoken to me of these poems, latterly, with invariable depreciation. When I have told you that they were praised and liked, you have expressed doubts as to the fact. My Flag poem, which you praised very much at first, you seemed afterwards to think poorly of, and besides long delaying, you gave me the pain of feeling that you had on hand an article of mine which did not suit you. You told me that my manner of reading made these poems seem better than they were, and this you have often said to me. Now when Emerson told me: "I liked the Flag when you recited, but I liked it much better when I came to read it over." I thought you might be mistaken as to its' merits. Others have told me the same thing. So much for the charge of want of appreciation which, after all, is not a very grievous one. I think that I have now gone over the whole ground of the two letters, your's and mine. I have done this in haste, but with care. I have only to say in conclusion that by returning me the Lyrics, you do me an injury which would not be warranted by a petulant and unreasonable word from me, even if I had sent you such an one. And this is all, I believe, that needs to be said, to explain what I did mean, and what I do feel.

    I am in town today upon family business, but return to Newport this afternoon. Believe me

Your's sincerely
Julia W. Howe

Despite Mrs. Howe's protest, Fields had had enough. He printed "Play," which she had recommended in her letter of July 9, instead of the poem that was in proof at the time and that she had disapproved of. But "Play," in the September 1863 number, was the last of the series to appear and the last contribution from Mrs. Howe during Fields's editorship.

The collapse of their business relationship did not make them enemies. Mrs. Howe's increasing participation in clubs and charities became a subject of ridicule in the Fields household, but it was not very malicious ridicule. An entry in Annie Fields's diary for August 1869 will illustrate:

We have had Bleak House with us & have revived our picture of Mrs. Howe in Mrs. Jellyby. Jamie laughed heartily over a description Tom gave him from a college friend of his who had been visiting at her house in Newport. He said the order of the house seemed to be "the Devil take the hindmost."[12]

Yet Annie, being something of a club woman herself, met Mrs. Howe fairly often in their later days, and the evidence indicates no lack of cordiality between them. Nevertheless there is a singular brevity in the published journals and reminiscences of both Mrs. Howe and the Fieldses in referring to each other.

---

[12]MS in the Massachusetts Historical Society.

Chapter VII:
Edward Everett Hale

Reverend Edward Everett Hale became through the *Atlantic Monthly* one of the popular writers of his time. It was his "The Man without a Country" in the December 1863 number that certified his fame, but his other articles, though less celebrated, were usually appreciated. He was especially valuable to the *Atlantic* editor because of his skill at light sketches—a thing that was always in demand.

A friend of Lowell's since their school days, he was among the early contributors to the magazine under its first editor. His first contribution, "The Dot and Line Alphabet," appeared in the October 1858 issue and attracted little attention. His only other work to appear during Lowell's time, "My Double; and How He Undid Me," was one of his best stories. It appeared in the September number of the following year. A third contribution, "The London Workingman's College," was submitted during Lowell's editorship, but its publication was postponed until the first issue that Fields edited, July 1861. Hale related the circumstances in *Memories of a Hundred Years* in a passage that illustrates his general unreliability as to facts:

> I was, so to speak, on the staff of the *Atlantic*. This means that I was very intimate with Phillips and, indeed, with Sampson who published it. I was in and out of their publication office till they died, I had been for twenty years on the closest personal terms with Lowell, and when the firm of Fields and Osgood [that is, Ticknor and Fields] took the magazine, I was very intimate with dear Fields. So it happened that when in January, 1860, I came home from England I wrote for them an article on the "Working-men's College" which had, just then, been founded by Frederic Denison Maurice.

The article told incidentally of Hale's being asked to participate in a marching squad at the college.

This story I told, not to my own advantage, in my article on the "Working-men's College," and sent the article to the editor of the *Atlantic* who accepted it. I forgot it, and I suppose he did. Imagine my disgust, when the number for April [actually July], 1861, came out—that fatal April,—when I was drilling and being drilled, when I wore a uniform jacket, and could drill men who were to be major-generals—this venerable article appeared revealing to a cynical world the fact that I did not know my facings![1]

According to Hale, he wrote one or two articles during the Civil War that were never attributed to him, but he does not tell what they were.[2] At any rate, the next article to bear his name in the *Atlantic* Index was "Solid Operations in Virginia," which appeared in June 1862. Belittling the part of Virginia in the Revolutionary War, it was the first of several war pieces by Hale. "I had a standing agreement with Fields," he wrote, "that I would write for the *Atlantic* articles to keep up people's courage."[3]

In January 1863 Hale became indignant over the proofreader's handling of one of his articles. It was unusual to hear a complaint about George Nichols, who was something more than a proofreader, being largely responsible for accuracy of statements as well as of spelling and punctuation in the Ticknor and Fields publications. For Nichols' work was highly regarded by most writers, particularly the meticulous Lowell. Hale wrote to Fields:

Jan. 13 1863

Dear Fields,
    This proof is a piece of impertinence of Mr. Nichols's.
    If the article is mine the "corrections" will not be made.
    If it is his he may do what he chooses with it.
    I will not attempt to explain his steady commonplace ignorance to him.
    To you I am willing to say that I know the responsibility I take as a writer for the press well enough not to be as careless as Mr. Nichols supposes. He has made a list of states on p. 247, supposing I cannot count. In this he counts Delaware among the "oligarchies" spoken of

---

[1]Edward Everett Hale, *Memories of a Hundred Years* (New York, 1902), II, 216-17.
[2]Ibid., II, 219.
[3]Ibid., II, 218-19.

by Gouverneur Morris, (whom he and all his proof readers misspelt *Governor* Morris in face of the MS. till I corrected it.) Delaware, on the other hand, is always properly ranked among the *Middle*, not the Southern States,—because tho' she held slaves—so did every state when the constitution was made,—the slave-holding interest has not been absolutely supreme. Thus, at this moment, Delaware has republican congressmen. On the other hand "When this thing began" Kanzas Minnesota and Oregon were not states. In the whole discussion regarding the admission of Kansas the balance was what I have stated, seventeen republics & fourteen oligarchies. I hesitated whether to say *sixteen* or *seventeen* which depends on Minnesota. But I took the familiar phrase of that period.

So on p. 249. Mr. Nichols supposes I cannot add figures. He has counted *in* Virginia, where Gov. Pierrepont's government is *established* among the states where free governments are to be established.

This explanation is for you. Truly Yrs.
Edw. E. Hale

It is this sort of superficial view of a subject by a man un-acquainted with it which reduces every thing to a dead, common place mediocrity.

It was a full year later when the article, "Northern Invasions," appeared in the *Atlantic*, without Nichols' corrections.

This is the only letter of complaint from Hale, although he had more reason to complain than many contributors because of the delays in printing some of his articles. These delays, as well as the infrequency of early articles, indicate Hale's standing with his editor. Until he wrote "The Man without a Country," he was classed among the second-rate contributors. His article "The Queen of California" is a case in point. It was submitted in May 1863 but published in March 1864. Hale had written a paper on the source of the name "California"—which he found to be in an old Spanish romance—for the American Antiquarian Society of Worcester, Massachusetts. He now wrote a second version, less scholarly than that prepared for his fellow antiquarians, and sent it off to Fields.

May 9, 1863
My dear Fields,
I have finished my California article,—and send it to you. I have delayed it that I might make the translations myself. I hope you will

not object to the fullness of them,—as I have thought it essential to put on record *in English* every word of this curious matter,—& there are but five copies of the Spanish in the country, three of which belong to Mr. Ticknor.

 The Antiquarians have all urged me to make a complete thing of it,—and *complete* this is. I send you, for your own eye, the paper which I sent to the Antiquarian Society. They print only a few copies —which they do not publish, so that the whole matter is really wholly new to the public.

Truly Yours
Edward E. Hale

The article would make 15 or 16 Atlantic pages.

Although Hale wrote "The Queen of California" because he thought the public would be interested in information about one of their most colorful states, Fields may have delayed it because he thought it too scholarly, in spite of the author's popularization.

But "The Man without a Country" changed everything. Hale's contributions rose from about one a year to five in 1864. He was praised by Lowell, and he became one of the desirable few. According to the author, the story was written primarily to influence the elections of October 1863 in Ohio, where C. L. Vallandigham was running for governor on an anti-Lincoln platform that Hale considered most unpatriotic. Hale conceived the idea of the story about August, basing it on material he had discovered while working at the American Antiquarian Society library. He described the circumstances of composition in his autobiography:

> I told Fields of the *Atlantic* at once, that I had in my inkstand the story of "A Man Without a Country," that this would be a good time for it; and that if he could print it in his September number, he should have it in time for the Ohio election....
> Accordingly, the article was in type before September. But alas! not printed, not even in October or November. And Mr. Vallandigham was hopelessly defeated in the October election with no credit to poor me.[4]

But again Hale's facts are twisted. In spite of this explanation, the delay in printing was for once not due to Fields. The truth of

[4]Ibid., II, 218.

the matter is that Hale did not send his manuscript to Fields until September 29—too late for the September or the October number. Nor does Hale's account mention the fact that he had offered the story to *Frank Leslie's Weekly*, which would have printed it had he not meanwhile given it to Fields.[5] He wrote to Fields shortly before the story was finished:

Saturday; Sept. 26. 1863.

Dear Fields

My story "The Man without a Country" has been hindered in its completion. If I send it to you Monday p. m. or Tuesday, and you like it,—can it go into November's Atlantic?

I am curious about time, because it is a caution to Vallandighams and Lunts, and so far my contribution to the political crisis.

Always Yours
Edward E. Hale

Probably by this time even the November *Atlantic* was made up, and Fields postponed the story to December, since it was already too late for it to influence the election. In November Hale wrote, asking that his story be put under the pseudonym Frederick Ingham in the magazine's semi-private list of authors:

My dear Fields,—

Will you place in your list of Atlantic authors for December the name of Frederick Ingham Esq. U. S. N. as responsible for my story?

This I write, lest the matter should have escaped your memory.

Truly Yrs.
E. E. Hale.

Nov. 12. 1863.

The popularity of "The Man without a Country" is too well known to reiterate. The tale is still to be found in almost any anthology of the short story, and its influence on American nationalism has probably been greater than most of us suspect. Shortly after its appearance Lowell wrote to Fields, praising Hale's work as "the cleverest story in the *Atlantic* since 'My Double'" and suggesting that Fields "get more of him." Fields followed Lowell's advice.

[5] Edward Everett Hale, Jr., *Life and Letters of Edward Everett Hale* (Boston, 1917), p. 357.

The editor's business tactics are amusingly illustrated by what followed. Diplomatic as he was, Fields would have been far less successful in business without the aid of his wife, who could be counted upon to charm into compliance anyone whom her husband wished to impress. Hale had suddenly become a writer of importance, and Annie Fields began her campaign. The next letter in the present collection is Hale's acknowledgment to her for the gift of one of her poems, an ode that had been delivered by Charlotte Cushman at the dedication of the new organ at the Boston Music Hall in November:

Dec. 18. 1863 67 Worcester St. Boston

My dear Mrs. Fields,

Your husband was so kind as to give me a copy of the pretty edition in which, in maiden white and gold what I am told is your maiden poem appears. I should have offered to you some expression of the great satisfaction it gave me on its delivery, if I had not imagined there was an incognito to be respected. It has rung in my ears ever since I heard Miss Cushman recite it,—and will be always most pleasurably associated to me with the great organ.

You were one of a few people who expressed some interest in my "exaggeration" called *The Children of the Public*. It has come to a second edition in its modest way,—and I shall be glad if you will accept a copy.

Very truly Yours
Edward E. Hale

And a few weeks later Hale wrote that he must decline an invitation from Annie but would send his wife.[6]

There were articles by Hale in the February, March, June, September, and October issues of the *Atlantic*. Three of these were designed "to keep up people's courage." "Northern Invasions" (February) begins with the hypothesis that all "Northern Invasions, when successful, advance the civilization of the world," and urges Northerners to emigrate to the South after the war, for the sake of the economic and social salvation of the conquered region. "How to Use Victory" (June) concerns the "Anglo-Saxon policy"—or rather lack of policy—that the North exercised

[6]Hale to Annie Fields, January 7, 1864.

in its prosecution of the war: "we have not adapted our actions to any preconceived theory, nor to any central idea." The point is that a sound, positive plan must be settled upon before victory could be of any use. The short story "Paul Jones and Denis Duval" (October) concerned the Civil War less directly. A realistic narrative based upon historical facts, it exploits the moral potentialities of an American hero while it disparages the English. It was written at a time when British-built ships were harassing the Northern blockade and the *Alabama* incident had just occurred. Hale sent the story to Fields in August, shortly after receiving his pay for the September contribution on domestic economy, "What Shall We Have for Dinner?" He wrote:

Milton;—Aug. 20. 1864

Dear Fields,

I send you Paul Jones & Denis Duval. It has taken a deal of work, and lacks dramatic interest badly now;—but I hope the double interest in Denis Duval and in frigate actions off England may make people read it.

The truth is whenever I got into the shadow of Thackeray's mighty ghost I was, of course, paralyzed & afraid. I did not dare make Denis Duval utter a word. I would not have felt so, I think, about any man there is left living.

I see the September number is out. Will you post me one here. For now I have revised this,—which I did in Boston yesterday,— I shall be as far from Boston as from Quebec till September is well under way.

I have your firm's check for a balance which I am glad to find is due me. For which thanks. If you can pay me a little on this paper I should like it, for I am short & Uncle Sam has taxed me.

Truly & always Yrs.
Edw. E. Hale

Hale received the proofs some time after September 11[7] and the story went into the October number with no time wasted.

During 1865 and 1866 Hale contributed only one article, but he was partly responsible for introducing S. Weir Mitchell to the magazine. The introduction took place in a roundabout way.

[7] Hale to Fields, September 11, 1864.

Without naming the author, Mrs. Annis Lee Wister sent a manuscript to Hale, who sent it on to Fields for the *Atlantic*. The manuscript was Mitchell's "The Case of George Dedlow." Hale wrote to Fields:

My dear Fields:—
    Mrs. Wister (Dr. Furness's daughter) a very bright and intelligent person, sends me this, asking me to send it to you for the Atlantic. I have not read it,—preferring to wait for print—but she says it is amazing good. If she said she had written it herself, I should print it blind. She does not say that—but says she did not write it.
                                      Always Yrs.
March 28. 1866.   Edward E. Hale

Fields accepted the story as the leading article in the July *Atlantic*, paying only fifty dollars for it—very small pay for a leading article. The check, in turn, was sent to Hale, who forwarded it to Mrs. Wister, who forwarded it to Mitchell. Hale acknowledged receipt of it on the first of July:

                              July 1. 1866 Address *Milton*
Messrs. Ticknor & Fields:—
    Gentlemen, I have received and sent to Mrs. Casper Wister, (not Weston) of Philadelphia your check for $50.00 on acct. the story George Dedlow.
    She is not the author. She told me who was but I have forgotten and do not know. The story came through her hands however and the check will go right.   Always Yrs.
                                      E. E. Hale
I hope to send you my story "How Mr. Frye would have preached it"—before the summer is over.

In August he reported that Mrs. Wister had not acknowledged the check, but he mentioned the real author's name:

Dear Fields:—
    Mrs. Wister never acknowledged your check sent to me,—and by me to her—for Mitchell's story Geo. Dedlow.
    Will you look on your bank-book and see if the check ever came in?—   Always Yrs.
                                        Edw. E. Hale
Aug. 11. 1866

But Mitchell did receive his pay. Taking advantage of his success with Fields, he was in less than a year receiving twelve dollars a page for his contributions—more per page than Hawthorne had been paid.[8]

Hale was one top-rank writer who did not write exclusively for Fields. He contributed frequently to the *Boston Daily Advertiser* under his brother Charles, and had at least one piece, "The Children of the Public," in *Frank Leslie's Illustrated Weekly Newspaper* in 1863. But he had to explain to Fields in July 1866 when he sent an article to the *Galaxy*. His explanation was flattering: the article was not good enough for the *Atlantic*, he said.

Milton, July 11. 1866.

Dear Fields:—

I sent the hoop-skirts to the Galaxy only because it was too absurd to print anywhere. I told Church he might have it if he would tell no one who wrote it. Accordingly he or Perkins told your Mr. Osgood,—my brother in law Gilman—and I do not know how many other people.

I shall always send to you anything you would care to have.

Everybody compliments me on George Dedlow—as if I wrote it. I suppose this impression comes from you. I did not write it,—and have forgotten the name of the man who did.

Always Yrs.
E. E. Hale

I will thank you and Mr. Osgood not to speak of me in connection with the Galaxy article.

Probably partly because of this incident, Fields came forward with an offer of $150 apiece for a series of sketches to be written by Hale during the following year. It was a good thing for the editor as he was always looking for the kind of light, optimistic material that Hale could produce, and it was a good thing for the author as it promised him three times what he had been receiving per contribution. He explained the details in a letter to his mother on August 29, 1866:

I have had no chance to tell you of a flattering offer I had from Fields Monday,—to furnish for the *Atlantic* six or eight sketches of

---

[8] Mitchell to Fields, April 1867? (FI 3213) and May 8, 1867.

any length or subject I choose, for which he will pay me one hundred and fifty dollars apiece. This is three times what he has ever paid me before. I declined furnishing so many, but have undertaken four or five before December 1867. The first of these, "How Mr. Frye would have preached it," I have had on the stocks for a year or two. The second "My week in Sybaris," for a longer time.[9]

Hale put a considerable amount of work on his contributions and they usually took him longer to complete than he expected. So the first "sketch," "How Mr. Frye Would Have Preached It," did not appear until the February number of the *Atlantic*. It is a short story about an embezzler who has learned that "The Way of the Transgressor is Hard." Hale later disclosed that it was based on the lives of General Banks and General Butler. Like all the stories of the author, it was written for the sake of the moral and exemplifies Hale's belief that a concrete narrative makes a better sermon than an ocean of abstractions.

Meanwhile Hale had read Charles Janeway Stillé's recent *History of the United States Sanitary Commission*, and because of his own part in the "Sanitary" during the Civil War he felt compelled to say something about the book.

Dear Fields:—
I have been looking through Stillé's History of the Sanitary Commission.
I had a good deal to do with that matter and know a good deal about it. I think there are things to be said about it, which are not likely to be said by a Reviewer. Will you not let me give you an article on the Book—and on the Sanitary.
If I send you such an article by Dec. 15 can it go into the February number?
I will not let this interrupt the series of "sketches" of which you have the titles. The work on "My visit to Sybaris" is largely done—but I like to keep such things on the anvil.
Always Yrs.
E. E. Hale
Nov. 12. 1866.

Concerning the Sanitary Commission—the voluntary organization designed to supplement governmental provisions for hospital

[9] E. E. Hale, Jr., II, 48.

facilities, recreation, food supplies, and occasional quarters for soldiers—Hale was filled with zeal. His article, a patriotic rhapsody on the achievements of the Commission and on its official history, was ready for Fields early in January. He explained his purposes in writing it when he sent it in:

Boston Jan. 8. 1867.

Dear Fields:—

I send you at last this Article on the Sanitary, which I have re-cast,—and much of which I have written,—since I supposed it was virtually done.

I want you to understand why I am so much interested in it. The public has never understood that the *preventive* work of the Sanitary was its victory. The officers themselves, the *Commission*, knows that all the stores might have been thrown into the sea,—& yet that its great victory would be the same. At last here comes Stillé's book, their own history by their own historian, and it proves that *he understands this as little as the public*.

To set the public a little right can only be done by the Atlantic. That is why I asked you to let me write. I cannot attack Stillé's book. But to thousands of people who will not read it, I can *say* what it does not say.

Why should I say this? Simply because from the first I knew all the working men at the Sanitary though I was not one of them. I was intimate with Bellows and Knapp. I was in the confidence, at least, of Olmsted. I can say some things therefore that they could not,—and I know some things that another man might not know.

I believe therefore that this dull and rather harmless looking article contains a statement or two which ought to be made in print that this extraordinary social movement may have justice done it now & hereafter.

Always Yours
Edward E. Hale

Hale's article, "The United States Sanitary Commission," was not printed immediately but appeared in the April 1867 issue.

The "Sybaris" article that Hale said he had had on hand for more than a year or two kept growing under the author's care. He had intended it as the second of his promised sketches, but by March 1867 it had become too long for a single contribution, and it was still not completed. Hale wrote to Fields:

Dear Fields:—

At every revision Sybaris grows so much longer that I am afraid it will have to be divided into two numbers.

I will take it to Worcester with me tonight,—read it carefully tomorrow,—and send it to you Monday night or Tuesday morning.

Always Yrs.

March 22. 1867.   E. E. Hale

Accordingly the first part of the work appeared in the *Atlantic* for July 1867 under the title "My Visit to Sybaris." In August Hale thought he could have the second part ready soon, but "A Week in Sybaris," as it was finally called, did not appear in the magazine until the February 1868 issue. The Sybarian sketches are interesting in that they are Hale's first Utopian writings and are among the first of those that became so popular in America in the late nineteenth century. Naïve they certainly were: Hale was more interested in comfortable resting places at street intersections and abolishment of wine than with economic problems or international security, which he ignored. Yet he favored such radical reforms as women's suffrage and women's conscription, and hinted at such socialistic principles as governmental control of public utilities and education. In this sense Hale anticipated future literary and intellectual trends, though he otherwise represented old-fashioned Bostonian morality at its utmost refinement—the Sybarites, for example, refrained from mentioning chiropodists at the dinner table.

The Sybarian sketches together with "How Mr. Frye Would Have Preached It" made up three of the promised sketches. For the fourth Hale had intended "The Rag-Man and the Rag-Woman," a story meant to teach frugality. On April 19, 1867, he had written to Fields, "I can send you 'The Ragman' on the 27th of April if you want it. It will make thirteen pages." Sometime after that he sent it, but Fields decided to hold it for the first number of the *Atlantic Almanac*, to appear at the end of the year. Hale was preparing another article for the *Almanac*, but when Fields chose the "Rag-Man" for it, Hale offered the other for the *Atlantic*. He sent "Dinner Speaking," as the new sketch was called, in August:

Edward Everett Hale

Dear Fields:—

This is the little "exaggeration" I had intended for the Annual. Perhaps you will still think it is best for that. If not you can use it for the Atlantic,—where it will make four pages.

Always Yours
Edw. E. Hale

It is founded on fact as Miss Edgeworth says.

Aug. 4, 1867.

If we get a rainy day I will string together the fragments of "My Journal in Sybaris" to follow up "My Visit to S."

A slight, witty satire on after-dinner speaking, the sketch appeared in the October number, coming between the two parts of "Sybaris."

His contract fulfilled, Hale continued to contribute frequently to the *Atlantic* for the next two years. His most important contribution during this period was the four-installment tale "The Brick Moon," a fantasy in which Hale expressed more of his opinions on the betterment of society. In 1870 his contributions stopped, for he had taken on the editorship of a new magazine, *Old and New*.

Throughout Fields's editorship of the *Atlantic*, Hale had contributed an average of two pieces a year. Many of his contributions were collected in his three books—*If, Yes, and Perhaps* (1868), containing the earlier short stories; *The Ingham Papers* (1869), containing stories and sketches; and *Sybaris and Other Homes* (1869), containing the Sybarian sketches. His work had made its mark upon the public. The fact that he was a minister and the charitable motives that distinguished all his work had a great deal to do with the *Atlantic*'s reputation for high purpose and refinement. On the other hand, the facileness of his writing and his actual lack of depth counterbalanced for *Atlantic* readers the strained and over-serious tone that characterized much of the magazine's content.

Chapter VIII:
John Townsend Trowbridge

THE STORY OF J. T. Trowbridge's relations with Fields stands as an example of how the publisher got the most out of an average writer. Trowbridge was frankly aware of his mediocrity:

> The fish in the pool of anticipation has (with few exceptions) appeared vastly larger than when I caught and took it from the hook. The fame and good fortune I cast my line for, which hope and imagination magnified to such alluring proportions, proved but modest prizes, when landed in the light of common day.... Instead of great epics and works of fiction that all the world would be waiting to acclaim, I have written some minor poems cared for by a few, half a dozen novels, and a large number of smaller books, that have been successful enough in their way.[1]

But his timely and original contributions gained many readers for himself and for the *Atlantic*, and it was mostly during the years of Fields's editorship of the magazine that Trowbridge achieved his place in literature.

Born in backwoods New York in 1827, Trowbridge was just beginning to consider himself established as a writer when the *Atlantic* was launched in 1857. Having become acquainted in the early fifties with Underwood, the assistant editor, he was among the first contributors. "Pendlam: A Modern Reformer" appeared in the first issue, November 1857. A rather light story about a character that reminds one of Hawthorne's Hollingsworth in *The Blithedale Romance*, it was the kind of thing that *Atlantic* editors always wanted. One of Trowbridge's earliest contributions, "Nancy Blynn's Lovers," a New England story, was re-

---

[1] John Townsend Trowbridge, *My Own Story* (Boston, 1903), pp. 332-33. The facts in this chapter, unless otherwise specified, are from this source.

jected by Lowell after it was already in type because the author "had allowed my principal character to accept money from his father in a manner that might befit the scamp of a piece, but not the hero."[2] The story was printed in *Harper's Monthly* for May 1858. Nevertheless, four more contributions by Trowbridge appeared in the *Atlantic* in 1858 and one in January 1859. When Ticknor and Fields bought the magazine shortly afterward, Lowell continued as editor but Underwood lost the place of assistant. Significantly, there was only one contribution from Trowbridge after that, until Fields took Lowell's place.

In the October 1861 issue appeared Trowbridge's first contribution under Fields, "The Name in the Bark," a poem on the transience of human achievement which elicited praise from Longfellow.[3] Now Trowbridge's contributions gradually increased until he was writing almost exclusively for the *Atlantic*. He averaged about three contributions a year from 1861 through 1870.

"The Vagabonds," one of his most popular poems, appeared in the March 1863 number. It was hopelessly sentimental and concerned the love of an old wandering fiddler for his dog:

> We are two travellers, Roger and I.
>   Roger's my dog.—Come here, you scamp!
> Jump for the gentlemen,—mind your eye!
>   Over the table,—look out for the lamp!—
> The rogue is growing a little old;
>   Five years we've tramped through wind and weather,
> And slept out-doors when nights were cold,
>   And ate and drank—and starved—together.

The poem had been written some time before, but Trowbridge had been reluctant to submit it to such a dignified periodical as the *Atlantic*:

I was then at a loss to know what to do with it; for I did not imagine that the only magazine I was in those days sending poems to would

---

[2] John Townsend Trowbridge, "An Early Contributor's Recollections," *Atlantic Monthly*, C (November 1907), 583-84.

[3] James C. Austin, "J. T. Fields and the Revision of Longfellow's Poems: Unpublished Correspondence," *New England Quarterly*, XXIV (June 1951), 244.

welcome anything so vagabondish as The Vagabonds. I read it to a few friends, who listened to it with moist eyes, but who confirmed my misgivings as to its having sufficient dignity for The Atlantic. So it went back into my desk, to lie there two or three years longer, until one who had come to be nearer to me than all others, reading it or hearing it read, with joy and tears declared that it must be published at once. I took her advice, but in sending it forth I was careful to accompany it with another poem, sufficiently literary, By the River [printed in the July 1863 number], which I thought would serve to keep my Vagabonds in countenance. Proofs of the one in which I had least confidence were the first to come to me for correction, and on a margin appeared the surprising note in blue pencil,—"Perfectly beautiful, nothing could be finer in its way—whom by?" the proof-reader's query addressed to the editor, The Atlantic contributions in those days being unsigned.[4]

Fields made a minor change in the poem, the naming of the dog, "Roger," but all in all he was much pleased with it. He had it read by an elocutionist before a private group at Longfellow's house and "predicted for it a great success on lyceum platforms; astonishing me by saying that, for public recitation, there had been nothing like it since Poe's Raven."[5] The poem received wide acclaim and was read by public lecturers in the United States and abroad.

Most of Trowbridge's contributions to the *Atlantic* were prose, but one other poem deserves mention. This is "The Jaguar Hunt," an allegory upon the conclusion of the Civil War. Although more passionate than "The Vagabonds," it is bitter rather than sentimental. The jaguar represents the Southern rebels:

> The dark jaguar was abroad in the land;
> His strength and his fierceness what foe could withstand?
> The breath of his anger was hot on the air
> And the white lamb of Peace he had dragged to his lair.

The Farmer and his sons track down the jaguar, which we learn had been a family pet until it turned wild. One of the sons, rep-

---

[4] Trowbridge, *My Own Story*, pp. 251-52.
[5] Ibid., p. 252.

resenting the Copperheads, counsels lenience toward the wounded beast:

> Then up spoke the slow eldest son, and he said,
> "All he needs now is just to be fostered and fed!
> Give over the strife! Brothers, put up the knife!
> We will tame him, reclaim him, but take not his life!"

But the Farmer is ruthless, as Trowbridge thought the North had a right to be, and releases the hound—perhaps General Sherman—to finish the jaguar:

> But the Farmer flung back the false words in his face:
> "He is none of my race, who gives counsel so base!
> Now let loose the hound!" And the hound was unbound,
> And like lightning the heart of the traitor he found.

Now the lamb of Peace is restored and an angel descends to augur lasting peace in the land. "The Jaguar Hunt," which appeared in the June 1865 number of the *Atlantic*, was written upon Fields's request, as were "The Last Rally," a poem, and "We Are a Nation," an article on the second election of Lincoln. In a way, Trowbridge was the logical person for Fields to ask for a commemorative ode: he was a rising author whom the editor wished to encourage, and he was a Ticknor and Fields employee whose office was close by the *Atlantic* headquarters.

His job had begun six months before, when the firm had established *Our Young Folks*. Trowbridge was one of the editors of the new magazine along with Howard Ticknor, Gail Hamilton, and Lucy Larcom. His chief duty was to contribute an article a month to the magazine's pages. But it was not long before, one by one, the other editors dropped out, leaving him as chief editor in 1870. His contributions were numerous: a series of articles on coal miners, glassmakers, and shipbuilders; one on natural history, written under the pseudonym of Harvey Wilder; and one on natural phenomena, under the name Augustus Holmes. There were also poems by Trowbridge, among them "Darius Green and His Flying Machine." But his most important contribution was a series of novels about Jack Hazard, which began after his assumption of the full editorship and continued in other magazines after the break up of *Our Young Folks* in 1874. The Jack Hazard novels were Trowbridge's chief claim to popularity.

Meanwhile Trowbridge's most popular prose contributions to the *Atlantic, Coupon Bonds,* appeared in the September and October 1865 issues. It was written, like Hale's stories, with a specific aim; the aim of *Coupon Bonds* is the stimulation of the sale of government bonds. Also like Hale's stories, it is both humorous and moralistic, involving a miserly couple, the Ducklows, who lose their cherished bonds and upon finding them are caused to bestow them upon a needy Civil War veteran and his family. One of the concluding paragraphs, though among the worst in the story, illustrates the author's attitude:

> Among the rest, the Ducklows rejoiced not the least; for selfishness was with them, as it is with many, rather a thing of habit than a fault of the heart. The catastrophe of the bonds broke up that life-long habit, and revealed good hearts underneath. The consciousness of having done an act of justice, although by accident, proved very sweet to them: it was really a fresh sensation; and Reuben and his dear little family, saved from ruin and distress, happy, thankful, glad was a sight to their old eyes such as they had never witnessed before. Not gold itself, in any quantity, at the highest premium, could have given them so much satisfaction; and as for coupon bonds, they are not to be mentioned in the comparison.

The story was too long to appear all together in one issue and too short to be serialized, and after it had been accepted the author wrote to Fields, "What do you say to dividing 'Coupon Bonds', into chapters?" (FI 4256). It was thus divided when it later appeared as a book, but in the magazine it was printed in two parts. The story was extremely popular and "had an appreciable influence in stimulating confidence in the government and its securities."[6] After its appearance in the *Atlantic* Fields published a paper-bound edition. It also appeared in several dramatic versions, one by the author.

Trowbridge's next contributions to the magazine were the re-

[6]Ibid., p. 255.

sult of arrangements he had made with L. Stebbins, a Hartford publisher who had approached him in August 1865 with the idea of writing a series of sketches about the South and the battlefields of the Civil War, to be published by subscription in book form. The author was to make a short tour of the South to gather material. He was reluctant to accept the offer because of his responsibilities toward *Our Young Folks,* but Fields consented to let him go, especially since he planned to send back five or six of the sketches for the *Atlantic* and *Our Young Folks*. He left immediately, and by August 23 was sending back the first of the articles, "The Fields of Gettysburg," which appeared in the November *Atlantic*. He wrote to Fields from Harper's Ferry:

Harper's Ferry, Va. Aug. 23rd 1865.
My Dear Fields
I send you some notes on the field of Gettysburg. If they suit, I may do something more for you of the same kind. If not, please preserve MS. carefully. In either case, let me know at your earliest convenience. It is my intention now to go through the southern states, & no doubt I shall find many things to make note of which might interest readers of the Atlantic. I shall remain here a few days—long enough perhaps to hear from you, if not, the postmaster will forward your letter to me.

Ever truly yours
J. T. Trowbridge

Within two weeks another article was ready. In the meantime Trowbridge's relations with Fields had progressed to the point where he was considering putting all his publishing into the hands of Ticknor and Fields:

Washington, D. C. Sept. 5th 1865
My Dear Fields
I will send you "The Field of Antietam" in a day or two. These papers—& others probably—you can use, if the Atlantic can give them room soon enough; but I intend issuing them with other matters in a volume about Jan. 1st., after which, of course they will be useless to you. The volume, by the way (& all this consider as *inter nos*) is not to be thrown upon the trade, but sold by agents only. One of the Hartford publishers is the originator of the project.

Furthermore, speaking of books, Mr. J. E. Tilton is withdrawing from the firm of Tilton & Co.; & now is the time for me to pull up my roots there. I shall not probably return to Boston before the last of November; but I have a book stereotyped which ought to be published in October: therefore, either they must issue it, or it must lie over until another year, unless I can make some arrangement to transfer it, with all my books in their hands, to you,—for of course I should prefer you before all other publishers. As I wish you to read the book before deciding anything in its favor, I enclose an order for the proofs on Mr. Ramsay, foreman, at Rand & Avery's. The title I had thought of was "Dr. Biddikin's Treasure." Tilton will sell all my plates at cost. N. B. If you like "Dr. Biddikin," & get it into your hands, then it may lie over until you find it convenient to publish.
              Yours
              J. T. Trowbridge[7]

"The Field of Antietam" was sent on September 11, along with another paper, "A Visit to Mount Vernon," for *Our Young Folks*. On the fifteenth Trowbridge wrote from Richmond, requesting the proofs of the Gettysburg article:

           Richmond, Va. Sept. 15, 1865
My Dear Fields,
 Any proof mailed to me here, I could probably read & return to you in a week. I do not consider it so very important, however, to see the proofs: (but would prefer to.)
 I shall remain here 2 weeks or so.
 Do you care for relics? shall I send you a shell? a round shot? a skull? or anything of that sort picked up from the battlefields?
 I sent you by express last Monday a paper on Antietam,— & a "Visit to Mount Vernon" with illustrations, for the Y. F., to Mr. Ticknor. Were they received?
            Every way yours
            J. T. Trowbridge

Then Trowbridge suddenly changed his plans and decided not to put the two articles on Gettysburg and Antietam in the *Atlantic* after all. Since he was shortly returning to his home in West Cambridge, he did not bother to explain to Fields in his letter:

---

[7]*Dr. Biddikin's Treasure* evidently became *Lucy Arlyn*, a novel, which was published by Ticknor and Fields in 1866.

John Townsend Trowbridge

Monumental Hotel Richmond, Va. Oct. 1st 1865

My Dear Fields

Please withhold from publication the Antietam paper; also the Gettysburg, if not too late. I will furnish you something different in their place. I am coming home, & will see you in a few days.

Yours

J. T. Trowbridge

It was too late to withdraw the paper on Gettysburg. But the one on Antietam never appeared in the *Atlantic*, Trowbridge replacing it with a new article, "The Wilderness."

At home Trowbridge was confined to his bed; he had contracted a violent fever in the South that kept him off his feet for several weeks. But he continued to carry on his business by letter. Negotiations had been pursued to enable him to transfer all his publishing from the hands of Tilton and Company to Ticknor and Fields. The latter firm was soon to bring out his novel called *Lucy Arlyn* as well as the book edition of *Coupon Bonds*. Trowbridge wrote of these matters on October 15, mentioning also that "The Wilderness" was ready for the *Atlantic* whenever Fields wanted it:

West Cambridge Oct. 15th 1865

My Dear Fields,

The contents of your gracious little note are very gratifying as they enable me to see my way towards the rending of a connection with a certain piratical firm, which has become exceedingly uncomfortable to me. Will you assume the plates? & then bring out the book at your own discretion and convenience.

I must confess also to the keen gratification it gives me to know that the story is commended by so practiced & competent a critic as your wife.

As for the "Coupon Bonds," it will of course be for my interest, as well as give me great pleasure, to see them brought out in the way you propose.

I will send you a paper on "The Wilderness" for the Dec. Atlantic when you are ready for it. As I may wish to put it in type before you do, I retain it for the present.

Mr. Stebbins (not Mr. Caxe) spent only one day here, last Tuesday, & returned the same evening to Hartford.

I have as yet but one leg in my trousers but I hope to be fully dressed in a day or two.

Sincerely your own
J. T. Trowbridge

Fields must have asked for "The Wilderness" immediately, for on October 20 Trowbridge sent it. In the letter accompanying the manuscript he referred to further complications in the transfer of his publications:

W. Cambridge Oct. 20, 1865

My Dear Fields,
 I send herewith "The Wilderness" paper & "Coupon Bonds" in chapters. Let me see proofs of both, if convenient. Of the former, please send extra sheet (*after* your proofreader has made his marks.)
 The Tiltons seem inclined to hold on to "Lucy" until they can dispose of all the plates of my books together. If you will permit me to refer them to your firm as a party willing to purchase at reasonable prices, an unpleasant business will be removed from my mind; while no obligation will rest on you to pay more for the plates than shall seem to you expedient.

Yours ever
J. T. Trowbridge

P. S. I am mending slowly.

There was still trouble enough for the author and the publisher before the transfer was completely effected,[8] but Fields published both *Coupon Bonds* and *Lucy Arlyn* in 1866. "The Wilderness" was published in the January 1866 issue of the *Atlantic*, the second and last of Trowbridge's articles on the South in the magazine. In these articles the author had described skillfully enough the beauty of the Southern landscape, the devastation of the war, and incidents of his journey, but he showed little awareness of the deep economic and social problems that faced the South. His book, *The South: a Tour of Its Battle-Fields and Ruined Cities*, was published as planned in Hartford in 1866, and was reasonably successful.

Trowbridge's relationship with Fields was always pleasant and

---

[8] Trowbridge to Fields, March 10, 1866.

he was one of the writers whom the editor relied upon most, but his contributions to the *Atlantic* were not always accepted. In one of his letters, written in 1865 or 1866 he mentioned a serial story he had offered to Fields three years before. Since the editor had rejected it, he now wished to print it in another magazine, but he was careful to consult Fields first:

W. Cambridge, Wednesday

My Dear Fields
  You will remember that 3 yrs. ago I offered the Atlantic a serial story, which was declined. I have now an opportunity to dispose of it to a new magazine, which, as it pays me a good price for it, wishes to place my name in its list of contributors, on the strength of it. Will such a use of my name clash at all with my obligation to the "Young Folks"? As the new mag. is for *adults*, the proposed arrangement will not come within the letter of my agreement with you,— but will it come within the *spirit* of it?
  It may seem idle for me to refer this matter to you at all,—but I desire to maintain the same relations of frankness & confidence which have hitherto existed between us, without casting so much as a shadow upon them by anything I may do.
  A word in reply *soon*, will oblige
Yours ever
J. T. Trowbridge
Glad you like the Meeting house story. I am busy on another humorous thing for you, which I think will be decidedly funny. J. T. T.[9]
[FI 4258]

"The Man Who Stole a Meeting-House," which Fields had approved, was an extravagant New England yarn, which was printed in the January 1867 number of the *Atlantic*. The other "humorous thing" may have been "Madam Waldoborough's Carriage," a fictitious anecdote about an American society lady in Paris, which Fields liked well enough to print in the April 1866 number.

After February 1867 nothing of Trowbridge's appeared in the magazine for more than two years. He submitted a poem he had

---

[9]The serial may have been *Neighbor's Wives*, published by Lee and Shepard in 1867.

prepared for a festival at Arlington, Massachusetts, where he now lived, but it was not accepted. He sent it to Fields with the following letter:

Arlington, Mass., June 18, 1867

My Dear Fields,

This ode, written for, & read at, our festival yesterday, is to be published in a pamphlet acct, of the day's proceedings, in the course of a few weeks. In the mean time, wd. you like to use it in the Atlantic? say in the Aug. No.? If so, I will furnish you with a revised copy, with brief notes explaining the local allusions.

Please return this copy, with any comments in pencil you may see fit to make upon it. And let me hear from it *soon*, & oblige

Yrs. ever, most sincerely,
J. T. Trowbridge

A few other of Trowbridge's *Atlantic* contributions are interesting because they illustrate an attempt to satisfy the popular demand for information about the more or less remote parts of the United States. The articles—"A Carpet-Bagger in Pennsylvania" (April and June 1869), "From Pennsylvania Hills to Minnesota Prairies" (March 1870), "Through the Woods to Lake Superior" (April 1870), and "A Week in Duluth" (May 1870) —were written from actual observation, Trowbridge's journeys being financed by Fields. Once again the author showed skill in observation. He visited the coal mines, the oil wells, the steel mills; he reported on the railroads, the scenery, and the points of interest. Though the result is superficial, it fulfilled its purpose of acquainting the reader with regions he might hardly hope to see.

Trowbridge was sorry to see Fields retire in 1871. He spoke sadly in his reminiscences of the disintegration of the firm under the management of J. R. Osgood, and he thought of the collapse of *Our Young Folks* in 1874 "as a personal bereavement." But the *Atlantic Monthly* still existed, though under a new publisher and a new editor, and it continued to receive contributions from Trowbridge.

Chapter IX:
William Dean Howells

ALTHOUGH William Dean Howells became the assistant editor of the *Atlantic* and the most prolific of its contributors during the latter half of Fields's editorship, his progress was not easy. Soon after the establishment of the magazine in 1857, he was one of its readers and aspired to become one of its writers. He frankly envied his Ohio friends Thomas Fullerton and John James Piatt, whose poems were accepted by the *Atlantic* before any of his.[1] In 1859 Lowell accepted Howells' poem "Andenken," but detained its publication until the January 1860 number in order to investigate its originality. Howells received twenty-five dollars for it, as he also did for "The Pilot's Story," a poem in the September issue.[2] The latter, a melodramatic narrative of a slave woman, was the most appreciated of his early contributions. Altogether Lowell accepted seven poems from Howells.

In 1860 the young writer made his first trip to Boston, where he met several of the New England literati, including Lowell and Fields. The purpose of his journey, aside from the desire to meet his heroes, was to find some kind of literary work. He even suggested to Fields that he would like to become assistant editor of the *Atlantic*, though he was only twenty-three and almost unknown. Fields did not give him a job, but he respected the sincere ambition of the young man and encouraged him to seek a place on the *New York Post*; nor did he forget Howells when he needed

---

[1] William Dean Howells, *Life in Letters of William Dean Howells*, ed. Mildred Howells (Garden City, New York, 1928), I, 15, 22-23.

[2] Robert Ernest Butler, "William Dean Howells as Editor of The Atlantic Monthly" (unpublished doctoral dissertation, Rutgers University, 1950), p. 8.

an assistant editor six years later. Besides, upon Howells' suggestion, Fields offered to accept a series of sketches of western cities that the Ohioan was to write from observation, but lack of funds prevented Howells from making the tour that the sketches entailed. He wrote to Ticknor and Fields from Columbus on June 10, 1861, to inform the firm of the failure of his plans: "If at some future time—in the autumn, or next spring," he said, "it should seem desirable to have me go on and make the articles, or sketches, as I proposed—I should be very glad, but for the present, it is impossible."[3] Howells' first eastern trip had not proved very successful, but in September 1861 he was back visiting his friends in Boston, having just accepted an appointment as consul to Venice. Then he left for Italy in November.

Meanwhile Fields had assumed the *Atlantic* editorship, and Howells was to find that in spite of his friendliness he was harder to please than Lowell. While in Boston in September 1861, the young writer had left several poems for Fields to consider, but without success. Fields wrote:

Boston Sept. 20 1861.

Dear Howell.
  I do not think I am wrong, but these poems seem to me not up to your mark. I therefore return them as you told me to do, if they were not what they ought to be coming from the pen that did "The Pilot's Story."
  I was sorry to see you for so brief a period only. All good things attend you to Italy.

Yours always
J. T. Fields.[4]

Howells was not happy about the rejection. One of the poems, "Bereft," he especially prized, and he said so to Fields when he replied from Ohio, where he was preparing for his departure to Italy.

---

[3] Howells, *Life*, I, 35.
[4] MS in Harvard University Library.

Dear Mr. Fields— Jefferson, Sept. 29th, 1861.
   You may be right in regard to the poems, but I cannot help thinking the one called "Bereft" to be the best thing I ever did. I don't know that I shall dare to send you anything again, and I can't help regarding the "Pilot's Story" in the present case as a misfortune.
   I suppose I'll be off now in a very short time. So I make you my adieux now, thanking you for kind wishes.
Very truly yours
W. D. Howells.

But none of the poems ever appeared in the *Atlantic*. In fact, only one of Howells' contributions, "Louis Lebeau's Conversion," was accepted by Fields before 1866, when Howells became a member of the staff. "Louis Lebeau's Conversion" was sketched in January 1862, and the author sent it to his father in Columbus, Ohio, shortly afterward. The elder Howells was to send the poem to the *Atlantic*, but before doing so he made some corrections of his own that Howells did not appreciate, for his father knew "nothing of the principles of the verse in which the poem is written, and I'm afraid his correction has been the death of it."[5] Nevertheless the piece appeared in the November number. It is a long narrative poem, skillfully written and moving, and it concerns a conflict between French Catholicism and the revivalistic religion of frontier Ohio. In its meter, its description of the wilderness, and its overdrawn pathos, it is strongly reminiscent of *Evangeline*:

> Autumn was in the land, and the trees were golden and crimson,
> And from the luminous boughs of the over-elms and the maples
> Tender and beautiful fell the light in the worshippers' faces,
> Softer than lights that stream through the saints on the windows
>   of churches,
> While the balsamy breath of the hemlocks and pines by the river
> Stole on the wind through the woodland aisles like the breath
>   of a censer.
> Loud the people sang old camp-meeting anthems that quaver
> Quaintly yet from lips forgetful of lips that have kissed them;
> Loud they sang the song of the Sacrifice and Atonement,
> And of the end of the world, and the infinite terrors of Judgment.

[5] Howells, *Life*, I, 49, 55, 57.

Howells' chief literary work while in Italy was *Venetian Life*, the series of informal sketches drawn from his observations. Some of the sketches were sent to the *Atlantic*, where they were rejected. However, Charles Hale, brother of Edward Everett Hale and editor of the *Boston Daily Advertiser*, accepted them with some new ones for his paper in 1863.[6] They were received handsomely by the public and were a credit to their author; Fields's rejection of them is to be classed among the editor's mistakes. A second series of Italian sketches, entitled *Italian Journeys*, was published in 1867 after appearing in part in the *Atlantic* and other magazines.

By the time he returned from Italy in 1863, Howells was firm in his determination to live by literature. The writing of *Venetian Life* had given him new confidence in his observational ability, but he still wrote poems which were invariably rejected by the *Atlantic*. One of these, a narrative poem, was submitted shortly after Howells' arrival in the United States. Though the editor rejected it, he offered to accept the descriptive portion alone.

Boston August 18 1865.

Dear Mr. Howell
   The poem is too long for the A. M. & I don't like the story part of it. If you will send me the merely descriptive portion of it (the part relating to Venice) I shall be glad to print it. But I presume you will not care to disconnect it. The story I cannot print, & I regret extremely that it does not seem to me up to your mark.
   Sorry you did not come to the sea-side. Tip-top day, & no Howells!
Yours Very truly
J. T. Fields.[7]

It was a month later when Howells replied that he was unwilling to break up the poem. At the same time he was undertaking the publication in book form of *Venetian Life*, which was brought out in England by Trübner and in America, upon the advice of Fields, by Hurd and Houghton:

[6]Ibid., pp. 76-78, 84-85.
[7]MS in Harvard University Library.

William Dean Howells

79 East 27th street, New York, Sept. 18, 1865.

My dear Sir:

Your letter of the 9th has been sent me from Jefferson, and I see the propriety of what you say. I thank you very sincerely for the suggestions made in regard to the book. The 500 copies will be taken by Messrs. Hurd & Houghton, of this city and will be published with their imprint over that of Trübner & Co.

The returned manuscripts came duly to hand. On looking over the poem, I did not see how I could separate the descriptive part from the rest, and so I have not sent it to you for the *Atlantic*. I've nothing else to try you with, unless I begin offering you over again all that you've rejected.

I think of bringing out a volume of four poems in hexameter, to be called "Rhythmic Ballads," and to contain Disillusion, another ms. poem, and The Pilot's Story and Louis Lebeau's Conversion. Have you any objection, as publisher of the *Atlantic*, to my using the two latter poems?

I suppose our sudden change from broiling hot to bitter cold weather comes from Boston.

I pray you to remember me to Mrs. Fields, and believe me

Very sincerely yours,
W. D. Howells.

But though Howells' own writing was eschewed, his literary judgment was valued, and because of this he was considered the best candidate for the assistant editorship of the *Atlantic* in 1866. Fields, whose health was beginning to bother him, needed a reliable man whom he could trust with the details of the magazine, especially while he was away during the summers. Fields's own interest in new writers was waning, and he was content to rely upon those who had helped him achieve his eminence, but he realized that new blood was essential for the future welfare of the magazine, and he supposed Howells to be alert to new developments in literature. He had the full approval of his counsellor Lowell, who had written just a few months before, "I hope you will do whatever you can, for Howells is sure to be somebody if he lives."[8] In January 1866 Fields made the offer of the assistant editorship to Howells, who had been engaged only the month

---

[8] Howells, *Life*, I, 97.

before to write regularly for Edwin Lawrence Godkin, editor of the *Nation* in New York. The generous Godkin encouraged Howells to accept, and Howells talked the proposal over with Fields's assistant James R. Osgood and later with Lowell.[9] He wrote to Fields on January 14:

My dear Sir: New York, January 14, 1866.

My engagement on The Nation is as permanent as anything in newspaper life, I suppose, but it is one that can be terminated at any moment either by the editor or myself. The question is whether I can be of sufficient use to justify you in offering me something better than I now have in the way of place and pay. My income is about fifty-five dollars a week and is nearly all from The Nation, for which I write reviews and articles on such subjects as I like.

I should be glad to have you write saying whether you could pay me the salary named, and stating more explicitly the duties you wish me to perform. I can then make you a direct answer.—I am gratified to have been first thought of for the vacancy on The Atlantic, and I beg to thank you for offering me the place.

                 Yours very truly,
                 W. D. Howells.

The editor, who had originally offered a salary of forty dollars a week, raised it to fifty upon Howells' request, with the possibility of extra pay for any contributions to the magazine other than reviews. At the end of the month he invited Howells to come to Boston to discuss the details:

My dear Sir.   Boston Jan. 27[?] 1866

If we could talk over the matter in Boston we could soon see if your residence hereabouts can be managed. Can you spare a day? If so and you will let me know what day this week (not Wednesday) you will be here I will be ready to see you. Come directly to my house, No. 37 Charles St. when you arrive. As you come on our business, as well as your own, your journey shall not be an expense to you. This I insist on.

                 Yours Very truly
                 J. T. Fields.[10]

[9] William Dean Howells, *Literary Friends and Acquaintance* (New York, 1901), p. 112.
[10] MS in Harvard University Library

Howells replied on January 29 with a promise to see Fields in Boston on Thursday evening: "I dare say we shall come to some understanding satisfactory to both of us." By February 6 negotiations were concluded and Howells had returned to New York, where he wrote a letter to Fields reiterating the duties of the position: "examination of mss. offered to the *Atlantic*; correspondence with contributors; reading proof for the magazine after its revisal by the printers; and writing the *Reviews and Literary Notices*, for which I am to receive fifty dollars a week, while I am to be paid extra for anything I may contribute to the body of the magazine."[11]

Beginning on March 1, 1866, the job was indeed a hard one, nor was it at first impressive in its responsibilities. The acceptance or rejection of manuscripts was left in Fields's hands, as was the correspondence with important contributors. Also it was made clear to Howells that one reason for his appointment had been his experience in the printing trade. In fact, the position was originally one of almost unrelieved drudgery. Neither Howells nor Fields expected this condition to last, but the rapidity with which the assistant proved himself was remarkable. He soon took over many duties which Fields was only too glad to relinquish. It was especially convenient, even in Fields's relations with some of the veteran writers, to be able to put part of the responsibility for the rejection of manuscripts upon another's shoulders. Howells worked hard. From 1866 to 1870 inclusive he wrote an average of twenty reviews and six other contributions per year—considerably more than any mere contributor—and his reading of manuscripts and proof was, in the *Atlantic* tradition, most meticulous.

His diligence did not go unnoticed, and he rapidly became known in literary and scholarly circles in Boston and Cambridge. In 1867 President Hill of Harvard granted him the honorary degree of Master of Arts, because of "that modest merit which has raised you to such deserved reputation in the world of letters, and endeared you personally to so many scholars."[12] He received a

[11] Howells, *Life*, I, 105.
[12] Thomas Hill to Howells, July 29, 1867, in Butler, p. 299.

more substantial reward from Fields in March of the following year, when his salary was raised from $2500 to $3500 per year, the latter sum to cover all his contributions. At the same time, Ticknor and Fields promised "that the proof-reading will be made less and less burdensome to me, because they all feel, as Mr. Clark told me, that my value to the *Atlantic* is in my writing."[13] Yet in spite of the recognition he received, it would be erroneous to suppose that Howells was the actual managing editor of the magazine before 1871.[14] He did most of the work and had an important part in the choice of articles, but the major decisions were mostly left to Fields, who not only controlled the purse strings but carried on the correspondence with the established writers and was responsible for the make-up of each issue except when he was out of town. Even when Fields was in Europe in 1869 and Howells was the acting editor, the *Atlantic* was chaperoned by both Lowell and Holmes, who reported on its progress in their letters to the chief editor; and Howells himself made a hobbling attempt to report regularly.

On the other hand, as early as October 1866, Fields was consulting Howells upon the selection of material for the magazine, and Howells was replying with a frankness that indicates the confidential nature of their relations. Fields had left him some foreign sketches and a review of Whipple's *Character and Characteristic Men* to consider for publication, and the assistant editor roundly condemned both:

Dear Mr. Fields: October 15, 1866.

I send back our cosmopolite's scenes of foreign life. I have seldom looked at anything more slangy, silly and vapid, and I think we could not possibly "find room for them." My examination of the Ms. has been very careful, and my judgment is decidedly against it.

—At the risk of being disagreeable I must say that I do not like

---

[13] Howells to William Cooper Howells and family, March 6, 1868, in Howells, *Life*, I, 126.

[14] See Butler, I, 21-22, and Clara Marburg Kirk and Rudolf Kirk (eds.), *William Dean Howells* (New York, 1950), p. lxiii. The exaggeration of the importance of Howells' position is due to his own statements in "Recollections of an *Atlantic* Editorship," *Atlantic Monthly*, C (November 1907), 594.

our reverend friend's notice of Whipple's book, which to my thinking is the best and strongest book you've published for a long time; whereas the review is diffuse and ineffectual. Are you hopelessly in for it?

Have you answered Stedman, accepting his poem, or shall I write him?

—I am suffering frightfully with influenza; but by keeping in the house I can keep at work. Please send me Bayard Taylor's poem, and whatever new books have been received for review.

Yours
W. D. H.[15]

Though he seldom wrote to Longfellow, Holmes, Lowell, or Whittier about their contributions to the *Atlantic*, Howells did correspond with writers of lesser repute, such as Edmund Clarence Stedman, who happened to be a personal friend. His judgment was usually final in regard to such authors as D. G. Mitchell or Harriet Prescott; when he recommended the rejection of their work, Fields usually accepted the decision:

Dear Mr. Fields: Cambridge, October 17, 1866.

Mr. Mitchell's discourse upon novels is only a very general generalization. He says nothing new, and does not enter deeply enough into the subject to recommend his antiquities. Miss Prescott's story is written with the spirit that seldom fails her, but I think neither you nor she can afford to print "Enoch Arden" over again. To be sure the plot was not original with Tennyson, but as his story is so fresh in the minds of every one, I think nobody can now profitably repeat it. Miss Prescott might be safely told this ground for the rejection of her story.   W. D. Howells.

Howells worked with Fields in these matters, and the handling of a particular writer's contribution was often the result of their joint efforts. In the case of Sara Hammond Palfrey's "Katherine Morne," beginning in the November 1866 issue, Fields had recommended some changes to which the author would not accede, but Howells considered the matter of little importance and preferred to let the author have her way. Presumably Howells' opin-

---

[15] A brief, anonymous review of Whipple's book appeared in the December *Atlantic*. The "scenes of foreign life" may have been J. W. Palmer's "My Heathen at Home," also in the December number.

ion prevailed, though the matter was brought to Fields for final approval:

Dear Mr. Fields:

I wish to say again in regard to the proof of "Katherine Morne," that I think you had better let the author have her way on all points. It is not likely to meet severe criticism, and she seems very determined in regard to it. I should have Mr. Bigelow cast it at once, but think the last decision properly belongs to you.

Please to have all my letters sent out as usual. Mrs. Howells remains.
W. D. H.   [FI 2412]

Besides his relations with such minor writers as Mitchell, Harriet Prescott, and Sara Palfrey, Howells was responsible for most of the new talent that came to the *Atlantic* after 1866. His encouragement of Aldrich, Harte, and Twain, during his assistant editorship and his chief editorship which followed, is most notable. And one of the most striking features of his later régime is the increased proportion of new talent in the magazine.[16] His encouragement of Henry James, Jr., was one of his earliest and most happy acts. The following letter concerning James was probably written on January 4, 1867, though it is dated 1866, and if so, it may refer to *Poor Richard*, one of the first of James's stories to appear in the *Atlantic*. It was because of Howells' recommendation that this and other stories by James were accepted. The assistant editor wrote to his chief:

January 4th, 1866.

Dear Mr. Fields:

Mr. James has given me the manuscript of a story about which he has already spoken to you, and I find it entirely acceptable.

If you haven't made up the March number entirely yet, wouldn't it be well to get this story into it? I send you the manuscript in order that you may look at it if you like. The title is of course to be changed.
W. D. H.[17]

[16]Butler, pp. 57, 86-87. See Howells, "Recollections," p. 599.

[17]My surmise that this letter is incorrectly dated is based upon the fact that it is written under the *Atlantic Monthly* letterhead. Howells was not connected with the *Atlantic* on January 4, 1866. Such errors in dating, so early in the year, are of course frequent. See also William Dean Howells, "Henry James, Jr.", *Century Magazine*, XXV (November 1882), 25.

Poor Richard began in the June 1867 number of the magazine.

Howells had more to do with the editorial policy of the *Atlantic* than merely to encourage new contributors. Fields consulted him on the difficulty of finding light material for the magazine. "I wish you could have taken part," Howells once wrote to Mrs. Fields, "in the improving conversation Mr. Fields and I had on Sunday afternoon concerning a future state and the impossibility of finding men who could write little short lively sketchy things of from six to eight pages in length" (FI 2409). The assistant editor may also have had some influence upon the political policy maintained in the magazine.[18] After 1866, political contributions became more diversified, though they were still solidly Republican; but this may have been due merely to the complications in politics resulting from the war's end. The issues of the war itself seemed quite simple to most New Englanders, while matters of Reconstruction, resumption of specie payments, the protective tariff, and Washington lobbying were puzzlingly complex. At any rate, the *Atlantic*'s stand of the late sixties was the same as that of the seventies when Howells was on his own.

In the preparation of each issue of the magazine, Howells aided Fields, but it was primarily the latter's responsibility except when he was away. Furthermore the chief editor sometimes suggested last-minute changes in the contents of an issue, as the following letter indicates. Fields wrote from New Hampshire, where he was vacationing, having left Howells in charge of the *Atlantic* for July and August. The July issue was printed but not yet on sale, and the August number was in preparation:

June 12th 1867. Campton Village N. H.

My dear Howells.

Thank you for yours of June 7th & 4th likewise. Charles Sumner has just written to me to say that he has ready an article for the "Atlantic" for August & insists that it shall go in that month called "Prophetic Voices about America." He says it will occupy ten or twelve pages. Now judging from all he has told me about this paper

---

[18]Butler, pp. 199-206. Louis J. Budd, "Howells, the *Atlantic Monthly* and Republicanism," *American Literature*, XXIV (May 1952), 139-56.

in times past it will be a very curious & interesting one and we must get it in. I have asked him to send it direct to the printing office this week. I expect to be at home on Monday Aft. for a few hours and if you could drop in any time after two o'clock we will put our venerable heads together and see what can be done for mankind in the "Atlantic" way. We must consult about those articles by the author of The Campaign Life of Lincoln for he is a man for us to look well after.

What a capital number is the July issue of the A. M.! Did you write all the papers yourself?

Mrs. Fields sends kind regards.
Yours very sincerely
James T. Fields.[19]

Sumner's article did not appear until the September number. In that number too, Fields made a change at the last possible moment, just as it was going to press. Howells wrote:

Cambridge, August 3, 1867.

Dear Mr. Fields:

I have your note of yesterday, and shall see that "Themistocles" is laid over. But we shall require a shorter poem in its place, and I wish you would send out by Monday morning's express those verses entitled "The Blue and the Grey." You say nothing about the Notices. I've directed them all to be put in type, and shall preferably retain the notice of Emerson as something already past due.—I've been twice to see you about these matters, and now write in despair of ever hitting the day when you are in town. I wish you could let me know the composition of the October number. We have a quasi invitation to spend some weeks in the country, and I want to know if it will be possible for me to get away.

Mr. Houghton tells me that the publication of my book shall be postponed till October 1st. I can therefore let you have some material for the October Atlantic if you like. I should entitle my sketch "Stopping at Vicenza, Verona and Parma." This is the last book of the sybil—commonly spelt sibyl.
Yours
W. D. H.[20]

The October *Atlantic*, which was composed by Fields, did not contain the Italian sketch. Howells still submitted his own con-

---

[19]MS in Harvard University Library.

[20]Francis Miles Finch's "The Blue and the Gray" did appear in the September number.

tributions, aside from reviews, to the chief editor's judgment, and they were by no means always accepted. On June 8, 1866, for example, he had written to Charles Eliot Norton about a poem that Norton had praised but that Fields had rejected:

I set the trap of my poem for Mr. Fields, and temptingly baited it with your praise and Mr. Lowell's, but Mr. Fields, after nibbling cautiously about it, refused to go in. I must say that the affair was managed beautifully on both sides, and I hardly know which to admire more: myself or Fields. I'm so well satisfied with my own skill in the matter that I can scarcely persuade myself that I failed of success.[21]

Nevertheless a great deal of Howells' writing was accepted for the *Atlantic*. There were the Italian sketches that appeared before the publication of *Italian Journeys*; namely, "Forza Maggiore," "A Glimpse of Genoa," "At Padua," and "Minor Italian Travels." These as well as his other sketches, many of which appeared in the collected *Suburban Sketches* in 1871, revealed Howells' ability to observe and interest the reader in the commonplace but significant details he saw about him. His travels take him from the streets of Genoa to the Negro quarter of Cambridge, and from the galleries of Italy to the secondhand shops of Massachusetts; always his descriptions are accurate but gentle, and touched with mild humor. His other articles are on such various subjects as the presidential platform for 1868 in "The Next President" (May 1868), the history of the Moravian community at Gnadenhutten, Ohio, in "Gnadenhütten" (January 1869), the trends in the theaters of Boston in "The New Taste in Theatricals" (May 1869), and the Boston Peace Jubilee in "Jubilee Days" (August 1869). Two of Howells' short stories appeared during his assistant editorship, "Tonelli's Marriage" (July 1868) and "A Romance of Real Life" (March 1870). The latter provided the author, in the character of "a contributor," an opportunity to set forth rather hesitantly his ideas upon the art and techniques of fiction writing—ideas which bore fruit in his later fiction. For example:

[21]Howells, *Life*, I, 110-11.

This contributor had been lately thinking, whenever he turned the pages of some foolish traveler ... that nowadays the wise adventurer sat down beside his own register and waited for incidents to seek him out. It seemed to him that the cultivation of a patient and receptive spirit was the sole condition needed to insure the occurrence of all manner of surprising facts within the range of one's own personal knowledge; that not only the Greeks were at our doors, but the fairies and the genii, and all the people of romance, who had but to be hospitably treated in order to develop the deepest interest of fiction, and to become the characters of plots so ingenious that the most cunning invention were poor beside them.

Indeed, for Howells "the Greeks were at our doors"; as he sat in his office in Boston or in his study in Cambridge, the world of literature was opening before him. He printed one other story in the *Atlantic*, "A Day's Pleasure" (July, August, September 1870), which was the type of narrative sketch that he later utilized in *Their Wedding Journey*. As for Howells' poems, it is significant that the only ones to appear in the magazine before he became chief editor were printed during Fields's absence. These were "Before the Gate" (August 1869) and "The First Cricket" (September 1869).

Howells' book reviews in the *Atlantic* covered a broad cross-section of the respectable reading of the late sixties. The first review was of Bayard Taylor's *The Story of Kennett*. Fields wrote to the author shortly after Howells' appointment to ask for an editorial copy of the book: "Send an early copy of the new novel & Howells shall do it up for the A. M."[22] The review appeared in the June 1866 issue. Howells commended the novel as "far surpassing his [Taylor's] former efforts in extended fiction," and hinted that it might contribute "to supply the great want of an American novel."

Later Howells managed the reviewing almost without restriction. He wrote to T. W. Higginson on December 24, 1869, that the choice of books to review was left mostly to him, and that he tried to include all the important ones as well as those that

[22] Fields to Bayard Taylor, October 21, 1866.

especially interested him.[23] Consequently he reviewed poetry, fiction, travel and exploration, history, biography, and translations. There was a preponderance of belles-lettres. The old New England writers received their share of notices—Lowell's *Biglow Papers*, Second Series, as well as *Under the Willows* and *Among My Books*; Emerson's *May-Day and Other Pieces*; Longfellow's *The New England Tragedies*; Whittier's *Ballads of New England*; and Hale's *If, Yes, and Perhaps* and *The Ingham Papers*. In the review of the *Biglow Papers* (January 1867) Howells contrasted Lowell's scholarly use of dialect with the "typographical pleasantry" of Artemus Ward and Petroleum V. Nasby, and the New Englander won the laurels: "They are neither of them without wit; and for the present they have a sort of reality; but they are of a stuff wholly different from that of Hosea Biglow, who is the type of a civilization, and who expresses, in a genuine vernacular, the true feeling, the racy humor, and the mother-wit of Yankee-land." In the review of *May-Day and Other Pieces* (September 1867) the reviewer reaffirmed Emerson's place as a leader of the age, and cited the book as containing "something undeniably great and good." Longfellow's book seems to have disappointed Howells somewhat, but the review (January 1869) concludes with a tribute to the book's "strange, sad pleasure, that 'angenehmer Schmerz', which high tragic poetry alone can give." The English writers were not neglected. Charles Reade's *Griffith Gaunt*, which appeared in the *Atlantic*, was reviewed (December 1866) the month after its completion in the magazine, and there were also notices by Howells of George Eliot's *The Spanish Gypsy*, Thackeray's *Miscellanies*, Tennyson's *Holy Grail*, and finally Ruskin's *Mystery of Life and Its Arts* and D. G. Rossetti's *Poems*. The review of Rossetti (July 1870) is especially interesting. Howells yielded high praise to "The Blessed Damozel" and reluctantly to "Jenny," but he joined in the current disapprobation of the poet's fleshliness:

It is a curious thing in a poet whose purity of mind and heart makes such a very strong impression, that his imagination should be so often

[23]Kirk, p. lxiii, n. 159.

dominated by character and fact which are quite other than pure. We think there has been more than enough of the Fallen Woman in literature; we wish that if she cannot be reformed, she might be at least policed out of sight; and we have a fancy (perhaps an erroneous, perhaps a guilty fancy) that some things, even in "The House of Life," however right they are, had best be kept out of speech.

In the end, the reviewer denies Rossetti a place among great poets. Among the forward-looking American writers Howells reviewed two books by Aldrich, one by Stedman, and several by Taylor. But some of his most revealing criticism is to be found in his reviews of the less genteel writers. He finds Melville's *Battle-Pieces and Aspects of the War* (review of February 1867) vapid. De Forest, in his novel *Miss Ravenel's Conversion* (review of July 1867), is heralded however as perhaps "the first to treat the war really and artistically." The reviewer is overenthusiastic about Bret Harte's *The Luck of Roaring Camp* (review of November 1870), and it was partly because of Howells that the irresponsible Westerner rose so brilliantly, only to fall. The review of Mark Twain's *The Innocents Abroad* (December 1869) was Howells' happiest effort. He was among the first in the East to recognize Twain, and his perceptive criticism made him the humorist's lifelong friend. Though he consistently misspelled Clemens (Clements), he understood the author's irony and his Americanism, and submitted that Twain was "quite worthy of the company of the best."

To report on the expository literature of the day, Howells had to demonstrate a breadth of knowledge for which he is not always credited. His reviews of travel and exploration included Professor I. I. Hayes's *The Open Polar Sea*, Agassiz's *A Journey in Brazil*, and Mrs. Horace Mann's translation of Sarmiento's *Life in the Argentine Republic*. He reported on the histories of Motley and Parkman, not to mention the Durand translation of Taine's *Italy, Rome, and Naples*. He criticized such timely productions as Reid's *Ohio in the War*, Richardson's *Personal History of U. S. Grant*, Jenckes's *Report on the Civil Service*, and Higginson's *Army Life in a Black Regiment*. And he had his say about the two scholarly compilations, Bartlett's *Familiar Quotations* and Allibone's *Critical Dictionary of Authors*. Howells once wrote jokingly to Mrs. Fields, "It *is* very hardening to write the book-notices for the Atlantic."[24] But it was more than hardening, it was tremendously fatiguing. Both the quantity and quality of Howells' reviews in the sixties are amazing.

Howells' increasing part in the editing of the *Atlantic* worked out very smoothly in general. There were disagreements between him and Fields, but they created no difficulties in their relationship, though contributors were sometimes confused by the divided editorship. Mrs. Abby Morton Diaz, a New England writer of humorous short stories, submitted a story to the magazine in 1868 that was read and rejected by Howells. Some time later, Fields wrote the author with the intention of printing the story. He suggested some deletions to which Mrs. Diaz yielded, but the story never appeared in the *Atlantic*. One of the author's letters to Fields, written March 1869, explains the situation:

Plymouth, March 24

Dear Sir.
   I have been trying to think of a name but no very good one occurs to me. Here are what I have thought of.
   "The Old Pilot and his Boys."
   "The Pilot's Two Boys."
   "A Seaside Story."
   "The Two Brothers."
   "Was it 'Well' with him?"
   "An out of the way Story." (Alluding to the out of the way place.) If either of these is satisfactory will you please see that it is given to the story? No matter about writing me which is taken. I think the disagreement between yourself and the Ass't. Ed. arises from this. You saw what I aimed to do, and he saw the imperfect way in which it was done. I wished to show—or not quite show, suggest, that the true life of a man is that which he lives in and for himself, and that this true life is not dependent on surroundings. Most of the story readers are probably young people and I thought that just to intimate this, and also to strike a little bit of a blow for unselfishness, would do them no harm. I was much dissatisfied with the way it was done

[24]Howells to Annie Fields, September 29, 1867.

and don't wonder the Ass't. Ed. is also. The Ms. was tried on a few young people and they expressed themselves—not to me—so highly entertained, that I thought—well, if it interests them, it may others of their kind, and stories not perfect are sometimes printed. If it is in order I should like to thank you for understanding me.

Respectfully yours,
Abby Morton Diaz

If you meet the Nortons in Europe would you be kind enough to give them my love? [FI 1054]

By this time the assistant editor had been thoroughly tested, and Fields, with his longing for England, decided that he could put him in charge of the magazine while the editor traveled abroad. Leaving Lowell and Holmes as consultants for the young man, Fields departed in April. By that time the June number was in preparation, and Fields had given Howells directions as to part of the contents of the later issues; but aside from this, the numbers from July to December were Howells'. Shortly after the editor's departure Howells began a long letter in which he reported his activities in the editorial office. The letter, which was continued a few weeks later, reveals a great deal about Howells' editorial procedure. He tried to be quite careful in maintaining the standards of quality, tone, and morality that Fields had stood for, while at the same time he did not desert his own principles:

Dear Mr. Fields: Cambridge, May 8, 1869.

I address you this in the bold hope that the sea has not got all of you, but that your organization at least has arrived in Liverpool. Yesterday at lunch, Mr. Osgood owned to having lost a bit in regard to your arrival at a given time; but there was a general and very encouraging belief that you had not been shipwrecked.

With the magazine I believe matters have gone well since you left. The June number went duly to press, and strikes me as a good one—though this is what we always say. Bayard Taylor sent a long poem which would fill five pages with rather heretical reading and not very poetical. It was an epistle from some Arab devotee who had been shocked by a meeting of Jews, Christians, Mahometans and pagans who fraternized on the ground that it didn't make much difference about their differences, for their code of morals was the same. I didn't think we were prepared to accept this position, and so—as the poem was dryish to boot—I declined it in one of those complimentary letters that always make a man so much madder than mere No! would.—I have accepted another story by Mr. Woods of The Advertiser, called The Robbery of the Blue River Bank, which I thought good, and another by a new hand—a tale of Southern life which I thought admirable. Both are short.—Aldrich withdrew his poem, and I put in place of it a little two stanza affair by Mrs. Piatt who wrote To-Day.—Parton wrote to say that he should soon have ready three or four papers on The Lobby, and proposing as many on Napoleon's correspondence. Consulting Mr. Osgood, I've concluded to propose *one* on the latter subject.—Mr. John Hay, ex-secretary of Lincoln, has sent an account of the assassination of the Mormon prophet Jos. Smith, from facts gathered on the ground of the tragedy at Nauvoo. I think I'll take it if he can re-shape it. At present it is rather slangy, and is so personal that I'm afraid it might get you in for some libel suits.—The Reverend Clarke's fourth paper has come to hand, and so has Dr. Palmer's second. The doctor has just taken a turn at *delerium tremens,* and having got back to the Asylum, may be supposed to write with greater authority than ever.—But I don't think he writes profitably, this time, and after consulting Mr. Osgood I must either decline his paper or cut it down greatly. He really adds very little that is new to his first article, and it is more disjointed and inconsequent.

May 23. Mr. Osgood, feeling bound to Dr. Palmer, we use his paper with some changes. It read better in the proof than it did in the manuscript. Taylor took his rejection in the sweetest spirit, and Hay has empowered me to make what changes are necessary in his paper. Parton will give us an article on the Napoleon correspondence. Mr. Lowell half-promised me a poem for the July number, but he had to go off to Ithaca before he could give it. He seemed to view the approaching week to be past at that seat of learning without enthusiasm, but I hope he'll find some compensation in doing good to Goldwin Smith. Every one here is amused at Mr. Smith's extraordinary proclamation that America would ever become too hot on the Alabama question to hold Englishmen.

29.—I substituted Mr. Benson's paper on French and English Artwriters for The Hamlets of the Stage in the July number, and laid over Wettstein till August. Mr. Parton's first article on the Lobby has come. I am uncertain whether to put it in August or September: shall consult Mr. Osgood. I have used Mr. Trowbridge's poem for July.—I believe this is a pretty fair account of my stewardship so far. From time to time I'll write of how affairs go on.

Mrs. Howells joins me in regards to Mrs. Fields and yourself. Pray remember me also to Miss Lowell, and believe me
Yours faithfully
W. D. Howells.

Howells did not keep his promise to write periodically. He wrote another report, however, in August. By this time Harriet Beecher Stowe's article, "The True Story of Lady Byron's Life," had appeared in the September issue. The exposé of Lord Byron's incest, based upon the still questionable statements of Lady Byron, was written in Mrs. Stowe's most melodramatic style as a vindication of the reputation of Byron's wife. Not only was the article too strong for genteel sensibilities but it was incompetently done, and from a financial point of view its acceptance turned out to be the biggest blunder perpetrated during Fields's editorship of the *Atlantic*. Although Howells attempted to correct the article, he was unable to make it palatable to the public. He explained this among other things in his August report:

Cambridge, Aug. 24, 1869.
Dear Mr. Fields:
My resolution to keep a diary concerning the editorial business, and send it to you regularly twice a month was altogether too bright, too beautiful to last. Yet while it endured, you will own it must have had its fascinations—such a propriety in it—so amusing to me, so satisfactory to you. Well, we will check the unavailing tear: the business, though unrecorded has been promptly done, and we are already arrived at the time when we begin to look for the return of Autumn and of you. I am glad you liked the August number so well: I put in the things you directed and filled out according to my own judgment, from the mass of material, that seems to grow like the liver of Prometheus the more it is preyed upon. The September is equally good, though Mrs. Stowe's sensation of course benumbs the public to everything else in it. So far her story has been received with howls of rejection from almost every side where a critical dog is kept. The Tribune, and one or two western papers alone accept it as truth; but I think the tide will turn, especially, if its publication in England elicits anything like confirmation there.—As to stories, you know the Foe in the Household ends in December. Mr. Hale brought in a curious thing, a week or two ago called The Brick Moon, which will run

from October till December inclusive; and besides this, I've taken five or six short things, of 10 or 12 pp. each; but the accepted Mss. have mainly been sketches and essays—a capital essay by Sheldon, among the rest. I've taken one poem, "by and with the advice and consent of" Mr. Lowell, and another upon my own judgment from Bayard Taylor. It's extremely fine, I think (An August Pastoral) and I get it into the October. And then—shut your eyes and open your mouth!—Lowell has written for your pet January number, a glorious poem of 12 pages. He read it to me yesterday, and I thought it magnificent—an opalescent beauty with every sort of intellectual light and color in it, and full of all dreamy tendernesses, too. It's ready now; and think of my denying myself the triumph of putting it in at once and waiting for you to get the glory later. Think, and blush, for having put off those two lectures of Henry Giles on me and my numbers! It's some comfort to remember that I've told everybody you made up the magazines before you left.—I've begun Dr. Jarvis's papers on the Increase of Life in the October; Clarke closes with Mahomet in November (a very successful and honorable set of papers); Shaler ends his earthquakes in Dec.; Mrs. Thaxter, though her first paper was greatly praised, has not followed it up; Goldwin Smith has sent nothing; (and small loss to us as things have fallen out,) I haven't got to Prof. Wilder's things yet—we had so much other science. Mrs. Agassiz has two charming papers on dredging in the Gulf, (Oct. and Nov.); Mr. King has not yet sent any of his sporting articles.—I followed up the "Recent Travels" in the Sept. with a similar article on "A Poetical Lot," and I'm glad that the first struck you favorably: I won't repeat what Lowell said of the second because pride is sinful. My notion was to vary the monotony of the notices by a sort of paper that would give me more elbow-room. In Nov. and Dec. I'll have notices; and in Nov., also, a study of some parts of Cambridge, called "A Pedestrian Tour."—I've had such a streak of good luck in volunteer contributions, that I don't lament your bad luck in England so much as I otherwise should. You won't perhaps value the suggestion any more because I offer it unasked; but I don't think it pays at all to take English stuff unless it's first chop: Minor Shows of London and Mrs. Lynton's paper are *not* first chop, and I hope you'll fail in the attempt to get anything more of like quality.—The Morris sonnets are very pretty, and the other little poem will go into the October.—I enclose a list of the articles accepted, that may possibly be interesting or useful to you, and also the Contents of the November number as it has gone to the printers.

I believe I haven't got into difficulty with any one, made you enemies or changed the general policy on the magazine; so there will be no occasion to repeat the scene which took place on the return of the chief editor of the San Diego Herald.—Concerning this last sentence, Mr. Kirk would have written on the margin: "A *scene* cannot *take place*," which reminds me that he is no longer reading proof at the University Press. I lament him for some reasons, but I believe on general principles that we're proof-read too much.—The Parton articles are interesting, but have on the whole been received with something more than the usual misgiving. I suppose that they are more popular than otherwise. Shaler's papers have been a very fair success; and Clarke's have been liked nearly everywhere. The Foe in the Household has lost ground a little, I think; Harry James's story is a great gain upon all that he's done before, in the popular estimation. —Dr. Holmes is a firm believer in Mrs. Stowe's article: Mr. Lowell if no longer a doubter of it, still a disliker. It seems to be pretty generally allowed it was awkwardly done. I see this, but I think the story is true and ought to have been told. People say Mrs. Stowe should have given names, dates and places in full. You saw that she made one mistake, stating the Byrons lived two years together instead of 18 months. We'd the greatest difficulty with her in getting to read her proof at all. Kirk and I both read it carefully, and sent it to her; *and she wouldn't return the proof!* but sent a copy which Dr. Holmes had gone over. I then read it again, and enclosed it to Dr. Holmes, who accepted all my corrections; but this was done hastily, with the printers at my back, and with a view to leave everything, as nearly as possible, just as Mrs. Stowe had written it. She had misquoted wherever she could, nearly—the (last) conversation as she gave it between Byron and Fletcher was all wrong.

Mrs. Howells joins me in cordial regards to you and Mrs. Fields. I know you must be enjoying yourselves, and I hope you feel easy about the "Atlantic" here. Our family has been uncommonly well; but Mrs. Howells has lost her father: the kind old man died July 5.— There is nothing new in Cambridge. So adieu!   W. D. Howells.[25]

Howells was never blamed for his part in the Byron controversy. In fact, it was little more than a year later that he was given the full editorship of the *Atlantic*. Fields returned from abroad in December 1869, and Howells became officially the editor in January 1871. The old editor remained to advise him

[25]Printed with slight omissions in Howells, *Life*, I, 146-49.

until September, while the responsibilities were gradually shifted. Fields did everything he could to insure Howells' success. "You will find Howells a good editor, I think," he wrote to Bayard Taylor on April 26, 1871, "and all will go on smoothly as ever with him."

The magazine continued smoothly enough during the ten years that Howells reigned. He carefully maintained its serious tone and high aims. His reverence for the old writers together with his desire to encourage the newer ones made what ought to have been a perfect combination. He gratefully accepted whatever contributions he could get from Holmes, Lowell, Longfellow, and Whittier, and at the same time increased the representation of new writers. Under his administration the political and social policies of the *Atlantic* were at least as praiseworthy as in either of the preceding editorships, and he tried to increase the magazine's range of subject matter by introducing a wider coverage of art and music and a full account of important foreign literature.[26] Yet the periodical never prospered as it had for Fields. The loss of fifteen thousand subscribers, which occurred in 1870 largely because of the Byron article, was not fully recovered until long after Howells' editorship had ended.

In the years following Fields's retirement, he and Howells frequently saw each other and occasionally corresponded. Their friendship was not injured when in 1875 Fields contributed an essay "Barry Cornwall and His Friends," to *Harper's Monthly*, but the author explained apologetically to Howells, at the same time that he complimented him on his new novel, *A Foregone Conclusion*:

Continental Hotel Philadelphia Nov. 20. 1875.
My dear Howells.
I have been about many a day from home & do not return for many a day yet, I am sorry to say,—but I cannot wait to tell you how your new story delights the very cockles of my heart. It seems to be, so far, the author's best as regards a good many points of excellence. I rejoice over it, & the magazine generally.

"Harper" made me such a regal offer I "caved," the sea-side hut-

[26]Butler, passim.

builders have to count up the shekels when the carpenter & mason are making out their bills under your very eyes & charging like "Chester"!

With best regards to you all within the Sacred precincts of Cambridge.

>Cordially Yours.
>James T. Fields.[27]

Howells replied promptly and banteringly:

>Nov. 22, 1875.

Dear Mr. Fields:

I'm exceedingly pleased that you like my story, and I thank you for thinking to say so. It's more of an experiment upon my public than I've ever ventured before, and I shall not consider it a successful till I have their approval of it in book-form. But it's immensely heartening to have a shake of the hand like yours.

—I supposed the Harpers had been corrupting you, but I didn't blame you—I would hail corruption, myself, with open arms. Besides, it was a great advantage to have the papers so nicely illustrated.

I will send this to Boston, and I hope Mrs. Fields will look into it and see that we send ever so much love to both of you.

>Ever sincerely yours
>W. D. Howells.

An interesting note of 1880 reveals Howells criticizing one of Fields's efforts—and none too gently. If Fields's essay was intended for the *Atlantic*, it fell short of its goal:

>August 12, 1880

Dear Mr. Fields:

I like the matter of this and enjoy it as I do all your literary reminiscences; but I think the manner of it is against it—a little too daringly fancied.

>Yours ever,
>W. D. Howells.

Upon Fields's death the following year, Howells was one of the mourners. He owed a very special debt of gratitude to Fields, and he was not prone to forget it. When Annie Fields's Biography, *James T. Fields, Biographical Notes and Personal Sketches*, was published in December 1881, he was sorry that he was unable to make use of the occasion by recording his feelings toward his

[27]MS in Harvard University Library.

old chief for the *Atlantic,* though he had already resigned the editorship earlier that year. He wrote to Mrs. Fields:

Belmont, Dec. 10, 1881

Dear Mrs. Fields:

I have now been nearly four weeks in bed, with fever, and a thousand other things; but I am slowly getting better.—The first week of my sickness was the time I had meant to give to a review of your beautiful and interesting book; and I know that you will believe that I deeply grieved at being prevented from writing of it. Of course Aldrich has had it well done; but I cannot cease to regret that I should not have been able to do it.

The reading gave me a sad but constant pleasure: it kept dear Mr. Fields continually before me; I saw him; I heard him speak and laugh. Could I say more in praise?

Write me a line to say you forgive my delinquency, and excusing this shapeless note—the best I can do—believe me

Ever sincerely Yours
W. D. Howells.

In another letter, written at the time of Fields's death, Howells had expressed himself more fully to Mrs. Fields. His words imply something of the importance of the older man's influence upon an author who was to attain considerable stature in American literature:

Perhaps I have never told you, and may fitly tell you here now, how affectionately and with what unalloyed gratitude I have constantly remembered my connection with him. A look or word of depreciation from him would have made me very unhappy, in the place I held under him; but in all the years I was with him, I had nothing but delicate kindness from him—forbearance where I failed, and generous praise where he thought I succeeded in my work.... I shall cherish the recollection of the little half hour he spent with me in the reception room, that night, before he felt able to go up-stairs. ... He would not let me feel heavy or sad about him. He was still as he always has been,—the genius of cheerful hospitality. There is no one left like him![28]

---

[28] Annie Fields, *James T. Fields,* p. 266. Further testimony by Howells of his respect for Fields occurs in "Recollections of an *Atlantic* Editorship" and *Literary Friends and Acquaintance.*

Chapter X:
The Other Bostonians

THE *Atlantic Monthly* in the sixties is most closely associated with the names of Lowell and Holmes and a few others. But they could not write the whole magazine, and for the bulk the editor relied upon the rather intimate group of Bostonians who did not contribute often individually but who wrote a great deal altogether. As a group they had as much to do with the magazine's character as the regular contributors. For instance when the *Atlantic* spoke on science, it was through the pen of Professor Agassiz; on religion, James Freeman Clarke or Cyrus Bartol. And there was usually someone in Boston who could manage whatever subject the editor called for.

The most important development in science during the magazine's early years was the theory of evolution. The controversy that followed the publication of Darwin's *Origin of Species* in 1859 naturally found its way into the *Atlantic*, where it was supported by the Harvard botanist Asa Gray and opposed by Louis Agassiz. Gray, whose series of three articles appeared in 1860 before Fields's editorship, took a cautious but nonetheless definite stand: "We find ourselves in the 'singular position' acknowledged by Pictet,—that is, confronted with a theory which, although it can really explain much, seems inadequate to the heavy task it so boldly assumes, but which, nevertheless, appears better fitted than any other that has been broached to explain, if it be possible to explain, somewhat of the manner in which organized beings may have arisen and succeeded each other."

Gray's report was appreciated by Darwin, who saw to the republication of the articles in England the following year.

Unfortunately Fields was a rather close friend of Agassiz, a fellow member of the Saturday Club, and in the *Atlantic* it was Agassiz rather than Gray that dominated the scene after 1861. Agassiz made sixteen contributions, one of which, "Methods of Study in Natural History," was a comprehensive exposition of modern biological theory in nine installments. The Darwinian theory frequently arose in these articles to haunt the professor; he seemed to feel himself on the defensive at every turn. His chief objection to the theory of evolution was his belief in the "permanence of types combined with repeated changes of species." He saw a constant divine plan appearing in the general types of living things in all ages, while specific characteristics of species were infinitely variable according to the Creator's whim—"to maintain the organic plan, while constantly diversifying the mode of expressing it." In "The Silurian Beach" (April 1863), Agassiz condemned the Darwinians' attempt to "belittle the Creative work, or say that He first scattered the seeds of life in meagre or stinted measure":

> I am fully aware that the intimate relations between the organic and physical world are interpreted by many as indicating the absence, rather than the presence, of an intelligent Creator. They argue, that the dependence of animals on material laws gives us the clue to their origin as well as to their maintenance. Were this influence as absolute and unvarying as the purely mechanical action of physical circumstances must necessarily be, this inference might have some pretence to logical probability,—though it seems to me unnecessary, under any circumstances, to resort to climatic influences or the action of any physical laws to explain the thoughtful distribution of the organic and inorganic world, so evidently intended to secure for all beings what best suits their nature and their needs. But the truth is, that, while these harmonious relations underlie the whole creation in such a manner as to indicate a great central plan, of which all things are a part, there is at the same time a freedom, an arbitrary element in the mode of carrying it out, which seems to point to the exercise of an individual will; for, side by side with facts, apparently the direct

result of physical laws, are other facts, the nature of which shows a complete independence of external influences.

Here speaks the Bostonian mind of the mid-nineteenth century at very nearly its worst. No one doubts Agassiz's importance to American science, but on this point he was blinded by preconceived notions of religion and propriety. And this was the fundamental fault in the intellectual community of which Boston was the center. The writers for the *Atlantic* and the editor himself often failed to look far enough into matters of science, politics, religion, sociology, and psychology because of intellectual blocks imposed by the culture to which they were loyal. Cultural taboos and the niceties of decorum sometimes limited their capacity to comprehend the problems that were rising before them, such as economic depressions, the exploitation of the laboring class, and the treatment of insanity. Although the struggle against these evils enlisted their sympathies, they sometimes—though by no means always—refused to see to its roots and were powerless in it. But this is condemning them for not being consistently able to transcend their age, and such an ability is ever rare.

On the other hand, in education the *Atlantic* achieved a certain distinction in printing some of the early utterances of the progressive President Eliot of Harvard. Eliot wrote to Fields on November 10, 1868, six months before his inauguration, and offered him three articles on education and science to be printed as soon as possible so as to influence college curriculums for the following year. The earliest possible date was the February 1869 issue, and after some consideration Eliot promised them for that time:

My Dear Sir,
I will send the first part of my manuscript to Mr. Howells tomorrow with the understanding that, if he finds it suitable for the Atlantic, the first paper can appear in the February number and the succeeding shorter ones in March and April. You will excuse my urgency about the time of printing. It really makes a considerable difference in the usefulness of the papers. They are meant to influence the programmes and methods of scientific and technological schools and of the preparatory schools. They will not be in time for effect next year unless they appear during the winter. It occurs to me that Mr. Howells

may not read the manuscript very carefully, and that I ought to say to you, that there are comments in the first article on nine different colleges and scientific schools. There is not a personal allusion of any kind in the article, but the comments are not all favorable, and may be distasteful to the parties concerned.

Sincerely Yours
Charles W. Eliot

3 Chestnut St. 12 Nov. '68[1]

Only two of the articles appeared, one in the February and the other in the March issue. Entitled "The New Education," they predict and encourage the rapid rise of technological schools in the United States. The closing paragraph gives an inkling of the reformation Eliot was about to inaugurate in American education for the sake of "progress for the world":

> Americans must not sit down contented with their position among the industrial nations. We have inherited civil liberty, social mobility, and immense native resources. The advantages we thus hold over the European nations are inestimable. The question is, not how much our freedom can do for us unaided, but how much we can help freedom by judicious education. We appreciate better than we did ten years ago that true progress in this country means progress for the world. In organizing the new education, we do not labor for ourselves alone. Freedom will be glorified in her works.

Although one of the effects of the new education was to free the schools from the dominance of the churches, it had not yet begun in the 1860's to destroy the position that religion held in the educated mind. Christianity still swayed the majority of the people in the United States, but more and more it was being questioned and examined. The spirit of questioning showed itself frequently in the *Atlantic*. In the first volume (May 1858) appeared an article by Theodore Parker on "Henry Ward Beecher." Both author and subject held progressive views of religion; in fact, nearly all religious articles in the *Atlantic* were liberal Unitarian (Fields himself belonging in this category), though Beecher, the subject of this article, was an orthodox

---

[1] See Eliot to Fields, November 10, November 11, and December 29, 1868.

Congregationalist. In 1858, however, it was still possible for Parker to say:

> The Puritans founded an ecclesiastical oligarchy which is by no means ended yet; with the obstinate "liberty of prophesying" there was mixed a certain respect for such as only wore the prophet's mantle; nor is it wholly gone....
> No class has such opportunities for influence, such means of power; even now the press ranks second to the pulpit.... No man of science or letters has such access to men.

Had he been living a decade later, Parker would probably have hesitated before making such statements. The Puritan respect for the clergy was beginning to weaken; an amoral civilization was beginning to replace the old morality; and the scientist was usurping the place of the minister.[2] Even "the eternal principle of Right" was to be questioned. The alert ministers of the late sixties expected Christianity to grow and change with the progress of civilization, and Parker might have been suspected of reactionary tendencies had he said then, as he did in 1858:

> The minister is not expected to appeal to the selfish motives which are addressed by the market, the forum, or the bar, but to the eternal principle of Right. He must not be guided by the statutes of man, changeable as the clouds, but must fix his eye on the bright particular star of Justice, the same yesterday, to-day, and forever.

Parker died in 1860, but only a few years later Cyrus A. Bartol, Fields's own minister and personal friend, was writing in "The Preacher's Trial" (February 1863):

> The pulpit has lost something of its old sacredness in the general mind. There is little popular superstition to endure its former dictation.... Is the minister's concern and call of God only, with certain imposing formalities and prearranged dogmas, to greet in their Sunday-clothes his friends who have laid aside their pursuits and delights with the gay garments or working-dress of the week, never reminding

---

[2] In Eliot's paper "The New Education," mentioned above, the author deplored the fact that college presidents had heretofore been almost invariably ministers. It is time, he said (and his own presidency of Harvard was a case in point), that colleges be directed by men trained in science and education.

them of what, during the six days, they have heard or where they have been? "No!" let him say; "if this is to be a minister, no minister can I be!" ... O preachers, beware of your sentimental descant on the worth of goodness, the goodness of being good, and the sinfulness of sin, without specifying either! ... The pulpit is to teach religion in application to life.

Bartol was not a profound thinker, but he saw that Christianity could not survive by ignoring the changes in society. It was not enough to appeal to the "eternal principle of Right" which was "the same yesterday, to-day, and forever." Religion must be practically adapted to modern needs.

In 1869 James Freeman Clarke, probably the foremost minister in Boston, tried to synthesize the recent trends in the progressive religion in a series of articles on the religions of the world as compared to Christianity. His aim was to prove that Christianity, especially Protestantism, was the culmination of the others, including and fulfilling them to form a universal creed: "The condition of progress is that nothing shall be lost. The lower truth must be preserved in the higher truth; the lower life taken up into the higher life" ("Mohammed," November 1869). The influence of Darwin is apparent in Clarke's belief in the chain of existence as applied to religion. Here is also the influence of Emerson, which shows itself continually in religious thinking of the sixties. Emerson's eclecticism is largely responsible for the interest in the Oriental religions and the origin of what Clarke called comparative theology. In his introductory article, "A New Chapter of Christian Evidences" (March 1869), Clarke set forth the conclusions that were to be drawn from the succeeding articles on Buddhism, Brahmanism, Confucianism, Mohammedanism, and others: "Christianity alone is ... a fulness of truth, not coming to destroy but to fulfil the previous religions; but being capable of replacing them by teaching all the truth they have taught, and supplying that which they have omitted." And he recognized the need for Christianity to adapt itself to a changing society: "Christianity, being not a system but a life, not a creed or a form, but a spirit, is able to meet all the changing wants of an advancing civilization by new developments and adaptations, constantly feeding the life of men at its roots by fresh supplies of faith in God and faith in man."

"Faith in God and faith in man" might well have been the watchword of the Bostonians and their allies. Religious faith is abundantly illustrated in these pages. Humanistic faith revealed itself in science and social theory by belief in progress, and in literature by the glorification of character and sentiment. In politics, the whole democratic tradition and tendency were hinged to this faith in ultimate human goodness. The North's crusade against slavery was a further manifestation.

From the very beginning the *Atlantic* took a firm humanitarian stand in politics. As the first editor, Lowell accepted his post with the understanding that he would speak out against slavery. The publishers' statement on the cover of the first issue read: "In politics the *Atlantic* will be the organ of no party or clique, but will honestly endeavor to be the exponent of what its conductors believe to be the American idea." That it did not evade its political responsibilities is evidenced not only by its early support of Lincoln, but also by the inclusion of the United States Senator from Massachusetts, Charles Sumner, among its contributors.

Sumner was an old friend of Fields and had long been published by the firm. When in his later years the senator fell from public favor, Fields's loyalty to him almost paralleled that of Hawthorne to Franklin Pierce. In 1863, however, Sumner was still a member of the Senate, working for the Northern cause and looking forward to a sound Reconstruction policy, when the North should have won its inevitable victory. He secured for Fields one of the most virulent articles to appear in the *Atlantic*, "Who is Roebuck?" by W. J. Austin, an attack on John Arthur Roebuck, a member of the British Parliament who sided with the Confederacy.[3] The article was printed in the September 1863 issue, at which time Sumner's first contribution also appeared.

---

[3]Fields to Sumner, June 13, 1863, MS in Harvard University Library.

Sumner's article, "Interesting Manuscripts of Edmund Burke," is a scholarly report on the manuscript of Burke's "Observations on the Conduct of the Minority," which shows Sumner to have been an antiquarian as well as a politician. He later utilized his antiquarian interest in "Monograph from an Old Note-Book," "Clemency and Common Sense," and "Prophetic Voices about America," in which he drew timely morals from the past. Sumner was originally paid five dollars a page for the paper on Burke—approximately the minimum rate—but upon receiving his cool acknowledgment of the check, Fields quickly wrote again: "That check for $20 was for the paper on the Burke Mss. Was it too little? Then I will make it larger."[4]

Sumner's second contribution is far more important, and brought the author two hundred dollars for twenty-three and a half pages.[5] Entitled "Our Domestic Relations; or How to Treat the Rebel States," it is a lengthy and copiously documented argument for Congressional control of the conquered South. Fearing military government on the one hand and a return to the *status quo ante bellum* on the other, Sumner believed that Congress had the legal right and duty to set up a provisional government for the Reconstruction period.

> The relations of the States to the National Government must be carefully considered,—not too boldly, not too timidly,—in order to see in what way, or by what process, the transition from Rebel forms may be most surely accomplished. If I do not greatly err, it will be found that the powers of Congress, which have thus far been so effective in raising armies and in supplying moneys, will be important, if not essential, in fixing the conditions of perpetual peace. But there is one point on which there can be no question. The dogma and delusion of State Rights, which did so much for the Rebellion, must not be allowed to neutralize all that our arms have gained.

Of Senator Sumner's three other articles in the magazine, the most interesting is "Clemency and Common Sense" in the De-

---

[4] Fields to Sumner, August 31, 1863, MS in Harvard University Library. See Sumner to Fields, August 30, 1863.

[5] Fields to Sumner, September 3, 1863, MS in Harvard University Library.

cember 1865 issue. Referring to the Reconstruction program, he warns against over-leniency toward the South in attempting to avoid vindictiveness: "*Alas! that, escaping from Charybdis, we should rush upon Scylla!*" And he predicts the economic decay that will lead to barbarism if the North continues its indulgence of the rebels: "By natural consequence, that same Barbarism which has drenched the land in blood will continue to prevail, with wrong, outrage, and the insurrections of an oppressed race; the national name will be dishonored, and the national power will be weakened."

In politics, the *Atlantic* maintained and still maintains its original purpose. In its coverage of art, it never arose to the expectations of its founders, despite its subtitle, *A Magazine of Literature, Art, and Politics*. The publishers' statement in the first issue said: "In the term Art they intend to include the whole domain of aesthetics, and hope gradually to make this critical department a true and fearless representative of Art, in all its various branches, without any regard to prejudice, whether personal or national, or to private considerations of what kind soever." But the founders' dream was never realized. Lowell made an effort to attain it during his editorship, and occasionally set out a separate art department in the magazine. During Fields's early years as editor, however, the department disappeared entirely and there were fewer articles. In his last four or five years, while Howells was his assistant, the number increased, especially through the contributions of Eugene Benson, a New Yorker residing in Paris.[6] Altogether there were four or five articles per year on painting, sculpture, and architecture during the magazine's first decade and a half, and articles on music were much rarer. Though the Boston Brahmins were great eclectic amateurs, they were either incompetent or unwilling to write on the fine arts in the sixties.

Such was not the case in belles-lettres, where Boston still ruled. The *Atlantic*'s attitude toward literature was enunciated by its four chief critics, Lowell, Whipple, Higginson, and Howells.

[6] See Eugene Benson to Fields, January 5, 1868.

Lowell, as first editor, and Howells, as third, made criticism a major part of their jobs, writing an enormous number of book notices as well as full articles on books. Fields, busy with publishing duties, did not have time for this while he was editor, though he probably wrote some reviews in the magazine which he never acknowledged. T. W. Higginson wrote much of the criticism for Fields; but the most representative critic was Edwin Percy Whipple, who wrote twenty-eight articles and at least twenty-six literary notices before 1871. Born in Gloucester, Massachusetts, in 1819, Whipple had lived in Boston since 1837. He was one of the foremost critics of his time, and one whom Hawthorne considered the best in America. A study of his critical opinions is a study of Bostonian literary taste.

One would expect then to find him preoccupied with the moral implications of the books he reviewed, and so he was. In "Beaumont and Fletcher, Massinger, and Ford," one of a series of articles on Elizabethan literature which appeared in 1867 and 1868, he constantly repudiated qualities in the dramatists which "offend our artistic and shock our moral sense." Of Beaumont and Fletcher he said:

They agreed in being tainted with the fashionable slavishness and fashionable immorality of the court of James. They believed in the divine right of kings as piously as any bishop, and they violated all the decencies of life as recklessly as any courtier. The impurity of Beaumont, however, seems the result of elaborate thinking, that of Fletcher the running over of heedless animal spirits. They agreed also in certain leading dramatic conceptions and types of character; and they agreed, in regard to the morality of their plays, in subordinating their consciences to their audiences.

But when he wrote of Spenser, he said:

We are in communion with a nature in which the most delicate, the most voluptuous, sense of beauty is in exquisite harmony with the austerist recognition of the paramount obligations of goodness and rectitude. The beauty of material objects never obscures to him the transcendent beauty of holiness.

Spenser had the ideal combination of "spiritual vision" and "artistic taste." The ultra-refined delight in beauty shows itself in Whipple's criticism in recurring expressions such as "poetic feeling," "grace," "sweetness," "high imagination," "freshness." This was inherited from the English romantics and developed into the sterile beauty-worship of Stedman, Stoddard, and Taylor. It is an impressionistic gourmandism in literature, exhibiting itself whenever the writer introduces a quotation—for example: "Who that has read it can ever forget the thrill that went through him as he completed the first stanza [of *The Faerie Queene*]?" and "How simple and tender, and yet how intensely imaginative, is this exquisite picture of the bride [in Spenser's *Epithalamion*]!"

Whipple's criticism was intensely of his own epoch, and it represented the blindness as well as the pride of the age. Deep in his mind, he felt that the nineteenth century had reached the ultimate point in the progress of culture. Again in "Spenser," he disparaged the nondramatic poets of the English Renaissance:

> Spenser is a great name; but he is the only undramatic poet of his time who could be placed above, or on a level with, Wordsworth, Byron, Shelley, Coleridge, or Tennyson. There is a list, somewhere, of two hundred names of poets who belonged to the Elizabethan age,—mostly mere nebulous appearances, which require a telescope of the greatest power to separate into individual stars. Few of them can be made to shine with as steady a lustre as the ordinary versemen who contribute to our magazines. Take "England's Helicon" and the "Paradise of Dainty Devices,"—two collections of the miscellaneous poetry written during the last forty or fifty years of the seventeenth [sic] century,—and, if we except a few pieces by Raleigh, Sidney, Marlowe, Greene, Lodge, Breton, Watson, Nash, and Hunnis, these collections have little to dazzle us into admiration or afflict us with a sense of inferiority.

Among the poets whom Whipple did not deign to mention here, but whom he included in "Minor Elizabethan Poets," is John Donne. He condemns Donne for intending "to surprise rather than to please"; "his muse is thus as hostile to use as to beauty." "The intention is, not to idealize what is true, but to display the writer's skill and wit in giving a show of reason to what is false." "His amatory poems, accordingly, are characterized by a cold, hard, labored, intellectualized sensuality, worse than the worst impurity of his contemporaries, because it has no excuse in passion for its violations of decency."

Although Whipple measured everything by the standards of his own age, still he prescribed a biographical interpretation of a writer's works. "The man is the measure of the poet," he said in "Beaumont and Fletcher," and Fletcher cannot equal Shakespeare because of the inferiority of his personal character. And the interaction of Donne's writing with his personality made him a scurrilous writer and a perverted man. The whole theme of Whipple's two articles on Francis Bacon is to reconcile Bacon the man with Bacon the writer. The conclusion is that he must have been basically moral though he lacked a certain warmth of humanity:

> But while this man was without the austerer virtues of humanity, we must not forget that he was also without its sour and malignant vices; and he stands almost alone in literature, as a vast dispassionate intellect, in which the sentiment of philanthropy has been refined and purified into the subtle essence of thought. Without this philanthropy or goodness, he tells us, "man is but a better kind of vermin"; and love of mankind, in Bacon, is not merely the noblest feeling but the highest reason. This beneficence, thus transformed into intelligence, is not a hard opinion, but a rich and mellow spirit of humanity, which communicates the life of the quality it embodies; and we cannot more fitly conclude than by quoting the noble sentence in which Bacon, after pointing out the mistakes regarding the true end of knowledge, closes by divorcing it from all selfish egotism and ambition.

The "love of mankind," upon which Whipple bases his evaluation of Bacon, is the last criterion of his critical system. Literature exists for the glorification of man. Hence, the Elizabethan dramatists are valuable despite their immoralities:

> They are all intensely and audaciously human. Taking them in the mass, they have much to offend our artistic and shock our moral sense; but still the dramatic literature of the world would be searched in vain for another instance of so broad and bold a representation of the varieties of human nature,—one in which the conventional restraints both on depravity and excellence are so resolutely set aside,— one in which the many-charactered soul of man is so vividly depicted,

in its weakness and in its strength, in its mirth and in its passion, in the appetites which sink it below the beasts that perish, in the aspirations which lift it to regions of existence of which the visible heavens are but the veil.

The poetry in the *Atlantic* followed Whipple's literary criteria —the austere ethics, the proper passion for beauty, the belief in progress, and to some extent the humaneness. The poets who wrote the most were Longfellow and Lowell of Cambridge, Holmes of Boston, and Whittier of Amesbury, Massachusetts. But there were other Bostonians who did most of the filling in so as to vary this four-part diet somewhat. Whether they actually offered any variety, other than mediocrity, is questionable. Their work is largely formalized and the choice of themes severely limited. The war, the death of a friend or lover, the illustration of a moral principle (such as the virtue of poverty), the desire for escape, and occasionally a story in verse were the subjects. Incidentally, these are in the order of their frequency, war poetry being the most frequent.

Despite the quality of the verse, it is incorrect then to say that the Bostonians ignored the distress of their country or that the *Atlantic* in the sixties was a magazine for escapists. In its pages appeared Holmes's "Brother Jonathan's Lament for Sister Caroline," Longfellow's "The Cumberland," Lowell's "Ode Recited at the Harvard Commemoration."[7] Mrs. A. D. T. Whitney wrote "My Daphne" in the August 1862 number, celebrating the coming emancipation of the slaves. T. W. Parsons, one year later, printed "Love's Challenge" about a patriotic girl who tells her lover:

> If thou have music in thy soul,
>   Yet have no sinew for the strife,
> Go teach thyself the war-drum's roll,
>   And woo me better with a fife!

---

[7] The articles on the Civil War by John Weiss and C. C. Hazewell must not be omitted from notice. These writers, both Bostonians, contributed many expository articles to the *Atlantic* on topics of timely interest.

Lucy Larcom did her bit with the maudlin "Reënlisted," May 1864:

> You would not pick him from the rest by eagles or by stars,
> By straps upon his coat-sleeve, or gold or silver bars,
> Nor a corporal's strip of worsted, but there's something
>   in his face,
> And something in his even step, a-marching in his place.

And in July 1865, T. B. Aldrich in the sonnet "Accomplices: Virginia, 1865" employed the graveyard strain in bewailing the war-dead on the Potomac.

After Howells became assistant editor in 1866, a few more poets from outside Boston contributed, such as E. C. Stedman and Helen Hunt, but the old guard continued to rule.

The Bostonian writers of fiction were few but good. Holmes's *The Professor's Story* (*Elsie Venner*) and *The Guardian Angel* were the most talked-about novels in the magazine. Among Aldrich's nineteen contributions there was some fiction, always highly readable. Aldrich was an excellent story teller, but he was too busy with the editing of *Every Saturday* to write much for the *Atlantic* after 1866, while before that time he was known chiefly as a poet. His "Struggle for Life" in the July 1867 issue is about a man who was buried alive. The theme is slightly reminiscent of Poe but with a pleasant twist at the end, exactly the kind of thing Fields needed to lighten the magazine. "A Young Desperado" in December of the same year is an anticipation of the *Story of a Bad Boy*. The little ruffian with a good heart whom Aldrich depicted here invites comparison with Harriet Beecher Stowe's attempt at a similar characterization in "Little Captain Trott." While Aldrich's story is still amusing, Mrs. Stowe's repels the modern reader with its sentimentality. Aldrich strove for realism, whereas Mrs. Stowe sought to play on the reader's emotions. Though "A Young Desperado" appeared first in the magazine, it is an early representative of the trend toward realism, while "Little Captain Trott" is a product of decadent romanticism.

There were eleven contributions during Fields's editorship

from the young Henry James. They are extremely interesting as studies in the development of the writer, and they show a deliberate progress even in the short space of time under consideration. *Poor Richard*, in the June, July, and August 1867 issues, for instance, is a somewhat diverse and episodic story set in America. Though there is some comparatively good characterization, there is much more dependence upon plot than we find in James's later works. Richard the protagonist, is interesting if superficial—an over-impetuous character given to drinking, until he reforms. Gertrude, the woman of the story, cannot make up her mind, and fortunately for the plot, does not until it is too late. The conclusion is not tragic but avoids melodrama by failing to unite the chief characters. *Gabrielle de Bergerac*, another three-installment novelette, published in 1869, ends melodramatically in marriage. Here, too, plot is prominent, often involving considerable histrionic action. The characters are even more superficial, Coquelin being a scholar-hero worthy of Cooper or Scott, and Gabrielle a heroine with scruples equal to those of the characters of Corneille. Yet the story shows an advance in technique. A French setting gives James a chance to show his understanding of old-world mores, while the use of an on-the-scene narrator gives the story a central point of view. Both the setting and technique are ones the writer employed to great artistic advantage in later years. Here, as author, he introduces the narrator, who tells the story in the first person. The narrator has but a minor part in the plot, as in James's later work, but his presence on the scene is often obviously contrived. He relates the happenings of many years ago as he understands them at present; hence, there is no growth or increasing awareness of the situation on his part—the latter technique being a later development of James's method. *Travelling Companions*, in the November and December 1870 issues, displays a greater proficiency in the same techniques. The narrator of this story is a major character, an American expatriate who meets and eventually marries an American girl in Italy. James is in his true métier, the American abroad. The story is strikingly similar to *Daisy Miller* except that the ending is spoiled by the marriage of the two. Miss Evans is an early example of James's delightful portrayals of the self-reliant American girl. The characterization of her father is equally good, though minor, and is typical of James's sympathetic portraits of practical American businessmen abroad. The use of short bits of pertinent conversation is a further anticipation of a later technique. *Travelling Companions* is by far the best of these stories. What it lacks in subtlety is partly made up by a simple and direct style, ideal for *Atlantic* readers of that time.

The contributions of Henry James were an indication of the direction that *Atlantic* fiction was to take under the editorships of Howells and Aldrich. Realism was replacing the fantasy of Hale, Trowbridge, and Holmes; settings, though usually localized, were not restricted to New England; and the writer of fiction was concentrating self-consciously upon his art rather than his message. Although Lowell, Holmes, and Whittier continued to hold exalted positions in the magazine, the old guard was gradually being replaced by younger writers with newer and less provincial ideas. Yet it was a long while before the tone established by Lowell and fixed by Fields gave way, and it is not too much to say that the serious open-mindedness in the *Atlantic* of the 1950's owes much to the efforts of the early Bostonian contributors.

PART THREE

FROM THE RIM

FOREWORD TO PART THREE

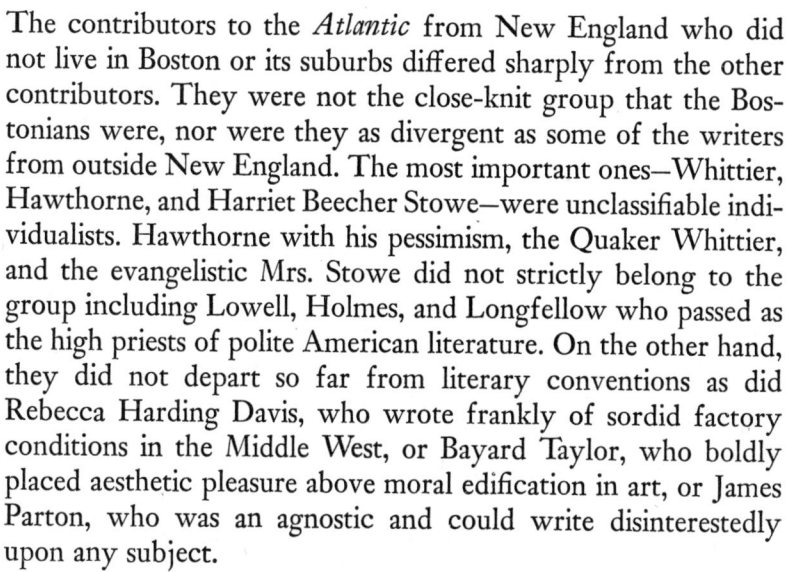

The contributors to the *Atlantic* from New England who did not live in Boston or its suburbs differed sharply from the other contributors. They were not the close-knit group that the Bostonians were, nor were they as divergent as some of the writers from outside New England. The most important ones—Whittier, Hawthorne, and Harriet Beecher Stowe—were unclassifiable individualists. Hawthorne with his pessimism, the Quaker Whittier, and the evangelistic Mrs. Stowe did not strictly belong to the group including Lowell, Holmes, and Longfellow who passed as the high priests of polite American literature. On the other hand, they did not depart so far from literary conventions as did Rebecca Harding Davis, who wrote frankly of sordid factory conditions in the Middle West, or Bayard Taylor, who boldly placed aesthetic pleasure above moral edification in art, or James Parton, who was an agnostic and could write disinterestedly upon any subject.

Thomas Wentworth Higginson, one of the three or four major literary critics and essayists of the magazine, wrote decorously and somewhat stiltedly, but he had strong opinions on such subjects as abolition and women's rights, and he was apt to defend them stoutly in both actions and words. He was perhaps more like the Bostonians than any of the other New England contributors from outside Boston. David Atwood Wasson was also a critic, and his criticism showed traces of an underlying philosophy which was not Bostonian. His informal essays on ethics showed a strong individuality.

Then there were the Transcendentalists, chiefly Emerson and Thoreau, who influenced *Atlantic* literature tremendously though they contributed little themselves. Emersonian self-reliance and Emersonian philosophical eclecticism cropped up persistently in the writings of many widely separated contributors, and nature writing like that of Thoreau, followed by John Burroughs and paralleled by Higginson, turned out to be standard *Atlantic* material.

Most of the magazine's women writers came from New England. There were fiction writers as different as Louisa May Alcott, who wrote lightly and frivolously, and Rose Terry Cooke, who honestly portrayed New England character. There were female essayists like Gail Hamilton, not to mention Mrs. Stowe. And there were poets, especially Celia Thaxter, who followed Whittier in attempting to paint New England landscape in verse.

One thing nearly all of these writers had in common: they were intensely New Englanders. New England attributes showed in the settings of their stories and poems, their rugged individualistic and moralistic attitudes, their love of the land. These things set them apart, but these things also caused the prevailing tone of the *Atlantic* in the sixties to be regional rather than cosmopolitan.

Chapter XI:
John Greenleaf Whittier

For many years John Greenleaf Whittier was the steadiest and one of the most respected of the early contributors of poetry to the *Atlantic*. According to a recent commentator,[1] Whittier's work falls into three divisions: antislavery poems, New England ballads and idyls, and personal and religious lyrics. Each of these had an influence upon the magazine, though the antislavery poetry had nearly all been written by the time the *Atlantic* began. The poet wrote almost nothing of a political nature during Lowell's editorship, but the mere fact of his inclusion among the first contributors, along with Harriet Beecher Stowe, indicated to readers that the editor was not going to shrink from controversial subjects. When Fields became editor the Civil War had begun, and Whittier showed his public spirit by writing war poems in place of antislavery propaganda. With his native ballads Whittier helped create the predominantly New England flavor of the *Atlantic* that was maintained throughout Fields's editorship. And the moral preoccupation in his lyrics befitted and supported the respectable tone that characterized the magazine; his humble faith and sentimentality satisfied the desires of the most sensitive reader.

The advent of the *Atlantic* had come at a convenient time for Whittier and marks the beginning of his fame in pure literature. He had been contributing generously to the low-paying antislavery publications, but without much personal gain. As he depended solely upon his writings for his living, he had found himself in an uncomfortable financial position in 1857. In May,

[1]George F. Whicher, "Literature and Conflict," *Literary History of the United States*, ed. Robert E. Spiller et al. (New York, 1948), I, 576.

Fields, who had been his friend and publisher since 1843, had offered to lend him money.[2] He had thought of mortgaging his house. And finally he had accepted aid from his English friend Joseph Sturge. The high pay of the *Atlantic* was therefore most opportune. He contributed "The Gift of Tritemius" to the first issue, "Skipper Ireson's Ride" to the second, and six more poems in 1858, including "Telling the Bees." After his long apprenticeship in hortative verse, he had reached a level of excellence almost his highest, and these poems are among his best. Only one of his contributions during Lowell's editorship, "Le Marais du Cygne," had had a political aim. By the time Fields became the *Atlantic* editor in 1861, Whittier had contributed fourteen poems, and throughout the first four editorships he was the chief contributor of poetry.[3]

Whittier was notorious for the roughness of his rhymes and meters, and Fields, a stickler for mechanical accuracy like Lowell before him, often revised and sometimes rejected his poems. Unlike Howells, who was Whittier's editor after Fields's retirement, Fields was unawed by the poet's not yet world-famous name. Of course, Fields always consulted him before making any revisions. One of the editor's first letters after assuming the chair suggested a change in the poem "Franconia from the Pemigewasset," one of a pair of "Mountain Pictures" which appeared in the March and April issues in 1862. The poem consists of a romantic description of New England mountains after a storm and the scene inspires the author to hope that the Civil War,

[2]Fields to Whittier, May 1, 1857, MS in Harvard University Library: "Let me whisper to you, if at any time you find your pocket light it will give me great pleasure personally to shovel in a few rocks to be returned at any time when most convenient to you, or if they should never come back it would be better still. My hand is still lame, but I can sign a check at any time if a friend needs it." See Samuel T. Pickard, *Life and Letters of John Greenleaf Whittier* (Boston, 1894), II, 403-405; and John A. Pollard, *John Greenleaf Whittier, Friend of Man* (Boston, 1949), p. 242.

[3]See Robert Ernest Butler, "William Dean Howells as Editor of The Atlantic Monthly" (unpublished doctoral dissertation at Rutgers University, 1950), p. 50; and Donald R. Tuttle, "Thomas Bailey Aldrich's Editorship of The Atlantic Monthly" (unpublished doctoral dissertation at Western Reserve University, 1939).

"the battle-storm that beats the land," may pass and leave "a greener earth and fairer sky behind." Whittier had written:

> Last night's thunder-gust
> Roared not in vain: for where its lightnings thrust
> Their tongues of fire, the great peaks seem so near,
> Lapped clear of mist. . . .

Fields objected to the use of the word "lapped," and Whittier, with characteristic mildness consented to change the line so that it read "Burned clean of mist":

Amesbury 12th Mo. 20. 1861

My dear Fields,
    See what it is to trust an author with his own proofs!
    I defer to thy judgment. I shrink from the feline suggestiveness of my figure of speech. The tongues of fire shall *burn* up the mist, & not "*lap*" it.
    For the rest, I hope the poem is none the worse for the changes, I have thought it best to make.
    I have written to C. G. Leland about the use of my name in the prospectus of the Continental Maga. *alias* the Knickerbocker.
    Our Govt. needs more wisdom than it has thus far had credit for, to sustain the national honor & avert a war with England. What a pity that Welles endorsed the act of Wilkes in his report. Why couldn't we have been satisfied with the thing without making such a cackling over it? Apologies are cheap, and we could afford to make a very handsome one, in this case.
    A war with England, could ruin us. It is too monstrous to think of. May God in his mercy save us from it!   Thine ever & truly
                                     John G. Whittier[4]

As for the use of Whittier's name in the prospectus of the *Continental Monthly*, the poet had written a letter in the fall of 1861 to James Roberts Gilmore, publisher of the *Knickerbocker Magazine*, which the recipient had construed as a promise of a contribution. When Gilmore soon afterward founded the *Continental Monthly* with Charles Godfrey Leland as editor, it was assumed that Whittier would write for the new magazine, which was to take the place of the old *Knickerbocker*. But it was a shock to the poet to find his name in the *Continental*'s prospectus

---

[4]Printed with a number of changes in Pickard, II, 443-44.

Fields of the Atlantic Monthly

for 1862, and it was almost as great a shock to Fields, who considered it an act of disloyalty for one of his authors to write for a potential rival. Whittier asked Leland for an explanation, and in his next letter to Fields he told what had happened:

My dear Fields:
    I am glad to know that thee like my last piece of rhyme. The *substantial* manner in which the approbation was given by Messrs. Ticknor & Fields, was particularly opportune, & satisfactory.
    I have had a letter also from Mr. Leland (who by the way I think was not responsible for the use of my name). He thinks I gave Mr. Gilmore some encouragement in a note to him some 3 months ago; I enclose a copy of my note which was written with the reference to the *anti-slavery* articles of the Knickerbocker. I wanted to encourage the publisher in his stand on the subject, & I think, on reflection, that there was some ground for his inference that I would, if able "add my word" to that of Mr. Leland on the great question in which I feel so deep an interest. At that time I knew nothing of any new magazine, or of any rivalship with the Atlantic, on the part of "Old Knick." I regarded the two magazines as so entirely different, that the idea never occurred to me. Mr. Dana of N. Y. introduced Mr. Leland to me as a gentleman & man of ability, & I have seen nothing to the contrary.
    What do we not all owe you for your edition of De Tocqueville! It is one of the best books of the century. Thanks too for Allingham's poems. After Tennyson he is my favorite among modern British poets.
    A happy New Year!   Ever thy
                                        J. G. W.
I send another verse for the Negro Song.
I send a word for Dr. Brown[5]   [FI 4660]

The Negro song that Whittier mentioned was "Song of the Negro Boatmen" from "At Port Royal, 1861," a poem on the coming liberation of the slaves, and it appeared in the *Atlantic* for February 1862. Whittier reworded one stanza before the poem reached its final version.[6] One of his idiosyncrasies was the continual changing he did in the proofs of his poems. Often he

---

[5] The dating of these manuscripts is frequently a matter of conjecture because of Whittier's omission of dates. Pickard's dating is of little value because it is often obviously wrong in cases where it can be tested.
[6] Pickard, II, 449, shows how the poem was altered.

would write two or three times to Fields, altering and adding, even in the case of short poems. The reason for this seemed to lie in his method of writing. Constantly suffering from headaches and eyestrain, he dashed off his first draft and sent it in as quickly as possible so as to avoid excessive fatigue; hence his revisions were nearly all made in the proof or later.

Whittier's ill health was always a hindrance to him, and it was especially distracting during these years. He was unable to read, write, or even talk for long at a time without suffering for it, and occasionally he had to stop working for periods of several weeks. Although he was intensely concerned over the war and wanted to do his part for the Northern cause, he often found it impossible. In April of 1862 he wrote to Senator Sumner: "It is hard to be a mere looker-on at a time like this. But such is my condition, I am not allowed to write—indeed I cannot without great suffering."[7] Nevertheless he contributed many war poems to the *Atlantic* and also to the weekly *New York Independent*, and even his less timely poems often reflect his underlying concern, as his authorized biographer, Pickard, has pointed out. Such poems as "In War-Time" (August 1862), "The Battle Autumn of 1862" (October 1862), and "Barbara Frietchie" (October 1863) were exceedingly popular; their influence on morale is one of those things that cannot be measured.

One of Whittier's chief efforts in 1862 was the poem "Andrew Rykman's Prayer." Supposedly the prayer of a Dutch Christian, it is really a statement of Whittier's own faith in the omnipresent grace of God:

>Scarcely Hope hath shaped for me
>What the future life may be.
>Other lips may well be bold;
>Like the publican of old,
>I can only urge the plea,
>"Lord, be merciful to me!"

When it was submitted to Fields, he discovered a bad rhyme which he mentioned to the poet. Whittier was not concerned

[7] Ibid., pp. 449-50. See also pp. 442-43.

about the rhyme, and left it alone, but he managed as usual to make an addition to the poem before it was published. "I know that 'pearl' & 'marl' do not jingle together well," he wrote in a letter of December 2, 1862, "but the lines have a meaning in them, & if the reader will roll his *r*'s a little they will do. I add a verse at the tail of it."[8] When the poem was printed in the *Atlantic* for January 1863 the false rhyme remained:

> [I] Never dreamed the gates of pearl
> Rise from out the burning marl.

In March 1863 Whittier was at work on "The Countess," a "ballad" relating the legend of a French count who marries a New England girl. The author wrote to Fields on March 6 before the poem was quite finished: "I shall send in a day or two a ballad 'La Comtesse'—the scene at 'The Rocks' on the Merrimac—which I am sure thee will like. I think it better by far than 'Amy Wentworth', if I am a fit judge."[9] Included with "The Countess" was an introductory dedication to the poet's old friend and physician Elias Weld, and Whittier asked for Fields's criticism of both the poem and the dedication when he wrote:

My dear Fields

I hope thee will like my little pastoral piece:—I am sure Mrs. F. will. The introduction I think had better be printed with my heading.
To E. W. x x x M. D.
and let the title come after. If thee see, on looking over it that its simplicity crosses the border line and becomes silliness, do me the favor to say so, & it shall go hard if I don't make it as dignified as Pope's "Essay on Man" or Dr. Johnson's "Vanity of Human Wishes." Wasn't it unwise for thee to send me the $50 in advance for it?
Thine ever
J. G. W.[10]   [FI 4564]

It was difficult to decide upon titles for both the poem and the introduction, and Whittier was still uncertain when he wrote the following note:

[8]Printed in Pickard, II, 450.

[9]Printed in Pickard, II, 453.

[10]Part printed in Pickard, II, 453.

John Greenleaf Whittier

Dear Fields
 Would it not be better to give the title in English "The Countess"? As to the introduction why not print it as you did that to Amy Wentworth. "To E. W." is not a good title for the poem, of which it is simply the prelude.   Thine truly
                                    J. G. W.   [FI 4577]

"To E. W." and "The Countess" appeared together in the May 1863 number of the magazine.

"Barbara Frietchie," in the October 1863 number, was one of the most important of the Civil War poems published in the *Atlantic*. Based upon a supposedly true story reported to Whittier by a friend in the District of Columbia, the poem was sent to Fields in August. Fields's admiration for it proved to be well founded; he wrote to the author on the twenty-fourth, enclosing payment of fifty dollars: " 'Barbara' is most welcome, and I will find room for it in the October number, most certainly.... You were right in thinking I should like it, for so I do, as I like few things in this world."[11] Fifty dollars was a moderate sum for a poem of the value and length of "Barbara Frietchie." If Whittier received this much for each contribution, he averaged two or three hundred dollars a year from the *Atlantic*, not a great deal to live on even when added to his book royalties and his pay for contributions to the *New York Independent*. Fields was doing what he could in the way of collected editions of Whittier's poems, and in May 1864, he doubled Whittier's royalties.[12] Nevertheless, until the publication of *Snow-Bound* in 1866, the simplicity of the Quaker poet's way of life was not entirely a matter of his own choosing.

Whittier's generosity in aiding young writers, especially women, is well known; for example, he had been instrumental in introducing Lucy Larcom, Alice and Phoebe Cary, and Grace Greenwood to the public. In 1863 his interest was directed toward Charlotte Forten, a part-Negro woman, who had gone

[11] Pickard, II, 458.
[12] Whittier to Fields, April 1864 (FI 4571) and May 2, 1864. Also Fields to Whittier, April 29, 1864, in the Oak Knoll Collection, Essex Institute, Salem, Massachusetts.

to St. Helena's Island, South Carolina, to teach the Negroes. He persuaded Fields to print her account of the place, he himself cutting it down to fit the limitations of space in the magazine. The recommendation that he sent was printed at the head of Miss Forten's article, "Life on the Sea Islands," when it finally appeared in May and June 1864:

> To the Editor of the "Atlantic Monthly."—The following graceful and picturesque description of the new condition of things on the Sea Islands of South Carolina, originally written for private perusal, seems to me worthy of a place in the "Atlantic." Its young author—herself akin to the long-suffering race whose Exodus she so pleasantly describes—is still engaged in her labor of love on St. Helena Island.—J. G. W.

By December 25, 1863, Whittier had received for Miss Forten a check for fifty dollars for the article, four months before it was published. Fields was happy to print it.[13]

One of Whittier's closest friends was Bayard Taylor, but Taylor did not have the Quaker poet's moral sensitiveness. The point is well illustrated in a letter from Whittier to Fields in which he suggests the reconsideration of one of Taylor's poems that Fields was considering printing. Whittier wrote in December 1864:

> 29th 12th Mo. 1864
> My dear Fields
> I have been thinking of Bayard's fine poem which thee showed me, & somehow, I fear there are one or two views in it touching "wine & women" which "beautiful exceedingly" as it is will give occasion for the Philistines of the Commonwealth & one or two other papers to say evil of it & him. Let me take the responsibility of advising thee to keep the Poem until thee see or hear from Bayard. He knows that I love him too well to advise anything which I do not think will be for the best. What an admirable picture he gives us in the last Atlantic of the semi-barbaric splendor of the Russian Fair? I wish he would continue these papers. They are liked by everybody.
> In haste ever & truly Thy fd.
> John G. Whittier

[13] Whittier to Fields, December 25, 1863.

John Greenleaf Whittier

The following letter seems to relate to the same situation, though we have no date or names to go by. At any rate, it illustrates Whittier's attitude and implies Fields's toward "sensuous" poetry:

Dear F.

I showed B's poem to a pure-minded & intellectual woman, last night, & she returned it with the remark that its *vagueness* was its best quality. I think it good, for a poem of that sensuous school,— but perhaps the best way to dispose of it wd. be to send him my note enclosed.

With love to thee & thine
J. G. W.   [FI 4677]

The fact that Fields considered Whittier's judgment in this matter of taste implies a new confidence in him on Fields's part. The same idea may be gathered from the price paid for Whittier's "Peace Autumn." It was a poem of thanks for the war's end:

> Thank God for rest, where none molest,
>   And none can make afraid,—
> For Peace that sits as Plenty's guest,
>   Beneath the homestead shade!

This poem brought twice as much as had the more popular "Barbara Frietchie" two years before:

Boston Sept. 5. 1865

My dear Whittier

Thank you for sending me your "Peace Autumn" poem. I am sorry it cannot go into the October number, that issue being all printed. It shall go into the Nov. No. which you know will be ready on the 20th of October. It is full of your earnest and beautiful expression and will be greatly welcomed by all. I am rejoiced to hear you are writing a snow-piece. Tell me all about it & let me know when you intend sending it to me. We are very unlucky not to have you to the shoals when you perched there, but we hope to go some day this week.

Annie sends kindest love.

So do I.

Yours Ever
J. T. F.

Enclosed is our check for $100. for "Peace Autumn."[14]

The "snow-piece" referred to was *Snow-Bound*, which Whittier sent to Fields on October 3, 1865. After many corrections

---
[14]Oak Knoll Collection, Essex Institute.

and revisions by Whittier the book went to press later that year, but even after that, Whittier sent some changes to be added to the second edition. The great popularity of the book amazed everyone. Pickard asserted that the first edition brought Whittier ten thousand dollars. Fields wrote to the author on April 2, 1866: "We can't keep the plaguey thing quiet. It goes and goes, and now today we are bankrupt again, not a one being 'in crib.' I fear it will be impossible to get along without printing another batch! I do indeed. Pity us."[15] It was finally possible for Whittier to feel himself financially secure.

Another of Whittier's best known poems, "Abraham Davenport," was printed in the *Atlantic* in 1866. A further enunciation of Whittier's religious convictions, it extols steadfastness to duty in the face of calamity. The line "Let God do his work, we will see to ours" expresses one of the fundamental principles of Whittier's life; despite war, sickness, and privation, he persevered in doing good. In the last letter cited Fields had promised to print the poem in the May number. Whittier did not understand when it was to appear and added another stanza in the proof. He wrote to Fields to explain:

My dear Fields
   I recollected after sending back the proof on Saturday that the sheet had "*May*" on its margin instead of "*June*"; & it occurred to me as possible that it was intended to go into this number. If so, my additional verse was unfortunate as it might cause delay. If it will help the matter any now, omit it altogether. I am sorry that my wits did not serve me sooner, & save thee the bother of the thing.
In haste, thine Ever
J. G. W.

Monday.   [FI 4580]

The poem appeared in the May issue as planned.

   As early as April 1866 Whittier had begun his book *The Tent on the Beach*, a collection of poems strung together in the form

---

[15]Oak Knoll Collection, Essex Institute. See also Whittier to Fields, October 3, 1865; and an undated letter from Whittier to Fields concerning corrections for the second edition, a copy of which letter is in the Oak Knoll Collection. See also Pickard, II, 501; and Pollard, p. 266.

of a conversation among three friends.[16] He paid tribute to Fields and Bayard Taylor by making them the friends with whom he himself conversed. His description of Fields is vague but not inaccurate:

>One, with his beard scarce silvered, bore
>   A ready credence in his looks,
>A lettered magnate, lording o'er
>   An ever-widening realm of books.
>In him brain-currents, near and far,
>   Converged as in a Leyden jar;
>The old, dead authors thronged him round about,
>And Elzevir's gray ghosts from leathern graves
>   looked out.
>
>He knew each living pundit well,
>   Could weigh the gifts of him or her,
>And well the market value tell
>   Of poet and philosopher.
>But if he lost, the scenes behind,
>Somewhat of reverence vague and blind,
>Finding the actors human at the best,
>No readier lips than his the good he saw confessed.
>
>His boyhood fancies not outgrown,
>   He loved himself the singer's art;
>Tenderly, gently, by his own
>   He knew and judged another's heart.
>No Rhadamanthine brow of doom
>Bowed the dazed pedant from his room;
>And bards, whose name is legion, if denied,
>Bore off alike intact their verses and their pride.
>
>Pleasant it was to roam about
>   The lettered world as he had done,
>And see the lords of song without
>   Their singing robes and garlands on.
>With Wordsworth paddle Rydal mere,
>Taste rugged Elliot's home-brewed beer,
>And with the ears of Rogers, at fourscore,
>Hear Garrick's buskined tread and Walpole's wit
>   once more.

[16]Letter previously cited, Fields to Whittier, April 2, 1866, Oak Knoll Collection, Essex Institute.

The manuscript was submitted on December 28. Fields, of course, was delighted and said so. Throughout January 1867 there was the usual scramble to make corrections and additions and revisions and get the poem ready to print. Whittier wrote more than seven letters containing alterations during January and February. When the poem was set up for the press on February 1, Whittier wrote to Fields, urging him to get a copy of the proof to Taylor before the latter left for Europe on the ninth. This was a strain, but it was accomplished by the indefatigable Fields. The book was another success. According to Pickard, twenty thousand copies were soon sold, at the rate of a thousand a day.[17] But by now Whittier was already established among the foremost poets of his time in America, and Ticknor and Fields had even published a cheap edition of his poems to go along with that of Longfellow for the benefit of the poorer reading public.[18]

Being very busy with book publications, Whittier sent only three poems to the *Atlantic* in 1867. One of these, "G. L. S.", a memoir of Major George Stearns, was submitted in April upon Fields's request for a contribution. "I have nothing I could venture to send you for the 'Atlantic,' " Whittier wrote, "unless the lines inclosed, on the death of Major Stearns, will serve your purposes." He protested that the poem was "rather ragged and unkempt" and that the first line was "all out of proportion as to length," but he did not offer to make any changes.[19] Fields replied that he would print the poem in the June issue, and sent a hundred dollars for it, a large sum for such a short and casual poem:

Boston April 17. 1867

My dear Whittier,
We are sorry you did not come up as you intended, but don't stay away much longer. The poem you sent is very strong & good throughout. It will come in the June No. (Here is a cheque for it) or rather here is a cheque for $600.—500 on a/c & 100 for the poem. The first

---

[17]Pickard, II, 512. See also the letters from Whittier to Fields, from December 28, 1866, to February 28, 1867.

[18]Fields to Whittier, September 27, 1866, Oak Knoll Collection, Essex Institute.

[19]Pickard, II, 526.

line is too long, but I shall print a blank line under the 1st. verse which will make of it a sort of solemn introduction to the poem. You will have proof shortly. I have made all the changes in "The Tent" we could stop to make. Please examine the Edn. sent, & see if you demand others. A. F. sends love. We have been to N. Y. & had a good week.
Yrs. ever
J. T. F.[20]

The proof was sent to Whittier immediately, who as usual made a few alterations:

20th 4 Mo. 1867

My dear Fields

I return the proof by the first mail. I add a verse, which occurs to me as needful, or at any rate, true. If you wish to get it into one page make the spaces less between the verses, & begin a little higher up on the page. It reads well I think in the proof. There is life in it if not poetry.

I have *doctored* the first line, & it is better every way. My love to Annie Fields. I got a line from Phebe Cary last night. She says, "We saw Mrs. F. & found the half had not been told us of her: she is prettier than her picture & her manner is charming." I always thought Phebe Cary remarkable for good sense & discrimination and isn't this an evidence of it?

Thine ever
J. G. W.

In May 1867, upon the announcement of the abolition of Negro slavery in Brazil, Whittier wrote "Freedom in Brazil" commemorating the event: "With clearer light, Cross of the South, shine forth." Fields accepted it but suggested the elimination of several feminine rhymes:

Boston. May 15. 1867.

[M]y dear Whittier

Thank you for sending me "Freedom in Brazil." It is a most timely and admirable poem. I think all the double rhymes you have employed in the piece take from the dignified movement of the poem and if I were you I would change them. They are as follows:

[20]Oak Knoll Collection, Essex Institute.

> Environ
> *iron*
> Curses
> *Rehearses*
> Springing
> *Swinging*

I wait to hear from you before I set the piece in type.
  In great haste, and lame handed,

J. T. Fields[21]

When the news report proved to be false, Whittier wanted the poem dropped:

Sat. Morning

My Dear Fields
  I find this in the Journal of yesterday. [The clipping itself follows, pasted to the letter.]

> —The news received here, by way of England, that the Emperor of Brazil had, on the 8th of April, issued a decree of emancipation, is not confirmed by late advices from Brazil.

If this is so—if we have "halloed before out of the woods," "Freedom *in Brazil*" must be stopped where it is. I know nothing about it except this brief paragraph. It may be that *it* is a mistake & not the original statement. I am sorry every way, if the "good news" proves false. But, pray enquire into it, & if I *have* anticipated matters in Brazil, the poem must be suppressed & something better put in its place.

In haste
J. G. W.   [FI 4659]

But it was printed anyway, in the July 1867 *Atlantic*. All the feminine rhymes were changed.

  Though he still criticized Whittier's versification, Fields now considered the poet one of "our emperors in literature," and when the first volume of the *Atlantic Almanac* was in preparation, he sought a contribution from Whittier to go along with those of Holmes, Lowell, and other major *Atlantic* writers. From Plymouth, New Hampshire, where he was beginning his vacation, the editor wrote:

[21] Oak Knoll Collection, Essex Institute.

John Greenleaf Whittier

Pemigewasset House. Plymouth, June 21st 1867.
My dear Whittier,

I wrote you some days ago asking you to come up to Campton Village, but get no reply. We have shifted our quarters as you see and are now on our way to Burlington, the Adirondacks, Canada and Mt. Desert. Send a line to the store marked, "to be forwarded immediately" telling us in which of these places we may expect you!

We are to publish for 1868 an "Atlantic Almanac" somewhat after the manner of the German one which Auerbach has edited for so many years. We intend to have original contributions from all our emperors in literature. All the papers will be brief and of course as far as possible be appropriate to some one of the four seasons. We look to you for either a bit of prose or a poem which shall have reference to either Spring, Summer, Autumn or Winter, or to one of the months in the year. We should like your contribution by the twentieth of July and sincerely hope you will comply with our request. Holmes is already at work & the other crowned heads are nibbling away at their ink-stands. (Payment same as for Atlantic articles)

If you will send your answer to the store at once addressed to me marked "immediate" it will be forwarded.

(With sincere and affectionate regards of the amanuensis)
Yours ever
J. T. Fields[22]

When it appeared that Whittier was too busy and too ill to write anything, Fields suggested that he use his "Laurel" poems. These were poems Whittier had written, commemorating some of the annual "laurel parties," social gatherings that had become an institution at Newburyport. Perhaps because the poems were too personal, Whittier decided not to use them. A few days before the deadline of July 20, he thought that he would not be able to contribute at all:

Amesbury 18th 7th Mo. 1867.
My dear Fields

I have just got back from the "Shoals" & find thy note. My "Laurels" are dry & sere—not worth keeping; & I don't like to put them into the Atlantic or the Almanac.

I can readily believe you had a pleasant & profitable excursion. I had a great desire to be with you, but was obliged to content myself with my little sea-voyage, & a week on the Shoals.

[22]Oak Knoll Collection, Essex Institute.

I want to run up to Boston soon, when I hope to see thee.

Love to Mrs. Fields. We wished you could have been with us on White Island on Tuesday—one of the sweetest days I ever knew. Mrs. Thaxter came out charmingly, with her sea-shore fancies & stories, & drolleries.
Thine ever
John G. Whittier

I fear I shall not be able to write anything for the "*Almanac*." I can't read or write much just now, owing to my old trouble of head & eyes.

Regardless of his protests, Whittier did contribute two poems to the *Almanac*: "A Winter Moonlight" and "Building the Fire." They were the only contributions he made to the annual publication while Fields was its publisher.

In August Whittier completed "The Wife: an Idyl of Bearcamp Water," a poem on "the simple life, the homely hearth ... where toil abounds." It was later greatly enlarged to form "Among the Hills." With customary modesty, he wrote to Annie Fields to get her and James's opinion of it before considering printing it:

My dear Mrs. Fields Amesbury 18 8 Mo. 1867

Will you not be able to run up & make me a visit this month or next. I recall so pleasantly your little visit of last year, that I long to see you once more under my roof.

I have written a little ballad which I am quite doubtful of—and wish I could consult thee & James T. about it. If my head will allow me to copy it & correct it I shall send it to you, if you do not anticipate me by coming yourselves.

The miserable wet weather—hard for everybody—is particularly so to me. I have spent some little time at the Shoals—the only place where I can fully escape dog-days. Mrs. Thaxter spoke of thee in terms of warm admiration. It surely must be pleasant to thee to feel that all who really know thee love thee. To be thus surrounded by an atmosphere of affectionate interest, is one of those blessings which should call forth the deepest gratitude to the Giver of all mercies.

I suppose friend Fields is working hard as ever, in spite of the weather. He must greatly enjoy his sea-shore evenings after the heat & labor of his office.

Lucy Larcom was at the Shoals a few days when I was; and I hope & think, enjoyed the change very much. I saw Aldrich & wife at Portsmouth a few days ago. Ever & truly thy fd.
John G. Whittier

Three days later, in a letter concerning other business, Fields expressed his eagerness to hear the new poem: "Yr. letter to Annie makes me hungry for the new ballad. When shall we come & hear it? Next week?"[23] The poem was accepted in its short form and published as the lead article in the January 1868 *Atlantic*. The enlarged version was done later that year and published as part of the book entitled *Among the Hills, and Other Poems* in 1869.

Whittier's illness reached a peak in 1868, and he was not permitted to write for a month. It was probably just before this that he wrote to Fields to postpone the publication of "The Meeting" because of its flaws or to make corrections in it himself if postponement was impractical. "The Meeting" was another religious lyric—to "testify to the oneness of humanity." Fields must have altered it himself, because the poem appeared in the February issue, before Whittier had recovered. Whittier's letter indicates his confidence in Fields:

Amesbury Monday 1st Mo.

Dear Fields,
 I wish thee could let "The Meeting" go over another month, as I feel my alterations will otherwise make trouble & delay for you. If, however, it is necessary to have it in yr. next No. there will be no time to send it back to me, & you must see to it as well as you can in the proof.

In haste
J. G. W.   [FI 4638]

He did not send another contribution until March, when he submitted "The Clear Vision," a contemplative lyric on nature and God. Fields responded on March 7: "I am rejoiced to see your handwriting once more especially as it comes to me in the form of an exquisite poem. 'The Clear Vision' is one of your best, and will touch deeply your large audience of readers throughout the country."[24] When he sent the proof to Whittier, Fields suggested some improvements in the poem, which Whittier accepted. The poet returned the proofs on April 2: "I send back the proof with

---

[23] Fields to Whittier, August 21, 1867, Oak Knoll Collection, Essex Institute.
[24] Fields to Whittier, March 7, 1868, Oak Knoll Collection, Essex Institute.

deference to thy suggestions. I think, as it now stands, the poem is good—considering who wrote it."[25] (FI 4639) "The Clear Vision" was printed in the May 1868 issue.

In June, Whittier was at work on "The Two Rabbis," "a fantasy of mine—which I like better than most things I have written of late."[26] He sent it to Fields for the *Atlantic* early in July, and Fields replied on the ninth:

"The Two Rabbis" came walking in with the postman last night, having been forwarded from Boston. They are beautiful persons and you have embalmed them in an exquisite poem. It seems to me one of your great successes and I thank you heartily for sending it to me.[27]

The poem was printed in the October 1868 number of the *Atlantic*. The concluding prayer of Rabbi Nathan, as Whittier wrote it, is one of the best statements of the poet's ideal of humility and good works:

>Hope not the cure of sin till Self is dead;
>Forget it in love's service, and the debt
>Thou canst not pay the angels shall forget;
>Heaven's gate is shut to him who comes alone;
>Save thou a soul, and it shall save thy own!

In August Whittier still had not sent anything for the *Almanac*. He had considered writing a ballad upon Abraham Lincoln, but his health prevented it. "I have nothing fit for your 'Almanac,'" he wrote to Fields on August 20, 1868. "The Lincoln Ballad I would try if I had health & strength enough, but at present I am quite unable to write. If I could get one good night's sleep I should be another man." Neither the ballad nor anything else by Whittier appeared in the *Almanac*.

An incidental event in the Whittier-Fields correspondence of 1868 was Annie Fields's attempt to get the poet to read one of his own poems before an audience in Boston for the benefit of edu-

---

[25] Quoted in Pickard, II, 530.
[26] Whittier to Fields, June 29, 1868. Quoted in Pickard, II, 531.
[27] Oak Knoll Collection, Essex Institute.

cation of Southern Negroes. Fields, who was partly responsible for the plan to have several eminent authors read their works for the worthy cause, left the impossible task of persuading Whittier to Annie, who was better qualified because of her youth and charm. Mrs. Fields's powers of persuasion were acknowledged, and the feminine appeal was one to which Whittier was known to be particularly susceptible. Her main argument was that "Mr. Bryant, who is already past the first blossoming of the 'almond in his hair' finds it a great sacrifice and trouble, especially as he must make the journey from New York, and he will not consent to do it without others will make the same effort and *secure success*. Dear Mr. Whittier," she pleaded, "will you bring your warrior spirit now to act a poem while reading one? I mean, the action will be arduous and heroic enough to be a poem for those who understand you."[28] Notwithstanding her valiant effort, Whittier declined. It was no doubt true that a public reading was for him physically impossible without a great deal of consequent suffering:

Amesbury 9 Mo. 5 1868

My dear Mrs. Fields,

Thee ask a miracle of me. Any thing within the bounds of my possibilities I would do, as thee very well know, not only for the cause's sake but for thine. Ask me to dance the Polka—or walk a slack rope from Park St. steeple to the State House dome—but don't ask me to stand up & read my rhymes to a Boston audience. I fancy I see myself doing it!

And yet how I wish I could! I am *so* sorry to have to say no & disappoint thee. But, it would [be] utterly impossible. I could not do it if I tried.

Besides, the performance would not, if it could be carried out, be very profitable. We must try some other method to help "The Man & the Brother."

I hoped to see thee and James T. at our house this summer. I have had an immense number of "pilgrims," mostly strangers, for the last few weeks; and as they are thinning off I trust I shall have some of my old friends in their place.

[28] Annie Fields to Whittier, September 3, 1868, Oak Knoll Collection, Essex Institute.

Don't blame me too severely, dear Mrs. Fields, for my inability to do what thee wish. It has given me real pain to refuse the request of one whom I so love & honor.

With love to J. T. F. I am ever & most truly
Thy friend
John G. Whittier[29]

The dedication to Annie Fields of Whittier's next book, *Among the Hills*, was partial atonement for her disappointment. He suggested the dedication the same month, September 1868.[30]

Prominent as Whittier had become, Fields did not think it necessary to accept his contributions indiscriminately. "The French Neutral," a narrative poem maintaining the parity of Catholicism and Protestantism and submitted in November 1869, failed to come up to standards and was rejected. Whittier was not sure of its quality when he sent it,[31] but then he often showed the same modest hesitation when submitting something new. When the poem was rejected, Whittier acquiesced most humbly, promising to try again:

Dear Fields   Amesbury 30 11 Mo. 69

I was by no means satisfied with the "French Neutral," when I sent it, & had misgivings about it afterwards. I shall let it lie by awhile & then see if it can be made anything of. In the mean time I am glad to have it again in my possession. The subject is a good one, if treated rightly. One Hundred of the Neutrals, you know, were scattered over Masstts.

I am not sure when I can be in Boston. I have been sick nearly all the month.
Thine truly
J. G. W.[32]

Eventually the poem was revised, and sent, not to Fields, but to his wife, a year later.[33] This time, when Fields saw the poem, he accepted it and published it under the title of "Marguerite" in the March 1871 *Atlantic*.

[29]Part printed in Pickard, II, 531.
[30]Whittier to Fields, September 26, 1868.
[31]Whittier to Fields, no date (FI 4671).
[32]Part printed in Pickard, II, 547-48.
[33]See Pickard, II, 549.

John Greenleaf Whittier

The contribution in October 1870 of the poem "The Sisters" was one of the last *Atlantic* contributions of Whittier while Fields was editor. It was a narrative on the theme of love more permanent than life. Fields's letter of acceptance is interesting because it shows that Whittier continued to receive a hundred dollars apiece for his poems, the price that had been established in 1865.

Boston, Oct. 27, 1870.

My dear Whittier,
 Annie promised to write to tell you how much we both liked "The Sisters." 'Tis a ballad after my own heart, and I predict for it great popularity. The proof will be sent to you in due time.
 Enclosed, please find our check for one hundred dollars, in payment for the poem.

Ever sincerely yours,
James T. Fields[34]

"The Sisters" was printed in the January 1871 issue of the *Atlantic*.

By January 1871 Fields had given up the editorial chair to Howells but was still assisting the young editor. With a little more time on his hands, he undertook the long-cherished project of making himself known as a writer, contributing something of his own each month to the *Atlantic*'s pages. In the May and June issues he had a series of humorous verses under the general title "Bubbles from an Ancient Pipe," designed to fill the need of frivolity that he had so often noticed during his editorship. Along with a piece called "Hiram Hays in Stratford" in the May issue, he printed twelve lines of doggerel entitled "Fame" on John G. Whittier:

> "Colored son of Carolina,
> John G. Whittier was thy friend;
> In thy darkest days of danger
> He stood by thee to defend.
>
> "To thy cause he gave his genius,
> And the influence of his fame;
> Speak, and tell me, dusky brother,
> Hast thou ever heard his name?"

---

[34] Oak Knoll Collection, Essex Institute.

Spake the son of Carolina,
  With an elbow on each knee:
"Neber heered the name o' Whityar,—
  T'ink I heered, tho', o' John G."

Before anyone else had seen it, Fields submitted it to Whittier for approval:

Dear Whittier: Boston, March 2, 1871.

   The Atlantic needs lightening and I am thinking of now and then putting in a skit of rhymed fun, under the head of—Bagatelles—
   I enclose Hiram Hays, that you may see the sort of thing I have in mind. I have got half a dozen more written, and among them is one which I like best of all, but I wish to ask you if there is any offense in it to my friends in Amesbury. If there is the slightest objection, you have only to say so, and the three verses will never have existed. Please return the printed and unprinted nonsense, with your reply to this.   Ever yours,
                                                       J. T. F.

Of course no one has seen the rhymes but Annie and my amanuensis.[35]

   When Fields retired completely from the magazine late in 1871, Whittier was naturally sorry to see the close of their long years of cordial business relations. He wrote to Annie on November 18 that he was afraid his loyalty to the *Atlantic* would depart with Fields: "I am afraid I shall lose all interest in the Atlantic if it passes out of James T. hands. I can't seem to adjust myself to these changes." Nevertheless he continued to contribute as regularly as ever, and except sentimentally, he was affected very little by the change.
   Like the other writers with whom Fields had dealt, Whittier continued to correspond frequently and in the friendliest way. He engaged Fields to lecture for the Amesbury Lyceum early in 1874. He sent poems to both James and Annie for criticism. He exchanged gifts with the Fieldses and received their visits. In 1880 he persuaded Fields to help in a campaign to raise money for the impoverished Donald Grant Mitchell. And he was always prompt in congratulating Fields on the latter's literary efforts.[36] He ex-

---

[35]Oak Knoll Collection, Essex Institute.
[36]Letters of Whittier to James and Annie Fields, 1873-1880.

pressed his gratitude for the encouragement and inspiration he had received from the Fieldses when he wrote to acknowledge their congratulations upon his seventieth birthday:

Oak Knoll Danvers 12th Mo. 24 1877

My dear Annie Fields,

    I ought before this to have acknowledged thy kind note, & the beautiful wreath, which is fresh as ever. But, I have had some hundreds of letters & tokens, from everybody & everywhere, and I have not been able to tell thee before how glad & happy your remembrance of me made me. I missed J. T. F. at the dinner at the Brunswick. In the midst of so much congratulation I do not forget his earlier appreciation & encouragement, and every kind word of thine which assured and cheered me, when the great public failed to recognize me. I dare not tell thee, for fear of seeming to exaggerate, how much these words have been to me. I never think of thee without a feeling of thankfulness that I can call thee my friend.

    With every good wish of the season for thee & J. T. F. I am always & gratefully thy friend.
John G. Whittier

Upon Fields's death in 1881, the editor of the *Atlantic*, T. B. Aldrich, who had succeeded Howells, asked Whittier to write a poetic memoir. Whittier, again ill, was unable to write at the moment:

Danvers 4th Mo. 28 1881

My dear Aldrich

    I wish I could say all I feel about our friend, but I am too unwell at this time to write anything worthy of him or myself. But who could so well speak as thyself? His fellow townsman & life long friend, no one could so properly say the fitting words in verse. Ah me! It is a sad loss to us—an unbroken friendship of 40 years so suddenly ended. No, *not* ended! for there was too much life in our friend to be utterly lost. I will only think of him as still living in the universe of God. Very forcibly comes to my mind thy wonderful line in "Identity." "I do not know; I only died last night." God help us all!

Thine truly
John G. Whittier[37]

About a month later, however, Whittier found it possible to send a few lines on Fields, entitled "In Memory," which appeared in the *Atlantic* for July 1881.

[37] Tuttle, I, 199, from MS in Harvard University Library.

Chapter XII:
Nathaniel Hawthorne

"My literary success, whatever it has been or may be," wrote Hawthorne to Fields toward the end of the former's life, "is the result of my connection with you."[1] This was Hawthorne's own opinion, perhaps slightly exaggerated in the warmth of gratitude, of his debt to his publisher. Unfortunately Fields's contribution to Hawthorne's success has been obscured by most Hawthorne biographers because of a quarrel between the publisher and the writer's widow over the profits from his works. Randall Stewart's biography, as well as his several articles on Hawthorne's relations with Fields, is an exception. Fields's "Hawthorne" in *Yesterdays with Authors* tells much about their friendship, but nineteenth-century discretion caused the writer to omit much of importance. Annie Fields's *Nathaniel Hawthorne* (Boston, 1899) adds somewhat to her husband's account.

Field's acquaintance with Hawthorne began about 1839. By 1849 the publisher was attempting to use his influence among the Whigs to forestall the displacement of the author from his Salem surveyorship. Fields's description of his discovery of the manuscript of *The Scarlet Letter* in Hawthorne's bureau drawer, his immediate enthusiasm for the work, and the success of its publication are well known.[2] At any rate Hawthorne's fame was not definitely established until Ticknor and Fields took him in hand and managed the effective distribution of his works. The year after the publication of *The Scarlet Letter* the author already had gained a reputation as far away as England. Fields wrote of it to Mary Russell Mitford, whose interest had been roused:

---

[1] Hawthorne to Fields, February 27, 1861, copy in Harvard University Library.
[2] Fields, *Yesterdays*, pp. 47, 48-49, 49-52.

Nathaniel Hawthorne

You ask me particularly about Hawthorne. He *is* young I am delighted to say. His hair is yet untinged by time's sure silver. His form is only second to Daniel Webster's in robustness, and his step is like a war horse tramp. You would not meet a more splendid specimen of manhood in a day's travel through New England. Holmes is a small compact little figure. Hawthorne would cut up into three or four patterns a-la-Holmes. A few days ago the author of The Scarlet Letter came to Boston after an absence of many months. Every eye glistened as it welcomed an author whose genius seems to have filled his native land quite suddenly with his fame. You would be charmed by Hawthorne. He blushes like a girl when he is praised, and thinks himself the most over rated man in America. I sent you a few weeks since his earliest work "The Twice Told Tales" in the preface to which you will read something of his career. He is wrong I think in supposing himself so little known in the early days of his literary history. I shall send you shortly a new Juvenile Book from his pen, as fine reading by the way for grown people as I happen to remember from the press for many a day. Speaking of your writings to me not long ago Hawthorne said "Miss Mitford's works are sweet in my memory as new mown hay."[3]

Fields's handling of the English publication of *The Blithedale Romance* in 1852 illustrates the effectiveness of his promotion of Hawthorne. In March Ticknor and Fields were asking a hundred pounds for Hawthorne for the rights of publication in England simultaneously with the American publication. But Fields, who was in England at the time, wrote to Hawthorne on May 21 that he had persuaded the English publishers Chapman and Hall to take the book for two hundred pounds: "I put it high and spread it thick."[4] When he later wrote to inform Hawthorne of the successful completion of the arrangements, Hawthorne replied: "You have succeeded admirably in regard to the 'Blithedale Romance', and have got £150 more than I expected to receive."[5]

While in Europe from 1853 to 1860, Hawthorne frequently

---

[3] Fields to Mary Russell Mitford, September 30, 1851.

[4] Tryon and Charvat, pp. 218-19. In a letter to Bayard Taylor (June 6, 1852), Fields spoke of Hawthorne's flattering reply: "By this mail I got a long letter from Hawthorne but it is so filled with flattering and too exaggerated mention of one of his publishers that I do not enclose it. The 'firm' wd. blush."

[5] Fields, *Yesterdays*, p. 71.

wrote to Fields, and after resigning his consulate in England in 1857, he relied on Ticknor and Fields to keep him supplied with money while he toured the continent. His custom was to leave his earnings with the firm until such time as he should need them. On February 3, 1859, he wrote from Rome of his financial worries and his dependence upon Fields: "Barings have sent me their % by which it appears that my debit is about £56 up to the 31st Dec. I have a credit of theirs on hand, of which £150 remains to be drawn; and I shall want £200. or £250. more, to bring me back to London; so that our respected senior partner will have to supply about £400 to meet my further expenditure on the Continent."

As early as July 18, 1859, Lowell was seeking Hawthorne as a contributor to the *Atlantic Monthly*. "If you should see Hawthorne before I do," Lowell wrote to Emerson, "will you put in a good word for the Atlantic. He brings home a honey-bag, I hear."[6] But Fields, who was also in Europe at this time, got to Hawthorne first. In the meantime, Ticknor and Fields had purchased the magazine, and Fields as well as Lowell wanted Hawthorne to contribute. It appears from the following banter of Hawthorne's that Fields had previously advised him not to write for Lowell but changed his tune when it became a matter of the publisher's own interest. "I had not *heard* of the purchase of the Atlantic Monthly; but my prejudging spirit had foreseen the event," Hawthorne wrote on November 17, 1859. "I cannot but admire your wishing me to write for it, after all your friendly advice to the contrary. However, I will—that is, after I get home. I mean to spend the rest of my abode in England in blessed idleness," he continued, replying to Fields's request for some bits from his notebooks, "and as for my *Journal*, in the first place, I have not got it here—secondly, there is nothing in it that it will do to publish." The moment Hawthorne's *The Marble Faun* was in the hands of the publisher, Fields began doggedly urging the writer to put his journals to use. It was largely because of this

[6] James Russell Lowell, *New Letters of James Russell Lowell*, ed. M. A. De Wolfe Howe (New York, 1932), p. 97.

urging that Hawthorne produced what he did during his remaining years.

Fields also asked for contributions from Hawthorne's wife, whose *Notes in England and Italy*, by the way, would have made good copy. Hawthorne wrote:

Leamington, Nov. 28th 1859.

Dear Fields,

You are quite right in wanting Mrs. Hawthorne for contributress; and perhaps I may yet starve her into compliance. I have never read anything so good as some of her narrative and descriptive epistles to her friends; but I doubt whether she would find sufficient inspiration in writing directly for the public. I don't know how the Romance [*The Marble Faun*] comes on; but I have a suspicion that they must have decided on deferring the publication till the spring. This will suit me just as well, provided it comes out before June—and provided they pay me an instalment of the copy money within a month or two.

Are you coming over?   Your Friend,
Nathl. Hawthorne.[7]

Sophia Hawthorne did not contribute anything of her own to the *Atlantic*. Hawthorne's first contribution appeared about a year later, and he did not write again until October 1861. Meanwhile, the publication of *The Marble Faun* (or *Transformation* as it was called in England) was progressing, and the English edition was published by Smith and Elder on February 28, 1860, Hawthorne receiving the highly satisfactory sum of six hundred pounds for it.[8] At the same time Ticknor released the American edition.

His work completed, Hawthorne leisurely prepared to return to America. He made arrangements for himself and his family to sail along with Fields and Mrs. Fields on June 16: "I consider it my duty, towards Ticknor and towards Boston, and America at large, to take you into custody and bring you home; for I know you will never come except upon compulsion. Let me know at once whether I am to use force."[9] Fields agreed to go without being forced:

[7] Copy in Harvard University Library.
[8] Fields, *Yesterdays*, pp. 86-88.
[9] Hawthorne to Fields, April 26, 1860, ibid., p. 88.

Fields of the Atlantic Monthly

London. 41 Jermyn St. May 20 1860

My dear Hawthorne.

I seize my only moments this morning by their throats and won't let them go till I say how much I regret not being able to meet Bennoch on his way to you this week. I find myself deep in a business plot with Murray and do not dare to move off the ground till the whole matter is settled. So I forego the pleasure of a visit to Bath. Thank you very much for your letter of the 26th April. Intending to be with you on Sunday I have not answered it. On the 16th of June then we will sail away together and find America if we can. You know what a dead-gone sailor I am, having no power at all over my legs during the whole voyage. But we will do our best on this occasion. I hope my state room has a sofa in it, for half the time I have not strength to tell my name to the steward. I am delighted with the Marble Faun as I knew I should be and will not allow that there was the slightest occasion for yr. explanatory P. S. at the end of the 3d Ed. On all hands among the best people I hear golden opinions, and your Publishers here are very proud to have sent out your book. Your Boston Publishers hold up their heads higher than ever now. You can't imagine what lots of attention I get in London from the fact that I am one of the boys who publish for you in America. I am sure that I have eaten the last week two dinners on the strength of my title page notoriety.

Giles wrote that article in the Boston Courier, Whipple tells me in his last letter.

Do come up to London. Among others who wish to meet you is Trollope the novelist whom I met at dinner yesterday. I told him you were a reader of his books and he seemed really delighted that you praised his novels. He is a good fellow. With our kindest regards to you all,

Ever yours,
James T. Fields.

Mrs. F. is glad of our chance of all going home together.

The "P. S. at the end of the third edition" was, of course, the rather unsatisfactory explanation of the ambiguities of the book that Hawthorne appended to *The Marble Faun*. The Henry Giles article in the *Courier* was a review of *The Marble Faun* which Hawthorne had liked. As for Trollope, for whose works Hawthorne had expressed great admiration, Hawthorne finally did meet him, although it was the next year in America.

In 1861, Fields was preparing a new edition of Lockhart's *Memoirs of the Life of Sir Walter Scott*, and, knowing Hawthorne's reverence for Scott, he decided to dedicate the volumes to him: "One night last December I read aloud your 'Artist of the Beautiful' from the 'Mosses' (always a great favorite of mine) and I said as I closed the book 'the Novels we inscribed to Washington Irving, and the Life shall be dedicated to the Artist of the Beautiful.'"[10] Hawthorne's acceptance was written two days later:

Concord, Feb. 27th 1861.

Dear Fields,

I am exceedingly gratified by the Dedication. I do not deserve so high an honor; but if you think me worthy, it is enough to make the compliment in the highest degree acceptable, no matter who may dispute my title to it. I care more for your good opinion than for that of a host of critics, and have excellent reason for so doing; inasmuch as my literary success, whatever it has been or may be, is the result of my connection with you. Somehow or other, you smote the rock of public sympathy on my behalf, and a stream gushed forth in sufficient quantity to quench my thirst, though not to drown me. I think no author can ever have had publishers that he valued so much as I do mine.

Julian will have a vacation in two or three weeks, and nothing would delight the old fellow so much as to spend a few days with Mrs. Fields and yourself; but I have great scruples (on your account) about letting him come to you in this periodical fashion, like a fit of the ague. Unless he is a quieter member of society, with you, than we find him at home, he must be a great deal of trouble.

We have been expecting Ticknor and General Pierce, this week:— that is to say, they promised to come; but I know the General too well not to have anticipated that other engagements would shove him aside from this one.

Your friend,
Nathl. Hawthorne.

"I am so proud [of this letter] that I keep it among my best treasures," wrote Fields.[11]

---

[10]Fields to Hawthorne, February 25, 1861.
[11]Fields, *Yesterdays*, p. 102, where part of the preceding letter is quoted.

The long and frequent visits of the Hawthorne children to the Fieldses, as mentioned in the preceding letter, indicate the friendship of the two families. The following letter from Fields, written upon the publication of part of the life of Scott, shows the sentimental affection that James and Annie felt for Nathaniel and Sophia:

My dear Hawthorne,
 You will see by the blue sign hanging at the top of this sheet that we are again in our hut by the river. By the Express you will receive some books which I hope you will care to have. Among them are the remaining volumes, save one, of that Life of Scott by Lockhart which it gave so much pleasure to your publishers to dedicate to you. The last one of the set will be pubd. in a few more weeks & you shall then have it to complete your copy. I send back your volume which you lent me some months(?) ago. I have found many good old thoughts in verse therein & thank you for trusting the book away from its brethren so long. We enjoyed, we always do, our visit to the Wayside. Annie says it is worth twenty visits elsewhere to sojourn under your roof. Long ago she fell in love with Mrs. Hawthorne and it does her a world of good to go to Concord. I think as I write of Hawthorne "on the Hill"; of the two trees, the locust and the oak, living apart yet so near to each other to all outside appearance; of all the pleasant moments of our ramble to the "Old Manse"; of our couch on the grass and the young voices singing to the river as we lay in the cool shadows. It was all very lovely, & I do not forget such happy thrills as you gave me and mine of real delight.
 Since dinner I read the Introduction to the "Mosses" to Annie as we sat in our window overlooking the bay. I wish you were all here in this twilight to see with us the boats go tilting by. It was like having you however, for your words in that delicious paper sounded like a talk under the trees. Childe Hawthorne to his bright Tower came!
 With all our kindest love to all the dwellers in the Wayside Paradise,
                              Ever yours, dear Hawthorne,
                                      J. T. Fields.
Don't forget you are to send me that paper for an early "Atlantic."
[FI 2126]

In September 1861 Anthony Trollope was visiting America and Fields finally managed to bring about a meeting between the American "romancer" and the English "realist." The editor wrote:

Nathaniel Hawthorne

Tuesday Sept. 11.

Dear Hawthorne.

    I send you enclosed a letter brought as an introduction by Anthony Trollope. He is a jolly good fellow & you will like him. Now he is in Newport & will return for a few days only to finish his visit here. On Monday he will dine with us at *3* o'clock at our house. We make the hour 3 that Emerson may get back to Concord. But you must stay with us & return next day if you wish to. Let me know on receipt of this if you will come. I really hope you can, for Trollope is a fine boy and wishes to meet you very much.

                                 Yours Ever,
                                 J. T. Fields.   [FI 2128]

Hawthorne and Trollope met on September 16. Lowell, Holmes, and Emerson were also present, and Lowell wrote a lively account of the interview in which he described Trollope as "a big, red-faced, rather underbred Englishman of the bald-with-spectacles type."[12] Trollope was much pleased with Hawthorne. Fields relayed the Englishman's impressions when he wrote on September 18:

                             Boston. *Wednesday*

My Dear Hawthorne.

    I wish very much to begin your new story (about the house) in our *January* number. Now dip your pen steadily and briskly to that end. When shall I have the first instalment? I shall depend upon seeing the early chapters of yr. story "right away." Did you get home safely? Trollope fell in love with you at first sight and went off moaning that he could not see you again. He swears you are the handsomest Yankee that ever walked this planet.

                               Yours Ever
                               J. T. Fields.

"Near Oxford" is admirable. Do the Cathedrals at your pleasure and oblige T. & F. The sooner the better.   [FI 2119]

    "Near Oxford," which appeared in the October 1861 issue of the *Atlantic*, was Hawthorne's second article in the magazine. It later appeared along with his other contributions, descriptive sketches gathered from the journal he had kept in England, in

---

[12]Scudder, II, 82-84.

the volume entitled *Our Old Home* in 1863. But Hawthorne considered this bread-and-butter writing; his heart was in the ideas he was considering for a romance. Fields had been goading him for some time to write a novel that could be printed serially in the *Atlantic*, though long before, Hawthorne had planned a romance of England but had been unable to get it on paper. Upon his return from Europe, he began work on *Doctor Grimshawe's Secret*, but dropped it early in 1861. By the fall of that year he was working on a new version of the same general theme, *Septimius Felton*, and Fields believed that it might be ready to begin serially in the January 1862 issue of the *Atlantic* as is indicated in the preceding letter. Actually, however, there were only the briefest notes at this time;[13] and Hawthorne wrote that he could not have the story ready in time for the January number:

The Wayside, Oct. 6th '61.

Dear Fields,
In compliance with your exhortations, I have begun to think seriously of that story, not as yet with a pen in my hand, but trudging to-and-fro on my hill-top. It has shaped itself into something like a plot, though undeveloped in many parts; but I will try it in black and white pretty soon. I shall *not* be ready by the first of December; for I don't mean to let you have the first chapters till I have written the final sentence of the story. Indeed, the first chapter of a story ought always to be the last written. Perhaps it will come to nothing. I have known hopefuller plots fail utterly, but I will give it a fair trial for I want to do something to earn my bread. And speaking of that, I must again apply to our unhappy Ticknor for $100—having a bill to pay this week, for painting my house on the outside. I was given over to Satan, surely, when I first had to do with carpenters and painters.

Geo. P. Bradford will call for my watch.
With best remembrances to Mrs. Fields,
Yours ever,
Nathl. Hawthorne.

P. S. Mrs. Hawthorne has just returned from a visit to Brattleboro![14]

[13]Edward H. Davidson, *Hawthorne's Last Phase* (New Haven, 1949), p. 74.
[14]Copy in Harvard University Library. Part printed in Fields, *Yesterdays*, p. 96.

In November he still hesitated. He disliked the idea of publishing serially, though he needed the money that this would bring:

Concord, Nov. 6th 1861

Dear Fields,

When the story is finished you may have it for the magazine if you think best. My hesitation is not so much on the score of comparative profit, as because I think my chapters have not the characteristics that produce success in serial publications; and, moreover, a monotony results from my harping on one string through the whole book, and when prolonged from month to month, it will be likely to tire the reader out. If published in a volume, he may finish the infliction as briefly as he likes. The story certainly will not be ready for the first months of the year, and I don't know precisely how soon it will be. Judging from appearances, it will be a pretty long story, though I cannot answer for two volumes. Unless I can get something for it from an English magazine, it would be better for me to go to England to secure the copyright there. Do you think Smith & Elder would like it for the Cornhill?

Can't you announce it conditionally, or hypothetically?

If you want me to write a good book, send me a good pen; not a gold one, for they seldom suit me; but a pen flexible, and capacious of ink, and that will not grow stiff and rheumatic the moment I begin to get attached to it. I never met with a good pen in my life; so I don't suppose you can find one. The one I write with was made in H—— and it is d——tion to write with it.

Truly yours.
Nathl. Hawthorne.[15]

In spite of Fields's encouragement, the novel was far from ready in January, and even Lowell's friendly counsel failed to spur the writer on. "You owe us your English romance," wrote Lowell. "You are of the few men in these later generations whose works are going to *keep*, so make as many of them as you honestly can for the credit of our side of the water."[16] Hawthorne continued to work away on *Septimius Felton* until early in 1863, but he produced only a collection of hopeless fragments.

[15] MS in Massachusetts Historical Society.

[16] J. R. Lowell to Hawthorne, February 26, 1862, in Lowell, *New Letters*, pp. 103-104.

One reason, of course, for Hawthorne's inability to finish a novel was his despondency over the war. "I see no reason," he wrote in April 1862, "to think hopefully of the final result of this war."[17] Disheartened at his own powerlessness to help in the Union cause, he tried to make up for it by writing. He sent his article "Chiefly about War Matters" to Fields in May. It was this article that contained the amusing description of Lincoln in which he spoke of "Uncle Abe's" "tall, loose-jointed figure, of an exaggerated Yankee port and demeanor . . . about the homeliest man I ever saw," of his "lank personality" and his apparent "impulse to throw his legs on the council-table, and tell the Cabinet Ministers a story." Fields thought it best to suppress these comments, and his position illustrates his official attitude toward political subjects during the Civil War. He wrote of it nine years later: "The paper, excellently well done throughout, of course, contained a personal description of President Lincoln, which I thought, considered as a portrait of a living man, and drawn by Hawthorne, it would not be wise or tasteful to print. The office of an editor is a disagreeable one sometimes, and the case of Hawthorne on Lincoln disturbed me not a little."[18] Feeling that Hawthorne's lines would only serve as ammunition for Lincoln's enemies at home and abroad, Fields importuned the author to soften them:

May 21 1862.

Dear Hawthorne.

I have just returned from New York and at once went to the Printing Office of the A. M. as a loyal Editor should do. I found yr. article all ready to send to you in proof and sat down to read it. I knew I shd. like it hugely and I do. But I am going to ask you to change some of it if you will. Ticknor & I both think it will be politic to alter yr. phrases with reference to the President, to leave out the description of his awkwardness & general uncouth aspect. England is reading the Maga. now & will gloat over the monkey figure of "Uncle Abe" as he appears in yr. paper. On p. 77-79 you will find I have drawn a line about another as a mark for you to re-read & consider if we are not right in our fears. I wd. not speak of the Presi-

---

[17]Hawthorne to Fields, April 2, 1862, copy in Harvard University Library.
[18]Fields, *Yesterdays*, p. 98.

dent as *Uncle Abe*, but wd. call him the President in every instance where he is mentioned. On p. *92-93*, also notice my mark. I don't like* the way you speak of the Southerners there & hope you will let me strike out the expressions that seem to me wd. outrage the feelings of many Atlantic readers.

Pray you ameliorate your description of the President, and change the other passages I have marked, or allow me to suggest in the proof what I think wd. be better changed. The *whole* article is piquant & tip top in all other respects.

Yours truly
J. T. F.

*as an Editor & Publisher.

And this was Hawthorne's good-natured reply—he complied though unconvinced:

Concord, May 23d '62

Dear Fields

I have looked over the article under the influence of a cigar and through the medium (but don't whisper it) of a glass of arrack and water; and, though I think you are wrong, I am going to comply with your request. I am the most good-natured man, and the most amenable to good advice (or bad advice either, for that matter) that you ever knew; so have it your own way! The whole description of the interview with Uncle Abe, and his personal appearance must be omitted, since I do not find it possible to alter them; and in so doing, I really think you omit the only part of the article really worth publishing. Upon my honor, it seems to me to have a historical value —but let it go. I have altered and transferred one of the notes, so as to indicate to the unfortunate public that it here loses something very nice. You must mark the omission with dashes; so— X X X X X

I have likewise modified the other passage that you allude to; and I cannot now conceive of any objection to it.

What a terrible thing it is to try to let off a little bit of truth into this miserable humbug of a world! If I had sent you the article as I first conceived it, I should not so much have wondered.

I want you to send me a proof-sheet of the article in its present state, before making any alterations; for, if ever I collect these sketches into a volume, I shall insert it in all its original beauty.

With kindest regards to Mrs. Fields,

Truly Yours,
Nathl. Hawthorne.

P. S. I shall probably come to Boston next week, to the Saturday Club.

A few weeks later Hawthorne sent Fields the manuscript of "Leamington Spa," the fourth article in the series of English sketches. He was paid a hundred dollars for it. As the article was twelve pages long, he was evidently receiving a flat hundred dollars per article, not the ten dollars per page he later got. Hawthorne had utter confidence in Fields's fairness and was always satisfied with whatever he received; in his letters to Fields he seldom mentioned money matters except to apply for advances. Fields sent the check for "Leamington Spa" in July. In the accompanying letter the editor suggested collecting the sketches in a volume, which later turned out to be *Our Old Home*:

July 24. 1862

My dear Hawthorne.

I always settle at once upon a new Mss. from "The Wayside" like a famished host upon miraculous bread, and so I can tell you this morning how much delight the "Leamington Spa" has given me in the perusal. I don't think even your pen ever did a better thing in its way. It is truly a bit of England broken off from one of the best spots by a most skillful master-hand. Do break off some more pieces and hand them to me for exhibition in the Atlantic Crystal Palace, for you will make it one by sending such rare specimens.—What a delectable *Book* you are building up out of these capital papers. Let us, Author and Publisher, be thinking of a sleek volume, for pretty soon we shall have made one. *We!*

Will you and Julian be here on Tuesday in season to dine with us? Tell me when you intend arriving and at what hour we shall have the pot boiling with your dinner.

Our best love to all your nest.

Ever yours
James T. Fields.

[Written in at head of letter:] Check for $100, enclosed for "Leamington Spa" article.

As encouragement to write more, Fields told Hawthorne of the popularity of the Leamington paper, which was printed in the October number of the *Atlantic*, making its appearance on the twentieth of September. Especially relished was Hawthorne's description of the typical English dowager whose "awful ponderosity of frame [was] not pulpy, like the looser development of our few fat women, but massive with solid beef and streaky tallow":

Nathaniel Hawthorne

Boston: Sept. 24. 1862.

Dear Hawthorne.

I wish to tell you how greatly admired yr. paper on Leamington is; how every body swears it is one of your or anybody's best; how I am stopped in the street to laugh with friends over your fat dowager; how the papers all praise the article & ask for more of the same sort.

You must send me a paper for my December No. & my January issue also. I can't get on without them, & I beg you will on receipt of this let me know the subjects of both articles.

Hereof fail not!

Fields's letter elicited the desired response: Hawthorne wrote immediately that he planned to send articles for both January and December:

The Wayside Sept. 27th '62

Dear Fields,

I mean to send you an article on Old English Towns—and another one in time for the January No.

I am glad that the Dowager meets with *a* kind reception in American Society.

Best regards to Mrs. Fields.

Truly Yours
Nathl. Hawthorne.[19]

On October 5 Hawthorne sent the first of the articles, which, when it appeared in the December *Atlantic*, bore the title "About Warwick." "Here is the article for December," he wrote. "I hope you will like it; for the subject seemed interesting to me when I was on the spot, but I always feel a singular despondency and heaviness of heart in re-opening those old journals now."[20] He continued to re-open the journals, however, for as his letter revealed, he needed money.

Choosing a title for the December article was troublesome, and Hawthorne suggested several possibilities for Fields to consider:

---

[19]MS in the Henry W. and Albert A. Berg Collection, New York Public Library.

[20]Copy in Harvard University Library. Part printed in Caroline Ticknor, *Hawthorne and His Publisher* (Boston, 1913), pp. 254-55; part in Fields, *Yesterdays*, pp. 102-103.

Concord. Oct. 9th '62.

Dear Fields,

    I have bothered my brains in vain, and can think of no better title for the Article. It is really of no consequence. Name it anything you like, provided the title shall promise no more than is to be found in the paper. This is the merit of my title; it expresses just what the article is. But call it "Warwick"—which implies a fuller description than I give—or "An Old English Town"—or "Leycester's Hospital"—which does not cover everything, and yet suggests a detailed description of the Hospital and full account of it, which I do not pretend to—or "About Warwick"—which is unexceptionable, and better than the present title, as being shorter. In a word, suit yourself. I wash my hands of it; though I think the title last suggested is the best, on the whole. I have not had the last volume of Scott's life, and did not know it was published.

    Julian arrived a little after midnight, somewhat footsore. Thank you for giving him a dinner.

    With kindest regards to Mrs. Fields,

                              Your friend.
                              Nathl. Hawthorne

    We are having the finest of summer weather here. You had better come.[21]

    The next article in the series of English sketches was "Recollections of a Gifted Woman," concerning Delia Bacon, for whose *Philosophy of the Plays of Shakespeare Unfolded* (1857) Hawthorne had written a preface. The sketch must have been submitted about the first of December, for Fields wrote to Hawthorne on the fourth:

Boston December 4. 1862

My dear Hawthorne.

    I am so much obliged to you for enriching our January Number with that glorious paper the "Recollections of a Gifted Woman" that I cannot help telling you so again as I finish re-reading it this evening. In future you must receive $100. for all articles of *ten pages or less*, and for all over ten pages, $10. pr. page additional. This last paper occupies 15 pages, so I gave Mrs. Hawthorne $150. to day. You must tell me if this is satisfactory. What is to be the subject of yr. next? And when will you send it? Have you not almost enough for a book prepared? And when will you like to publish a volume?

[21]Copy in Harvard University Library.

Julian has gone under the blankets. He and I walked several miles in Dorchester this afternoon, and had our tea at a friend's table at the end of our tramp.

         Yours Ever
         J. T. F.

P. S. We have never printed an article in the "Atlantic" that has been more applauded than "About Warwick." That absolutely perfect paper is hailed with delight all over the land. Curtis had his cup of coffee with us today and he joined the chorus with enthusiasm. Lowell & Longfellow chanted high praises to me last night, and Holmes swears you are the Prince of English writers. He holds his own plume straight into the air as you know, but he knocks under to you. Charles Street bows to Hawthorne-den. Oliver kneels!

The new rate of payment was designed to encourage Hawthorne, who, more than most writers, needed encouragement in his later years. But in spite of his gratitude for both pay and praise, and in spite of his desire to increase his income, he was physically unable to produce as he would like. Though he continued to write the English sketches, he was not forwarding his more serious literary plans. His reply to Fields mentions his recurrent illness:

Dear Fields,   Concord, Dec. 6th '62

 I am delighted at what you tell me about the kind appreciation of my articles; for I feel rather despondent about them myself. As to the increased rate of payment, it is more than satisfactory, for I was satisfied before; but I am glad to know that you think my work worth its price, and the money comes into a pocket where it finds plenty of room. I have been quite ill for some days past, and so have been interrupted in an article which would otherwise have been nearly finished. You will not get it in season for the February No.; but that is no matter—there will be room for "other novelty," as the play bills say. I think of calling it "A Suburban Residence," or some title to that effect; and it will describe my summer's abode at Bennoch's house, with sketches of Greenwich Park & Hospital, and Greenwich Fair, and other notable things in the neighborhood of London.

 I hope Julian's visit has not bored you intolerably. It is certainly a relief to us to get rid of him occasionally; he is too big for a small house. Don't tell him so, however.

 With kindest regards to Mrs. Fields, Your friend,
                Nathl. Hawthorne.

The article, which was finally called "A London Suburb," appeared in the March *Atlantic*. Upon sending it to Fields in January, Hawthorne revealed his wavering self-confidence when he asked Fields not to show the manuscript to Una, Hawthorne's daughter, who was visiting the Fieldses. The time had been when Hawthorne's family were his favorite critics.

Dear Fields,   The Wayside, Jan. 4th 1863.

    I herewith bore you with another article. I am sorry that it runs to such length but I have left out what would have made a sheet or two more in order to bring it within reasonable compass. Don't read this to Una nor let her hear it, for it always plagues me to have my wife and children read my productions before they are printed and if I could prevent it afterwards, I would. I trust Mrs. Fields and yourself are in jolly condition. We are very well here. Una writes to her mother as if she were in a state of high enjoyment.

                                        Your friend,
                                        Nathl. Hawthorne.[22]

Fields was prompt, as usual with Hawthorne, in sending payment for the article. Hawthorne responded:

Dear Fields,   Concord, Jan'y. 8th 1863.

    I rec'd your note with the $150 cheque, which came as opportunely as possible—satisfying (and 50 per cent over) a demand which I had just made on Ticknor. I have not thought of any title for the next article; but I think I shall dip into London a little, being so near it in the one just sent you. It will require, I believe, as much as three more articles, including "A London Suburb," to make up a volume of, say 325 pages. Methinks it would be better to defer publication till the autumn—at least, till summer; though perhaps it may be desirable to make what harvest we can while the war lasts; for when that comes to an end, I look for utter ruin—at all events, so dark a gloom that nobody can see to read in it, and so no more books will be bought. Not that I really believe this, but I should not wonder if it were true. Una seems to be very happy. I hope you like her. We do.

    If my pen were not so horribly stiff, I should scribble over this whole sheet. Give our kind regards to Mrs. Fields, and believe me

                                Sincerely Your friend,
                                Nathl. Hawthorne.[23]

[22]Copy in Harvard University Library.
[23]Copy in Harvard University Library.

Toward the end of January, Fields sent the proofs of "A London Suburb," and again he had high praise for the author. Perhaps he exaggerated a little, but it is true that Hawthorne's articles were one of the chief attractions of the magazine:

Boston Jan. 26. 1863.

My dear Hawthorne.

I send this to warn you that in a day or two your proof of the "London Suburb" paper will be sent to Concord & that you must send it back to me very soon after you get it as it comes early in the No.—Have I told you how delighted I am with it? If I have not, I am a knave of the darkest dye. You will be tired of my enthusiasm over these charming papers, but this last one is so excellent from beginning to end I must roar again. I declare to you it is the best of the series. But this I always say of the last one I read. All the felicities of the English tongue seem to have been created for yr. use alone. I sent you a box of pens the other day in Una's trunk that you may go on forever with these admirable articles. I have six gross more for you when you get out. It shall not be my fault that you have no instruments to proceed in this glorious series. The "Atlantic" is lifted into quite another region by your rich contributions to its pages.

Are you not coming to Boston? We long to see you once more & Longfellow always asks when you are to be here. Your room looking on the bay is really pleasant this winter, and we have chowders frequently. Una did not get one, but her father shall not fail to eat several if he will come down and live a week under our hut's roof.

With kindest remembrances, Ever Yours sincerely

J. T. Fields.

Hawthorne knew Fields well enough to recognize flattery when he saw it, but he appreciated the basic sincerity of Fields's friendliness. He replied on January 30: "I am much encouraged by what you say about the English Articles—not but what I am sensible that you mollify me with a good deal of soft soap, but it is skillfully applied and effects all that you intend it should."[24]

When he sent the sketch for May, "Up the Thames," on February 22, Hawthorne feared that it was too long and gave Fields permission to cut as he saw fit. Suffering under the "unshakable conviction that all this series of articles is good for nothing,"[25]

[24]Copy in Harvard University Library.
[25]Hawthorne to Fields, February 22, 1863, cited in Fields, *Yesterdays*, p. 103.

the author proposed doing only two more sketches for the *Atlantic*, and this plan was eventually carried out. The editor's reply, with a check for "Up the Thames," was sent the following day. The description of Hawthorne's meeting with Leigh Hunt, "a beautiful old man," naturally appealed to Fields, who was an idolator of Hunt:

Boston February 23. 1863.

My dear Hawthorne.

Enclosed I send you the narrow strip which usually follows your papers.

This being Washington's Birth Day I went home early with your Mss. of "Up the Thames" in my pocket to read to my wife. So we sat in our room by the bay, and I read your delightful and not a bit too long paper. From beginning to end it is admirable and will prove among the most liked. What you say of poor dear old L. H. I like extremely and I am sure all his lovers will accept in full. You brought back the kindly old poet very vividly. You remember I too was present at B[arry] C[ornwall]'s dinner party and sat near the old boys, Barry & Leigh. That dinner I shall not soon forget.

You write of only two more! We will talk that over when you come here, but I shall not let you stop then. However, now listen to a plan for your visit.

Imprimus. We all hunger to see you. Mrs. F. says you must come on Friday or Saturday and stay over Sunday and as many days onward as you choose to be contented with us. Now, my friend, do come, and do stay some days with us. It is a long time since you were here, and you need some change. Besides I wish to talk book with you a little. It is time we made arrangements for the forthcoming volume. The little room on the bay is swept and garnished for you. The Claret is waiting in the closet for your advent. The house is cleared of visitors, and no one is here to molest. Come then, and the sooner the better.

With kindest regards to Mrs. Hawthorne & the children,
Yours always
James T. Fields.

Some time in April Hawthorne submitted "Outside Glimpses of English Poverty" and began the article that was intended as the last of the series, "Consular Experiences." Upon receipt of his payment for the former, he wrote to Fields of his plans:

Nathaniel Hawthorne

Wayside, April 18th '63

Dear Fields,

I received the cheque, and pocket it with great satisfaction. I shall begin to write the last article (which will come first in the volume) in a day or two. I don't think the public will bear any more of this sort of thing.

I had a letter from Bennoch the other day. He has a fit of the gout, but seems to be comfortable enough now. He sends me the enclosed verses, and, I think, would like to have them published in the Atlantic. Do it if you like. I pretend to no judgment in poetry, and shall therefore refrain from recommending or dissuading.

Bennoch also sent this Epithalamium by Mrs. Crasland, and I doubt not that the good lady will be pleased to see it copied into one of our newspapers with a few laudatory remarks. Can't you do it in the Transcript (let Michael Angelo [Fields's valet], write the remarks, if you have not the time) and send her a copy? You cannot imagine how a little praise jollifies us poor authors to the marrow of our bones. Consider, if you had not been a publisher you would certainly have been one of our wretched tribe, and therefore ought to have a fellow-feeling for us.

Your friend,
Nathl. Hawthorne.[26]

Hawthorne, like most of the great writers of the time, was often the reluctant recipient of the literary productions of would-be writers who wanted him to use his influence in getting their works published.

At the end of the month Hawthorne submitted "Consular Experiences" but suggested that instead of putting it in the *Atlantic*, it might be printed for the first time as the initial essay in the new volume, in which case he could "concoct another article" for the magazine.[27] Fields approved of the plan, and Hawthorne went to work on "Civic Banquets," which appeared in the August number.

The plans for the publication of *Our Old Home* were progressing smoothly. But an obstruction appeared: Hawthorne insisted on dedicating the book to Franklin Pierce, the unpopular

---

[26] Copy in Harvard University Library. Part printed in Fields, *Yesterdays*, p. 104.
[27] Hawthorne to Fields, April 30, 1863, in Fields, *Yesterdays*, p. 105.

ex-president, who had been Hawthorne's schoolmate, and to whom Hawthorne was faithful in spite of public disapproval. At first the writer's idea was to dedicate either to Pierce or Francis Bennoch, a friend at whose house Hawthorne had stayed when in England:

Wayside, May 3rd '63.

Dear Fields,

I am exceedingly glad that you like the "Consular Experiences." It will certainly be better to keep them fresh for the volume, which otherwise will be likely to come into the world without having a new word said about it. I will write another in season for the August No.—in which this article was to have appeared.

I am of three minds about dedicating the volume. First, it seems due to Frank Pierce (as he put me into the position where I made all those profound observations of English scenery, life, and character) to inscribe it to him with a few pages of friendly and explanatory talk—which also would be very gratifying to my own life-long affection for him. Secondly, I want to say something to Bennoch to show him that I am thoroughly mindful of all his hospitality and kindness; and I suppose he might be pleased to see his name at the head of a book of mine. Thirdly, I am not convinced that it is worth while to inscribe it to anybody. We will see hereafter.

As I have most or all of the unbound Nos. of the magazine containing my articles, I will look over them and make such corrections as seem desirable, and send them to you, probably in the course of a week. You shall likewise have the re-written copy of "Uttoxeter" [originally published in 1857, not in the *Atlantic*] with additions, before the press is ready for it. How soon do you mean to get the volume out?

If you can get anything for the sheets in England, do it by all means —even if it were only five pounds. I don't see why anybody should give more, or so much, for a book that a dozen pirates will be ready to seize upon, if it prove to have any sellable value. However, it will not take in England, being calculated (by the objects which it describes, and the sentiments it expresses) for the American market only.

Truly Yours,
Nathl. Hawthorne.

As for printing the book in England, Fields went to work on it and managed to get an offer of £150 from Smith, Elder, and Company:

Nathaniel Hawthorne

Boston June 30. 1863.

My dear Hawthorne.

At last I have got back to my desk, but my wife is still in the country for a few days more. Smith & Elder are to reprint "Our Old Home" & are to pay 150 Pounds for it (£150), so you see England has not given up yet their favorite American authors. Smith & Elder say in their letter of reply to mine they expect the first offer of your new *Romance* when it is ready. They also say they must have Our Old Home in *their hands* thirty days before the book is published in the States. This of course will delay a little, but it is best to do as they desire seeing they pay for what is by no means copyright.

If there is to be any Introductory matter to "O. O. H." send it please at once as the printer is quite ready for it now. I will of course attend to the sending of sheets to S. & Elder & give you no trouble in the matter. Leave it all in my hands.

How admirably you have done the "Civic Banquet." I read it all in proof last night at the P[rinting] Office, and had such delight over it that the men nudged each other & thought me sun-struck; and I was, but not by the luminary so far away as they had reckoned.

Dear Hawthorne, you shall not stop sending to the Atlantic these glorious things from your journal. So pray be at work getting others ready just as soon as the weather will let you to appear after the Vol. comes out, which I think now will be in Sept. to accommodate Smith & Elder.

"English Poverty" is attracting great attention. Holmes kept me on his door-step last night half an hour talking over its qualities. You are doing us an immense benefit in the Maga. Your papers make us stronger every month. Pray give our best love to your household & tell me how Gail [Hamilton] got on under the skies of Concord. Her letter to me telling of her visit is so glowing that I think the girl wishes to go back and *live* at the Wayside.

Ever Yours
J. T. Fields.

Hawthorne was overjoyed with Smith, Elder, and Company's offer. "On my own behalf," he wrote to Fields the next day, "I never could have thought of asking more than £50, and should hardly have expected to get £10."[28]

In the same letter Hawthorne announced his intention "to dedicate the book to Frank Pierce, come what may." A dedication to

---

[28]Hawthorne to Fields, July 1, 1862. Printed in Fields, *Yesterdays*, p. 106.

Pierce, the compromising pacifist, was of course bad business in the middle of the war. Fields wrote to Hawthorne on July 3 to caution him about one paragraph that the publisher feared would be especially offensive to enemies of Pierce:

My dear Hawthorne.

 A cool room is waiting for you always at No. 37 whenever you choose to come to it. This is July 3d & we remain in Rye till Monday when we return to our bay-side again. Your dedication to F. P. has a paragraph in it I shd. be glad to talk over with you when you come here. But it is a charming bit of writing, that same dedication.

Ever yours
J. T. Fields.
in hot haste.

Boston, Friday morning.   [FI 2125]

Sensing that Hawthorne could not be persuaded to disavow his friendship for Pierce, Fields did not insist upon deleting the whole dedication. However, he thought it prudent to advise the writer of what might be the consequences of printing it, and again he suggested omitting one paragraph:

Boston. July 15. 1863.

My dear Hawthorne.

 Bravo Julian! The old fellow has just been in to tell me "he is through," & now on his way to be noticed by the sun in the way of a photograph. I shall carry him home to dine if we have dinner in season to day. Una came in on her way to Canton & left on my desk such a spray of lilies that their perfume now fills No. 37 with the rarest odor, even after so many days. As I am writing comes yr. letter of yesterday. Here are the proofs of Dedication & Letter just in from the printer. It is the opinion of wiser men than I am in the "Trade" that the Dedn. & Letter to F. P. will ruin the sale of yr. book. I tell you this, in season that you may act upon it if you elect so to do. A large dealer told me he shd. not order any copies, much as his customers admired yr. writings, and a very knowing literary friend of yours says it will be, in these days, the most damaging move you could possibly make. So, this is what I feared. Now you must decide whether you will risk the sale of "Our Old Home" by putting a friend's name to it.

 At any rate let me call yr. attention to the whole passage I have marked X as a part to be omitted with safety. You can cut as you choose in this proof.

Rough days we live in. Cannons are resting in Dock Square & the soldiers today are under arms in our city. Last night we had blood in the streets. Where it will land us all, God alone can tell. It looks smoky to my dim vision.

Kind love from both of us to you all.

Yrs. Ever,
J. T. F.

P. S. I will hold Stephen away from Concord if possible, & I think I can do it.

Hawthorne replied with finality that the dedication would remain, though he rewrote the last paragraph. "If the public of the North see fit to ostracize me for this, I can only say that I would gladly sacrifice a thousand or two of dollars rather than retain the goodwill of such a herd of dolts and mean-spirited scoundrels."[29] Fields's advice was certainly right from a commercial point of view, and admirable as Hawthorne's action was, it was also impractical. There is little doubt that many people refused to buy the book because of the dedication. The story of Emerson's tearing out the offending pages from his copy of *Our Old Home* is representative of the popular reaction. And Harriet Beecher Stowe wrote to the Fieldses: "I never read the preface, and have not yet seen the book, but ... I can scarcely believe it of you, if I can of him [Hawthorne]. I regret that I went to see him last summer."[30]

With *Our Old Home* in the hands of the printers, the author and the publisher once again began to talk of a novel. Hawthorne, having given up *Septimius Felton*, began in June 1863 on a new approach to the same theme, *The Dolliver Romance*. His inability to write during his latter years was certainly not due to a lack of incentive. He needed money for his growing family, as his letters show, and Fields never relaxed in offering encouragement to write, both pecuniary and personal. In August 1863 the editor made the handsome proposal of two hundred dollars a month for a serialized romance for the *Atlantic*:

[29] Hawthorne to Fields, July 18, 1863, MS in possession of Mrs. Z. B. Adams. Printed in Fields, *Yesterdays*, pp. 107-108.

[30] Annie Adams Fields, *Life and Letters of Harriet Beecher Stowe* (Boston, 1898), pp. 293-94.

Fields of the Atlantic Monthly

Boston August 31. 1863.

My dear Hawthorne.
In the event of your sending that story, of which we spoke this morning, for publication in the "Atlantic," let it be understood between us that we shall pay you *$200*, for each monthly instalment.
Yours Ever
J. T. F.

But Hawthorne's health, mental as well as physical, was declining rapidly and he wrote only with extreme effort. He tried to comply with Fields's request, but on October 24 he wrote that he would be unable to meet the editor's deadline.[31] He contemplated writing a prefatory sketch of Thoreau, whose tale of a deathless man was the germ of the plot of Hawthorne's novel. But the sketch of Thoreau was never written—or at least has never been found.[32]

When Fields replied to Hawthorne's letter a few days later, he urged the author to let him promise the new novel to the readers of the *Atlantic* in the December issue:

Boston October 28 1863.

My dear Hawthorne.
Ticknor sent the money at once the day yr. letter came. Now I think of it, did Una & Julian walk up last Saturday & did they do it dry shod? I have been very much worse in health than I have been in ten years the past week, & so I could not join them in the Cambridge Square. A wretched cold has got me between its jaws and crunches me so that my whole body roars. But to day I can breathe, and actually spoke a pleasant word to a friend just now.
Would that we could help you to a title, but who wd. dare meddle in that way over a book of yours! No, Sir Knight; only yourself can christen your brain-children.

The New Tithonus.
The Deathless Man.
The Modern Tithonus

Such names as these wd. at once occur to everyone, but you will prefix a title that will sound on long after it is spoken. So begin, mon Emperor, and it is done!

[31]Fields, *Yesterdays*, pp. 109-10.
[32]See Davidson, pp. 77, 80.

I wish very much to announce in our Decr. No. that you will have a story in the Maga. early in the year. May I?

At any rate you must send me something for our Jany. No. as a sweetener to the whole volume.

When are you coming down? Why not next week and see Charlotte Cushman. She will be with us on Monday. So will Una. Come with her.
Kind love to all. Yours always
James T. Fields.

Your Thoreau idea is excellent. Carry it into execution. "Our Old Home" continues to sell bravely. You may safely count on a handsome sum out of that book. Make another series. You cannot do better.

Will you write your name under this Photog. It is for a friend of ours.

Fields wanted the novel to begin in the January 1864 *Atlantic*, but in his next letter Hawthorne put it off until February.[33] Still wanting a title, he proposed calling the installments "Fragments of a Romance" and deciding on a better name when the novel was finished and ready to publish as a book. He was still in need of money. "Tell Ticknor that I want a hundred dollars more," he wrote, "and I suppose I shall keep on wanting more and more till the end of my days." The next day Fields replied with a check and further encouragement. He was overjoyed with the prospect of beginning the novel in February, and he advised Hawthorne not to worry about a title until the first chapter was written:

Boston Nov. 9. 1863.

My dear Hawthorne.

Here is the bit of paper you send for. Plenty more like it for you when you choose to call on the Old Corner.

I am delighted that you see a chapter for me resolutely determined on for our Feb. No.—Won't I be glad to get it? Touching the name of the story, don't bother about that for several days to come. When you send me the first instalment we will muse together. Your autobiographical prefaces are always hailed with pleasure, so when the story is finished for a book you must not omit that part of it.

I have promised to go to Concord & see Miss Thoreau about some business matters. Perhaps I shall take a few hours *this* week. If I do

---

[33]Hawthorne to Fields, November 8, 1863. Printed in Fields, *Yesterdays*, p. 111.

the "Wayside" will see me plunging in for a call only, as I am over pressed with work here.

Did you ever have the *Neuralgia*? I have got it fastened upon me for the first time in my life & I don't like it for a companion.

With kind love to all from both of us,

Yours always,
J. T. Fields.

Within a month Hawthorne had completed the first chapter of the novel and sent it to Fields, who immediately sent him a check for the whole first installment, although there was more to be added before the installment would be complete. On December 9 Hawthorne wrote in acknowledgment:

I recd. the cheque for $200. and thank you for it, but there must still be a further consideration forthcoming on my part, because the first instalment of the Dolliver Romance is not completed. I want you to send me that chapter in print as soon as possible in order that I may write the rest in a similar strain, and so conclude this preliminary phase of Dr. Dolliver. You must not think of publishing it so soon as the Feby. No.[34]

Again the novel had to be postponed. In his reply to Hawthorne, written on December 10, Fields agreed to publish the first installment in March instead of February: "Always consult yr. own convenience and mood with me. Your pleasure is mine & I trust you know me well enough by this time to feel this is so in every enterprize." Hawthorne had had Fields print proofs of the first chapter of the romance so that he could get a better idea of how it would look in print, but he wrote on December 15: "I have not yet had courage to read the Dolliver proof-sheet, but will set about it soon, though with terrible reluctance—such as I never felt before."[35]

On January 17, 1864, he had still not completed the whole installment. "I am not quite up to writing yet," he declared to Fields, "but shall make an effort as soon as I see any hope of

[34]Copy in Harvard University Library.
[35]Copy in Harvard University Library.

success."[36] Finally toward the end of February he had to admit defeat: "I hardly know what to say to the Public about this abortive Romance, though I know pretty well what the case will be. I shall never finish it."[37]

By this time it was obvious that Hawthorne's health was declining dangerously, and his friends were becoming anxious, but there seemed to be nothing to be done for him. In April he started a trip to Washington with Ticknor, during which the latter became ill and died. The night before the death Hawthorne wrote to Fields:

Philadelphia Continental House. Saturday evening.

Dear Fields,

I am sorry to say that our friend Ticknor is suffering under a severe billious attack since yesterday morning. He had previously seemed uncomfortable, but not to an alarming degree. He sent for a physician during the night, and fell into the hands of an allopathist, who of course belabored him with pills and powders of various kinds and then proceeded to cup and poultice, and blister, according to the ancient rule of that tribe of savages. The consequence is that poor Ticknor is already very much reduced, while the disease flourishes as luxuriantly as if that were the Doctor's sole object. He calls it a billious colic (or bilious, I know not which) and says it is one of the worst cases he ever knew. I think him a man of skill and intelligence in his way, and doubt not that he will do everything that his views of scientific medicine will permit. Since I began writing the above, Mr. Burnett of Boston tells me that the Doctor, after this morning's visit, requested the proprietor of the Continental to telegraph to Boston the state of the case. I am glad of it because it relieves me of the responsibility of either disclosing the intelligence or withholding it. I will only add that Ticknor, under the influence of a blister and some powders, seems more comfortable than at any other time since his attack, and that Mr. Burnett (who is an apothecary, and therefore conversant with these accursed matters) says that he is in a good state. But I can see that it will not be a very few days that will set him upon his legs again. As regards nursing, he shall have the best that can be obtained; and my own room is next to his, so that I can step in at any moment, but that will be of about as much

---

[36] MS in possession of Professor Norman Holmes Pearson.

[37] Hawthorne to Fields, February 25, 1864. Printed in Fields, *Yesterdays*, pp. 115-16.

service as if a hippopotamus were to do him the same kindness. Nevertheless, I have blistered, and powdered, and pilled him, and made my observations on medical science and the sad and comic aspects of human misery.

Excuse this illegible scrawl, for I am writing almost in the dark. Remember me to Mrs. Fields. As regards myself, I almost forgot to say that I am perfectly well. If you could find time to write to Mrs. Hawthorne and tell her so, it would be doing me a great favor, for I doubt whether I can find an opportunity just now to do it myself. You would be surprised to see how stalwart I have become in this little time.
Your friend,
N. H. [FI 2318]

Hawthorne claimed to be "perfectly well" but he was not, and the shock of Ticknor's death affected him greatly. Early in May his daughter Una wrote regarding her father's health:

Dear Mr. Fields;

Mamma forgot to tell you in her note that it is at the Bromfield Papa is to meet General Pierce when he goes down on Wednesday; so they will go straight there, and as Papa now intends to leave here at half past eight A. M. they will probably be there about ten o'clock, and Mamma says you could perhaps despatch a little messenger to see if they have arrived.

Mamma is very anxious to have Dr. Holmes see Papa. He has so visibly lost in every way this week, and grows so very weak, that we have longed for a physician's eye to be upon him, but he has refused all along to see a doctor. Today, however, Mamma discovered that it is only to a homeopathic physician he has an objection, so we are very glad, because I suppose learned doctors in these days of whatever belief, do not drug their patients as absurdly as they did in old times, and very likely Papa only needs to be directed in diet and mode of life to recover. So we hope Dr. Holmes will be able to see him.

With love to Mrs. Fields

Sincerely yours
Una Hawthorne.

May 8th Concord[38]

On May 11 Hawthorne came to Boston to meet Franklin Pierce, who was going with him for a trip into New Hampshire. Holmes met Hawthorne on that day and casually observed his physical

[38] MS in Boston Public Library.

condition. The report of Holmes's observations were later published in the *Atlantic* for July.

On May 19 Hawthorne died in Plymouth, New Hampshire. Pierce telegraphed the news to Fields immediately, and then wrote a letter asking the publisher to notify Mrs. Hawthorne: "I cannot write to dear Mrs. Hawthorne, and you must exercise your judgment with regard to sending this and the unfinished note, enclosed, to her."[39] Upon Fields devolved the duty not only of informing Sophia Hawthorne of her husband's death but also, in one case at least, of announcing the funeral.[40] The funeral took place on May 23. Fields, along with Longfellow, Lowell, Holmes, Emerson, and others, was a pallbearer.

The manuscript of the first chapter of *The Dolliver Romance* lay on the coffin during the funeral service. "H's romance is unfinished," Fields wrote to Bayard Taylor on May 26. "The fragment I placed on his coffin & it was borne to his grave. It is now in my possession & will appear shortly in the 'Atlantic.' I count it one of his best as far as it goes."[41] The chapter appeared in the July *Atlantic*.

Sophia Hawthorne's acceptance of her husband's death was little less than saintly, but she relied a good deal upon the Fieldses' friendship. On May 29 she wrote to Fields: "Tell Annie I have not yet measured the power of her ministrations to me that day."[42] Perhaps she referred to the day the message was delivered.

After Hawthorne's death Fields received numerous writings on him for the *Atlantic*. First, of course, was Holmes's medical report published in the July number. And there was Longfellow's poem "Hawthorne" (originally called "Concord, a Poem on Hawthorne's Funeral") in August. Fields wrote to Longfellow late in June to thank him for it:

Although I am hoping to see you soon I must thank you for sending me that poem in answer to my wish for something from Cambridge.

[39]Fields, *Yesterdays*, p. 123.
[40]Fields to [?] Clark, no date, MS in Harvard University Library.
[41]See Davidson, pp. 11, 137.
[42]MS in Harvard University Library.

Fields of the Atlantic Monthly

How beautiful that tribute is, and how it will soothe the hearts of those who are left lonely at "The Wayside." I am rejoiced that you were in the mood to give expression to your own and all our feelings in such a perfect lyric. Now we shall always connect your poem with that divine day when we took leave of dear Hawthorne on his mount of transfiguration. [FI 1806]

Meanwhile, G. W. Curtis sent an article which Fields rejected out of respect for his late friend because Curtis had found fault with Hawthorne's politics. In rejecting the manuscript, Fields offered to pay for it anyway, but Curtis, who understood the editor's feelings, declined:

North Shore. Staten Island, N. Y. 22nd June 1864.
My dear Fields.
Today I recover your letter from the Eaton House, which cannot explain where it has been.

I can perfectly understand that your personal feeling should have made the article impossible for you to print; and Holmes's tender & admiring words which I have just read, are doubtless more timely and becoming in your pages, yet warm with Hawthorne's hand.

But I cannot let you pay me. I do not know that I shall make any use of the *ms*, but, if I should, your most generous money would burn my pocket and my conscience.

You are always most prompt and kind. Please return me my *ms*. by mail, & believe me
as always Yours
G. W. Curtis.

I wonder if Mrs. H. has told you the great romance of all in H's life![43]

Curtis' article was printed in the October 1864 number of the *North American Review*.

Fields was still eager to print the remains of Hawthorne's works, and by November he had persuaded Mrs. Hawthorne to let him print the remaining fragment of *The Dolliver Romance*. He paid her well in advance of publication and at the rate he had previously promised Hawthorne, two hundred dollars per installment, although when the promise was made it was assumed that the story would some day be finished:

[43] See Randall Stewart, *Nathaniel Hawthorne, a Biography* (New Haven, 1948), p. 239.

Nathaniel Hawthorne

Boston Nov. 9. 1864.

Dear Mrs. Hawthorne

Enclosed I send our cheque for $200, being for the 2d Scene from the Dolliver Romance which you brought to me and which is to go into the Jany. No. of the Atlantic. I send the cheque thus early thinking you might need it for bills &c coming in (if such there be). You know you have only to present the cheque to *any* bank & it will be cashed.

Yours always,
J. T. Fields[44]

"Another Scene from the Dolliver Romance" appeared as scheduled in January 1865. In 1876 Fields's successor in the publishing business printed the two fragments together with a third in book form.

During the years immediately following, Fields remained on the friendliest terms with Hawthorne's family. But the income from the estate left by Hawthorne proved inadequate, in a time of rising costs, to keep the widow and children properly. It was partly for this reason that Mrs. Hawthorne allowed Fields to persuade her to print Hawthorne's journals. With Fields's help, she prepared them for the press, which meant that she omitted and altered as she thought Hawthorne would have done if he were alive. To Fields she applied for editorial advice, and he was responsible for a few of the expurgations, the most important being the omission of the description of the drowned girl whose body had been found in the Concord River.[45]

Also assisting in the editing, at least to the extent of giving advice, were Longfellow and Lowell. A letter from Fields to the former reveals that Mrs. Hawthorne sought the poet's approval of one section of the journal:

---

[44]MS in the Henry W. and Albert A. Berg Collection, New York Public Library.

[45]Randall Stewart, "Editing Hawthorne's Notebooks," *More Books*, XX (September 1945), 299-315. See Fields to Una Hawthorne, March ? 1865 and April 2, 1865, MSS in Boston Public Library. Also the articles by Randall Stewart, "The Hawthornes at the Wayside," *More Books*, XIX (September 1944), 263-79; "Hawthorne's Last Illness and Death," *More Books*, XIX (October 1944), 303-13; and "Mrs. Hawthorne's Financial Difficulties. Selections from her Letters to James T. Fields, 1865-1868," *More Books*, XXI (February 1946), 43-53.

Boston Sept. 4. 1866,

Dear Longfellow.
  Here is Hawthorne's charming journal of his days with the child Julian. I send it pr. Mrs. Hawthorne's request for yr. judgment as to its publication.
  How are you these gray days? And when do you come up for good?
                                   Yrs. Ever
                                   J. T. F.

Another section of the notebooks was sent to Lowell, but Mrs. Hawthorne decided not to publish it and it was returned.[46] *Passages from Hawthorne's American Note-Books* appeared monthly in the *Atlantic* throughout the year 1866, Mrs. Hawthorne receiving twelve hundred dollars for the twelve installments. One selection from the English journal was printed in the July 1867 issue.

It was in 1868 that the misunderstanding occurred that put an unfortunate end to the friendship of the Hawthorne and Fields families. Because of her financial straits, Sophia Hawthorne, encouraged by her friend Gail Hamilton, began to suspect Fields of withholding some of the royalties on Hawthorne's books that rightfully belonged to her. When she asked to see Ticknor and Fields's records, Fields stalled: it was not customary to show the books to an outsider and besides they were in no condition to be read. Mrs. Hawthorne became more suspicious. Finally, through the offices of her more business-like sister, Elizabeth Peabody, she got access to the books and found she had not really been cheated. What had happened was that Fields, in a perfectly legal manner, had lowered the royalties on Hawthorne's books from fifteen per cent based upon the retail price, to twelve cents a volume. The twelve-cent rate was in accordance with a contract that had been written in 1864; but Sophia, unaware that this contract was in effect, still thought in terms of fifteen per cent. Miss Peabody related the circumstances in a letter to Fields:

---

[46]On October 31, 1867, Lowell wrote to Fields (MS in Harvard University Library): "I never had any part of Hawthorne's journal except the one volume about the Iles of Shoals, & that, you will remember, I at once returned."

Nathaniel Hawthorne

My dear Sir— Jan. 4th 1869 Cambridge. Follen Str.

I ought not to delay saying to you that Mr. Clarke [a member of the firm of Fields, Osgood and Company] explained satisfactorily, so far as the accuracy of his account goes, the discrepancy between the amounts credited for copy right to Mr. & Mrs. Hawthorne in them; and the results of my analysis—

I did not know, nor did the papers he gave me *hint* that the Contract for 12 cents a volume went into operation in 1864. I knew there was such a contract, which Mr. Hillard [Hawthorne's executor] signed, and which afterwards was given up, because when Mrs. Hawthorne came to know it she objected, & it was found that Mr. Hillard had signed it under the erroneous impression that *she* had been consulted beforehand. But I had carelessly taken the impression that it never went into operation at all—but had *just* been arranged (in 1868). I find that—reckoning the copy right from the date of this contract to 1868 at 12 cents per volume—*the great deficit* which I had found no longer exists;—and Mr. Clarke's accounts are consistent with each other. And it will be my *pleasure*, as well as duty to testify this, on all occasions & to all persons.

Had it not been for this mistake of mine, I should not have thought of asking for a verification by printers of the *accuracy* of the *entries* of the numbers manufactured; which did not seem to me to be unreasonable, when I thought there was an inaccuracy of several thousand dollars proved—by manipulating carefully your own (or Mr. Clarke's) figures.

I shall therefore, as Mr. Clarke desires it, go in after he comes home, and with my own eyes *see* the verification of his entries by the printer's bills and examine the reports of Trades Sales—proving that the sales of Mr. Hawthorne's books have been surprisingly small. And I trust you need not be told that I shall be *happy* to give my testimony that the business transactions between your firm and the Hawthornes, are legally righteous; and to give my assurance of the same to Mrs. Hawthorne,—relieving her mind of any doubts she may have entertained of not receiving her legal rights. But as that 12 cents a volume contract is proved by this examination to have been a great deal worse bargain for her, than even to have received only *ten per cent* during those four years, when she thought she was receiving 15 per cent, I do not suppose she will ever feel that affectionate confidence in your disinterested *friendship* that she once had; and I suppose she will always feel that it was not right for the firm to have paid only ten per cent for the Wonder Book & Tanglewood tales at the time Mr. Hawthorne believed he was receiving 15 per cent. But I shall advise her not to think of changing her American publisher for the remaining volumes of Mr. Hawthorne's works, since Mr. Hillard's arrangements are such there never can be any room for misunderstanding in future, & *the interests* of both parties are identical in the profits & losses that must accrue.

Yours, in the same friendly spirit as before

Elizabeth P. Peabody

I shall tell Mrs. Hawthorne that the sales of her husband's books are *not* according to their merit or the general impression—and this I am sure I can make her *believe* if she sees that I am convinced of it.[47]

The controversy would not have occurred if Hawthorne and his wife had kept records of their accounts with Fields or if Fields had done business upon an orderly instead of friendly basis. Mrs. Hawthorne felt that her husband was underpaid. A thorough comparison of his pay rate with that of other writers of the time awaits the researches of Professors Tryon and Chavat, who are examining the business relations of Ticknor and Fields. But from the information at hand, it appears that he was receiving about as much as other Ticknor and Fields authors of comparable popularity.[48] Also, it should be understood that Hawthorne himself was always completely satisfied with his pay. And the present writer can add that, as far as Hawthorne's relations with the *Atlantic* were concerned, he was treated as generously, both financially and editorially, as any *Atlantic* contributor. Longfellow and a few others were occasionally paid more but they were worth it on the score of popularity. Annie Fields commented: "Hawthorne loved and trusted his publishers, while they in turn were generous to him, though their wishes far outran anything

---

[47]MS in the Boston Public Library. For the details of the dispute, see Randall Stewart, " 'Pestiferous Gail Hamilton', James T. Fields and the Hawthornes," *New England Quarterly*, XVII (September 1944), 418-23; and "Mrs. Hawthorne's Quarrel with James T. Fields," *More Books*, XXI (September 1946), 254-63.

[48]In 1863 Whittier was receiving royalties of only five per cent of the retail price for the "Blue and Gold" edition of his poems (Whittier to Fields, March 6, 1863). The same year Miss Thoreau was offered ten cents per copy for the first edition of H. D. Thoreau's *Excursions* (Ralph L. Rusk [ed.], *Letters of Ralph Waldo Emerson* [New York, 1939] V, 339). And in 1864 Emerson received ten cents per copy for the "Blue and Gold" edition of his *Poems* and twelve and a half cents for the more expensive "Cabinet Edition" (ibid., p. 377).

they could do for him . . . and all the devotion of his publishers—proved by the constant reprinting of his books in varying forms, by newspaper articles, by private letters and conversations—was needed to create the popularity he achieved."[49]

Regardless of the right or wrong, the quarrel resulted in permanent alienation. Sophia was no longer inclined to confide in her old friends, and her departure for Europe in 1868 may have been partly due to this. In fact, the feeling remained in the Hawthorne family, and in the biographies of Hawthorne written by his descendants, little credit is given to James T. Fields.[50]

---

[49] Annie Fields, *Nathaniel Hawthorne* (Boston, 1899), pp. 88-89.

[50] See Julian Hawthorne, *Nathaniel Hawthorne and His Wife* (Boston, 1885), and *Hawthorne and His Circle* (New York, 1903); Rose Lathrop, *Memories of Hawthorne* (Boston, 1897). Upon the publication of *Nathaniel Hawthorne and His wife*, T. B. Aldrich, who was then the *Atlantic* editor, asked T. W. Higginson to review the book and to be especially severe with it because of Julian Hawthorne's malicious neglect of Fields. Higginson gladly complied; his review appeared in the February 1885 number. See Donald Reuel Tuttle, "Thomas Bailey Aldrich's Editorship of the Atlantic Monthly" (unpublished doctoral dissertation at Western Reserve University, 1939), I, 275.

Chapter XIII:

Thomas Wentworth Higginson

ONE OF THE most prolific of the *Atlantic* contributors was Thomas Wentworth Higginson, who contributed fifty-one regular articles and essays and twenty-five reviews by 1870. Before Howells joined the magazine, he was the man whom Fields relied upon for advice, special articles, and reviews when they were most needed. In *Cheerful Yesterdays* Higginson outlined his position: "I happened to be one of his favorites; he even wished me, at one time, to undertake the whole critical department, which I luckily declined, although it appears by the index that I wrote more largely for the first twenty volumes of the magazine than any other contributor except Lowell and Holmes."[1]

Higginson had not prospered as he wished under Lowell, "who strained at gnats and swallowed camels," and he was greatly relieved when Fields became editor of the magazine:

It was a change of much importance to all its contributors, and greatly affected my own literary life. Lowell had been, of course, an appreciative and a sympathetic editor, yet sometimes dilatory and exasperating. Thus, a paper of mine on Theodore Parker, which should have appeared directly after the death of its subject, was delayed for five months by being accidentally put under a pile of unexamined manuscripts. Lowell had, moreover, some conservative reactions, and my essay "Ought Women to Learn the Alphabet?" which would now seem very innocent, and probably had a wider circulation than any other magazine article I ever wrote, was not accepted without some shaking of the head, though it was finally given the place of honor in the number.[2]

---

[1] Thomas Wentworth Higginson, *Cheerful Yesterdays* (Boston, 1898), pp. 185-86.
[2] Ibid., p. 184.

Fields, on the other hand, saw in the writer a man who could be trusted with many of the keynote articles and reviews that he himself was too busy to undertake.

Reviewing was an endless job, and it was especially important to Fields, for one of the greatest advantages of operating the magazine was the publicity it afforded to books published by Ticknor and Fields. The reviews in the *Atlantic* were not fraudulent; in fact, the magazine had a considerable influence upon the book trade largely because of its deserved reputation for honesty; but the editor usually chose sympathetic reviewers for the firm's own publications. Higginson was one of the best reviewers of the period, and his reputation for plain speaking was not the least of his qualifications. During Fields's editorship he reviewed such diverse books as Thoreau's *The Maine Woods, Cape Cod,* and *Letters to Various Persons*; Max Müller's *Lectures on the Science of Language*; John Stuart Mill's *Dissertations and Discussions*; Horace Mann's *Lectures and Reports on Education*; William Morris's *The Earthly Paradise*; and Emerson's *Society and Solitude*. The review of *The Maine Woods* (September 1864) is representative. Higginson found faults in the author: his provincialism, his insistence upon seeing the best side of nature and worst side of man, and his lack of discipline in form and style. "In truth," Higginson wrote, "he never quite completed the transition from the observer to the artist." But then the reviewer proceeded to commend Thoreau's growing popularity, and concluded with the tribute: "Nature has awaited many years for Thoreau."

Higginson's articles are generally of four types: editorials on the Civil War, meditative essays on nature, literary essays, and special articles upon subjects of a current but non-political interest. As would be expected, the war articles show a firm faith in the Northern cause. "The Ordeal by Battle," published at the beginning of the war in July 1861, reviews the prevailing situation and emphasizes the advantages on the side of the North. "Regular and Volunteer Officers" (September 1864) praises the conduct of the regular army officers in the war and approves the increasing cooperation between regulars and volunteers: "It is pleasant to see how much the present war has done towards effacing the traditional jealousy between regular officers and volunteers." Higginson's most important contribution on the war is of course his "Leaves from an Officer's Journal," the record of his command of the first regiment of freed slaves. Published in three installments from November 1864 to January 1865, it is a first-hand account of the troubles, the skirmishes, and the heroism of the Negroes in the war: "I wish to record, as truthfully as I may, the beginnings of a momentous experiment, which, by proving the aptitude of the freed slaves for military drill and discipline, their ardent loyalty, and their self-control in success, contributed somewhat towards solving the problem of the war, and towards remoulding the destinies of two races on this continent."

Higginson's meditative essays are less timely and also less substantial. Like many of his contemporaries he felt or thought he felt a bond of sympathy with trees and flowers, birds and beasts, but his over-civilized diction prevented him from expressing it very effectively. Yet though he faltered in trying to communicate the feeling, he could say what he meant in theory, as he did in "My Out-Door Study" (September 1861): "Once separated from Nature, literature recedes into metaphysics, or dwindles into novels. How ignoble seems the current material of London literary life, for instance, compared with the noble simplicity which, a half-century ago, made the Lake Country an enchanted land forever!" One of Higginson's best nature essays was "Snow" (February 1862), which was commended by Thoreau.[3] The nature writings gradually gave way to literary essays, but as late as 1870, Higginson could still write them; "Footpaths" in the November issue is an example.

Such an essay as "Sunshine and Petrarch" (September 1867) shows the close connection between Higginson's essays on nature and those on literature, for this concerns both. It is a less serious discussion of literature, however, than "Literature as an Art" (December 1867) and "Americanism in Literature" (January

---

[3] Thomas Wentworth Higginson, *Letters and Journals of Thomas Wentworth Higginson, 1846-1906*, ed. Mary Thacher Higginson (Boston, 1921), p. 114.

1870), which together set forth the author's theories of the past and future of literature in the United States. In the latter, Higginson prescribes "Americanism" as potentially "the basis of all culture":

No, it does not seem to me that the obstacle to a new birth of literature and art in America lies in the Puritan tradition, but rather in the timid and faithless spirit that lurks in the circles of culture, and still holds something of literary and academic leadership in the homes of the Puritans.... How can any noble literature germinate where young men are habitually taught that there is no such thing as originality, and that nothing remains for us in this effete epoch of history but the mere recombing of thoughts which sprang first from braver brains?

The remaining group of articles by Higginson represents the topics of the times. A calm pronouncement against tobacco—"the use of tobacco must, therefore, be held to mark a rather coarse and childish epoch in our civilization, if nothing worse"—is the subject of "A New Counterblast" (December 1861). "The Health of Our Girls" (June 1862) is an essay on the unhygienic absurdities of civilized women's clothing and health habits. Another of these articles, "Letter to a Young Contributor" (April 1862), lists the usual precautions for the submittal of manuscripts to a magazine, neatness, care in mechanical details, condensation, and courtesy to the editor, and there is also an apology on the editor's behalf for the necessity of rejections. The article was a boon to Fields, but it resulted in many letters to Higginson from aspiring writers who wanted advice—among them Emily Dickinson.

Higginson's letter which accompanied the manuscript of "Letter to a Young Contributor" in January 1862 reveals the freedom with which he criticized Fields for the good of the magazine:

Dear Friend:
   I send the "Letter to a Young Contributor," which will cover nine or ten pages.
   I am sorry to say that this household unites in the opinion that February is a decidedly poor number. Mrs. Howe ["Battle Hymn of the Republic"] is tedious. "To-day" [Rebecca Harding] grim and

disagreeable, though not without power; "Love and Skates" [Theodore Winthrop] trashy and second-rate; and Bayard Taylor ["The Experiences of the A. C."] below plummet-sounding of decent criticism. His mediocre piece had a certain simplicity and earnestness, but this seems to me only fit for the "Ledger" in its decline. I could only raise one smile over the "Biglow" ("rod, perch, or pole"), but I suppose that will be liked. Whittier's poem ["At Port Royal, 1861"] is daring, but successful; Agassiz ["Methods of Study in Natural History"] has covered the same ground often. Whipple uses "considerable" atrociously at beginning of last critical notice, and "Snow" [Higginson] has a direful misprint on page 195 (end of paragraph)— *South* for *Earth*. I liked "Ease in Work" [D. A. Wasson], "Fremont and Artists" in Italy ["Fremont's Hundred Days in Missouri" and "Our Artists in Italy"].

The thing that troubled me most, though, was the absence of a strong article on the war, especially as January had none. I see men buying the "Continental" for its strong emancipatory pieces, and they are amazed that the "Atlantic" should not have got beyond Lowell's timid "Self-Possession." For the "Atlantic" to speak only once in three months, and then *against* an emancipatory policy, is humiliating. Perhaps I ought to have written and offered one, but I could not write when busy about regiments and companies, and after that I supposed you had a press of war matter on hand, as no doubt you did some months ago; but public sentiment is moving fast if events are not, and it is a shame that life should come from the "Knickerbocker" and not from the "Atlantic." You always get frank criticisms from me, at least, you know.

P. S. I see the papers treat the number well—but so they always do. At the lowest point ever reached by the magazine, just before your return from England, the newspaper praises kept regularly on.[4]

Higginson's part in the *Atlantic* is not to be passed over lightly. Though he is often overshadowed by the illustrious poets and essayists who were his colleagues, he had more to do with the serious prose style that was a chief characteristic of the magazine than any other writer between the resignation of Lowell and the appointment of Howells. This included the war period, wherein Higginson's matter as well as manner was authoritative *Atlantic* policy.

[4]Ibid., pp. 113-14.

Chapter XIV:
David Atwood Wasson

One of the ministers on the contributing staff of the *Atlantic Monthly* was David Atwood Wasson—"one of the ablest essayists of the decade," according to Mott.[1] His presence represented again the pervading moral consciousness which was characteristic of the times. Furthermore, he was part of the New England setting in which the *Atlantic* was rooted. Like many another New England clergyman, he took part in the revolt against orthodox religion—the spirit of questioning which began with Emerson and the Transcendentalists, came to a sort of peak in the sixties with such men as John Weiss, C. A. Bartol, and Henry James, Sr., and eventually led to the breakup of intellectual genteelism and to the religious chaos of the twentieth century. Nominally a Unitarian, Wasson was influenced by Carlyle and Emerson and Theodore Parker, and he renounced the established forms of religion and their formulas for salvation. Born in Brooksville, Maine, in 1823, he was educated at North Yarmouth, Andover, Bowdoin, and the Theological Seminary at Bangor, Maine, where there had been some hesitation about his ordination because of his radicalism. After serving as Unitarian minister at Groveland, Massachusetts, he soon broke away to form an independent church there in the 1850's. Though a hopeless cripple from the fifties onward because of an injury sustained in his youth, he was active as one of the organizers of the Free Religious Association, as a regular member of the Boston Radical Club, and as a contributor to the religious periodicals, the *Index*, the *Radical*, and the *Christian Examiner*.

He contributed at least twenty-seven poems, essays, articles, and reviews to the *Atlantic* during the editorships of Lowell and Fields. The essays, on such subjects as "Light Literature," "Individuality,"

---
[1] Mott, III, 302.

and "Originality" and their moral implications, were in the mode of Emerson or of Matthew Arnold but stylistically influenced by Carlyle. They were perceptive essays, showing considerable awareness of the philosophical trends of the time. When Wasson later took up reviewing, this awareness and his inclination to look at the whole of a subject at once, stood him in good stead. Still, for the *Atlantic* he was a minor writer except in quantity. He got nowhere with his poetry; his essays, though usually accepted, paid him very little. Only his book reviews were noticeably successful, and they did not contribute a great deal to his reputation because they were unsigned, even in the yearly index to the magazine.

The title of his first contribution, submitted while Lowell was editor, "The New World and the New Man," symbolized both his and the magazine's interest in the spiritual renascence thought to be in the making. One of his best essays, it was sent to the *Atlantic* through the efforts of Wasson's friend T. W. Higginson. It "received widespread attention."[2] Three other contributions followed in short order, and by the time Fields became editor in 1861, Wasson had had five essays and poems accepted.

The first contribution to Fields, submitted in 1861, drew a rejection. "The Sword in Ethics" was a patriotic plea written in the early stages of the Civil War, and when it was returned, Wasson rewrote it and submitted it to the *Christian Examiner*, which printed it early in 1862.[3] Another contribution, sent to the *Atlantic* at about the same time as "The Sword in Ethics," was not rejected however. It was a sonnet, "Time's Household," in which the author likened death to the assumption of a royal estate:

>Yet doth a voice in every bosom say,
>"So perish buds while bursting into bloom."

Sent September 1, the poem was printed in the October number. Wasson wrote at the time of submittal:

[2]"David Atwood Wasson," *The National Encyclopaedia of American Biography* (New York, 1907), IX, 99. O. B. Frothingham, "Memoir," in David Atwood Wasson, *Essays, Religious, Social, Political* (Boston, 1889), p. 58.

[3]Wasson to Fields, July 4, 1861.

David Atwood Wasson

My Dear Mr. Fields   Water Cure, Worcester Sept. 1: 1861

The accompanying poem insisted on pushing its way through my brain yesterday, in spite of many protests from me that I was just now too weak to be its conduit. Now it is done, I like it: perhaps you will. I think it is finished, but do not detain it for cooler inspection, because it occurred to me as barely possible that you could, & would like to, crowd it into the Oct. Atlantic,—as now is the time for this talk, so far as it is the time for any. I am afraid you will laugh when I tell you that the thing turned me out of bed ever so many times last night, & that I have got to be sick a few days—that is, *more* sick,— to pay for writing it; but if the *montes parturiunt* &c comes to your lips pray don't let it get over them.

I fear the "Sword in Ethics" proves longer than I supposed. It made but 36 pages in my writing, but covered more in the copy, as I learn. I hope bye & bye (not too soon) to send you an essay under the title (perhaps) of *Pro Patria Mori*, which shall *not* be long.

I am always truly yours   David A. Wasson

The essay "Pro Patria Mori" never appeared in the *Atlantic*.

In spite of rejections, Fields managed to retain Wasson's good will, and he soon received two essays he was glad to accept, "Light Literature" and "Ease in Work," which were printed in the January and February 1862 issues. Their brevity was one of their chief virtues, being less than three pages apiece. In the former, the writer attacked the escapist notion of "light literature": "The drunkard dreams of flying, and fancies the stars themselves left below him, while he is really lying in the gutter. There are those, & numbers of those, who in reading seek no more than to be cheated in a similar way." Equally felicitous figures of speech abound in Wasson's prose. "Ease in Work" propounds the theory that great works come from the "heart," and though they are the fruits of almost infinite labor, they appear as the casual effusions of a mind at ease. When he submitted the essays, Wasson proposed writing several more on "quite a number of thoughts and conceptions," if Fields was agreeable:

My Dear Sir   Water Cure. Worcester Nov. 1861

You will tomorrow, I think, receive two very little essays of mine, upon "Ease in Work" & "Light Literature" respectively. I at first thought of covering them by one common title, with the thought—to confess the truth—of slipping in others bye & bye under the same head. But on the whole I would prefer their being published under their proper captions only, without any profession of continuance, provided you do not object to contributions so very short—from one to three pages, say. Is this brevity objectionable to you?

In course of several years I have set aside quite a number of thoughts & conceptions to be treated in this brief way. My essays will resemble rather those of Lord Bacon than the papers of the Spectator in being not comments upon manners, but statements of thought. I mean that each shall be as complete in itself as any more extended treatise, & shall be strictly popular without any sacrifice of the thought itself.

I am now getting a trifle more strength, & think I will take up this branch of my work & go through with it. When I am more fully restored I shall return to the longer enterprises which were broken off by my breaking down. In the meantime these short pieces of work will interest without exhausting me, & will at the same time give me the feeling that my existence is not wholly useless. If therefore you like contributions so short, & if you like the execution of those I send you, then I think that this shall be the kind of work I will offer you, whenever I offer any, for some while to come.

Should these please you, as I trust they will, can you give one of them place in the Jan. number?

I require no answer by lettter. I shall pass through Boston on Wednesday & will call at your place of business between half past eleven & twelve o'clock. I write now namely to bring the matter up.

I should have long since thanked you for your courtesy in sending my MS to me; but first illness, then other causes & then *no* sufficient cause, prevented me. I was sorry that my "Sword" failed to meet your wishes, but on the other hand was glad to feel assured that you would print no line of mine for any other reason than such as your own judgment & desire should furnish.

Yours very truly
David A. Wasson   [FI 4357]

On November 7 Wasson wrote: "It is good that you like my little essays, & contents me much. You were kind to let me know so promptly." And in little more than a week his check came, well in advance of publication.[4] It was extremely small, only twenty dollars for the two essays, but Wasson was satisfied. Not primarily a writer by profession, he was happy to receive any

---

[4] Wasson to Fields, November 16, 1861.

compensation from a magazine with the *Atlantic*'s prestige. Lesser magazines were paying as little as a dollar a page for contributions by unknown writers at this time.

The next contribution brought more money. Submitted on January 3, 1862, Wasson received twenty-five dollars for it within a week,[5] although it was not printed until April. It was called "Individuality," the third of five contributions by Wasson in the 1862 *Atlantic*. An essay of a little over five pages, it begins with an affirmation of something very like the Transcendental oversoul: "There is an imperishable nature of Man, ever and everywhere the same, of which each particular man is a testimony and representation." It is the universal character of man that is important to Wasson, and individuality is merely "an accompaniment, an accessory, a red line on the map, a fence about the field, a copyright on the book." Wasson wrote his pieces for the *Atlantic* as well as contributions for other magazines, besides doing his usual public lecturing, despite a permanent illness that was particularly irksome now and kept him virtually imprisoned in his house and unable to work a great deal of the time. He spoke of his illness in the letter which accompanied the manuscript of "Individuality."

Water Cure Worcester Jan. 3: 1862

My Dear Sir

I send you herewith an essay for the March Atlantic, if you choose to print it then. It is longer than I wish, but I could not make it shorter & at the same time secure artistic comp[l]eteness—& I would rather write for nothing than write below my best. I feel pretty sure that you will like this piece. Miss Loring, who copied it, thinks I have never written anything, perhaps, quite so good. However, do not think I wish to forestall or bias your judgment. You will recognize two hands in the copy; for a f[e]rocious squall broke into my room & wetted the MS. But I think you will find it mended legibly.

Though this essay be longer than was proposed, you may depend upon my adhering to the plan of *short* essays. I shall try also to furnish one each month for a while as you kindly write me.

The fates were against me on my passage to Boston. I called at your place, but was almost glad not to see you, for I was that day

---

[5] Wasson to Fields, January 9, 1862.

suffering such extreme pain as totally unfitted me for conversation. I remained in the city over night, hoping to get release from pain before next morning, but was disappointed, & so gave up & came here. Some day, however, my wishes will be fulfilled, & in the meantime I may gain strength, & be able to bring more of myself to the meeting than my weak body is now willing to bear about.

I guess that my little piece in the Jan. No. was pretty nearly ignored by the papers. If this does not trouble you, it does not trouble me. To be a burden upon a periodical that I earnestly desire to assist & upon a man for whom I covet success, would indeed cause me some chagrin. Other than this I have no care about the matter. I long ago saw that if I should work purely as a thinker & artist & upon themes of permanent interest, I could attract little immediate attention from the public generally; & I long ago made up my mind what I would do in the premises. My illness & consequent limitations as to work combine with straitened circumstances to make adherence to that choice more difficult than it would otherwise be; but I seldom know what it is to feel discouraged, & now never know what it [is] to waver in my election. Meantime generous friends & sometimes a large-hearted publisher help me on. As for me, I really wish nothing but to do my work & do it *well*. I wish no *pay* for it, & what one piece brings me in money is valuable as it enables me to complete another. If I can do justice to my boy & find strength & means for giving shape to my habitual ideas, all that I ask for myself in life will be given me.

The "Sword in Ethics" with considerable modifications will appear in the Examiner. I wrote it when my life-tides were very low, & on reviewing it, found it very unequally written, as well as in some parts unnecessarily harsh; & felt that you were right in rejecting it. But as it is now, I do not dislike it, & some of the prominent views in it are ones that I have deeply considered.

As I lost the opportunity of seeing you, I thought you would allow me to write thus much to you, especially as my letter will require no answer.

Very truly yours,
David A. Wasson

P. S. I have an essay partially written & susceptible of speedy completion on "Hindrance" or "Help by Hindrance," which would be a little more pat to the times than this. If, for this reason, you would prefer it for the March No. I could have it ready, I think, by the middle of the month—though I *like*, when I can as well as not, to have a larger margin of time for elaboration & finish. However, a little work would make this ready.

In regard to the new essay "Hindrance," Fields replied that there was no need to hurry its completion; so Wasson detained it until February 12. Here again the writer showed the influence of New England Transcendentalism, by reiterating in his own terms the Emersonian doctrine of compensation. Wasson's view is extremely optimistic; all things in the universe, he says, tend toward final good; "All that occurs on a universal scale lies in the line of a pure success." In view of Wasson's own physical distress, this was indeed a courageous outlook. The manuscript of the essay itself was copied by Wasson under considerable strain, his copyist being ill and unable to write. The author apologized to Fields for his handwriting in the letter of submittal:

Water Cure, Worcester Febr. 12: 1862

My Dear Mr. Fields

At first sight of my MS. you will think the essay wickedly long, but a little inspection will show you that it is not so—only spread over a great deal of space. I cannot give you any such copy as our mutual friend Miss Loring prepares, but I hope you will acquit me of carelessness or want of consideration for your eyes & the printer's, seeing that writing still costs me a deal of pain.

Yours with cordial regard
D. A. Wasson[6]

On the same day that he sent this letter, Wasson received one from Fields explaining that "Individuality," the essay intended for the March *Atlantic*, must be postponed a month. Wasson answered with characteristic complaisance, for he was a most humble contributor: "Don't hesitate a moment to do with 'Individuality' just what may prove convenient, & next month do what shall be convenient then. Whatever you do will be right & best."[7] If "Individuality" was to be deferred until April, it meant that there would be two of Wasson's contributions in the April number or else "Hindrance" would have to wait until May. Never overeager to see his work in print, the author chose the second alternative. "The season of the year approaches which is critical for me," he

[6] See also Wasson to Fields, February 8, 1862.
[7] Wasson to Fields, February 12, 1862.

wrote, "& I shall not be unwilling to forget for a month that there is any such thing as work in the world."[8]

The last of Wasson's essays in the 1862 *Atlantic* was finished under difficulties even more severe than usual. "It would have come sooner," he said in his letter of submittal on April 2, "but that a foolish horse attempted to run with me, & compelled me to such an exertion of my strength as quite bankrupted my unsound spine, & prostrated me for some days." Entitled "Originality," the essay develops the thesis that there is no new truth, but that what we call originality is merely the rediscovery of ancient and timeless truth:

The great poets tell us nothing new. They remind us. They bear speech deep into our being, and to the heart of our heart lend a tongue. They have words that correspond to facts in all men and women. But they are not newsmongers.

"Originality" was accepted for the July *Atlantic*. As usual, Wasson received twenty-five dollars in advance for it, which he considered a "liberal allowance."[9]

But not all of Wasson's contributions were accepted; his poetry was especially ill fated. He submitted one of his poems on June 4, 1862, with some misgivings. He reiterated his faith in the justness of Fields's discrimination in his letter of submittal: "I am always simply grateful to you when you withhold from publication anything that you judge ought not to go out, even though my own judgment should differ." Except for "Time's Household" in 1861, not one of Wasson's poems appeared in the *Atlantic* after Fields became editor. Because of his philosophical turn of mind, his poetry, like his prose, lacked the lightness desired by editors of the sixties and later.

"Mr. Buckle as a Thinker," Wasson's next contribution to the *Atlantic*, was a reply to Henry Thomas Buckle's *History of Civilization in Spain and Scotland* (1861). Buckle's theory of history was based upon social determinism, derived from Comtian Positivism, which Wasson felt to be pernicious. When he sent his paper to Fields, Wasson explained his intentions:

[8] Wasson to Fields, February 24, 1862.   [9] Wasson to Fields, April 11, 1862.

David Atwood Wasson

Lawrence, Sept. 17: 1862

My Dear Sir

Here is the result of my six weeks in Maine. The essay is fearfully long, I know; & in parts it has to be closely reasoned; for I did not wish to grapple with Mr. Buckle's book to no purpose; but I believe you will find it clear & alive throughout. I have spared no pains to make it so, for I much desire that it may be acceptable to you; since the main positions assumed are such as I have for some while wished to bring before the public. The application, in particular, of the scientific method & the doctrine of homology to human belief, & the criticism of social averages, are points that I have long had in mind. They are hinges upon which much turns quite outside of my personal thought. I have no doubt which way the door will open in due time; but why may it not open rightly now?

Theodore Parker gave Buckle a great start among the liberals of America. This is the more to be regretted because the liberalism of America has not been associated, like that of England, with a nationalistic philosophy,—a fact for which many thanks are due to Mr. Emerson. I had congratulated myself no little upon this, & saw in the gradual implicit acceptance of a spiritual philosophy as the basis of American energy one chief sign of a great future for us. It is for this reason, above all others, that I address myself to meet this work.

Mr. Buckle's book is widely read now,—I did not know how widely until lately; & no one, to the best of my knowledge, has taken hold of him at all in this way. If they have not abused him, they have dealt in little but desultory criticism; which, of course, left matters just where they were before.

I had a delicate task before me in treating him as I desired so soon after his death; but I think his warmest friends will not deem that his ashes are rudely disturbed; while on the other hand I have freely spoken my mind.

If you *can* find a place for this ponderous paper, please do so. But you know well how it is with me—that I am heartily glad you are editor, not I (nor anybody else); & that at last my only desire is that you should obey your own judgment.

Cordially yours
David A. Wasson.

My place of address will be *Worcester* for the present.

"Mr. Buckle as a Thinker" begins with a statement of the three basic assumptions of Buckle's theory: a denial of free will, a denial of human knowledge beyond that of the senses, and an avowal of a social law that determines individual actions. "The question of free-will," Wasson asserts, "has at sundry times and seasons, and by champions many and furious, been disputed, till the ground about it is all beaten into blinding dust, wherein no reasonable man can now desire to cloud his eyes and clog his lungs." Immediately following this statement, he launches into a metaphysical diatribe on free will such that the present writer has no intention of following him. The real conclusion is simply that Wasson did not accept Buckle's premises. Such were the straits in which many New England religious thinkers were beginning to find themselves. It was well enough to disavow faith in Positivistic premises, but to try to disprove them by wrangling over Aristotelian categories and distinctions merely beclouded the issue. Yet Wasson's desire to see history in a spiritual light made it hard for him to confess, at the end of his paper, that Buckle's application of his theory cast a new light on history and extended the limits of human knowledge as they could not otherwise have been extended.

The fifteen-page essay on Buckle was appreciated by Fields, who printed it in the January 1863 issue of the *Atlantic*. Long before it appeared, however, Fields had sent the author a remuneration of forty dollars,[10] considerably more than he had been receiving for his short essays. Wasson's talent for conscientious reviewing of books was beginning to assert itself.

In the case of a minor writer like Wasson, Fields had little objection to his printing articles outside the *Atlantic*. Nevertheless Wasson frequently submitted his things to Fields first and did not print elsewhere unless Fields declined them. Such was the case in February 1863, when Wasson, upon receiving a rejection from Fields, sent one of his essays to the *Christian Examiner*, which printed it a few months later.[11]

As for matters of editorial trimming, no troubles arose, because Wasson was willing to let Fields cut what he pleased. When he sent his article "Shall We Compromise?" an attack upon the Cop-

---

[10] Wasson to Fields, October 13, 1862.

[11] Wasson to Fields, February 2, 1863, and Wasson to Annie Fields, May 22, 1863.

perhead movement, to Fields in March 1863, he half expected some objections to his remarks on General McClellan and gave Fields a free hand with them:

32 Dorne St. March 23:

Dear Editor,

Here's the Compromise. If you prefer to knock McClellan out of the last page,—& he isn't worth making anybody about,—do so. Say, suppose, During that month of (disastrous) delay at Yorktown. I am afraid it is a page longer than I intended. Perhaps I could have done better at condensing but for this horrid cold.

Cordially & always yours,
D. A. Wasson

Violent as the article was in its attack on Southern "barbarity," it contained no personal allusions. The reference to McClellan was wholly omitted and the following line was supplied: "During that fatal month's *siesta* at Yorktown. . . ." The paper appeared in the May *Atlantic*.

The remainder of Wasson's contributions were mostly book reviews. The Emersonian essay was passing out of style, and Wasson found Fields more eager to accept and pay for his criticisms.[12] The marked change in his type of writing indicates a rather sudden awareness on Fields's part, if not on his own, of his potentialities in this new work. Never having written reviews for the *Atlantic* before, he suddenly began in the latter half of 1863. His critical aims differed markedly from those of the impressionistic critics which were so prevalent at the time and to which Fields himself subscribed. Wasson's fundamental concern with artistic structure and overall meaning faintly anticipated the views of later critics, most notably James—and likewise his perception of literature as a projection of the writer's whole self. He wrote, for example, in his essay on "Whittier" in the March 1864 *Atlantic*:

---

[12] A letter from Wasson to Fields, November 23, 1863, acknowledges the receipt of $150: "Your note containing a cheque for one hundred & fifty dollars has come to hand, & will do my *heart* to live on a while." Whether this was for one contribution or several, it was by far the largest single sum Wasson had received from Fields, so far as the letters reveal.

We shall consider Whittier's poetry in this light,—as a vital effluence, as a product of his being; and citations will be made, not by way of culling "beauties,"—a mode of criticism to which there are grave objections,—but of illustrating total growth, quality, and power. Our endeavor will be to get at, so far as possible, the processes of vital action, of spiritual assimilation, which go on in the poet, and then to trace these in his poetry.

The point is not that Wasson's criticism was especially good, nor even that he had occasion to exercise these theories very often in the *Atlantic*, as most of his reviews covered expository works. But he was a critic with a critical theory, and his presence among the writers in the *Atlantic* is thus significant.

Usually Wasson chose the books he wanted to review. In February 1864 he prepared two of his own choosing, on John William Draper's *A History of the Intellectual Development of Europe* and Ernest Renan's *De L'Origine du Langage*. He wrote to Fields:

Worcester Febr. 1: 1864

Dear Friend,

If you have engaged no one to notice Draper's "Intellectual Development of Europe," please leave that work to me. I shall have to rap Dr. Draper's knuckles a little, I shall. He is able, indefatigable, & his statement is unexceptionable in form—creditable, in truth, as to manner & ability to American literature; but I have no notion of seeing History & Mind & Soul swamped in Physiology. This way of using smaller truths to strangle nobler truths is a kind of intellectual garrotting which isn't altogether to my mind.

I am also reading Renan *De L'Origine du Langage*, & shall like to furnish you a little notice of that. Not theological at all, you know.

You needn't write me. I shall be in Boston two or three weeks hence, & will see you. I write merely to prevent any engagement with another, unless some one will do the work who can do it better.

Yours as ever
D. A. Wasson.

Again in these reviews Wasson had a chance to ride his favorite hobby, exposing the limitations of the Positivistic tendency in philosophical inquiry. Draper's book was a rather abortive attempt to interpret intellectual history in terms of physiological cycles, and Wasson, who at all times insisted upon a distinction between body and soul, considered it shockingly inadequate. With Renan he could sympathize, for the French philologist attributed the origin of language to the spiritual essence of man, quite apart from physiology.

In May, reviews of both books appeared in the *Atlantic*. The second was never attributed to Wasson in the *Atlantic* Index, but presumably is his. He did not actually send it to Fields until a month after this letter was written, but meanwhile he wrote two others of his own choosing which were accepted.[13] They concerned Francis William Newman's translation of the *Iliad*, which Wasson proposed "not to criticize, but to bury," and Charles Kingsley's *The Roman and the Teuton*, which the reviewer conditionally approved for its humane and moralistic approach to history. The reviews, both quite brief, appeared respectively in the July and August issues of the 1864 *Atlantic*.

On the other hand, when Samuel Longfellow wanted Wasson to write a review of *Hymns of the Spirit*, one of the most popular hymn books of the century, by Samuel Longfellow and Samuel Johnson, Wasson did not write it.[14] And another time Wasson declined Fields's request for a review because he could not make anything of the book:

Dear Friend,
 I give up this book. The author has, I think, an idea, perhaps a great one. But he skips & bobs about so amazing that now I have him & now I don't; he is here; no, he is there; Lord save us, where is he? To a sober roadster like me, with small faculty for anything but going straight on, it is hard work to keep up with these flying gymnastics. So pray let me off.
Yours always,
David A. Wasson [FI 4348]

During this period Wasson was busy lecturing throughout the country on philosophy and religion, and when he was in Boston, as he often was, he always visited the Fieldses. His visits and his

---

[13] Wasson to Fields, February 27, 1864.
[14] Samuel Longfellow to Fields, June 1, 1864.

letters to Annie Fields show what friendly regard they had for him. One of his lectures, "Character and Historical Position of Theodore Parker," was written up as an article similar to those he used to contribute to the *Atlantic*. But he did not send it to Fields, though he spoke enthusiastically of it to Annie; instead he sent it to the *Christian Examiner,* which still printed essays of that type and which published this one in July 1864.[15]

The current course of lectures completed, Wasson had time in September 1864 to think of writing something bigger than reviews. Having sold his last straight essay to Fields, "Communication" (October 1864), a treatise on the propagation of moral truth, he felt that he had arrived at a place of greater importance, and he began to look around for new subject matter:

Worcester, Sept. 15: 1864.

Dear Friend,
    I'm your man: hard at work. No more preaching at the Melodeon & much more leisure to work for the "little Magazine" in consequence. I'll report myself before long. Two hundred dollars received: it looked encouraging!
    What a capital book that of Boker's is! I am delighted with it.
Cordially yours
D. A. Wasson

The new subject turned out to be an account of a trip to Labrador with an artist, William Bradford. Fields was glad to accept it because of the interest his readers were showing in travel literature, especially when it concerned the United States or nearby regions. The result was a series of five sketches, "Ice and Esquimaux," running from December 1864 to May 1865.

Ordinarily Wasson did not annoy his editor with last-minute changes in his articles; one case in which he did was therefore of some importance. He wanted to revise some remarks concerning his companion Bradford that occurred in one of his Labrador papers, but the manner of change was left entirely up to Fields:

---

[15] See the letters from Wasson to Annie Fields, March to October 1864.

On about the fourth page, perhaps, from the end of my concluding paper about Labrador I spoke of Bradford as "this true man of genius." It now occurs to me that I expressed an opinion to that effect in my first paper, & its reiteration in the last is superfluous. Will you do me the favor to have the words I have quoted exchanged for some neutral expression? I forget how the context runs, & therefore cannot suggest the change more definitely.[16]

In September and October 1865 appeared two essays by Wasson on Goethe's *Wilhelm Meister's Apprenticeship*. Three years before, Wasson had mentioned his work on this subject, which had then been on his mind for over six years.[17] He wrote to Fields in March 1865, shortly before the essays were completed:

Dear Friend,   Worcester March 6: 1865
Mrs. Wasson had mislaid your letter, but gave me, as she supposed, the substance of it. It has now come to light, & I see that you propose *either* a book-notice *or* an article. When we talked of it two years ago you thought it would do to allow me *two* essays of ten pages each. Are you still of that mind? I shall have to squeeze to get it even into that compass. But I *will* squeeze. I think I can give two essays that will not be altogether heavy & that will constitute a piece of real criticism, good for today & for another day too. It will help you the more because all will see that it is not written to order, but from conviction. I am already well advanced in the preparation of these, & can let you have them at no distant day. Suppose you let me try & see what I can make of it.
                Yours faithfully
                D. A. Wasson

On the twentieth the author sent the first of the essays and prepared to send the second within a few days. "I have risked being dry in the effort for brevity," he wrote, "but perhaps you will think have not risked it enough."[18] The papers were indeed a serious piece of criticism. Beginning with the proposition that *Wilhelm Meister* is "the typical history of growth in a human spirit," Wasson proceeded to enumerate the factors of spiritual growth as pictured by Goethe. The criticism concludes with

---
[16] Wasson to Fields, February 17, 1865.
[17] Wasson to Fields, October 13, 1862.
[18] Wasson to Fields, March 20, 1865.

an evaluation: *Wilhelm Meister* is "the one prose epic of the world, up to this date," for it succeeds in reconciling contemporary life with the eternal ideals of mankind.

Before the essays on *Wilhelm Meister's Apprenticeship* were printed, Wasson had, in May 1865, accepted the ministry of Theodore Parker's church, which he held until the end of 1866. His writing for the *Atlantic* came nearly to an end; two reviews in the December 1865 number and one in 1887, the year of his death, were all he contributed to the *Atlantic* for the rest of his life. In November 1865 he submitted a poem, but as usual with his poetry, it was rejected. He wrote to Fields somewhat disappointed:

South Boston Nov. 27: 1865

Dear Friend,

I thank you for your frankness. I like to deal with men who meet me in this frank & manly way.

But I shall not agree with you as to "The Mystic." I have kept it, not merely a week, but four years. The immediate occasion of my sending it to you was this: one of the finest men I know, who never uttered an empty compliment in his life, happened to see it, & "froze" to it astonishingly,—carried it off to bed with him & wellnigh got it by heart, & next morning urged me in a tone that in many years acquaintance I have never heard before to send it to the *Atlantic*.

I say this, not to urge its acceptance, for that question is closed, but simply to make it apparent that in sending it I have expressed my respect for the Atlantic rather than the contrary.

Shall I confess the whole truth? It is that, in my opinion, I have in this poem—if you will allow the word,—touched a deeper point than ever before.

But your frankness & straightforwardness are not the less admirable to me, that I must make bold for this time to differ from your judgment.

Yours with cordial regard
David A. Wasson.

I will call & get the MS. as soon as I get over a miserable cold which has shut me up for some days.

Another contribution, "Suffrage in America," underwent a similar fate. When he submitted it in December 1866, Wasson hinted that perhaps his usefulness to the *Atlantic* was past:

David Atwood Wasson

Sommerville, Dec. 25: 1866.

Dear Mr. Fields,

I am just completing a paper on "Suffrage in America," strenuously advocating qualified (of course impartial), as opposed to unconditional & indiscriminate suffrage. It is a matter on which I have meditated seriously for many years, & which I have now much at heart, not only because of its immediate practical interest, but because it involves the basis on which our government & all government rests. So far as I can judge of my own work, this paper is, in respect to literary execution, force of reasoning & breadth & originality of thought, as good as anything I could reasonably hope to do. It is somewhat long, but the number of special topics covered will prevent it, I think, from being tedious. I cannot but trust that it will attract, at least deserve, some attention in our country, & perhaps abroad. However, it is somewhat more important than literary success that I am thinking of.

Have you a place for a paper of this character. And if so, shall I send it?

Perhaps you do not attend to these matters now. If so, you will know what to do with this letter.

The Galaxy is open to me,—at any rate, I am invited to write for it. But whether they would wish such a paper as this I do not know, & do not care to learn until I hear from the Atlantic.

I have quitted the pulpit & betaken myself for good & all to literary labor of a more deliberate & reflective kind. If forced out of this, as I will not be easily, I shall go into business.

Yours as ever
D. A. Wasson.

Wasson's remaining years were marked by continued suffering. Though he worked for a few years in a customhouse, and then went to Germany to study, he shortly became partially blind and, for most of the rest of his life, was confined to his home in West Medford, Massachusetts, where he continued to study and write. After his departure from the *Atlantic,* he wrote not only for the *Galaxy,* but also for the *Radical Review,* the *Journal of Social Sciences,* the *International Review,* and the *Unitarian Review.* And after his death two books, *Poems* (1888) and *Essays, Religious, Social Political* (1889), were compiled from his collected writings.

Chapter XV:

Harriet Beecher Stowe

HARRIET BEECHER STOWE was the least dignified of the important contributors to the *Atlantic Monthly* during its first decade. In a magazine with a reputation for "austerity," her presence among the contributors must be accounted for by her popularity with the reading public. She was not only a rabble rouser, as *Uncle Tom's Cabin* and *Dred* had already proved, but a fanatic who could be expected to pursue relentlessly any cause to which she attached herself. In fact, her outburst in defense of Lady Byron, published toward the end of Fields's editorship, lost the *Atlantic* not only a great deal of dignity but also a great deal of circulation. Yet Mrs. Stowe subscribed to most of the principles that the magazine represented; only in her crusades did she go beyond the limits of dignity, and only one of her major crusades, the Lady Byron matter, was waged in the *Atlantic*. She believed in conventional Christian morals, and demonstrated it in everything she wrote. She furthered the magazine's emphasis on New England material with *The Minister's Wooing* and the *Oldtown Fireside Stories*. And she catered to the popularity of the Italian setting with *Agnes of Sorrento*.

Her feminine touch was of no little importance to the magazine. An examination of the advertisements alone suggests that at least half the *Atlantic* readers were women, and Mrs. Stowe in the sixties was the North's leading representative of rising womanhood. She wrote the "Reply to the Address of the Women of England" and the "Tribute of a Loving Friend to the Memory of a Noble Woman," in which she spoke directly of the social and cultural responsibilities of women, and she initiated in *House and Home Papers* the feminine movement for beautifying the home which continues to this day in such magazines as *Good Housekeeping* and *Better Homes and Gardens*. Indeed, even her fiction was notable for the prominence of female characters.

Except for Longfellow, Mrs. Stowe was the most popular writer in the magazine. For this reason, and because Fields really liked her, she was permitted many extravagances. She generally left all correction of her manuscripts to the editor and the proof-readers, and her inaccuracies in grammar, punctuation, and facts were so bad that "the text was largely rewritten on the margin of the proofs."[1] She usually insisted upon writing for other magazines as well as for the *Atlantic*, and she was one of the few major writers whom Fields permitted to do so. She frequently asked for advances in pay, and Fields granted them liberally, yet she could never be relied upon to produce her copy when expected, often taking on five or six other engagements before fulfilling one. Or when Fields needed one kind of article, she would be likely to produce another and insist upon its being accepted. Despite all this, Fields accepted virtually all the prose she sent him, for fear of alienating her if he did not. Her poetry alone he did not print in the magazine.

As one of the original group that began the *Atlantic* in the fall of 1857, Mrs. Stowe had contributed "The Mourning Veil," a short story, to the first number, and *The Minister's Wooing*, a serialized novel ending in December 1859. In 1859-60 she was in Europe, where she met Mr. and Mrs. Fields, and upon her return with them in June of the latter year, she began a correspondence with Fields concerning her contributions to the magazine, even though he was not yet editor.

She planned *Agnes of Sorrento* for the *Atlantic* shortly after her return from Europe.[2] The story had come to her while she was in Italy and was a special favorite of hers. She explained to Fields:

---

[1] William Dean Howells, *Literary Friends and Acquaintance* (New York, 1901), p. 138.

[2] Annie Fields, *Life and Letters of Harriet Beecher Stowe* (Boston, 1898), p. 283.

My dear Mr. Fields

Agnes of Sorrento was conceived on the spot—a spontaneous tribute to the exceeding & wonderful loveliness of beauty of all things there.

One bright evening as I was entering the old gate way I saw a beautiful young girl sitting in its shadow selling oranges—she was my Agnes. Walking that same evening thro the sombre depths of the gorge I met "old Elsie" walking erect & tall with her piercing black eyes roman nose & silver hair, walking with determination in every step and spinning like one of the fates glittering silver flax from a distaff she carried in her hands.

A few days after our party being weather bound at Salerno—had resort to all our talents to pass the time & songs & stories were the fashion of the day. The first chapter was my contribution to that entertainment. The story was voted into existence by the voices of all that party—& by none more enthusiastically than by one young voice which will never be heard on earth more. It was kept in mind & expanded & narrated as we went on to Rome over a track that the pilgrim Agnes is to travel. To me therefore it is fragrant with love of Italy & memory of some of the brightest hours of life.

I wanted to write something of this kind as in an Authors Introduction to the Public. Could you contrive to print it on a fly leaf if I get it ready & put a little sort of dedicatory poem at the end of it.

I shall do this at least in the book if not now.[3]   [FI 3951]

Arrangements were made for the simultaneous publication of *Agnes of Sorrento* in the *Cornhill Magazine*, published by Smith, Elder, and Company in England. In January 1861, Mrs. Stowe promised Fields that she would have three numbers ahead by May, so that he could safely begin the story in the May issue. When she sent the manuscript of the first installment to Fields, she wrote again:

My dear Mr. Fields

I suppose you think it quite time to hear from me. In fact my story was prolonged thro the holidays—& I have delayed sending you the story as I promised first that I might get myself out of the immediate

---

[3] Mrs. Stowe's letters are actually written in three hands, indistinguishable except by technical analysis; they are probably the work of herself and her twin daughters. See Forrest Wilson, *Crusader in Crinoline: The Life of Harriet Beecher Stowe* (New York, 1941), p. 9. The disregard for punctuation and the idiosyncrasies in sentence construction are reproduced here as faithfully as possible; they add to the "character" of the writing.

pursuit of the Independent & second, that I might once more re read my little darling, for whom I have a peculiar love.

Authors are apt I suppose like parents to have their unreasonable partialities. Every body has—& I have a pleasure in writing this that gilds this icy winter weather. I write my Maine Story with a shiver & come back to this as to a flowery home where I love to rest.

I have received a letter from Smith & Elder which ratifies the treaty. I send it you.

By the bye do you suppose such instalments *as to length* as I gave in The Ministers Wooing will content them—They were ordinarily about ten pages. I am never profuse as to quantity. It is irksome to me to spin out.

I send you by this mail the first number or what I would like to have the first number of my story—because it comes to a good stopping place. I cannot tell however until it is printed how it will run. Can you set it up for me directly & favor me with the proof. I will forward the rest in a day or two. Meanwhile, can you find me a copy of a translation of the Decameron. I want to run it over for one or two ideas that I am in pursuit of. Also "Promenades Dans Rome" by Stendhal or some such name.

My manuscripts are always left to the printer for punctuation—as you will observe. I have no time for copying.

This story was begun at Salerno in an expedition which we made from Sorrento to Paestum & thence back to Sorrento—all the scene is fresh as yesterday in my mind.[4]

The delay in sending the manuscript was Mrs. Stowe's own fault. She had meanwhile contracted to write a New England story, *The Pearl of Orr's Island*, as a serial in the *New York Independent*, beginning also in May 1861. Because of her financial ineptitude, her need for money now, as usual, was great, and she had been tempted by a handsome offer. Fields too had wanted a New England story, but she had insisted on *Agnes* for the *Atlantic* because of her preference for it. The two serials proved too much for her, and she finally had to put off *Pearl* after two installments had been printed, postponing the continuation until December, while *Agnes* continued monthly until its completion in the April 1862 issue. Both stories suffered from the drain on

---

[4]Part printed in Annie Fields, *Life of Stowe*, p. 285.

her imagination as well as her energy, but in spite of the author's prejudice, Fields got the worst of the bargain. *Pearl* was a huge success, and the circulation of the *Independent* soared; *Agnes* was one of the author's worst productions and brought the *Atlantic* little more than the popularity of a famous name. "If the story did not discredit the *Atlantic*," wrote her biographer Forrest Wilson, "it was as poor a piece of fiction as that magazine ever printed in its early years under a celebrated name."[5]

While Fields stood patiently by, Mrs. Stowe was not worried by her own shortcomings. She was receiving two hundred dollars per installment for the *Atlantic* serial and looked forward to fifty per cent of the profits from its later publication in book form. A letter which she attached to the manuscript of the January 1862 installment stated the highly remunerative conditions of her contract:

Dear Mr. Fields
 I send you Smith & Elders letter & mine. You see that the two first lines expresses their satisfaction at my acceptance & it closes with arrangements for payment. I did not answer any further therefore supposing the immediate forwarding of copy would be *all* that was needed. I don't see how any thing *could* be more complete. Ought I to write now?
                                         Truly Yours
                                         H. B. Stowe

                                                                  (over)
I should like to have a memorandum in writing from you in regard to the terms for Agnes of Sorrento which I understood generally were to be such as Mr. Phillips offered for the Ministers Wooing— namely two hundred dollars for each number payable on issue & half share of profits in book form. Is this your understanding.
                                         Truly Yours
                                         H. B. S.   [FI 3924]

Like Hawthorne Mrs. Stowe maintained an account with Fields from which she could draw money whenever she needed it, regardless sometimes of whether the firm owed her anything at the moment. For example, when her son Fred was appointed

[5] Wilson, p. 464.

second lieutenant in the Massachusetts Heavy Artillery in 1862, she ordered $250 sent to him from Ticknor and Fields to buy uniforms and equipment.[6] Her popularity made it worth while for the firm to comply with her request.

Finally in April 1862 both her serials were finished and she breathed a short sigh of relief. She wrote to her friend Mrs. Howard, "At last I am free. Both stories are finished, and the last copy sent to England, thanks to the girls' busy copying fingers. I have been pressed and overdriven."[7]

After a few months of freedom, she set to work in November upon a new article, her "Reply to the Address of the Women of England." In 1853 she had been the recipient of a finely-bound, twenty-six volume petition, containing the signatures of 562,848 English women, entitled *The Affectionate and Christian Address of Many Thousands of Women of Great Britain and Ireland to Their Sisters, the Women of the United States of America*. Its purpose was to further the abolition movement in America. Now in 1862 the English were betraying their principles by showing increasing favor to the Southern cause in the war—even to the extent of supplying the Confederates with warships. As a Northerner, Mrs. Stowe was indignant, and seized the opportunity to reply to the long unanswered *Address*, in order to use her influence against the prevailing attitude in England. Lincoln's Emancipation Proclamation had already been promised to go into effect January 1, 1863, and it provided the occasion for the "Reply." Mrs. Stowe could say: "Sisters, you have spoken well; we have heard you; we have heeded; we have striven in the cause, even unto death. . . . Sisters, what have you done, and what do you mean to do?" But Lincoln's intentions were not always clear to his contemporaries, and Mrs. Stowe felt that she must assure herself of the effectiveness and extent of the promised Proclamation before vaunting it forth in her article. Having been invited to a Thanksgiving celebration for the freed Negroes in Wash-

---

[6]Stowe to Fields, no date (FI 3925).
[7]Annie Fields, *Life of Stowe*, p. 291.

ington, and wishing to see her son Fred, stationed in the Army nearby, she decided to go to the capital to investigate the matter and to see the President himself. She wrote to Fields:

Hartford Nov. 13 1863

Dear Sir.

I have taken the liberty to draw upon you for one hundred dollars on account. The cheque payable to T. C. Perkins will come to you in a day. A sudden emergency caused by the missending of some money causes me to apply to you. From your question "if I wanted money" I inferred I might safely do it. At any rate you will greatly accommodate me by honoring this draft.

I am going to send you that article *but* before I send it I am going to Washington to see the heads of department myself & to satisfy myself that I may refer to the Emancipation Proclamation as a reality & a substance not to fizzle out at the little end of the horn as I should be sorry to call the attention of my sisters in Europe to any such impotent conclusion. You may depend on three or four pages at least —perhaps double that.

I start for Washington tomorrow morning & mean to have a talk with "Father Abraham" himself among others—"Eyes & Ears" is a good thing. I like it especially "Dog Noble & the Hole"[?]. It is charming genial reading for these war times—one wants genial reading too— ones heart gets congested by reading the newspapers.

Well Good night—they are reading the papers aloud & discussing corn, Wilkes & the blockade so with best love to Mrs. Fields I am Ever lovingly & truly

Yours to serve
H. B. Stowe[8]

The journey begun, she stopped in Brooklyn a few days to visit friends. Here she composed the major part of her article, but she wrote to Fields that she would wait until she had collected her facts and then send the whole article to him at once:

Brooklyn Nov. 19. 1862

Dear Mr. Fields

I have been proceeding prosperously in my article and have already written eighteen large side pages of letter paper—it is about two thirds done—the last part is yet to be written. I would willingly send you

[8]Part printed in Annie Fields, *Life of Stowe*, p. 262.

the first part for the press before I leave for Washington but think it is best on the whole to wait till I have seen how things lie there and then send all together. There is most cheering news ahead in the way of assurances that our war is to be put right through & that the proclamation is to go with vigor. We shall see a great first & I think I am doing as well for my testimony to it as I could ask.

With love to Mrs. Fields I am very truly
Yours
H. B. Stowe

Messrs. Ticknor & Fields
Gentlemen
 Please send whatever balance may be due me to Mr. John T. Howard in check on N. York.
H. B. Stowe.

Post office box 1840 New York. Will you get up New Years & Christmas Editions of the Pearl & Agnes?

The meeting with Lincoln impressed Mrs. Stowe deeply. Previously dissatisfied with his cautious procedure, she returned from the interview his wholehearted supporter, as may be seen by her ardent defense of him in the "Reply." Without revealing his specific plans, Lincoln encouraged her to print the article, for he too was concerned about influencing Great Britain.[9] Pleased with her findings, Mrs. Stowe finally submitted her manuscript on November 27, leaving Fields barely enough time to correct it and put it into the January 1863 number of the *Atlantic*, which appeared twelve days before the official Emancipation Proclamation. She excused herself for the delay by complaining of the "many interruptions and disturbances" that had as usual beset her:

Dear Sir   Washington Nov. 27 1862
 I shall mail with this my letter. I have written it among many interruptions and disturbances & therefore must beg as a favor that you or Mrs. Fields, will read the proof sheets and correct any mistakes. I have delayed it that I might get the latest possible information of what is likely to be on the First of January. It seems to be the opinion here not only that the president will stand up to his Proclamation but that the Border states will accede to his proposition for Emancipation. I have noted the thing as a glorious expectancy.

[9] Wilson, pp. 484-85.

I am in doubt as to what year that letter came. In the Sunny memories you will find the date. I say *four* years—you must make the figure right four or five as the case may be.

Sec. Chase & his pretty daughters spent last evening with us. Fred is with us in good health & spirits has just received an appointment on the staff of Gen. S[?] second in command to Siegel. We are waiting for the formalities of passing it thro the War office.

Again—as soon as a clear proof is ready send it to my husband. I hope the usual press corrector of the magazine will do what he has done for me. I have been to day to the home of the Contrabands seeing about five hundred poor fugitives eating a comfortable Thanksgiving dinner & singing Oh let my people go. It was a strange & moving sight.

Good bye I am ever

      Truly yours & your wife's friend to serve
      H. B. Stowe[10]

The effect of the article in England, not to mention the Northern States, was considerable, as attested by the letters Mrs. Stowe received from John Bright and Archbishop Whately and by other letters that were printed in *Punch*.[11] In the April 1863 issue, the *Atlantic* reprinted Mrs. Frances Power Cobbe's *Rejoinder to Mrs. Stowe's Reply to the Address of the Women of England*, originally published as a pamphlet by the "printer and publisher in ordinary to Her Majesty" in England. Mrs. Cobbe assured Mrs. Stowe: "The failure of English sympathy whereof you complain is but partial at the most, and for that partial failure we deeply and sorrowfully grieve. But the nation at large is still true; and wherever it has been possible to learn the feelings of the great masses, no lack of ardent feeling has ever been found in England for the Northern cause."

The only other article by Mrs. Stowe in the 1863 *Atlantic* was "Sojourner Truth, the Libyan Sibyl." It was the true story of a Negro woman who had traveled in the North before the war, lecturing upon "When I Found Jesus." Some time after the article was published, the author wrote to Fields that she

---

[10] Part printed in Annie Fields, *Life of Stowe*, pp. 262-63.
[11] Annie Fields, *Life of Stowe*, p. 268. See also Stowe to Annie Fields, February 10, 1863.

had "heard from old Sojourner—She is alive—has had my article read to her & enjoys it hugely—wondered this Stowe could remember so much" (FI 3981).

In October Mrs. Stowe began one of her most important works for the *Atlantic*, the *House and Home Papers*. She and Mr. Stowe had recently undertaken the building of a new house in Hartford, and it occurred to her that she might capitalize on her experience. Hence she conceived the plan for several articles on "home-keeping," as opposed to "house-keeping," supposedly written by the fictitious Christopher Crowfield. When she wrote about it to Fields, her mind was already made up, even to the hundred dollars he was to pay her for each installment:

Oct. 27.

My dear Mr. Fields

I send you the first of a series of papers to be called "House & Home papers"—which will run thro six eight ten or twelve numbers. The plan of this tho having a general unity does not force one to have one in "de rigeur" every month—& yet if the vein takes one one can have one every month—you understand. I shall want about a hundred dollars a number for them & we will talk about a book later. I have several more in my mind now—a sort of spicy sprightly writing that I feel I need to write in these days to keep from thinking of things that make me dizzy & blind & fill my eyes with tears so that I can't see the paper. I mean such things as are being done where our heroes are dying as Shaw did. It is not wise that all our literature should run in a rut cut thro our hearts & red with our blood. I feel the need of a little gentle household merriment & talk of common things—to indulge which I have devised this.

Very truly yours
H. B. Stowe

I am in Hartford now Direct to care of T. C. Perkins.
Love to the Great Fields beyond the smiling flood.   [FI 4002]

The *House and Home Papers*, which began in the January 1864 issue, concerned thrift, efficiency, and beauty in furnishing and maintaining a home, but the author's main emphasis was upon the moral and sentimental aspects of home life. Common sense and familial consideration were the watchwords, and the tone of the papers could be anything from sermonizing to humorous narrative.

The Stowes' new house, "Oakholm," was costing more than had been expected, and, Professor Stowe having retired to engage in writing of his own, Mrs. Stowe saw that she would again have to write furiously to keep up with expenses. She began negotiations with the *Cornhill Magazine* for a novel the following year. The novel eventually turned out to be *Oldtown Folks*, which she had long had in her mind, but several years were to pass before it was actually written. Yet as early as March 2, 1864, she wrote to Fields with the idea of printing it simultaneously in the *Atlantic* and the *Cornhill*.

With the *House and Home Papers* appearing every month and the plans for the novel pending, other opportunities to make money presented themselves, and Mrs. Stowe could not resist them. A Philadelphia publisher wanted to do a new edition of *Uncle Tom*; this was easily disposed of by referring it to Fields. The popularity of the *House and Home Papers* suggested the expediency of printing them as a book, which might well be got out for the Christmas season. The *Watchman and Reflector* had made her a generous offer for a series of short biographies, and in spite of her other work she accepted it at a hundred dollars a month,[12] thus bringing her income up to two hundred dollars, excluding book royalties. She wrote to Fields of her various undertakings:

Dear Mr. Field

I am going to write a letter now all about business in regular style first second & third. First then I got a letter to day from the Philadelphia publishers about the toy book Uncle Tom, which I answered by saying that so far as *I* was concerned, I was perfectly willing & referred them to you. I think it might be a good advertisement but I think they might agree to put your advertisement in as an offset. 2d I think from all I can collect that the H & H papers will make a popular holiday book (next Christmas) & that we had better make our calculation to get it out for that time.—What do you say to getting some illustrations for it?—3d The men of our time that I am now furnishing to the W. & R. with some additions might I think make another saleable book. What do you say? Now in regard to that story.

[12]Wilson, p. 499.

It is to be of New England life in the age after the revolutionary war & before railroads had destroyed the primitive flavor of our life—the rough kindly simple religious life of a Massachusetts town in those days when the weekly mail stage was the only excitement. It is something I have been skimming & saving cream for many years & I have a choice lot of actors ready to come onto the boards.

Of course you will represent all this as best seems to you in yr. letter to the Cornhill.

Business being over—How nicely Bayard Taylor's article was done. I am so glad he has set us right with Thackeray & Thackeray with us. Where & how is our Annie. We Fold our tents like Arabs in about 4 weeks & shall be preparing to silently steal away. The new house grows like the palm tree. I called on your place twice but you were not there.

Ever truly Yrs.
H. B. Stowe   [FI 3932]

But in spite of her industry, she was spending every cent of the considerable sum she earned, and had to write to Fields in May to collect what remained on account with the firm.[13]

The *House and Home* sketch for July 1864 is a plea to Northern women to buy more American products. It is Mrs. Stowe's contribution to the movement for keeping American capital at home during the war, and her paper lists some of the achievements of American manufacturers in imitating and often equaling French and English articles of clothing and household furnishing. Her letter of the third of June shows how much she depended upon Fields to bring her works to completion. As she requested, he added the date of G. W. Curtis' article "My Friend the Watch," an encomium upon the Waltham watch works in Waltham, Massachusetts; and he inserted the lines upon the Cambridge glass works that she included in her letter.

Dear Friend Fields   Hartford June 3. 1864
I wrote my piece in a sea of troubles—sick myself with a bilious attack husband sick & divers of the domestic trials of backwoods life piled on that. I had as you see, to write by Amanuensis—& yet my little senate of girls say that they like it better than any thing I have written yet.

[13]Stowe to Fields, May 1, 1864.

I have not the details or knowledge to do half justice to the subject but I hope it will prove *suggestive*. Please let Annie look it over & if she & you think I have said too much of the Waltham watches make it right—also—insert what I had to leave blank the number of the Atlantic in which that article occurs.

I wanted to add something on American glass—& if you could find any place where the following paragraph could be dovetailed in—do it—just after where I say a person might confine themselves in furnishing a house to American articles without much sacrifice—add

"We need go no further than our Cambridge glass works to see that the most dainty devices of cut glass chrystal ground & engraved glass of every color & pattern may be had of American make—every way equal to the best European & for half the price."

If Annie thinks of any other thing that ought to be mentioned & will put it in for me she will serve both the cause & me....

As the series drew to an end, Mrs. Stowe became more and more rushed. On July 26 she applied for an extension of time for her September article. As the paper had to appear on August 20, it was already late to be sending in manuscript, and because of the amount of correcting that had to be done upon all of the author's work, it was asking a great deal to postpone the deadline. At any rate, no paper appeared in the September issue. By September, still working feverishly, Mrs. Stowe found that she had more to say than she could squeeze into the intended twelve installments. At this time she proposed an extra installment;[14] as it eventually turned out, she wrote a whole new two-year series.

Since the popularity of the household papers was an established fact, a continuation of them seemed highly advisable to Mrs. Stowe. In fact, the rage for home-making columns can be said to have been definitely under way when a similar series began in September in the pages of the *Atlantic*'s arch-rival, *Harper's Monthly*, as Mrs. Stowe cheerfully pointed out to Annie. And at about the same time Madam Demorest asked Mrs. Stowe to write a column in her elegant *Mirror of Fashions* magazine. Not

[14]Stowe to Fields, ca. September 1864 (FI 3929). See Stowe to Annie Fields, July 26, 1864.

one to leave her successes unexploited, Mrs. Stowe had already arranged with Fields for the publication of the *House and Home Papers* as a book, [15] and now she wrote to him that she would begin a new Christopher Crowfield series in the *Atlantic* for double the price of the first:

> I want to write to you now, about my future engagements. I told you that Mad. Demorest had written to see if I would consent to write for her magazine. By looking over the prospectus of what she has sent me I see she intends adding a literary department, a family department, with her usual matters of dress & fashion. She has a very good woman who writes *well*, in the domestic department, she takes an interest in the ladys loyal league, & seems likely to have *good things said, in what people are* thinking of—& will infallibly, if she carries out her plan have a longer list of subscribers.
>
> You see whoever can write on home & family matters, on what people think of & are anxious about, & what to hear from has an immense advantage. The success of the H & H papers has shown me how much people want this sort of thing, & now I am bring[ing] the series to a close—I find I have ever so much more to say. In fact, the idea has come in this shape. How much easier to keep up a domestic & family department in the Atlantic than to try to add a literary department to Madame Demorest. Now I have projected the plan of a set of papers for the next year to be called Christopher's Evenings—which will allow great freedom, & latitude—a capacity of striking any where where a topic seems to be on the public mind & that will comprise a little series of sketches or rather little groups of sketches out of which books may be made. You understand Christopher writes these for the winter evening amusement of his family. One set will be entitled "An acount on the seven little foxes that spoil the vines"—This will cover seven sketches of certain domestic troubles. Another set is the Cathedral or the shrines of House saints—under which I shall give certain sketches of home characters in style contrasting with that of the legends of the saints—the shirt-making knitting whooping-cough-tending saints the Aunt Esthers & Aunt Marias.
>
> Now I could prepare my story for your magazine—but I do not feel that the public mind is just now in a state for a story. It is troubled unsettled, burdened with the *real*, the home nest is every where disturbed & the birds consequently flutter around that—& I myself having

---

[15] Stowe to Fields, November 9, 1864. See Stowe to Annie Fields, September 30, 1864.

these things now in my mind shall get them off piece meal for this & that paper if I don't do it for you.

I propose then, to keep up a domestic department—for the same price which I should want for a romance—two hundred a month. I have made just about that, this year dividing my forces here & there on different papers but I would greatly prefer to spend all my time & strength on one thing and I am pretty sure that I could make this thing more popular just now than the others. The story would be amusing & funny—but have no *practical* bearing. I should keep a month or two ahead so as to have abundant time. *Home* is the thing we must strike for now, it is here we must strengthen the things that remain —& I feel sure that here we could do something worth doing.[16]

[FI 3937]

Impatient for a reply, she wrote again—again setting forth her plan for two hundred dollars monthly. This time she added something, however. Although her first loyalty had always gone to the *Atlantic*, she had often contributed to other magazines when good opportunities offered themselves. Fields had hardly dared contest her policy, though he always preferred that his favorite writers write for his pages alone. Now she offered to become an exclusive contributor if he would meet her on her own terms:

three

Dear Mr. Fields. I have written you four letters since I came home & have nothing in reply. The first, had the titles to my chapters for the book. The second I forget what but the third, was a proposal to you to write for the Atlantic alone for the next year at the rate of two hundred per number & furnish either the story I projected or another set of domestic papers including several stories sketches & other varieties of a domestic nature on the basis of the H & H.— I have since received an application to write for a magazine—which I deferred till I could hear from you. The man is pressing for an answer. If I consider this proposition with you to stand as accepted I shall decline & I would like to know as soon as possible that I may not keep him waiting. I had rather write, for the Atlantic sole & only have to write for several if I can do as well by it you understand.

Truly Yours

I sent you the H & H papers for the book:—asked for the new ones to be corrected. Why oh why not write? [FI 3934]

H. B. Stowe

[16]Part printed in Annie Fields, *Life of Stowe*, p. 300.

Although he was still looking for the promised novel, Fields accepted the new terms, for the willful Mrs. Stowe would write what she pleased.

The first article in the new series, finally entitled *The Chimney-Corner*, was sent at the last minute for the January number. In the letter accompanying the manuscript, Mrs. Stowe explained that the subject had changed in her hands—a thing not uncommon in her way of writing. Begun as a slight domestic sketch, it became a tedious and maudlin message of sympathy to those who had lost relatives and sweethearts in the war. It runs the gamut of truisms about death, and ends, in the true Stowe manner, by recommending active social work for those whose lives are left empty:

Nov. 29, 1864

My dear Friend

    I have sent my New Years article, the result of one of those peculiar experiences, which sometimes occur to us writers. I had planned an article gay sprightly wholly domestic but as I began & sketched the pleasant home & quiet fireside an irresistible impulse *wrote for me* what followed an offering of sympathy to the suffering & agonized, whose homes have forever been darkened. Many causes united at once to force on me this vision, from which generally I shrink—but which sometimes will not be denied—will make itself felt. Just before I went to New York two of my earliest & most intimate friends, lost their oldest sons—Captains & Majors—splendid fellows physically & morally —beautiful brave religious—uniting the courage of soldiers to the faith of martyrs—& when I went to Brooklyn it seemed as if I was hearing some such thing almost every day. This & that family had heard of the death of a son—& Henry in his profession as minister has so many letters full of imploring anguish the cry of hearts breaking that ask help of him. He had heard from Mrs. Shaw & that poor Effie Lowel, said that she had only to wait for the birth of her child & then all she asked was, to lie down & die....

    Now my dear Friend I want you to insure that I shall *get the proof sheets of this,* as there is a very important correction to be made, in what I have said in regard to Protestant sisters of Charity—I have been studying the subject & find there are many orders & some who have done this work quite as well as the Catholics. It seems to me that some such movement may spring up out of the multitude of bereaved women, whose hearts & hands have been emptied by this war. Do you see or hear of Elizabeth Comstock and her mission...."[17]

With her plans for the new year settled, Mrs. Stowe tried to get ahead of her deadlines and managed to finish the February *Chimney-Corner* by December 9, 1864. Her pledge of exclusive contribution to the *Atlantic* was mitigated when the new Ticknor and Fields magazine *Our Young Folks* came into being, for she could contribute to it without betraying Fields's interests. She began with "Hum, the Son of Buz," a story about her pet hummingbird, which was the leading article in the first number of the new magazine, January 1865; and she continued to contribute frequently, sending eight pieces that year. Her contributions were a major attraction in *Our Young Folks*. Although she received only fifty dollars for a sketch or story,[18] she enjoyed the work and appreciated the extra money. At one time she wrote to Fields, "The Young folks beats the Atlantic. We all write better off our stilts—all of us" (FI 3931).

During 1865 her contributions to both of the Ticknor and Fields publications appeared steadily, despite her ill health and the constant pressure of duties to her family. One of these duties was the preparations for the marriage of her daughter Georgina to Henry Allen in June. Amid the bustle of trimming the new house for the celebration, she took time to vent her crusading zeal again in the July *Atlantic*. "Our Martyrs," the July installment of *The Chimney-Corner*, was a bitter attack against the defeated Confederate leaders and those Northerners—among whom she might have numbered her own brother, Henry Ward Beecher—who advocated leniency toward the South. She sent the article to Fields in May:

Sunday Eve

My Dear Mr. Fields

I am in trouble—have been in trouble ever since my turtle doves announced their intention of pairing in June instead of August, be-

---

[17] Part printed in Annie Fields, *Life of Stowe*, pp. 273-74.
[18] Wilson, p. 504.

cause it entailed on me an immediate necessity of bringing every thing out of doors & in to a state of completeness for the wedding exhibition in June. The garden must be planted, the lawn graded planed harrowed rolled seeded & the grass up & growing—stumps got out & shrubs & trees got in conservatory made over—belts planted —holes filled & all by three very slippery sort of Irishmen who had rather any time be minding their own business than mine. Then back door steps to be made eve troughs skreens & what not, papering painting & varnishing hitherto neglected to be completed—also spring house cleaning—also dress making for one bride and three ordinary females—also Fred Charleys & Mr. Stowes wardrobe to be overlooked also carpets to be made & put down—also a revolution in the kitchen cabinet, threatening for a time to blow up the whole establishment altogether also lists of invitations to be made out cards written in the family—also articles for Atlantic & what not so that at this time [of] writing I am reduced to a condition bordering on idiocy. Now for my trouble—I received my accounts from you last week with a check for 250 which, being at the time busy in superintending two men & one woman I put in my pocket for future examination. That is the last I know of them—& two days after when the press was over & I got a clear moment to examine them the whole package had disappeared check & all. As I had not endorsed it it can however be of no special damage & if you can send me another in its place I will destroy that when I find it.

Most probably I have as I often do in a fit of extra caution put them away safely somewhere & entirely forgotten where. The renewal of the check however would be a great convenience and save the little wits I have from going off in searching.

By means of these distracted labors our grounds do look surprisingly advanced for a one year old place and I do wish you & Annie could see them. Georgie is going to write her acknowledgement of your kind presents herself. Nothing could have been finer than Hawthornes works—it is really a mine of beauty and she & Allen are both delighted.

I send you to day, a Chimney Corner on "Our Martyrs" which I have written out of the fullness of my heart & which Mr. Stowe & the girls say ought not to wait till August but be published as soon as possible because it is on events & issues now before the public. Would it be possible to get it into the July number? I fear not—if not then it must go in August.

Look it over & see. I am going to Dr. Dio Lewis at Lexington after the wedding to rest. Wouldn't Annie go there too & let us see each other a little while?

Yours Ever
H. B. Stowe

P. S. The Article I speak of is an account of the martyrdom of a Christian boy of our own town of Andover who died of starvation & want in a Southern prison on last Christmas day—and it gives me a chance to speak what I burn to say of Robert Lee & Jeff Davis—& I do *wish* it could be got before the public next month. I shall send it by afternoon mail.[19]   [FI 4022]

The wedding celebration, though very tiring, came off well. The Fieldses, as the letter above indicates, had sent as a wedding present a set of the works of Hawthorne, richly bound in white, which pleased Mrs. Stowe so much that she ordered several sets of her own works in similar bindings. She was still getting her *Chimney-Corner* articles in on time, and she was doing her best to further the influence of "Our Martyrs" by sending offprints to important people in politics. She wrote to Fields four days after the wedding and two days before the *Atlantic* containing "Our Martyrs" appeared on sale:

Is my August Atlantic number in type. It it is cant I have *now* half a dozen copies of it to send to different persons thro the country. There is a false maukish pseudo talk of humanity & magnanimity to these cruel assassins Davis & others which I have resolved to do what *I* can to bring up the more legitimate objects of pity—the hearths & homes which this wretch has desolated. I want to send this account to some influential persons.[20]

Early in September Mrs. Stowe was beginning the last installment of *The Chimney-Corner* for 1865, and wanted to talk to Fields about plans for the coming year. "I have applications on hand from other papers," she wrote, "& first, I wish to know whether you wish to make the same arrangement with me as the last year."[21] Not until the end of the year was a new contract

[19]Part printed in Annie Fields, *Life of Stowe*, pp. 297-98.
[20]Stowe to Fields, June 18, 1865.
[21]Stowe to Fields, September 6, 1865.

agreed upon. Mrs. Stowe determined to continue the *Chimney-Corner* series but demanded the right to publish in other magazines, because, she insisted, the rising cost of living made a larger income desirable.

New York Nov. 29

My dear Mr. Fields

    I have all the fall been hoping to get to Boston to have a little talk with you on business—but perhaps it may as well be done by letter.

    You will recollect our contract for last year embraced the understanding that I should write for no other paper. This I have adhered to, only reserving to myself the right of filling up these existing engagements with the W. & Reflector.

    This year I shall feel obliged to ask you to remit that portion of our contract, in respect of this one fact, that the high prices make the liberal terms you offer in fact less than I used to have—as a hundred dollars buys only fifty dollars worth of any thing. I do not ask however any increase from you only to allow me to make use of what time remains over & above the supply of my agreement with you to gain something from other papers.

    The W. & Reflector, have been always men wholly honorable & gentlemanly in their treatment of me and are anxious to have six pieces for the coming year for which they offer so good a sum that I would like to accept thinking you would make no objections—& referred them to you.

    Tell Annie I am coming to Boston this winter & shall then have something to say to her. I shall spend there the week that Br. Henry is there sometime in Jany.

Truly Yours Ever
H. B. Stowe[22]   [FI 4007]

Fields, still waiting patiently for the long-promised novel, had to give in to this new imposition, and permitted Mrs. Stowe to recommence her biographical sketches for the *Watchman and Reflector*.

    The following months were as busy as ever. During the winter, the 1865 *Chimney-Corner* was published under the title of *Little Foxes*, and the author began preparing a volume of poems to be printed in 1867. The new series of household sketches, *The*

---

[22]Part printed in Wilson, p. 510.

Chimney-Corner for 1866, began in the January *Atlantic* and continued regularly for nine months. In August 1866 Mrs. Stowe began to think seriously of her novel—so seriously, indeed, that she suddenly realized she had no October *Chimney-Corner* to send. She wrote to Fields of her intention to send the novel to the *Atlantic* the following year at her present rate of two hundred dollars per installment:

My Dear Mr. Fields
    I have not written the October "Chimney" because the time has at last come that I am endeavoring to begin my novel. This month I devote to the recollections & quietudes necessary for the imaging in the waters of what is to appear. For the same reason, I must decline your wifes much desired & valued invitation to come to you simply because it would disturb the composure & quietude needed for the inceptive stages of such works. To move my writing desk from its quiet corner & disturb my moorings by new scenes would be like sweeping down a half built spiders web. I must dream & weave a while in peace & stupidity. What do you say to "My Grandmother's Kitchen"—for the title.
    Finally dear friend let there be no doubt of the material understanding between us. I understand that you pay me for twelve months to come the same two hundred pr. month that I have been receiving for Atlantic articles—& I continue my series in the Young folks. This will about exhaust my capabilities of work for the year. Is this to be so?—& was it not your desire that I should do just as I have. I so understood it.
    With best love to your wife & meaning to see you this fall in Boston I am
                                Ever Truly, Yours
                                H. B. Stowe
I have been thus long in answering your letters because they waited in Hartford while I have been here in Stockbridge. Direct your answer to Care of Mr. Allen, Stockbridge. [FI 3940]

    The October 1866 *Chimney-Corner* was never written, but Mrs. Stowe continued to ponder the novel. Nevertheless, a great many interruptions occurred in the following years before the book was finally finished in February 1869. In the winter of 1866-67 she succeeded, with the connivance of Fields, in urging her procrastinating spouse to print his masterpiece, the *Origin and History of the Books of the Bible,* which turned out to be an immense success, adding ten thousand dollars to the family fortune.[23] In February 1867 she was drawn into a contract with the Hartford Publishing Company to publish *Men of Our Times* in book form, a collection of her *Watchman and Reflector* biographies with additions. The additions caused her a great deal more trouble than she had anticipated. She solicited the aid of the Fieldses in collecting material for her sketches of Andrews and Garrison, while at the same time she had to apologize again and again for postponing the novel. At the end of the year she stopped work on it entirely while she finished *Men of Our Times* for a publisher who was not so lenient as Fields. Fields therefore demanded something to publish and was rewarded with the *Chimney-Corner* papers of the year before, which Mrs. Stowe insisted upon taking time out to revise. She was absent and idle— as far as her writing was concerned—for months at a time on her estate in Florida, where her finances had suffered a setback due to poor management. In 1868 she planned an article on the spiritualistic diversion, planchette, without results. She undertook the co-editorship of *Hearth and Home,* contributing a regular column to that magazine. It is indeed a marvel that Fields did not give up in despair; if his generosity could survive this ordeal, it was invincible.

As a matter of fact, in the midst of the confusion he was always ready with kind encouragement. Mrs. Stowe wrote to him on one occasion: "I thank you very much for your encouraging words, for I really need them. I have worked so hard that I am almost tired."[24] But his encouragement was more than words. During this whole period he was "subsidizing" Mrs. Stowe, as she once put it. From 1866 to 1869 he paid her ten thousand

---

[23] Wilson, pp. 515-16. Further details in this paragraph are from Wilson, pp. 511-31, corroborated by the letters in the Fields Manuscripts, Huntington Library.

[24] Stowe to Fields (per secretary), December 28, 1868. Printed in Annie Fields, *Life of Stowe,* p. 317.

dollars, "much of it in prepayments, that she might write with a mind at leisure."[25]

In the end Fields was pleased with the novel *Oldtown Folks*, which was, as a matter of fact, one of her best. He offered her six thousand dollars outright for the rights of serial publication in England and America and all book rights for the first year after publication. This she rejected. After years of waiting, Fields was not to get the book in the *Atlantic* at all, for she believed she could make more by the usual system of royalties than by accepting the flat sum. Furthermore, she said, the story was unsuitable for publication in the *Atlantic*, for the magazine's liberal religious policy would prejudice the orthodox Congregational readers she wished to reach.[26] Her wishes were not to be questioned; Fields published the book in May 1869 without using it in the magazine. Its sequel, *Oldtown Fireside Stories* which was equally good, compensated for the loss to the *Atlantic* when it appeared in the magazine in 1870.

While the novel was in progress the author's contributions to the *Atlantic* were necessarily meager. Between September 1866, when the last of the *Chimney-Corner* pieces had been published, and September 1869, when her article on Lady Byron was the sensation of the day, she published only three pieces in the magazine. These were "Our Second Girl" (January 1868), an unrealistic short story extolling the womanly virtues of humility and domesticity; "Tribute of a Loving Friend to the Memory of a Noble Woman" (February 1869), a eulogy of the Duchess of Sutherland, whom Mrs. Stowe had known in England; and "Little Captain Trott" (March 1869), a hopelessly sentimental characterization, Theophrastian style, of a baby. Though she was busy enough with her other work, these contributions brought welcome cash when she was able to write them. She confessed her motive to Fields concerning one of them, probably "Little Captain Trott": "I have a story half done & tho I am at present in a great hurry I will look it up & finish it & send it to you.

[25] Annie Fields, *Life of Stowe*, p. 326. See Stowe to Fields, December 1867? (FI 4999).   [26] Wilson, pp. 530-31.

If it suits you you can have it for the usual price you have paid for my monthly articles. I write it just now because I want a little of the ready——" (FI 3967).[27] She also contributed once to the *Atlantic Almanac*; her essay upon art in the home, entitled "What Pictures Shall I Hang on My Walls?" appeared in the 1869 number. Once again her remuneration was an important consideration, and she complied with Fields's request for a contribution only after making sure that the terms would be satisfactory.[28]

In addition to her other enterprises, she was instrumental in getting an article of Professor Stowe's printed in the *Atlantic*. It was she who made arrangements with Fields, and it was she who did the final copying of "The Talmud," which appeared in the June 1868 number. It took her some time to get "her rabbi" worked into an agreeable state, but one day she wrote to Fields:

Dear Friend Fields

I told you that my Rabbi last winter was up to his chin in curious lore & that I tried in vain to make him give an article in the Atlantic of some of the things he used to tell me.

But latterly there has been an article on the Talmud in one of the English reviews that has set him to snorting & he told me to say that if you wanted an article on the Talmud & Rabbinic literature in the Atlantic he'd send you one. He has succeeded after keeping a standing order in Europe for ten years in getting a very rare work containing extracts from the Talmud,—which I believe is about twenty folios. The publishers at last negotiated with the Ducal library at Gotha and got him a duplicate copy of this resumé which has all the Talmud in it that one man cd. digest in a life time & so he is prepared to tell Americans all about it. When begun—by whom & all that, with some of the curious things in it.—I think it will make a spicy article on the subject and I like to show those foreign fellows that we over here know a thing or two & have now & then a book.

I am about through with my task & have ever so much *in my head* on The Old town folks—& shall resume directly after the Holidays.
Ever Yours
H. B. Stowe

The old Rabbi is quite worked up he stalks the study & says I'm going into this Talmud business hammer & tongs—& I'l make a fancy thing of it. [FI 3956]

[27]Ibid., pp. 522-23.   [28]Stowe to Fields, ca. July 1868 (FI 3934).

Altogether Mrs. Stowe exerted a great deal of pressure to get the article out, and in the end she had to do the copying. But she wrote exultingly to Fields on February 16 that it was finally on its way: "Thus I have ushered into the world a document which I venture to say condenses more information on an obscure & curious subject than *any* in the known world."[29] Professor Stowe, besides being the husband of the celebrated Harriet, had earned considerable respect in his own right through the successful publication of his book on the Bible. "Obscure and curious" as his subject was, therefore, his contribution helped maintain the somewhat erudite tone the *Atlantic* boasted.

It was in the latter half of 1869, while the Fieldses were in Europe, that Mrs. Stowe published the article that was to have so great an effect on her own fame and that of the *Atlantic*— the Byron article. Her reasons for writing the thing are as obscure and almost as interesting as the Byron story itself. She met Lady Byron in England in the spring of 1853, at which time she wrote in her journal to her husband: "She is of slight figure, formed with exceeding delicacy, and her whole form, face, dress, and air unite to make an impression of a character singularly dignified, gentle, pure, and yet strong. No words addressed to me in any conversation hitherto have made their way to my inner soul with such force as a few remarks dropped by her on the present religious aspect of England,—remarks of such quality as one seldom hears."[30] A remarkably close friendship sprang up immediately, though the women met only a few times. Their relationship has been described by an enemy:

An intimacy sprang up between the two ladies on the anti-slavery and negro question—the chief, though by no means the only, sympathetic bond between them. They were both literary; both what used to be called "blues"; both professional philanthropists,—both strong-minded women; both celebrated, though in very different ways; and of tastes, and of modes of looking at men and things, and at the world in general, that seem to have been remarkably congenial. The intimacy

---

[29] Printed in Annie Fields, *Life of Stowe*, p. 379.
[30] Ibid., p. 201.

thus formed soon expanded into an ardent friendship, such as commonly occurs only among gushing young ladies at school or among older ladies who think that they have suffered long at the hands of the other sex, or who look down upon that sex from the lofty pedestal of moral virtue to which they imagine that they have clambered.[31]

Mrs. Stowe's letter to Lady Byron following their visit in 1857 strikingly corroborates this interpretation: "I left you," it begins, "with a strange sort of yearning, throbbing feeling; you make me feel quite as I did years ago, a sort of girlishness quite odd for me."[32] It was at this last meeting that Mrs. Stowe had been entrusted with the tale of Lord Byron's incest. When asked whether it should not be revealed immediately, she replied that Lady Byron should not try to undergo the scandal during her lifetime but should leave the facts in the hands of "some discreet friends." "There is nothing covered that shall not be revealed, neither hid that shall not be known," she quoted.[33]

Lady Byron died in 1860. In the February 1861 issue of the *Atlantic*, Harriet Martineau published a purely laudatory memoir of her, but it was not until Mrs. Stowe took it upon herself to awaken a deluded world that any public mention was made of the ugly details. Mrs. Stowe said in her article that she had waited patiently for someone to vindicate her abused heroine, but finding no one, she felt called upon to do it herself. Her immediate incitement, she asserted, was the publication of the *Recollections of Lord Byron* by the Countess Guiccioli, Byron's mistress during his late Italian years. This book, of course, praised Byron at the expense of his wife. Later, in *Lady Byron Vindicated*, which was really an attempted vindication of Mrs. Stowe, written after the furor caused by the *Atlantic* article had made a reply imperative, Mrs. Stowe named a reviewer in *Blackwood's Magazine* as the real culprit who had drawn forth her tirade. The

---

[31] Charles Mackay, *Medora Leigh*, in John Drinkwater, *The Pilgrim of Eternity* (London, 1925), pp. 32-33.

[32] Annie Fields, *Life of Stowe*, p. 236.

[33] Ibid., p. 321.

Blackwood's review, she said, attempted to authorize the book and disseminate its falsities upon a guileless public. Actually, however, the *Blackwood's* article could have had nothing to do with it, for it did not appear until some time after Mrs. Stowe's was completed and sent to the editor.[34]

Her real reason for publishing the exposé was her infatuation for Lady Byron and her inability to conceive of any falsehood or error in her friend. It never occurred to her to question what Lady Byron told her, although her whole theory depended upon its truth. Forrest Wilson believes her inner motive was a desire to glorify her intimacy with the famous lady: "Whether she recognized it or not, a small, selfish voice was whispering to her that in telling this unsavoury story she was proclaiming to the world the glamorous, stupendous fact that she, Harriet Beecher Stowe, had been the bosom friend of Byron's wife and widow, the sharer of her most intimate secrets."[35] There is little doubt of the truth in this. Lady Byron was not only the wife of an immortal poet, she was also the wife of a lord; and Mrs. Stowe had a romantic respect for titles despite her democratic rodomontade. But in the end, she was motivated by her irrepressible zeal for crusading.

The fundamental revelation of the article, "The True Story of Lady Byron's Life," was Byron's incest with his half-sister, Augusta Leigh. This point has never been disproved, though it is still questioned. Almost everything else in the article was wrong. Critics were quick to point out the inaccuracy in the statement that Byron's marriage lasted two years, when in reality it was little more than one. Other supposed facts were highly questionable, and the quotations were nearly all inaccurate. Furthermore the details were made as vague as possible, for propriety's sake, and there was no attempt to prove the authenticity of the accusations. Incest was never actually named in the article, nor was the object of it; the following passage was the only hint:

[34] Wilson, pp. 550-51.
[35] Ibid., p. 536.

He fell into the depths of a secret adulterous intrigue with a blood relation, so near in consanguinity that discovery must have been utter ruin and expulsion from civilized society.

Until persuaded by Holmes or someone else who read her manuscript, Mrs. Stowe made no explanation at all of where her information came from. Upon consideration, she did add a note to the end of her article telling of her last meeting with Lady Byron.

But the grossest fault in the article was the hysterical over-dramatization into which Mrs. Stowe's fervor led her. She strove to rescue "the youth of America" from "that brilliant, seductive genius" whose "better feelings [were] choked and overgrown by the thorns of base, unworthy passions." The "angelic" Lady Byron, "with no one to help or counsel her but Almighty God . . . wrestled and struggled with fiends of darkness for the redemption of her husband's soul." On the whole, it was more than even the Victorian mind could take, and the reaction surprised everyone.

Because of Fields's absence, the responsibility for accepting or rejecting the article was Howells', though he relied upon the advice of Holmes, Lowell, and Osgood. Beginning the article shortly after her return from Florida in May 1869, Mrs. Stowe sent the first proofs to Dr. Holmes, whom she especially trusted as an adviser. In writing to him on June 26, she described the circumstances that had led her to act. She declared that Lady Byron had "lived under a weight of slanders and false imputations laid upon her by her husband." The afflicted woman had told her story to Mrs. Stowe, with "almost the solemnity of a deathbed confession," so that the American as an outsider could advise her impersonally as to publishing the truth. Mrs. Stowe had advised against it; but now that Lady Byron was no longer alive to suffer from the publicity, the authoress was determined to defend her memory against the "unsparing attack" of the Guiccioli book. She wanted from Holmes, she said, "*not* your advice as to whether the main facts shall be told, for on this point I am so resolved that I frankly say advice would do me no good. But you might help me, with your delicacy and insight, to make the *manner of tell-*

ing more perfect, and I want to do it as wisely and well as such story can be told."[36] After such an injunction as that, Holmes did not try to dissuade her from publishing, but he did make some revisions in her chaotic "manner of telling." In his letter to Fields in July he reported that "she asked me to look over the proofs which I did very diligently and made various lesser suggestions which she received very kindly and adopted."[37]

Howells seemed to approve of the article in general though he saw its faults as clearly as anybody, but his hands were tied. He was afraid to reject it for fear of losing one of the best contributors, yet he could not even get her to correct her proofs. He had Holmes's counsel to rely on, but Lowell disapproved utterly. He reported to Fields, a few days after the article came out in the September *Atlantic*, that he had done his best under the circumstances, but that his corrections were "done hastily, with the printers at my back, and with a view to leave everything, as nearly as possible, just as Mrs. Stowe had written it."[38]

The public reaction to the article was far beyond anything the *Atlantic* had ever gone through. Both the British and American presses were pitiless in their attacks on Mrs. Stowe. Justin McCarthy in a virulent review in the *New York Independent* said: "I do not think that Mrs. Stowe has done much to serve the memory of her friend, and I know she has done much to injure her own fame."[39] It was all too true. Abusive cartoons appeared in the *Tomahawk* and *Fun Magazine* among others.[40] Dickens wrote to Fields from Gad's Hill: "Wish you had had nothing to do with the Byron matter. Wish Mrs. Stowe was in the pillory."[41] Lowell, if he ever really believed the exposé, never approved the publishing of it. Holmes was one of the few who stood by the

---

[36] Annie Fields, *Life of Stowe*, pp. 319-20.
[37] Oliver Wendell Holmes to Fields, July 10, 1869.
[38] William Dean Howells to Fields, August 24, 1869.
[39] Wilson, p. 540.
[40] Ibid., facing p. 538. Drinkwater, facing p. 20.
[41] Charles Dickens to Fields, October 6, 1869, in Howe, *Memories of a Hostess*, p. 191.

authoress; his consolatory letter did much to keep up her spirits.[42] The *Atlantic*'s subscription list plunged.

The reviews demanded a reply, and Mrs. Stowe set furiously to work preparing a book in which she would array her evidence in a more complete and orderly fashion. During this period her correspondence was with Fields's partner, Osgood—as if she were afraid to face Fields—although the editor returned to Boston while the book was in progress. "After I have made my final revisions *on that* [proofsheets]," she wrote to Osgood, "then I must consult Henry & Mr. Fields & you may consult Dr. Holmes & any other men you choose to see it—before it is finally *cast*"[43] (FI 24351). Eventually Fields, seeing there was nothing to be done, was conciliated. The book, *Lady Byron Vindicated*, was published in January 1870 but did little to assuage the public feeling. The truth of the account of the Byron scandal still rested upon the words of Lady Byron—few doubted Mrs. Stowe's veracity in reporting them. Whether or not the charges are true, Mrs. Stowe's article and book are still indispensable as data for the study of Byron. She failed in whitewashing Lady Byron, however, and she did her own fame irreparable damage.

Months before the Byron article was written and even before Mrs. Stowe's trip to Florida in the spring of 1869, she had begun her series of New England tales, eventually called *Oldtown Fireside Stories*. Based upon the boyhood reminiscences of her husband, Calvin Stowe, in his native Natick, Massachusetts, it was composed of materials left over from the novel, *Oldtown Folks*. By March 2, 1869, shortly after arriving in Florida, she had completed two stories, which she sent to Fields with appropriate explanation:

---

[42] James Russell Lowell to Edmund Quincy, September 15, 1869, in James Russell Lowell, *New Letters of James Russell Lowell*, ed. M. A. De Wolfe Howe (New York, 1932), pp. 146-47. Oliver Wendell Holmes to Stowe, September 25, 1869, in John T. Morse, Jr., *Life and Letters of Oliver Wendell Holmes* (Boston, 1896), II, 228.

[43] See Wilson, pp. 541-42, 545.

Fields of the Atlantic Monthly

March 2. 1869

Dear Mr. Fields

I inclose you this week no. 2 of Old Town Firelight Stories. The origin of it is this. There was an amount of curious old Natick tradition & stories that I could not work into Old town Folks without making the book too bulky & still that has great attractions for my imagination.

Just for the sake of diverting myself & making myself laugh and dream I am writing out these. I do not know how far a series of yankee stories told in Yankee dialect may do—but to me it is very fascinating to write it. I send you by this mail the second of the series. The third is to be a story of the Indian Wars—& the fourth of the witchcraft & then there are some of *pure* fun like the adventures of old Father Horner of Newton.

Do you want to engage the set for the Atlantic?—I write more readily for the Atlantic—and the set ought to go into the same periodical.

The impulse to write them has come on me all of a sudden and I can finish & send them on rapidly if I keep on feeling as I do now. It strikes me that a series of short stories each complete in itself is a thing that the Atlantic needs. I should like to furnish twelve of them.

Whether I shall make Sam the only narrator or whether Aunt Lois and Grandmamma shall not each have a legend is not certain. There is one thing I wish to have you expound to my accurate friend & family connection Mr. Bigelow, when he reads my proof of yankee talk. The genuine yankee always calls things this ere, and that are.

This ere woman and that 'are man.

Now I always spell them according to the sound this *ere* & that *are* —but my accurate friend Mr. Bigelow always alters it & won't let me print "that *are*" simply because being a contraction of *there* it is more accurate to spell it "that 'ere." Now please ask him to let me have it printed *my* way in future. You see I have taken for granted that you will want the series for the Atlantic & if so please let me know & I will finish up now while the spirit is on me and get em into your hands.

I have heard of your box on the way. I wish I could send you and Annie some of our orange blossoms & oranges. We have both now.

Mr. Osgood thought of making a *childs* book of Pussy Willow. Will you do it this fall. If so if you will send me the numbers I will revise it.

Yours Ever
H. B. Stowe[44]

[44]Part printed in Wilson, p. 532.

Fields was happy to take the series, but because of the Byron trouble it was a full year before anything further was done about it. In the spring of 1870 the author agreed to send the rest of the stories. By this time she was again in Florida trying to escape the noise of the Byron controversy, and she wrote to Annie on March 9:

> I received within a few days a box of books—also a letter from you & one from Mr. Fields on business.
> Say to him that I will furnish the series as far as they go at the terms named. There may be twelve or there may be less—according as they come or as the spirits from the vasty deep hand them up. I am writing them as a pure recreative movement of mind to divert myself from the stormy unrestful present. The Byron controversy still rages as I am informed for I read nothing on that subject having departed all that. My Lord & head, who occasionally keeps me informed on how it is going—but I am being chatelaine of a Florida farm....
> But to return to those sketches, Mr. Fields objects to the title "fire light papers." I wanted to express the idea that these were the Chimney Corner stories related by fire light in the great kitchen. I would have said Old town Chimney Corner Stories, only I had had one "Chimney Corner book." Suppose we call them "Old Town fireside Stories (or legends.") This to be the title of the series, & then each one to have its title besides. The first story should be called "The Ghost in Old Cacks Mill." I forgot to put its specific title to it.

Some of the stories were in Fields's hands that same month, and he ventured to criticize them. As usual she accepted the criticism graciously:

> Mandarin March 21, 1870
>
> Dear Mr. Fields.
> The criticism that you make about some paragraphs in the mss which recall sentences in the book is a just one. I thought of it myself & think it would be reason enough for striking out these paragraphs if you would just do it for me. Please do.
> It is important for me in order to arrange for some business to know how much money is likely to be due on account in May. Will you be so good as have a rough estimate made & sent me that I may know how much I am likely to have. I wish with all my heart you and Annie were here to hear our birds sing and smell orange blossoms and eat oranges. We are having heavenly weather. Mr. &

Mrs. Howard are making us a visit. When we have friends here then only do we really fully enjoy our place & some time I hope we shall see you.

           Yours Ever
           H. B. S.

The writing of the stories proceeded rapidly in spite of the continual strain of her other activities. Again pressed for money, she had again overburdened herself with work. She had begun a novel, *Pink and White Tyranny*, intended for a new magazine, the *Christian Union*, which had been purchased by the Beechers and the Howards, and for which she also wrote articles. She was advertised as a contributor to the *Revolution*, a women's suffrage journal, and she was still writing for *Our Young Folks*. She still had the responsibility of her Florida investment, and she was trying to sell her house in Hartford. Nevertheless, by May 10, 1870, she had sent five of the stories and was planning an edition in book form.[45] The sixth and final story, "The Ghost in the Cap'n Brown House," though begun in the spring, was not finished until later in the year. "Bye the bye," she wrote to Fields, "I must delay sending you the Ghost in the Captain Brown house till I can go to Natick & make a personal inspection of the premises & give it to you *hot*" (FI 3939).[46] It turned out to be a good ghost story, told in a spirit of mock reproach toward those who have not enough imagination to believe in ghosts. "Why, Aunt Lois don't even believe the stories in Cotton Mather's Magnolia," says the Yankee narrator. All six of the *Oldtown Fireside Stories* appeared in the *Atlantic* between June and December 1870. They were among Mrs. Stowe's best productions—"excellent depictions of New England," according to Professor Walter Blair—and they had considerable influence upon the work of the later local colorists.[47] The amusing narrator, Sam Lawson, became a household favorite; and when the stories were published as a book in 1872,

---

[45] Stowe to Fields.

[46] Printed in Annie Fields, *Life of Stowe*, p. 324.

[47] Walter Blair, *Native American Humor (1800-1900)* (New York, 1937), pp. 124-43.

they proved that the author had not lost her following despite her Byronic escapade.

The *Oldtown Fireside Stories* were the last of Mrs. Stowe's contributions for several years. With Fields's retirement at the end of 1870, she gave up her yearly contracts and devoted her time to other publications or to none at all. In 1871 she wrote a novel, *My Wife and I*, for the *Christian Union*, but in August she wrote to Annie: "After this year I hope to have a little rest & above all things I won't be hampered with a serial to write."[48] She continued to correspond with the Fieldses, and in 1881 she hoped for a return of the old days when she heard that Fields was again to become editor of the *Atlantic*.[49] But the rumor of Fields's return proved false.

A few months later her old editor was dead. Writing to her son Charles, Mrs. Stowe enumerated some of Fields's virtues. "He had a habit of quiet benevolence," she said; "he did habitually and quietly more good to everybody he had to do with than common."[50] Mrs. Stowe had reason to be thankful for his "quiet benevolence." If he did not contribute greatly to her fame, he made it possible and pleasant for her to live securely by her writing.

---

[48]Stowe to Annie Fields, August 4, 1870. Printed in Annie Fields, *Life of Stowe*, p. 324.

[49]Stowe to Fields, January 1, 1881.

[50]Annie Fields, *Life of Stowe*, p. 380.

Chapter XVI:

The Transcendentalists

THE SIGNIFICANCE of the Transcendentalists in the *Atlantic Monthly* is hard to define for the same reason that it is hard to define Transcendentalism itself. To begin with, Who were the Transcendentalists? For our present purposes, an arbitrary grouping of those contributors whom most literary historians classify in this category will suffice: Emerson, Thoreau, Bronson Alcott, Mrs. A. M. Diaz, C. P. Cranch, and G. W. Curtis. What did they have in common? This is more difficult to resolve. American Transcendentalists usually were basically concerned with the development and expression of their individual character, in which they placed a sometimes exaggerated faith; they believed in a rather vague God who could be understood through mystic contemplation and who had placed a divine essence in every man; hence, their contemplation of nature was a sort of religious activity which they believed brought them closer to a realization of themselves and of life's mysteries; and since all things were possible to him who could achieve this realization, they were generally optimistic about the future of individuals and society. But these beliefs were shared by many *Atlantic* contributors, not all of whom appear in our arbitrary list. The truth is that the Transcendental movement in its many ramifications had a far greater effect upon the magazine than any single contributor. It is not too much to say that the literary flowering of the 1860's would have been impossible—or at least very different—without its influence.

The leading figure of the movement, Emerson, might be called a major contributor to the *Atlantic* under Fields except for two important considerations: he furnished only twelve contributions, and none of them was of primary importance. But to the editor and readers alike he was one of the leading

American writers, and he had been one of the original group of contributors. He had looked upon the new magazine as "an assuming to guide the age—very proper and necessary to be done, and good news that it shall be so." Yet, characteristically, he had not entered into it with the wholehearted enthusiasm of Holmes or Lowell: "But this journal, is this it? Has Apollo spoken?"[1] At any rate, there had been five contributions by Emerson in the first issue (November 1857), including "Days," one of his best poems, and "Brahma," which caused considerable discussion because of its seeming incomprehensibility. And the magazine had become "the most prized periodical in the Emerson study and parlor."[2]

Some of his most significant contributions to Fields were political. "The President's Proclamation" (November 1862) was an ecstatic appraisal of the Emancipation Proclamation, originally delivered as an address. It was followed in the February 1863 issue by "The Boston Hymn," the fiery poem read on the day of emancipation at the Boston Jubilee; and in December of the same year was the war poem "Voluntaries." His and the *Atlantic*'s concern with American culture was represented by the essays "American Civilization" (April 1862) and "Aspects of Culture" (January 1868). The latter appeared at the moment the magazine added "Science" to its subtitle, and expressed Emerson's joy in scientific progress:

Science surpasses the old miracles of mythology.... Who would live in the stone age, or the iron, or the lucastrine? Who does not prefer the age of steel, of gold, of coal, petroleum, cotton, steam, electricity, and the spectroscope?

Of the several poems contributed to Fields, "Terminus" was the last and best. It forecast as early as January 1867, however, the decline in Emerson's creative power that was soon to follow.

As a contributor Emerson was one of the privileged few; his work was always sought and always welcome when it arrived,

---

[1] Ralph Waldo Emerson, *The Heart of Emerson's Journals*, ed. Bliss Perry (Boston, 1926), p. 279.
[2] Ralph L. Rusk, *The Life of Ralph Waldo Emerson* (New York, 1949), p. 396.

and he received the top rate of pay. Fields, who also published his books, did not find him personally so congenial as others of his friends, yet he not only treated the author with great respect but did him all manner of favors. Not the least of his services was the handling of the sale of tickets for Emerson's lectures, during the sixties and the organization and management of his "conversations" in the seventies.[3]

One of the most important of Emerson's contributions to the magazine (August 1862) was his address read at the funeral services of Henry Thoreau. Thoreau was another *Atlantic* writer, although his quarrel with Lowell over the bowdlerizing of his first contribution, "Chesuncook" (July, August, September 1858), had kept him aloof from the magazine until Lowell's editorship had terminated. He had also been dissatisfied with the remuneration for his contributions; he thought he should receive as much for an essay as Emerson, even though his reputation was far inferior to Emerson's at the time.[4] Consequently, the payment he was to receive was one of the first subjects he broached to Fields upon again considering the possibility of writing for the *Atlantic*:

Concord Feb. 11th '62

Messrs. Editors,

Only extreme illness has prevented my answering your note earlier. I have no objection to having the papers you refer to printed in your monthly—if my feeble health will permit me to prepare them for the printer. What will you give me for them? They are, or have been used as, lectures of the usual length, taking about an hour to read & I don't see how they can be divided without injury. How many pages can you print at once? Of course, I should expect that no sentiment or sentence be altered or omitted without my consent, & to retain the copyright of the paper after you had used it in your monthly. Is your monthly copyrighted?

Yours respectfully,
S. E. Thoreau
for H. D. Thoreau

---

[3]Rusk, p. 451, and Ralph Waldo Emerson, *Letters of Ralph Waldo Emerson*, ed. Rusk, (New York, 1939), V, 247 ff.

[4]John Townsend Trowbridge, "An Early Contributor's Recollections," *Atlantic Monthly*, C (November 1907), 588.

On February 20 Thoreau sent "Autumnal Tints." The essay required special treatment because Thoreau wanted a line drawing of a leaf to go with the text. In his letter of submittal, he described the arrangement he wanted:

Concord Feb. 20th 1862

Messrs. Ticknor & Fields,

I send you herewith, the paper called Autumnal Tints. I see that it will have to be divided, & I would prefer that the first portion terminate with page 42, in order that it may make the more impression. The rest I think will take care of itself.

I may as well say now that on pages 55-6-7-8 I have described the Scarlet Oak leaf very minutely. In my lecturing I have always carried a very large & handsome one displayed on a white ground, which did me great service with the audience. Now if you will read those pages, I think that you will see the advantage of having a simple outline engraving of this leaf & also of the White Oak leaf on the opposite page, that the readers may the better appreciate my words—I will supply the leaves to be copied when the time comes.

When you answer the questions in my last note, please let me know about how soon this article will be published.

Yours respectfully,
Henry D. Thoreau.
By S. E. Thoreau.

On March 1 he sent the leaf itself—only one instead of the two he had mentioned—with further directions for printing. By March 11 he had corrected the proofs of the essay,[5] but he never saw it in the magazine—nor any of the essays that followed it—for he died in May. Fields saved it for the lead article of the October issue.

Meanwhile, Thoreau had contributed three other essays before his death. Liking "Autumnal Tints," Fields suggested more articles on the seasons, but Thoreau declined. Instead he sent on February 28 a paper called "The Higher Law," on the vanity of most human occupations. The editor was not quite so well pleased with this essay, especially with the title, which the author consequently changed to "Life without Principle." It was not printed

---

[5] Thoreau (per S. E. Thoreau) to Fields, March 11, 1862.

until the October issue in 1863, when Thoreau's posthumous fame made it desirable.[6]

The essay "Walking" was the first to appear in the *Atlantic*, though it was the third to be submitted to Fields. Sent on March 11, 1862, it appeared in the June number. It was the best of the lot—"perhaps the finest brief statement of what he [Thoreau] had lived for."[7]

Thoreau submitted his last contribution a month before he died. "Wild Apples," sent on April 2,[8] was the leading article in the November *Atlantic*. It was a dissertation in Thoreau's rambling style upon the superiority of wild apples over cultivated ones. Three more essays, from Thoreau's posthumous papers, appeared in the *Atlantic* in 1863 and 1864: "Night and Moonlight," "The Wellfleet Oysterman," and "The Highland Light."

Thoreau's writings on nature were of course the best in the *Atlantic*, though he had many rivals and imitators. One of his would-be rivals was Amos Bronson Alcott, whose only article, "The Forester" (April 1862), was a eulogy of Thoreau. When he submitted a second article the same year, he was first asked to make several alterations. Then, after amending and re-submitting it, he received a delightful letter of rejection, in which the editor advised him not to try to write:

Dear Mr. Alcott.   Boston. Sept. 23d 1862

I have read the amended version of your paper and must again decide against its appearance in print. For *you* to read to a circle of appreciating friends it fulfills all the requirements of a lecture on a most charming subject, but put it into printer's ink and I am sure it would fail of success. It lacks the trick of condensation and avoidance of repetition so imperatively demanded in these days by magazine readers. You *will* say your good things (so delightful to hear reiterated from your own lips) in so many different spots throughout the essay,

---

[6]Thoreau (per S. E. Thoreau) to Fields, February 24, 1862; February 28, 1862; March 4, 1862.

[7]Townsend Scudder, "Henry David Thoreau," *Literary History of the United States*, ed. Robert E. Spiller et al. (New York, 1948), I, 408. See Thoreau (per S. E. Thoreau) to Fields, March 11, 1862.

[8]Thoreau (per S. E. Thoreau) to Fields, April 2, 1862.

and follow up your eloquent statements with strokes as it were in the same place, again and again, that printing your paper would be like putting your thoughts three or four times over into the same number of the magazine. Depend upon it I am right in advising you to refrain from using type instead of your own voice.

Yours very truly
James T. Fields.

Needless to say, there were no more contributions from this pen.

When recognition was merited, Fields was usually prepared to give it. To Mrs. Abby Morton Diaz, a writer who deserved more permanent fame than she has received, he gave timely encouragement. A resident of Plymouth, Massachusetts, Mrs. Diaz had lived some years at Brook Farm, where her father was a member. Five of her contributions to the *Atlantic* were published in the sixties. The first, "Pink and Blue," was submitted to Lowell:

> Her cousin Edwin Morton urged her to write for publication. She scoffed at the idea, and said that there was "not enough in her." She stood in awe of people who wrote, and looked upon them as far above her. Her remarkable wit and brilliancy were accompanied with uncommon modesty. But her cousin kept encouraging her—she called him her "faithgiver," because he gave her faith in herself—and at last she wrote a story called "Pink and Blue," and sent it to the *Atlantic*, New England's leading magazine. Her brother told her she was too ambitious, and she herself had no idea that the *Atlantic* would accept it; but she said she meant to do with her manuscript as she would if she had a peck of potatoes to sell—offer it first in the best market, and then work her way down. To her surprise, the editor [Lowell] took it, and [Fields] took several other stories, sending her a check for each; and then sent her an additional check for $60, with a letter saying that he thought her contributions were really worth more than he had first paid her for them—a characteristic trait of generosity in Mr. Fields.[9]

Mrs. Diaz was a most tractable contributor. She permitted Fields to edit as he pleased, she revised and cut her work to suit

---

[9] "The Life Work of Mrs. Abby Morton Diaz," obituary notice in the *Woman's Journal*, June 13, 1903 (FI 1065). See letters of Abby Morton Diaz in Fields Manuscripts, Huntington Library.

him, and she was grateful for criticism. She became a good friend of the Fieldses and took part with Annie in feminist and social betterment activities.

Her contributions were all short stories built on the plan begun in "Pink and Blue," in which a group of people in a small New England town decided to relate how they happened—or didn't happen—to marry. Though coy, the love stories are often amusing because of Mrs. Diaz' ability to invent ingratiating characters, and they are free of the sentimentality and ponderous philosophizing which spoil many similar efforts of the period. In "The Schoolmaster's Story" (April 1864), for example, the author describes the heroine: "some would say ... 'a neck and throat pure and white as a lily-leaf'; and they would say no more than the truth, only I never like to put things in that way." And in "Some Account of the Early Life of an Old Bachelor" she announces: "Suppose it is not a pleasant story. Life is not all brightness." Her attitude was related to that of the early local colorists, especially Rose Terry Cooke, and in her own way she took part in the rise of the New England woman as a writer of fiction.

Another Transcendentalist, Christopher Pearse Cranch, though not a resident of New England, was an occasional contributor to the *Atlantic*. His father was a Massachusetts man and Cranch himself had lived many years in New England, but he was born in the District of Columbia and had been abroad for several years, returning to live in the United States on Staten Island in 1863. He was a friend of Emerson, who had published several of his poems in the *Dial*. A Unitarian minister, a critic, and a painter, he had some reputation also as a poet. Lowell published nine of his contributions in the *Atlantic*, but when Fields became editor in 1861 they stopped abruptly. Not until 1866 did Fields find any of his contributions worth accepting,[10] nor was his work printed again with any regularity until after Fields retired.

[10]George William Curtis to Fields, May 27, 1862. In this letter Curtis asks Fields for Cranch whether the *Atlantic* is going to publish any of Cranch's submittals.

From 1866 through 1870 he wrote five poems and three reviews of books on art, including *The Mystery of Life and Its Arts* by John Ruskin. The poems are metrically skillful, but that is about all that can be said in their favor. The first, "The Bobolinks" (September 1866), is probably the best. Beginning effervescently, it concludes with the sentimental philosophy:

> Hope springs with you [the bobolinks]:
>   I dread no more
>   Despondency and dullness;
>   For good Supreme can never fail
>   That gives such perfect fullness.

The "Ode, Read at the Festival, Celebrating the Birthday of Margaret Fuller Ossoli" (August 1870) is a five-page eulogy of

> the noblest woman of her time—
>   Whose soul, a pure and radiant chrysolite,
> Dims the superfluous arts our social forms invite.

Cranch's contributions in the sixties added very little of either fame or literary value to the *Atlantic*.

A friend and neighbor of Cranch's was George William Curtis, a Rhode Islander by birth, though he had not lived in New England since 1839 except for a two-year sojourn at Brook Farm. His appearance in the *Atlantic* was due to his friendship with Fields, for Curtis was a regular contributor to the rival *Harper's Monthly* and in 1863 became editor of *Harper's Weekly*. His contributions were few and miscellaneous: a memorial essay on Theodore Winthrop, the novelist (August 1861); a light description of a tour of the Waltham watch works, "My Friend the Watch" (January 1870), which was aimed at encouraging the consumption of American-made products; a criticism of Longfellow (December 1863), in which Curtis explained the poet's popularity as resulting from his "genial humanity ... independent of literary art and of genius, but which is made known to others, and therefore becomes possible to recognize, only through literary forms"; and a literary notice of Fanny Kemble's *Journal of a Residence on a Georgia Plantation* (September

1863), in which he praised the true picture of slavery recorded in the book. Probably the most respected critic among the Transcendentalist sympathizers of the decade. Curtis' importance in the *Atlantic* was as a representative rather than as a major contributor.

The Transcendentalists had a fair, though not voluminous, showing in the *Atlantic*. The peak of the Transcendental movement was past: Margaret Fuller and Theodore Parker were dead; Thoreau died in 1862; Emerson's writing was slackening. But their influence upon other writers can be seen on page after page of the magazine.

Chapter XVII:
Ladies, Militants, and Dilettantes

A REMARKABLE feature of the *Atlantic* in the sixties was the large number of female writers of fiction. Most of them were from New England, where educational opportunities were greatest. Standards of literacy among women had become such that by the time of the *Atlantic*, the majority of readers of all sorts of magazines were the housewives. The popularity of the sentimental domestic novel, that reached its peak in the fifties and sixties, was one phase of the movement. Another was women's rights. Between the extreme of sentimental domesticity and that of campaigning zeal, the women who contributed to the *Atlantic* showed generally an admirable levelheadedness, a shrewd ability to observe, and often a tonic sense of humor. Harriet Beecher Stowe, the most famous of the group, was a zealot. Like Mrs. Diaz and many of the others, she was in the midst of the abolition movement and the social reform movements that followed. But her contributions to the magazine were, more often than not, subdued and even humorous.

The quality of female writing in the *Atlantic* was due to Fields's judicious selection from the reams of manuscripts he received from women. Of no little importance to him was the example of Annie Fields, who represented the best of the feminine virtues of the time. Never overzealous and constantly mindful of woman's mid-century position as arbiter of refinement, she gave conscientiously of her time, money, and social influence to the numerous causes for social reform. She herself contributed eighteen poems to the *Atlantic*, and it was to women like her that Fields looked for the leavening of the magazine.

Mrs. Lydia Maria Francis Child (1802-1880), one of the oldest of the women contributors, was already well known as a writer of historical romances and an abolitionist by the time she began writing for the *Atlantic*. She had one story in the magazine while Lowell was editor in 1858. Four years later she wrote to Fields from her farm in Wayland, Massachusetts, sending another short story and an article on spiritualism:

Wayland, Feb. 26th, 1862.

Mr. Field,

You may call my story Willie Wharton, or a Romance of the Prairies, or anything else that you like better. On the other side of this sheet, I have, according to your request, written an introductory paragraph, which you can use if you like it; if not, I will alter it.

I herewith send you another article for the Atlantic. If you don't want it, you need not take the trouble to explain why, but merely send me the M. S. by Moore's Wayland Express, 6 Court *Square*.

It annoys me to have my M. S. S. lost, or unreasonably detained, when they are not to be published; but in all other respects, I am as reasonable a being as an editor could desire to deal with. The rejection of any article I send will never disturb me in the least.

Very cordially your friend
L. Maria Child.

P. S. I don't know what you will think of the *subject* of my article. For my own part, I find it a comfort to go out of *this* world, in these times.

I will tell *you*, though not the public, that the person who saw the first vision I mention was my old friend Miss Henrietta Sargent, a very sensible maiden lady, a near relative of Manlius Sargent and of Epes Sargent. Such things interest me a good deal, as psychological phenomena. I will make changes in the article if you wish.[1]

"Spirits" appeared in the May 1862 *Atlantic*. In this article, after relating three instances of spiritual contact, Mrs. Child affirmed the existence of some sort of spirit world, a subject in which she was intensely interested, though she was not fooled by "mediums." A spiritual vision occurs in her short story, "Willie Wharton," which appeared in the March 1863 number. Though taking place "in one of our Western States, a few years ago,"

[1] The introductory paragraph was printed with "Willie Wharton."

"Willie Wharton" is reminiscent of Mrs. Child's first popular novel, *Hobomok*. It is the story of a frontier boy who grows up with the Indians and marries one of them. Here Mrs. Child exploited the old contrast between the life of the "noble savage" and that of the civilized white man, not wholly to the advantage of the latter. "Poor Chloe, A True Story of Massachusetts in the Olden Time" (March 1866), her third contribution to Fields, is a sad story of Negro slavery in Massachusetts. Her last contribution reveals another of her interests, comparative religion. "Resemblances between the Buddhist and the Roman Catholic Religions" is exactly what its title suggests, an elementary comparison of the two religions for the purpose of partially justifying the former.

In contrast to Mrs. Child, the young Harriet Elizabeth Prescott (1835-1921), who became Mrs. Spofford in 1865, gained almost her first recognition in the pages of the *Atlantic*. Her first contribution, "In a Cellar" (February 1859), a clever and entertaining short story, brought immediate praise.[2] Through the aid of T. W. Higginson she was introduced to the Boston literary men, and became a frequent contributor to the magazine, publishing twenty-three stories, poems, and essays in it by 1870. She was not among the major contributors who gave the *Atlantic* its character but she could be counted upon for light, harmless fiction that would hold the readers without taxing their minds. Unlike many of her sister writers, she did not take part in reforms, though they had her sympathy. Accordingly her writing is freer from didacticism than that of the others.

Her short stories were her most frequent contributions, though she published four essays on such diverse subjects as Elizabeth Sheppard (the English novelist), Charles Reade, bees, and old age, and two effusive poems full of nature imagery. An excessively fluent prose style endeared her to many readers as a writer of fiction. Such stories as "Dark Ways" (May 1863) and "Ray" (January 1864), where she was not at home in her setting, were

[2] John Townsend Trowbridge, "An Early Contributor's Recollections," *Atlantic Monthly*, C (November 1907), 587.

bogged down in fine writing. Higginson, perhaps her strongest admirer and one who found her style almost faultless, was able to point out other faults: "... her plots have usually been melodramatic, her characters morbid, and her descriptions overdone."[3] Yet her characters could hardly be called morbid by a twentieth-century critic; in fact it is in her characterization that she excels. Stories like "The South Breaker" (May and June 1862) and "Little Ben" (September 1870), which concern the New England fisherman whom she knew, demonstrate her skill at localized characters, and place her among the early local colorists.

Harriet Prescott, being a docile girl and a favorite of the Bostonians, was happy in her relations with Fields and his associates. Not so "Gail Hamilton," whose real name was Mary Abigail Dodge and who was anything but docile. Aside from Mrs. Hawthorne's grievances and in connection with them, Miss Dodge's charges against Fields are almost the only explicit challenge to his reputation of honesty and generosity.[4] That her reputation had been made by Ticknor and Fields, and that she had published in the *Atlantic Monthly* and helped edit *Our Young Folks* did not deter her from suddenly rising up in a fury over her rate of pay, and, after a stormy private trial in which she won what she had wanted, she declaimed her wrongs to the world. Her satire of Ticknor and Fields, *A Battle of the Books*, a full volume that ran through several editions, makes interesting reading as an antidote to the unctuous publicity that—as she gloatingly pointed out—the firm caused to circulate without acknowledging its origin. Her story is apparently a true relating of the altercation, including much of the correspondence, with only the names and dates altered. Unfortunately for her case, the reader can read the book, and, disregarding her hysteria, accuse Fields of nothing worse than treating her as the poorer than

---

[3] Thomas Wentworth Higginson, review of *Azarian* by Harriet E. Prescott, *Atlantic Monthly*, XIV (October 1864), 515.

[4] See Randall Stewart, "'Pestiferous Gail Hamilton,' James T. Fields and the Hawthornes," *New England Quarterly*, XVII (September 1944), 418-23. Julia Ward Howe's quarrel with Fields (see Chapter VI), though hardly a quarrel at all, might be held a further instance of unfairness on Fields's part.

average writer that she was, instead of as a privileged friend. Like Hawthorne, she had trustingly left her royalties entirely up to Fields, hardly knowing how much she received and supposing it was at least average. Like Mrs. Hawthorne, she suddenly found that she was getting less than she expected, in Miss Dodge's case less than the average writer for other publishers. She could and did get more from others, but Ticknor and Fields had their prestige to offer, and besides they were as publishers most interested in selling the writers with established names, who gave them all the business they could handle. She confessed her naïveté in the business:

Perhaps I do not quite know what I am talking about. I suspect, on the whole, I do not. But my remarks are all the more valuable for that. If, after two years of clapper-clawing among a quartette of cats, a mouse is still unskilled in feline ways, in what state of helplessness must be those unadventurous little things who have never left their holes?[5]

When the case was brought before a private board of arbiters in 1868, it was recommended that Fields, Osgood and Company pay what Miss Dodge thought they owed her. This they had already offered to do. But they were not legally bound to any such action, and it was only because of her own implacability that matters reached such a crisis, for had she permitted it, Fields would have settled the matter satisfactorily without bitterness, as her own book makes abundantly clear. Nevertheless, the battle broke up the friendship and Miss Dodge severed all her connections with the firm.

She had contributed twenty-five pieces to the *Atlantic*. Besides a half-dozen literary notices, she wrote light essays on domestic situations, such as "My Garden" (May 1862) and "Moving" (July 1862); a few serious declamations, such as "A Call to My Country-Women" (March 1863); and several semi-serious meanderings on general subjects, such as "A Complaint of Friends" (September 1862) and "The New School of Biography" (No-

[5] Gail Hamilton, *A Battle of the Books* (New York, 1870), p. 260.

vember 1864). Her vigorous style is at its best when she has something to attack, as in "A Complaint of Friends," in which she condemns all sorts of presumptuousness allowed for friendship's sake; but she is seldom at a loss for a target. Her weakness was diffuseness, resulting from her frequent lack of anything important to say or any clear conclusion to be reached. She was highly indignant about woman suffrage but her ultimate statement (in the sixties) was that men were too much men to offer the ballot to women and she was too much a lady to ask for it.[6]

Another writer of the same generation, born in the early thirties, was Mrs. Helen Maria Hunt, who became Helen Hunt Jackson on her marriage to W. S. Jackson in 1875. She submitted a poem "The Zone of Calms," to Fields in April 1867,[7] but her first accepted writing was "Coronation" in the February 1869 number. It is a parable on kingship, in simple rhyme. Meanwhile she had left for Europe, to return in 1870, and her following contributions generally show the influence of her journey.

"A German Landlady," a sketch in the October 1870 issue, was actually named by Fields, as Mrs. Hunt's letter of July 29, 1870, indicates. "I am very glad you like my Fraulein," she wrote, "and very sorry you don't like her name. It seems to me a far more picturesque and appetizing title than any clause with 'Landlady' in it; but of course I yield to your judgement and Col. Higginson's." When her check came, she found that she was getting only five dollars a page instead of ten, which she thought was the standard *Atlantic* rate. She wrote to Fields the day after the sketch appeared, at which time she sent another article and suggested that the rate be higher for it.

Bethlehem, N. H. Sept. 21. 1870

Dear Mr. Fields,
    I send you my Gastein article, which I hope you will like. If not, may I ask you to be so very kind as to let me have it again at the earliest day, because I am sure of immediate use for it.

---

[6] Review of *Woman's Wrongs* by Gail Hamilton, *Atlantic Monthly*, XXI (April 1868), 509.

[7] Helen Hunt to Fields, April 16, 1867 and May 11, 1867.

And will you pardon me for asking also, if in case you do use it, it ought not to be paid for at a higher rate per page than the German Landlady? I have been told, perhaps erroneously, that the price per page of the Atlantic, is $10.

I believe that the price of $75 was marked on the Fraulein however; so I mean not the slightest dissatisfaction with that: but I had no idea it would be so long;—and neither did I have the good luck of her appearing in the Atlantic in my thought, when I marked her figure!

I send the article, paid through, by Express: please return it, by same way, to be paid here.

Yours very truly
Helen Hunt.

Actually she was receiving approximately the standard *Atlantic* pay; ten dollars per page was given only to established writers. For "The Valley of Gastein," Fields offered sixty dollars for thirteen pages, which Mrs. Hunt did not wish to accept:

Dear Mr. Fields,   Bethlehem—Sept. 27, 1870

I am very sorry, but I think I cannot let the "Gastein" go for $60. I am sure of $75. for it, and I hope, more, as it makes about fifteen pages.

At any other time, I would rather have it in the Atlantic, even at a lower price, than I should get elsewhere; but this fall, I am writing, (I mean printing.) for money to pay for publishing my verses!—

So I must ask you to be so good as to send the article back to me, by Express. I do not like to risk it by mail.

Address—
Mrs. Hunt
At Mr. Barrett's
Bethlehem. N. Hampshire.   Yours truly—Helen Hunt

But satisfactory arrangements were reached, and the travel sketch appeared in the January 1871 *Atlantic*. Altogether she contributed two poems, six sketches, and a series of letters from Italy, "Encyclicals of a Traveller," between 1869 and the end of 1871.

It is remarkable that all the New England women writers who contributed to any extent to the *Atlantic* were born within a decade of each other (1827-1836), with the exception of Stowe, Howe, and Child, who belonged to an earlier generation. Another of these younger writers was Louisa May Alcott, whose stories appeared in the magazine in 1860 and 1863. Having contributed two to Lowell in the former year, she contributed two more to Fields in the latter. They were "Debby's Début" (August), a frivolous story of young love and polite society, and "The Brothers" (November), which takes place during the Civil War and involves a Negro contraband.

Her "Thoreau's Flute," an elegy, which appeared in the September 1863 *Atlantic*, had an unusual history. It had been sent to Fields by Hawthorne, who got it from Miss Alcott's father, Bronson. The author was pleased when she learned that Fields wanted to print it, and she agreed to alter a line to which he had objected. She wrote to Annie:

Concord June 24th

Dear Cousin Annie.

Thanks for the bonny thought & the "Flute's" promotion. Kindly criticism never offends but to me is often more flattering than praise for if any one takes the trouble to criticize it seems to prove that the thing is worth mending.

Poetry is not my forte & the lines were never meant to go beyond my scrapbook. Perhaps the place in which they were composed may partly account for the halting rhyme, they jingled into my sleepy brain during a night watch beside the bed of a one-legged lad dying of wound fever in the Hospital last Dec.; were forgotten till father found them among my papers, read them like a partial parent as he is, to neighbor Hawthorne, who asked for them the other day & without telling me their destination sent them to sit in high places where they hardly belong.

I am immensely busy just now getting up some Scenes from Dickens for the benefit of the Fifty fifth colored regiment, & enriching the Commonwealth with my valuable contributions, but I will set my wits to work on the "forlorn" line & see if I can better it. How will this do?

"Spring mourns as for untimely frost,
The genius of the wood is lost."

Or is the r in frost as objectionable as in lorn? If my little ship is to be launched in the Atlantic I must attend her build & rigging & see that she does not founder for want of proper ballast as an honorable flag is flying at the mast head.

If you come to Concord shall we not see you at The Gables? mountains we cannot offer but poets & philosophers with very little snow upon their heads & the country pleasures we enjoy in this our "Happy Valley."

With best regards to Mr. Fields I am

very truly yours
L. M. Alcott[8]

The following year Miss Alcott was busy with her first novel, *Moods*, and in 1865 she departed for Europe. She contributed no more to the magazine.

Rose Terry, who became Mrs. Cooke in 1873, was possibly the best of the female contributors of the generation born in the thirties. A true local colorist, she set forth some of her literary ideals in her first story for Fields, "Miss Lucinda" (August 1861), and they are strikingly similar to those later propounded by Howells:

But if I apologize for a story that is nowise tragic, nor fitted to "the fashion of these [Civil War] times," possibly somebody will say at its end that I should also have apologized for its subject, since it is as easy for an author to treat his reader to high themes as vulgar ones, and velvet can be thrown into a portrait as cheaply as calico; but of this apology I wash my hands. I believe nothing in place or circumstance makes romance. I have the same quick sympathy for Biddy's sorrows with Patrick as I have for the Empress of France and her august, but rather grim lord and master. I think words are often no harder to bear than "a blue batting," and I have a reverence for poor old maids as great as for the nine Muses. Commonplace people are only commonplace from character, and no position affects that. So forgive me once more, patient reader, if I offer you no tragedy in high life, no sentimental history of fashion and wealth, but only a little story about a woman who could not be a heroine.

Unfortunately for our opinion of Fields, Miss Terry contributed only five pieces during his editorship, while she had printed sixteen during Lowell's short four years. Her second contribution to be printed by Fields was a poem that had been sent to Lowell in 1861. A year later she wrote to ask what had become of it:

[8] The excellent lines cited in the letter were printed in the *Atlantic*, with changes in the punctuation.

Fields of the Atlantic Monthly

Jan. 27th 1862

Editors Atlantic Monthly
Dear Sirs

I have nothing that I can send you directly, I am at work on a story for you which I shall probably finish in about ten days.

My health has been so unusually miserable for the last year that I could not write, and I cannot depend on it at any time so far as to promise the finishing of anything, which interferes with any work excessively. But as soon as I can I will send you what I can.

Nearly a year ago I sent a poem and a story to the Atlantic[;] the story was accepted & Mr. Ticknor sent me word that the poem was referred to Mr. Lowell. I have not seen or heard of it since, and if you are not going to use it I should like to receive the manuscript again, as I have only its rough copy, and would like to publish it elsewhere. It was called "Out of the Body."

Be so good hereafter as to direct to me Care of H. W. Terry, as our new post-office regulations demand this of box-holders.

Yours very truly.
Rose Terry.

Her poetry is not excellent, but it is definitely above the average for the *Atlantic*, and "Out of the Body to God," finally printed in the June number, is the better of the two she contributed to Fields. Through its conventional form and language, there appears a sincere religious feeling. The story referred to in the letter is "A Woman," which was printed in the December number. It concerns the psychological maturing of a girl whose bridegroom of a few months is killed in the war and who devotes herself to nursing war casualties. It is told through the agency of an amiable old maid, who keeps the narrative alive and sparkling.

"The New Sangreal," a war poem, was her next contribution, and it was accepted by Fields with editorial revisions. She permitted the revisions reluctantly; Fields had objected to some "deficient rhythms" which she avowed were intentional.[9] The poem was printed in the September 1864 *Atlantic*.

Miss Terry's final contribution to Fields was "Dely's Cow," in the June 1865 issue. Like most of her stories, this one takes place

---

[9] Rose Terry to "Editor of the Atlantic Monthly," July 23, 1863; see also manuscript of "The New Sangreal," with Fields's revisions (FI 624).

318

in New England, and it concerns the hardships of a young family during the war. It shows perhaps better than either of her previous stories her quiet humor of character, her skill at dialect, and her sound understanding of the New England temperament. Good-natured as her approach is, it is free from the optimistic extravagances of her sister writers. There was a need, she told Fields, of a "strong and original woman author in America, to efface the little prettinesses and commonplaces of us smaller fry."[10]

One of the small fry who abounded in prettinesses and commonplaces was Celia Thaxter, who contributed more poetry to the *Atlantic* than any other woman. She owed a great deal to the magazine, to Lowell, and to the Fieldses. It was Lowell who printed her first poem without her knowledge, it having been sent to him by one of her friends. "Land-Locked," as it was called, which was in the March 1861 number, is typical of her work. Her subject was the sea, with which she had a long acquaintance, having been raised in the lonely lighthouse-keeper's cottage on White Island in the Isles of Shoals. She never tired of describing and redescribing the waves and winds, the flora and fauna, the storms and sunsets of her childhood home—until the present-day reader (at least if he is a landlubber) loses patience.

She was a close friend of both James and Annie Fields, and her extant letters[11] to them alone would make a volume. Annie Fields's opinion of her as a writer is to be found in "Celia Thaxter," from *Authors and Friends*: "While White's 'Selborne,' and the pictures of Bewick, and Thoreau's 'Walden,' and the 'Autobiography of Richard Jefferies' endure, so long will 'Among the Isles of Shoals' hold its place with all lovers of nature."[12]

Among the Isles of Shoals was her only prose contribution to the *Atlantic*. It is a long description of the islands, running through four issues (August 1869 and January, February, and May 1870). Minute details abound concerning the history, the natural phenomena, the people, the villages, and the shipwrecks.

---

[10]Rose Terry to Fields, October 28, 1864.
[11]Now in the Huntington Library and the collection of Mrs. Z. B. Adams.
[12]Annie Fields, *Authors and Friends*, p. 230.

There is also a considerable amount of philosophizing on the value of hard work, the attitude of dwellers by the sea, God's manifestations in nature. Published as a book by James R. Osgood and Company in 1873, it was popular, and Osgood later printed it in a fifty-cent edition as a guidebook to be sold in railroad stations.[13]

Her poetry is all of a type. Of the fifteen poems contributed to Fields all but three concern nature directly and more than half concern the sea. There is a noticeable progression from pure description in the earlier pieces to didacticism in the later. Nature frequently reminded her of God's omniscience and of the spiritual compensations of suffering. In "Expectations" (September 1868) she laments the coming of winter.

> Yea, even so. Through this enchanted land,
>   This morning-red of life, we go to meet
> The tempest in the desert, hand in hand
>   Along God's paths of pain that seek his feet.

A few of her later poems are purely "philosophical," to the exclusion of nature. Such is "Courage" (April 1870), an apology for her optimism. Mrs. Thaxter was a pleasant contributor, always amenable to Fields's revisions, of which there were many. She wrote upon submitting one of her poems, "Sorrow" (May 1867): "I have copied my ballad for your dissecting knife."[14] She continued to contribute steadily to the *Atlantic* long after Fields's retirement.

Another friend of Annie's was Sarah Orne Jewett, who after Fields's death lived with Mrs. Fields for many years in the house in Manchester. She contributed only one story to the *Atlantic* during Fields's editorship, but its acceptance was her first recognition as a literary figure, for she was only twenty when it appeared in the December 1869 issue.[15] "Mr. Bruce" is not one of her best short stories, though it shows promise. Bounded by a highly artifical plot, it relates the love affair of an Englishman

---

[13] Celia Thaxter to Fields, October 29, 1877.
[14] Celia Thaxter to Fields, January 6, 1867.
[15] See Francis Otto Matthiessen, *Sarah Orne Jewett* (Boston, 1929), pp. 33-36.

with a New England girl. Miss Jewett became a frequent contributor to the magazine a few years later.

Three other New England contributors, as distinctly individualistic as any of their fellows, should not be omitted from a discussion of the *Atlantic Monthly* in the sixties: J. W. De Forest, H. H. Brownell, and D. G. Mitchell. De Forest began contributing in 1859 and had printed three pieces by 1861. During his years in the army he sent nothing, but within four months after his discharge on January 1, 1868, he was again in the *Atlantic* with "A Gentleman of an Old School" (May 1868). One of his first contributions (September and October 1868) was a review of his experiences as director of the Freedmen's Bureau in Greenville, South Carolina. Under the title "The Man and Brother," the article concerns the ignorance and incapacity of the Negro in his new status, the problems he has to meet, and the difficulties to be overcome by those that want to help him. The whole realistic picture of the situation is discouraging, and concludes with a question:

What judgment shall we pass upon abrupt emancipation, considered merely with reference to the negro? It is a mighty experiment, fraught with as much menace as hope.

To the white race alone it is a certain and precious boon.

De Forest took up the subject again a year later in his clever allegorical short story "The City of Brass" (October 1869), in which he likened the emancipated Negro to a gigantic oriental statue, brought to monstrous life by a well-meaning Boston philanthropist.

"Love in Mount Lebanon" (February 1869) is an exotic tale of Syria, where De Forest had visited in 1846, but all his other stories involve either the supernatural, like "The City of Brass," or the weird. Probably the best of the lot is "A Strange Arrival," about a hearty New England sea captain and his daughter who meet the Flying Dutchman. With delicious humor De Forest contrasts the realistic characterization of the "cap'n" with the romantic one of the Dutchman. A moralistic twist is involved when all the riches given by the Flying Dutchman disappear except for the necklace of pearls given to the girl because she pitied his plight; but the incident is treated merely as a normal element of a fairy tale. "The Drummer Ghost" (July 1869) and "The Taillefer Bell-Ringings" (August 1869) are ghost stories, told simply and effectively. "The Lauson Tragedy" (April and May 1870) is a very modern detective story, excellently told and involving some superb characters, likable and unlikable, and in which De Forest's understanding of the callous side of human nature is displayed to advantage. In all, he contributed eight times during Fields's editorship. And he continued fairly regularly after that.

The minor writer Henry Howard Brownell contributed twice to Fields. His reputation as a poet received a considerable boost when he was nominated "Our Battle-Laureate" in Holmes's article of the same name (May 1865). A month later, in the June 1865 issue, he contributed "Down!" a noisy poem descriptive of a sea battle. His other contribution was a thirteen-page poem, "Abraham Lincoln" (October 1865), a tribute to the dead president.

D. G. Mitchell serves to remind us of the amazing popularity of the discursive essay in the middle of the nineteenth century. His *Wet Weather Work*, in eight installments from 1863 to 1864, rambles interminably from crops to literature. Besides a short essay on Washington Irving, he also contributed *Doctor Johns*, an extended narrative with a New England plot, which Mitchell hesitated to call a novel[16] and which took seventeen installments.

With his love of the soil and his diffuseness of style, Mitchell represented growing tendencies in the literature of New England. The renaissance was about over by the end of the sixties. Hawthorne and Thoreau were dead; Holmes, Longfellow, Lowell, and Emerson had many years to live but had passed their peak; and a new generation was beginning to come to the foreground. In the writing of Rose Terry Cooke, Celia Thaxter, and J. W. De Forest could be seen the seeds of the future.

[16]Donald Grant Mitchell to Fields, November 11, 1864? (FI 3191).

PART FOUR

FROM THE HINTERLAND

FOREWORD TO PART FOUR

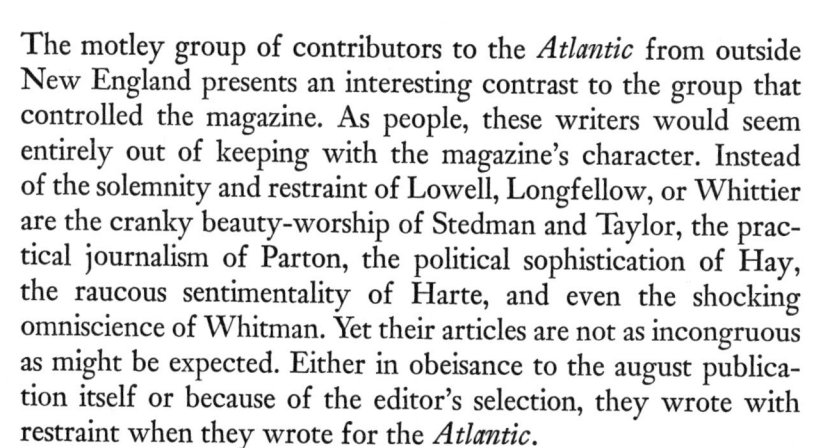

The motley group of contributors to the *Atlantic* from outside New England presents an interesting contrast to the group that controlled the magazine. As people, these writers would seem entirely out of keeping with the magazine's character. Instead of the solemnity and restraint of Lowell, Longfellow, or Whittier are the cranky beauty-worship of Stedman and Taylor, the practical journalism of Parton, the political sophistication of Hay, the raucous sentimentality of Harte, and even the shocking omniscience of Whitman. Yet their articles are not as incongruous as might be expected. Either in obeisance to the august publication itself or because of the editor's selection, they wrote with restraint when they wrote for the *Atlantic*.

Their only characteristic as a group is that they were not New Englanders; otherwise they had almost nothing in common. An acute observer in the sixties might have distinguished diverse trends of the future in the work of Taylor, Harte, Rebecca Harding, or S. Weir Mitchell; for these writers represented respectively the ideal of literature as a fine art, the portrayal of the West in action and humor, a concern with the social conditions of the laboring man, and a psychiatric approach to fiction. Though the contributions from the "hinterland" were decidedly in the minority, they added a variety to the *Atlantic* which enhanced its popular appeal.

By the end of the sixties it was becoming apparent that the literary center of the United States would one day move away from New England. Fields either did not see this or did not care, though Bayard Taylor saw it when he wrote to Aldrich on March 16, 1866:

Whatever may be the temporary changes, *here* [New York] will be, before long, the centre of Literature as of Art. If it were not for the damnable want of unity among our authors, we should have Ticknor and Fields in Broadway by this time. Even now, it is the best place for them, if they would but see it.[1]

Fields did a better job of recruiting writers from afar than Lowell, and the proportion of articles written outside New England increased during his editorship, but it remained for Howells, especially after Fields's retirement, to carry on the principle more energetically than ever before.

---

[1] Manuscript in Harvard University Library, quoted in Donald Reuel Tuttle, "Thomas Bailey Aldrich's Editorship of The Atlantic Monthly, A Chapter in the Belles-Lettres Tradition" (unpublished doctoral dissertation, Western Reserve University, 1939), I, 14.

Chapter XVIII:
Bayard Taylor

THE WRITER who contributed by far the most to the *Atlantic* from outside New England was Bayard Taylor. He and Fields had been friends since the forties, and each had written complimentary reviews of the other's publications and had used his influence whenever possible in the other's behalf.[1] Taylor was a contributor to the *Atlantic*, however, even before Fields became editor; three mediocre poems and a pseudopsychological short story were accepted and printed by Lowell before 1861.

Though Taylor had already established a reputation as a writer of many poems, and though he considered himself primarily a poet, he was most popular for his travel sketches, especially *Views Afoot* (1846), which had brought him his first considerable public recognition. To the *Atlantic* during Fields's regime, he contributed not only poems and travel sketches but also short stories and articles on literary figures, and Fields saw to it that there was not a preponderance of poems. In the new editor's first number appeared one of Taylor's stories, "The Haunted Shanty," although more than one poem had already been accepted and set aside for later issues.[2] "The Haunted Shanty" begins realistically with a description of Illinois prairie, but its subject is one of spiritualistic communion. Its mystery and suspense make it good popular reading. Seven months later, in the February 1862 number, appeared "Experiences of the A. C.," a story that had been sent to Fields at about the same time as "The Haunted

---

[1] Fields to Taylor, May 7, 1849; May 11, 1850; and undated, 1850 (FI 2052).
[2] Bayard Taylor, *The Unpublished Letters of Bayard Taylor in the Huntington Library*, ed. John R. Schultz (San Marino, 1937), p. 53.

Shanty." Here Taylor exploited a theme which Hawthorne had perhaps inaugurated in *The Blithedale Romance,* an unsuccessful utopian community. Like Hawthorne, Taylor depicted an egotistical crank as the guiding spirit of the community and showed the disintegration of the experiment in the self-centered bickerings of the members. But Taylor's treatment was whimsical and supposedly humorous. He was better at writing about the Quaker life that he had known as a boy. In "Friend Eli's Daughter," which was printed in the July 1862 issue, the sympathetic picture of a Pennsylvania Quaker family is convincing. The plot is not unusual—love temporarily thwarted by the strictness of a religious creed—and the characters are mostly romanticized, but Friend Eli himself, who "was at peace with himself and the world—that is, so much of the world as he acknowledged," is striking. Taylor also wrote a story of life in Russia, "Beauty and the Beast"; another Quaker tale, "The Strange Friend"; and an unusual and interesting kind of detective story, "Can a Life Hide Itself?" He commonly received $100 to $150 apiece for his short stories regardless of length, a price that had been established by Lowell in 1860.[3]

Taylor's poems in the *Atlantic* are all very much alike. He was so intent upon rising above the sordidness of life and achieving an other-worldliness that he avoided almost everything that makes for literary interest. His style, packed with poetic diction and affluent rhetoric, is extremely skillful but monotonous. Fields was wise in encouraging him to write more prose and in handling his poems gingerly. The first of the poems, "The Bath," expresses the creed of the group of poets, including Boker, Stedman, and Stoddard, of which Taylor was the most famous representative:

> Off, fetters of the falser life,—
> Weeds that conceal the statue's form!
> This silent world with truth is rife,
> This wooing air is warm.

[3] Ibid., p. 147. James Russell Lowell, *New Letters of James Russell Lowell,* ed. M. A. De Wolfe Howe (New York, 1932), p. 100. Fields to Taylor, April 7, 1861.

> Now fall the thin disguises, planned
>   For men too weak to walk unblamed:
> Naked beside the sea I stand,—
>   Naked, and not ashamed....
>
> But leave to me this brief escape
>   To simple manhood, pure and free,—
> A child of God, in God's own shape,
>   Between the land and sea!

"The Bath" was in the September 1861 number of the magazine. Taylor's second poetic contribution, "Euphorion," on the beauty of grief, did not appear until more than a year later. "The Test," his only contribution concerning the Civil War, was sent in December 1862. Fields pronounced it "charming"[4] and printed it in the February 1863 number. It glorifies the soldier who leaves his sweetheart to give his life in battle,

> For Love, forsook this side of danger,
>   Waits for the man who goes beyond!

Fields printed less than one poem per year by Taylor during the sixties though more than that were submitted.

   Occasionally Taylor wrote sketches of foreign writers who he or Fields thought deserved the American public's attention. Four of these appeared in the *Atlantic* during the sixties, "The German Burns," "William Makepeace Thackeray," "The Author of Saul," and "Friedrich Rückert." The first, in the April 1862 number, is on the German dialect poet Johann Peter Hebel. It contains little criticism but concerns itself with the life and character of the poet and includes translations by Taylor in a sort of hybrid Yankee dialect of some of Hebel's poems. The most interesting of the sketches is that of Thackeray, which was in the March 1864 issue of the magazine. It is a memorial notice of "the great master of English prose," who had just died. Having been well acquainted with Thackeray, Taylor was able to speak from personal knowledge, and he protested against the popular misconcep-

---

[4]Fields to Taylor, December 12, 1862.

tion that the satirist was callous or cynical. From Fields's letter acknowledging receipt of the article, it appears that he had suggested it to Taylor:

Dear B. Boston Jan. 26. 1864

Your paper is most charming through and through. It is *just* what I want and I thank you for being so prompt. If it be possible you shall have the proof, but I doubt. My space is waiting to be filled, and yr. copy is always so plain I shall venture the article with our reading if it be necessary so to do.

Behold! a slip of paper ($60.) for the excellent article you have sent to me. I don't know when I have been more gratified with a paper for the A. M.

The photo. is admirable & I shall have it sent to London to be engraved.

Yours always
J. T. F.

Sixty dollars was a rather small remuneration for the Thackeray article; the Hebel had brought a hundred, while "The Author of Saul," an article upon the obscure Canadian writer Charles Heavysege, brought even more.[5]

Travel sketches were popular in the sixties, and Taylor had a knack for picking out the picturesque and exotic in his travels that was pleasing to his public. Still, his first contributions of this kind to Fields were rejected. In July 1861 the author wrote from Germany, where he was on one of his frequent visits, that he had four such sketches in mind:

My Dear Sir: Gotha, Germany, July 8, 1861

I send you herewith an illustrated article about a little-known corner of Germany. I propose to make another about the Bohemian Forest, a very interesting region, and two of Hungary and the Carpathians—four in all, which is all I shall be able to do. I have chosen the subjects for illustration which seemed to me most interesting to American readers. The other articles will be fully illustrated, especially so far as the *people* are concerned.

The accompanying article will make 14 or 15 pages of the Magazine,

---

[5] Marie Hansen Taylor, *On Two Continents, Memories of Half a Century* (New York, 1905), p. 110. Fields to Taylor, July 1, 1865.

and, counting at the rate I receive for my newspaper correspondence, will be worth $250. I should be greatly obliged if you would send me draft (say of Duncan Thermar & Co.) for the amount, as I shall not leave here before the beginning of September, and may need it at that time. I shall start for Bohemia and Hungary about the 1st of August.

Please address as above, and oblige

Yours very truly,
Bayard Taylor.[6]

But none of these articles was printed, perhaps because Taylor was asking too much for them. Nor did a paper on Romania, which he sent to Fields in 1863, ever appear in the magazine.[7] "A Cruise on Lake Ladoga" was the first of Taylor's travel sketches to receive Fields's editorial approval. It was the leading article in the May 1864 number. An account of a journey from St. Petersburg to Serdopol among a group of pilgrims to the monastery of Valaam, it contained many of the elements of romantic travel literature that have since become so hackneyed. It did not conclude with a glowing sunset, but there were chiming bells: "Once more the bells of Valaam chimed farewell, and we turned the point to the westward, steering back to Nexholm. ... And now, as I recall those five days among the islands of the Northern Lake, I see that it is good to go on a pilgrimage, even if one is not a pilgrim." Like all of Taylor's papers on foreign travel, this one contained genial descriptions of the food, the traveling accommodations, and the scenery along the way. "Between Europe and Asia," in the January 1865 *Atlantic*, was less superficial. In describing an annual fair at Nijni Novgorod, Taylor commented upon the condition of the Russian serfs, the apparent degree of religious and racial tolerance, and the production of cotton, grain, and potatoes in European Russia. Fields liked the paper well enough to put it in his favored January number, and to pay a hundred dollars for it. He wrote to Taylor just after reading the manuscript:

[6]The *Atlantic* did not contain illustrations. Could Taylor have meant "illustrated" with words?
[7]Fields to Taylor, September 14, 1863.

> Boston October 8. 1864.
>
> Dear Bayard.
>
> Your paper arrived last night and I read it before going up stairs. It seems to me one of the best sketches of travel you have done, and I am very glad to get it now. It will go into our January No. because I want your name there. Enclosed you will find check for $100. in payment. Don't stop thinking about the other papers I spoke to you of when we met. Get into the vein of writing them as soon as you can for the idea is a good one.
>
> Whittier came to see me week before last looking sad, and paler than usual. He said little about his loss, but the scar shows.
>
> Kind regards to Marie from both of us. We go to New York next week.
>
> Yours always
> J. T. F.

Another article, "Travel in the United States," is really not a travel sketch at all but a discourse upon the inconvenience and inefficiency of the American railroad system. In the most plainspoken of Taylor's contributions to the *Atlantic*, he denounced the monopolistic rings that had made the railroads tyrants rather than servants of the people.

The proprietor, who makes from one hundred thousand to half a million dollars per annum, becomes sublimely indifferent to the comfort of his guests; and the railroad which employs all its rolling stock, and intends to buy but very little more until prices come down, puts on the airs of an absolute power. Corporations, with us, are controlled by a few individuals, and we endure in all the practical relations of life an amount of tyranny which would not be tolerated a single day were its character political. Our corporations are more despotic, dishonest, and irresponsible than in any other country of the civilized world. Our politicians, of whatever party, repeat the old phrases indicative of mistrust of corporations; yet we find the latter controlling entire States, electing their own legislatures and members of Congress, demoralizing voters, and exercising other dangerous privileges, in utter defiance of the public interest. We are silent under impositions of this kind which would raise a popular tempest in many countries of Europe.

A whole series of travel sketches by Taylor, *By-Ways of Europe*, appeared in the magazine during 1867-1868. Here Taylor reported on picturesque and out-of-the-way spots in France, Spain, Germany, Switzerland, and the Mediterranean. Except for the places described, these sketches were no different from his previous ones.

Though Fields could be severely critical of Taylor's writing, he was eager to help him as a friend. In 1862 he attempted to secure the writer's appointment as United States Minister to Russia. As chargé d'affaires for the minister Simon Cameron, Taylor had performed the duties of the post without the title, but he was in hopes of receiving the official appointment from the Lincoln government. Fields wrote pessimistically:

> The principal business of your letter has engaged my attention a good deal and I need not assure you that nothing we can do in Boston shall be left undone for your interest. Of course you are the man of men for the place and I sincerely hope your supreme fitness will be so apparent to the government that no failure can take place in your appointment. I was in New York last week and talked the matter over with influential people who all spoke of your ability as a thing undoubted, but some of them feared the politician-look of the matter, saying that many prominent men were already in the field to be provided for by Abraham and his surroundings. Stoddard spoke decidedly to the effect that political influence wd. deprive you of the appointment so evidently yours by every manner of fitness. But I know letters and documents, bearing upon your claims, are passing about and your friends will be active in your behalf. The country seems badly supplied with able men, and mediocrity gets notice where talent fails. I say very little about the future, but dark clouds gather fast enough to make us feel uneasy. I seem to see innumerable griefs ahead. But God knows. We must wait, but not cease working.[8]

Fields's political influence was not so great as he would have liked to suppose, and Taylor failed to receive the position despite his excellent qualifications. But Taylor was prepared to accept defeat by the time he wrote to Fields in January: "The fact is, I scarcely expect it, knowing so well the usual practice of our government to consider only party services, without regard to

---
[8]Fields to Taylor, November 8, 1862.

fitness or propriety."[9] In March Fields asked Taylor to write under strict anonymity "a 5 or 6 page article for the A. M. showing up the imbecility and ignorance of some of our Foreign Ministers. It seems to me you could paint them from your book of experiences in travel so as to make the nation wince."[10] But Taylor did not write the article.

In the early sixties Taylor was not an exclusive contributor to the *Atlantic*. He not only wrote travel sketches for the newspapers, but also contributed to the *Continental Monthly*. Besides, Fields cooperated with Thackeray, the editor of the *Cornhill Magazine*, in printing some of Taylor's pieces simultaneously in England and the United States. By 1864, however, Fields was encouraging Taylor to send all his work to the *Atlantic*: "Whenever you feel like handling any topic remember the A. M. is always glad to hear from you." And he suggested that Taylor was well fitted to write the type of thing the editor most needed: "I wish you felt like a series of short humorous papers for the A. M. to occupy 5 or 6 pages each. We can afford to pay well you know."[11] The plan was further elaborated in a letter that Fields wrote two weeks later, while the article on American diplomats was still being considered:

Boston March 31. 1864

My Dear Taylor.

With reference to the diplomatic article you shall be kept free of recognition as to authorship if we of the A. M. can help you. Your name will not be revealed by us.

Touching the other papers I suggested. It struck me you might have laid away for the public (in your brain cells at least) some humorous thoughts as to persons & places that might be worked up for the A. M. What we most need are *short* storyish papers that have fun as an element in them. You shall try one or two of those "subjects" (by way of experiment) that came into yr. mind when you recd. my letter requesting such things for the Atlantic. When I think of

---

[9] Marie Hansen Taylor and Horace E. Scudder, *Life and Letters of Bayard Taylor* (Boston, 1884), I, 407.
[10] Fields to Taylor, March 19, 1864.
[11] Ibid.

the laughable incidents I have listened to from yr. lips related as having befallen you in yr. rambles round the world, it has often occurred to me "what a chance for a series of papers to make people feel in good humor through the grim-est days, B. T. might write if he chose." For instance what an extraordinary experience you have had in *food* during your travel-life! What wonderful *beds* you have slept in! What funny *landlords* you have encountered! By what *servants* you have been ministered unto! The Catalogue of your Travel-Oddities, new to the great un-moving-about-world, is longer than the Atlantic ocean itself. Turn over Charles Lamb's "Elia" & see what drollery he made out of a voyage now and then to a ten-mile-away watering place.

We rejoice over the success of your "Hannah [Thurston]." Long may she circulate!

Our kindest loves to you both, and to the young lady, your daughter, whom I only know by report which gives her plaudits for excellence both in looks and actions.

Very Sincerely
J. T. Fields.

We don't forget the un-received water-color! when will it come?[12]

Though Taylor approved of Fields's idea in conversation, and though Fields urged him again in 1866, offering a hundred dollars apiece for the proposed sketches, only one such sketch appeared, "A Distinguished Character," in the September 1866 number of the magazine. It was an amusing catalogue of the annoyances a writer must suffer to be popular. "Now that I have written away my vexation," Taylor concluded, "I recognize very clearly that my object in writing this article is apology rather than complaint."

Fields, did, however, get Taylor to contribute regularly in 1867. The editor wrote on August 16, 1866, to ask permission to include the writer in the magazine's prospectus for the new year: "You must write for the A. M. regularly during 1867 & I wish to announce you among our certainties." In September he had a more specific plan; Taylor must begin a novel to be ready to publish serially in 1868 or 1869:

---

[12]See Fields to Taylor, March 24, 1866.

We wish to engage the author of "Hannah Thurston" to write a novel for the Atlantic Monthly, to be pubd. in 12 nos. of that moral monthly, the privilege of publishing in book-form after it is completed in the A. M. to be given T. & F. for 5 years. We shd. want the story for the year 1868 or 9. What amount in current coin of the Republic should we pay you for the novel, thus to be printed & published? We offer you Five Thousand Dollars ($5000), and beg you will keep this a secret. An early reply will oblige us, as we are looking ahead.[13]

Taylor replied immediately that "your proposal chimes in very well with my own plans." He already had a novel in mind, "a work illustrating a phase of American life which interests me profoundly, and which I want to make better than the former ones"; and he hoped to finish it by the end of 1868 or shortly thereafter. The plan of serial publication interested him, but "it must be completed from end to end before any part of it goes out of my hands." Also, he hoped that Fields would like his series of travel sketches on "a number of the most picturesque and least known corners and by-ways of Europe," such as Friesland, the monastery of Montserrat, Gruyère, and the Volscian Mountains, which he intended to visit and write up during the succeeding months.[14] *By-Ways of Europe*, the new series, began in the August 1867 number of the *Atlantic* and ended with the thirteenth installment in the March 1869 number. The novel, *Joseph and His Friend*, was postponed to the 1870 *Atlantic*, appearing in all twelve issues for that year. It was Taylor's last but not his best novel. A complicated and melodramatic plot and a cast of psychopathic characters without convincing motivation offer little to a discriminating reader. Taylor received two hundred dollars per installment for the publication of the novel in the magazine,[15] and the book publication was left to G. P. Putnam and Son in New York.

[13]Fields to Taylor, September 13, 1866.

[14]Taylor and Scudder, II, 463.

[15]Fields to Taylor, May 4, 1870, and August 27, 1870. From February 1867 until late in 1870 Fields suffered from a lame hand, and most of his letters during these years were written by a secretary.

Bayard Taylor

In September 1868, before *Joseph and His Friend* was published, Taylor sent Fields one of his most important works, the poem "The Sunshine of the Gods." Though it is far from being a great poem, it felicitously describes the passion of poetic conception as understood by the school of writers that Taylor represented. To Taylor, the poet's office was to catch the elusive bits of universal truth that were unattainable to others.

> 'Tis the Sunshine of the Gods,
> The sudden light that quickens,
> Unites the nimble forces,
> And yokes the shy expression
> To the thoughts that waited long,—
> Waiting and wooing vainly:
> But now they meet like lovers
> In the time of willing increase,
> Each warming each, and giving
> The kiss that maketh strong:
> And the mind feels fairest May-time
> In the marriage of its passions,
> For Thought is one with Speech,
> In the Sunshine of the Gods,
> And Speech is one with Song!

Fields, recognizing the poem's value, wrote that it was "an exquisite poem, and one of the best you ever wrote, and ever will write."[16] When the proof was returned to Taylor, the poet made a slight addition, but Fields would not accept it, preferring the original expression. "You have done wisely not to alter the 'Sunshine of the Gods,' " wrote the editor on September 16. "I do not think your additional lines for the eighth stanza, helps or strengthens the verse, and so I shall omit them." The poem appeared in the January 1869 issue of the *Atlantic*.

Its companion piece, "Notus Ignoto," did not fare so well, though it was a favorite of its author. Fields qualifiedly rejected it in his letter of January 7:

---

[16] Fields to Taylor, September 3, 1868.

Fields of the Atlantic Monthly

Boston. Jan. 7. 1869.

My dear Taylor:
    Is it really twenty-three years ago, since you and Whipple and I, first ate beefsteak together, at the old Coffee Rooms on Washington Street! Have you still that old cap, which you wore then, laid away in camphor at Cedarcroft?
    There are things in "Notus Ignoto" that I like very much, but I think you can make it all better, if you keep it by you a little time longer. I particularly don't like, the two last lines in verse one.—and the line in verse two;—"and I lead you" &c ("higher, deeper" is particularly bad)—and the last line in verse three—"*His nostrils warm* &c.";—and the end of the second line in verse five ("words assistance" is prosaic enough), and the rhymes in verse five, "starvest" and "harvest." The close of the piece seems to me very inadequate.
    I think you ought to make this poem very much better, and I do not think it of the slightest consequence that it should immediately follow "The Sunshine of the Gods."

                             Always yours
                             J. T. F.

But Taylor was insistent and Fields had to explain further, this time tempering his remarks with a reference to the success of "The Sunshine of the Gods":

    If you could hear, all I hear said about "The Sunshine of the Gods," your ears would burn. Whittier, Aldrich and the rest think it, perhaps, if not your best, one of your very best. I did not decide hastily on "Notus Ignoto," but submitted it to three competent heads, which, without prompting from me, decided against it, as it now stands. It should be a very perfect poem, that is a fitting companion for "The Sunshine of the Gods."[17]

But the poet felt slighted, and Fields had to write still another explanation:

                                   Boston, Feb. 3, 1869.

My dear Taylor:
    Thank you very much for your kind note of the 22nd of January. If my hand were not lame, and I could manipulate the pen with such perfection of chirography, as you have always done, I would gladly always shake my own fist over the paper at you. But nowadays I

[17] Fields to Taylor, January 20, 1869.

can just make out to sign my name, only, and this must be my excuse for all amanuensory letters, you get from me. I never quarrel with a poet's individuality, and offer any strictures on a piece of verse, with great editorial modesty, but, if the poem I returned is really better than "The Sunshine of the Gods," I will eat a complete set of your works, and have dear old George Putnam thrown in, for sauce. However, someday I hope to be out of this business, and quietly laid away in some uneditorial corner.

With our best love to the household at Cedarcroft.

Ever sincerely yours,
J. T. F.

Taylor did not forgive Fields immediately. When Howells asked the writer for another poem for the magazine later that year—Fields having departed for Europe—Taylor vented his wrath upon the assistant editor:

I should like to write a poem for—or, rather, *publish one in*—the Atlantic, now and then; but Fields poured a bucket of ice-water over my head last winter, and I am shy of repeated drenchings.... no person or power on earth shall induce me to change what *I* feel to be right. To be true to one'self is more—in Literature—than to be agreeable to others.

Criticize me as much as you like, but only let me speak my mind in return, and we shall never fall out.[18]

His anger was not as great as it seemed, however, for he not only continued to contribute frequently to the *Atlantic* for many years, but he completely rewrote "Notus Ignoto" in a different meter before finally printing it in his collected poems.[19]

---

[18] Taylor to William Dean Howells, May 10, 1869, in Robert Ernest Butler, "William Dean Howells as Editor of The Atlantic Monthly" (unpublished doctoral dissertation, Rutgers University, 1950), p. 90, from manuscript in Harvard University Library.

[19] Marie Taylor, *On Two Continents*, p. 196.

Chapter XIX:
James Parton

JAMES PARTON, the English-born husband of the authoress "Fanny Fern," was an important contributor to the *Atlantic Monthly* for several reasons. For one thing, he represented the non-literary writer at his best, and his articles, though timely, are historically important as they concern topics that were currently popular. Second, he was "the most successful biographer of his generation and a master of the reconstructional method"; he had a modern, disinterested thirst for facts and "a positive genius for imparting order and motion to great masses of fact."[1] Third, his tough inquisitiveness revealed to him conditions of society that were overlooked by most of his contemporaries.

In 1866, when Fields became interested in him, Parton was forty-four and had already written several books, among them *Life and Times of Aaron Burr* (1857) and *General Butler in New Orleans* (1863), each of which had gone through seventeen editions.[2] A resident of New York City, he was a frequent contributor to the *New York Ledger* and also to the *North American Review*, which had become a Ticknor and Fields publication less than two years before. It was in the *North American*, where he was writing biographical sketches and articles on politics, that Fields began to notice him. He invited him to send similar articles to the *Atlantic* and to collect some of his short biographies for publication in a volume with the firm. Parton was flattered with the attention and indicated that he might accept, but he explained that he put several months of research into his articles and would

---

[1] George Henry Genzmer, *Dictionary of American Biography*.

[2] S. Austin Allibone, *A Critical Dictionary of English Literature and British and American Authors*, II (Philadelphia, 1899), 1519-20.

not be able to send any for the magazine until he had had time to prepare:

New York, 182 E. 18th St. March 15, 1866

My dear Sir,

Your note of March 11—, which I received yesterday, gave me great pleasure, for I am so constituted as to need a little praise now and then. I not only like it, but it really seems to strengthen me.

With regard to the Atlantic Monthly, I will bear your invitation in mind, & if ever a good idea occurs to me for an article, which I can use, I will endeavor to do it. The great difficulty with me is that I depend wholly upon industry—upon the preliminary research—which takes a world of time. There are many subjects of the greatest possible interest which could only be properly treated after a long period of investigation—out-of-doors. For example, I am trying to get together the material for an article for the N. A. Review on Political Wirepulling. I could easily expend a year in merely getting the facts —facts which never get into print.

I have been half tempted to propose to you the publication in the Atlantic Monthly of a Life of Voltaire: as the Life of Napoleon was published in Harpers' Magazine. But, I have much doubt, whether it would be well for you to do it. I have been studying and collecting for this subject for more than two years, always hoping to be able some day to do it. I merely mention it—in case you should think it worth while to consider it. If you should, I will explain the plan fully.

I should be glad to have you publish the pieces to which you refer in a volume, when there is enough of them. At present, I only remember the following: Calhoun, Clay, Girard, Astor, Vanderbilt, Theodoria Bun, J. G. Bennett, John Randolph, Goodyear. Perhaps, in time, we shall have enough to pick from. John Randolph, I should add, is not yet done. To these I may be able to add, Martin Van Buren & Hunter Weed, before very long. The grand object of all is to show, how things work in America, and who work them. I meditate an article on Jefferson and Hamilton, to show the prodigious superiority of Jefferson, & that the only safety is in following *him*, not his rival.

No more, however, this morning. I thank you for your hearty encouragement, & am

Very truly yours
Jas. Parton[3]

---

[3]Part printed in Milton E. Flower, *James Parton, the Father of Modern Biography* (Durham, 1951), pp. 81-82. Ticknor and Fields published Parton's biographies as *Famous Americans of Recent Times* in 1867.

Fields proposed that Parton write several articles, the first of which was to be on the popular Congregationalist minister Henry Ward Beecher, Harriet Beecher Stowe's brother. It is noteworthy that the editor should pick Parton, an avowed agnostic at a time when agnosticism was in very bad repute, to write not only this but other articles on contemporary religion. And though Parton spoke very highly of Beecher, his radicalism was perceptible in the article. By August 1866 Parton was planning "Henry Ward Beecher's Church" and also a second article, "History of the Sewing Machine," for the *Atlantic*. He wrote to Fields:

Brattleboro, Vermont, Aug. 8, 1866

My dear Sir,
　I have received Mr. Beecher's book, long sought in vain.
　Mr. Bonner [publisher of the *Ledger*] behaves handsomely. He lets me off, but says he shall be glad of an article now and then, if I can squeeze one out, and raises the price a little. Perhaps, by getting half an Amanuensis I may do it. Meanwhile I have one or two done. My mornings are now spent in thundering away at the New York thieves; my afternoons, to reading Webster; my evenings to brooding over him.
　The last thing you said to me was: Do the sewing machine first. Did you mean, first after Beecher? Or, to omit Beecher.
　I suppose I must be governed by the sewing machine men. Elias Howe lives at Bridgeport. He is the great source. He may be absent. Perhaps, I had better keep Mr. Beecher to work on when an obstacle arises in the way of some other article. I shall be always dependent upon others in preparing the other articles.
　The vision of Mrs. Fields' costume and Miss Bartol's shoes haunts me still. They will never know what it cost me to refrain from calling them a pair of jolly Bricks.
　It is delicious here. I hope you and Mrs. Fields will come before we go.
　Please give my respects to,
　　　　　　　Mrs. Fields
　　　　　　　Mrs. Bartol
　　　　　　　Miss Bartol
　　　　　　　Dr. Bartol
　　　　　　　Mr. Daggett
　　　　　　　Mr. Clarke
　　　　　　　Mr. Ticknor

James Parton
    Mr. Osgood
    Mr. Howells
    Mr. Aldrich and
    the other young Lady.
And believe me your friend and ally,

                                        Jas. Parton[4]

    Parton did not actually begin to write the Beecher article until October. Meanwhile he was receiving requests for articles or books from numerous editors and publishers, but by this time Fields had impressed him with the advantages of loyalty to the *Atlantic* and he declined all offers. "H. W. Beecher is begun, and all is serene," he wrote on October 2, "except that I receive an invitation to write something for somebody twice a week. Yesterday, from the Hon. H. J. Raymond; to day, from D. Appleton and Co. I tell 'em all, I am yours; and so I am." A few weeks later the Beecher article was ready. Parton's first article for the *Atlantic*, printed in the January 1868 issue, represented a changing attitude not only in the magazine but in the whole country. People were becoming more interested in the facts about their country—not sugar-coated facts but the truth. Parton considered Beecher's church "simply the most characteristic thing in America," and he contrasted it with the elegant churches of the wealthy, which frightened the poor man away and made religion a luxury. He also showed his awareness of ugliness in the American scene—from corruption in politics and business to the evils of men's clubs and women's fashions:

    There are some reasons for thinking that the men and the organizations that have had in charge the moral interests of the people of the United States for the last fifty years have not been quite equal to their trust. What are we to think of such results of New England culture as Douglas, Cass, Webster, and many other men of great ability, but strangely wanting in moral power? What are we to think of the great numbers of Southern Yankees who were, and are, the bitterest foes of all that New England represents? What are we to think of the Rings that seem now-a-days to form themselves, as it were, spontaneously in every great corporation? What of the club-

[4]See Flower, p. 84.

houses that spring up at every corner, for the accommodation of husbands and fathers who find more attraction in wine, supper, and equivocal stories than in the society of their wives and children? What are we to think of that fact, that among the people who can afford to advertise at the rate of a dollar and a half a line are those who provide women with the means of killing their unborn children, —a double crime, murder and suicide? What are we to think of the moral impotence of almost all women to resist the tyranny of fashion, and the *necessity* that appears to rest upon them to copy every disfiguration invented by the harlots of Paris? What are we to think of the want both of masculine and moral force in men, which makes them helpless against the extravagance of their households, to support which they do fifty years' work in twenty, and then die? What are we to think of the fact, that all creatures living in the United States enjoy good health, except the human beings, who are nearly all ill?

With difficulty the author avoided the more explosive aspects of his own religious unorthodoxy. "The subject, has its dangers, in avoiding which I have scratched out almost as much as I have retained," he wrote to Fields in his letter of submittal on October 26. "To make all sure, I read it over to Mrs. Parton, who is a judge of what the religious people will stand. I hope we are right in thinking that it is now safe."[5]

Shortly before he sent the Beecher paper, Parton set forth his plans for future articles. He was still working on the sewing machine article, and he hoped, not vainly, that Fields would finance a trip to Chicago, Cincinnati, and St. Louis in search of material for papers on those cities:

New York, 182 E. 18th St. Oct. 24, 1866

My dear Sir,

I received your note of Oct. 4, at the proper time, and to day comes the firm's note of Oct. 23. I have several things to say and to ask, and will now endeavor to say and ask them in the fewest possible words. I shudder to think of the quantity of notes you have to read and answer.

I

The article on Henry Ward Beecher's church is nearly done, and I shall send it this week. I have been a little hurried with it, not supposing it wanted till Nov. 15th.

[5]Flower, p. 84.

II

Daniel Webster is done, all but one more going over, and I will send it to Mr. Norton in a few days.

III

I conclude, that an article for the February number must be in your hands by Dec. 15. Unless I should have wonderful luck in getting information about the sewing machine, it will take me until that time to do the article, and, consequently, I could not go to Chicago and write upon it by Jan. 15. To avoid crowding, and to give me a little needed change and rest (for I am writing too much) had I not better go to Chicago very soon, almost immediately, while the weather is good, and secure that? I could start by Nov. 5, or very soon after.

IV

While I am out there, would it not be well for me to spend a week at St. Louis, and, perhaps, another at Cincinnati, and so get the material for three articles? They could alternate with others. I think I could do all the travelling in a month. I do not urge this, nor even wish it, but only suggest it. The expenses would not exceed $250. I should suppose.

V

When do you wish to have the copy for the volume of Review articles? "Clay, Webster and Calhoun, and Some of their Contemporaries."

VI

With regard to your suggestion about the Boys and Girls Biography Book, I fear I could not do well the fictitious frame work, and I think the smart boys and girls now-a-days see through it, and don't like it. Besides; what time can I get for it? Will they do as they are? If so, when do you want them, and how many pages?

VII

If you should chance to see a pamphlet with my name on the cover, know, that the bulk of the work was done by others. My part of it was done without interrupting my other labors.

I believe this is all. You can answer this in a very few words, long as it is, and I beg you will do so.

That New York article continues to be talked and written about; yea, and even preached about; which only confirms me in the belief, that the old seventy four, called the N. A. R. *could* be lifted.

Very truly yours
Jas. Parton

With Fields's approval and $250 for traveling expenses, Parton set out for Chicago early in November. The paper on the sewing machine was postponed while he collected material for his series of articles on American cities. The subject was a popular one, for Americans were becoming more and more curious about the parts of their country they had heard of but were unable to visit. A survey of the content of the magazines of the latter nineteenth century indicates that Parton was one of the early exploiters of the local travel sketch.[6] On November 11, the author wrote that "All is well," and that he hoped to be able to stop in Pittsburgh upon his return and so add that city to his series. The whole expedition took a little less than a month. Parton returned to New York December 11 and the next day he wrote Fields a report:

New York, 182 E. 18th St. Dec. 12, 1866.
My dear Mr. Fields,
 I returned safely last night, after five weeks of the most incessant labor, but rested and refreshed by it. I have brought home a head and trunk full of knowledge, which I shall set to work upon immediately. If I have half as much success in using as in getting the material, all will be well.
 I shall now endeavor to have an article upon Chicago in your hands on or before the 15th of January, i. e. in time for the March number.
 After that is done, I will either go on with the other cities, St. Louis, Cincinnati and Pittsburgh, or I will alternate them with the other subjects, as proposed. Just as you prefer.
 When next you are tired, go to those western cities, and get below the surface of them. As man of business, as literary man, as American citizen, and as human being, you will be instructed and pleased. The United States is *there*.
 But no more to day, for I am in the midst of confusion, and write only to report myself.
 With my love to the Firm, and my respects to the sleeping partner.
Ever yours,
Jas. Parton

"Chicago" appeared in the March 1867 issue of the *Atlantic*. In it Parton noted with facts and figures the tremendous growth, the

---

[6]See John A. Kouwenhoven, "America on the Move," *Harper's Magazine*, CCI (October 1950), 97-144.

industry, and the enterprising spirit of the community. The papers on Cincinnati, St. Louis, and Pittsburgh are similar. Parton's concern was with the future effects upon American life of these booming Western cities, and he foresaw the possibilities of evil as well as the immense productive capacity created by their uncontrolled industrialization.

The plan of alternating the articles on American cities with others was put into effect. Thus the next to appear was the long-awaited "History of the Sewing Machine." It is another instance of Parton's attention to what was on the public mind. Introduced in the forties and fifties, the sewing machine soon became an industrial product. With the Civil War the industry boomed because of the demand for clothing. Returning veterans, however, preferred factory-made clothing to that made at home on the machine, so the demand for private machines slackened and competition between manufacturers increased. Naturally the manufacturers were interested in all the publicity they could get, as their advertising in the *Atlantic Monthly*, for example, testifies.[7] The public, then, was kept constantly aware of the industry and was curious for facts. Parton's research included an interview with the inventor of the machine, Elias Howe, and he reported his interview to Fields. If, as Parton says, Howe received a dollar on every machine sold in the United States, it was no wonder that he made two million dollars by the time he died in 1867.

New York, 182 E. 18th St. Jan. 29, 1867

My dear Chieftain,

First, I thank the House for its generous gift and polite attention in sending me a set of books bound in green cloth. Nothing could be more elegant. Nash so beautifully clad has a kind of merit and dignity.

In the second place, I have had such good luck in the Sewing Machine, that I expect to be able to send it to you by the 15th of February. I have access to 30000 pages of testimony taken in suits, and Elias Howe has told me his whole story. All the great makers

---

[7] Frank Presbrey, *The History and Development of Advertising* (New York, 1929), p. 57.

Fields of the Atlantic Monthly

have been very communicative, and only one has offered me a machine. With that exception, they have all behaved virtuously. The facts are startling enough. 52219 machines were made in the U. S. during the quarter ending Dec. 10, 1866, without counting the 20000 supposed to be made on the sly. Not many less than 1000 machines a day are now produced. Mr. Howe gets a dollar for each one returned. This is better than writing articles, and better even than publishing them. Let us invent something immediately.

Good subjects: N. P. Willis. "Is it wrong to go to the theatre?"

This last must be done by someone that respects the scruple, without sharing it. Such an article would go right home to thousands of families, in which the subject is a cause of contention between the elders and the young ones.

Your Dickens will be a hit, I think. But oh! my Shakspeare!

No answer required.

With my constant regards to Mrs. Fields and Miss Bartoll, I remain very truly yours

Jas. Parton[8]

The paper on the sewing machine was sent in February and printed in the May 1867 issue of the *Atlantic*. It was, as Parton suggested in a letter to Fields of February 13, "an important and interesting chapter in the history of the United States—that part of history which is so important that historians seldom say anything about it."

Sewing machines and pianos were by far the most advertised products, aside from books, in the *Atlantic*. It is not surprising, then, that one of Parton's next articles should have been upon pianos. Though magazine advertising was relatively insignificant as compared with today, Fields was glad to encourage contributions upon these subjects. Parton's article as usual is factual and concise, and it praises especially the American manufacturers of pianos, and their success in mass production methods without sacrifice of technical accuracy. It also notes the large and increasing number of pianos and organs in American middle-class homes. Though Parton complained that he knew nothing of the subject when he began, he had the article ready for the July 1867 number of the magazine. He wrote to Fields in March:

[8] "My Shakespeare" refers to a new edition which Parton suggested but which Fields did not undertake.

James Parton

New York, 182 E. 18th St. March 18th, 1867.
My dear Mr. Fields,

I expect to send you St. Louis to morrow, so that you will have it on Wednesday morning.

The 25 copies arrived, and I thank the illustrious House for its generosity and politeness. The book is very elegant.

I do not believe it will be possible for me to do the piano in time for next month. I know nothing of the subject, and have a constitutional difficulty in understanding such. I think, therefore, I will not try for next month.

I have much thought of the subject likely for the magazine: "Our Roman Catholic Brethren."

That is, an account of the Catholic Church in the U. S. Early mass, convent schools, Pushing in the west, converts, Ritualism, Protestant errors that help the Catholics,—such as Sabbatarianism, & severe orthodoxy, politics, servant-girls, etc. etc. etc.

Ever yours,
Jas. Parton

Parton eventually wrote the article on Roman Catholics, but it was not printed until the next year.

Occasionally Parton recommended new writers to Fields. One was Marshal Oliver, an actor and later a professor. As the following letters show, the recommendation worked out well for all concerned, but especially for Oliver. Parton wrote to Fields in behalf of the young man:

Highgate Springs, Franklin Co. Vt. July 10, 1867.
My dear Mr. Fields,

You will have received an article by Marshal Oliver upon the Drama in New York. Mr. Oliver is a young artist who was starved into going on the stage for a while, and I suggested to him to write out his experience for the Atlantic Monthly. If he has done this, his article may be valuable. All such articles are; if they are tolerably executed. If he has done something else, the chances are less favorable. You are the judge. I can only say, that the author is a very nice, intelligent young fellow, very modest, very well disposed, and very poor. All that is nothing to the point, however.

I am in the full tide of International Copyright. The subject interests me powerfully. It will be two weeks before I can send it.

I heard of you in Montreal, from a person who saw you there

and is now here. This is a good place, close to Lake Champlain. Come and take a sail.

Ever yours
Jas. Parton

No answer, except to say you are coming.

In July, when the Oliver article was brought to Parton's notice, he was working on a new subject, the need for an international copyright law. The evils arising from the lack of a suitable copyright arrangement with Great Britain had been apparent, of course, since post-Revolutionary War days, but there had not been enough political pressure to get anything done about it. In 1867 an international copyright movement was under way, in which Parton and Fields took an active interest. Parton's article, printed in the October *Atlantic*, was an attempt to publicize the situation. He sent it to Fields on August 3. "I have done my best with it," he wrote in the accompanying letter, "and now you must do with it just what you like. Cut it down, add to it, do anything you think likely to finish the object.... All I care for is, to have the cause promoted." Fields and his proofreaders cluttered the proof with many "marks and queries," but the editor gave the article his "warm approval."[9] It is no wonder that he approved, for, in the course of outlining the copyright situation as it stood, Parton heartily commended the firm of Ticknor and Fields for its generous remunerations to Tennyson, Browning, Reade, Arnold, Kingsley, Dickens, and others for publishing their works in America regardless of lack of legal protection. Parton concluded his eulogium:

We dare not comment upon these facts, because, if we were to indulge our desire to do so, the passage would be certain "to turn up missing" upon the printed page, since Messrs. Ticknor and Fields live two hundred miles nearer the office of the Atlantic Monthly than we do. Happily, comment is needless. Every man who has either a conscience or a talent for business will recognize either the propriety or the wisdom of their conduct. Upon this rock of fair-dealing the eminent and long-sustained prosperity of this house is founded.

[9] Parton to Fields, August 21, 1867.

While the copyright article was in progress, Fields had accepted the article by Oliver, "Four Months on the Stage." Parton wrote to ask that the young author be paid immediately, as he had just been appointed assistant professor of drawing at the Naval Academy at Annapolis and would need money to buy uniforms. Fields responded promptly, presumably with the money, though the article was not printed until the February 1868 issue. Oliver's success reminded Parton that he knew of another writer who could produce something that would make good material for the *Atlantic*. "Emboldened by this success," he wrote to Fields, September 22, 1867, "I have encouraged a nice young fellow in the Ledger office to put down all there is about The Fast Horses of America. He reads Kant, and hears horse-talk all the time. No one can be better placed for becoming learned in horses than he, for while Robert Bonner buys fast horses, David Bonner breeds them, and he hears both talk every day." John Elderkin's article, "The Turf and the Trotting Horses of America," was accepted for the May 1868 issue only after considerable revision by Parton, but it was characteristic of the kind of thing Parton favored for the *Atlantic*. It was his opinion as well as others' that the *Atlantic* was too literary and needed to be popularized. Amusingly enough, this was the identical criticism that Fields had handed Lowell some seven years before. Parton wrote:

N. Y. 303. E. 18th St. Sept. 27, 1867.

My dear Friend,
I have just received your note, enclosing one for Mr. Oliver. That modest youth has either gone to Annapolis, or is just going. If he is gone, I will send him his note, and much good may it do him. I will gladly read the proof.

Mr. Clark never fails to respond most promptly to the slightest intimation of my wants.

I, also, see and hear good things about the International [Copyright] article. It was an excellent thought of yours to leave off the ending. Now, the question is, will it do any good? Perhaps, it were well to send a copy to the ministers abroad, Mr. Bancroft, and the rest. To Mr. Seward, also. To some English authors, too.

I will do all I can to have the Fast Horses done properly. It will be one of the set-off articles, to make a relief for the Emersonian, Whippletonian, pieces, and keep the New Yorkers from saying you are "too literary."

Ever yours faithfully,
Jas. Parton

One of Parton's articles, "Does it Pay to Smoke?" was so popular that it was reprinted together with a later one, "Will the Coming Man Drink Wine," in a small book entitled *Smoking and Drinking* in 1868. Parton suggested the subject to Fields on September 14, 1867; two months later he wrote to say that he was making a survey of illustrious men to discover their opinions on smoking:

N. Y. 303 E. 18th St. Nov. 10, 1867

My dear Friend,

I want to know whether or not certain persons smoke: Does Mr. Longfellow? Does Mr. Emerson? Does Mr. Norton? Did Theodore Parker?

May I trouble you just to write yes or no, after each of those questions, tear off the leaf, and send it back? To save you trouble, I enclose an envelope all ready directed.

You see, I am making two lists: 1. of all the illustrious smokers; 2. of all the illustrious enemies of smoke. I hope the dinner went off in triumph. Having seen Mr. Longfellow, I no longer wonder at every body's loving him so. I often think of him in his becoming house, and seated so properly at the head of that table, nor am I ever forgetful to whom I owe the pleasure of having seen him in both situations. See Sunday's Herald for another of Bennett's digs at me. As in England, no one is of any consequence, till he has been caricatured in Punch. So, in America, to be attacked in the Herald is an evidence that the person attacked is of some account.

Ever yours very truly,
Jas. Parton

Could not the Atlantic Monthly avail itself of the sudden importance of General Grant? Say a full and true account of his life, in one, two, or three numbers, the materials obtained in places where he has lived.

He smokes 20 cigars a day. This I learn from one of his household. He has been trying of late to reduce his allowance, and *this* is the cause of his occasional indispositions, which keep him at home for a day or two. When he does not smoke all day, he *must* chew or be sick. He has thoroughly depraved his system by tobacco. This you may rely on as true, but, not publish.

J. P.[10]

Parton's verdict on the value of smoking was adverse. His paper, which was the leading article in the February 1868 issue, excited comment much as such articles do today—witness, for example, the sensational "studies" of tobacco publicized in the *Reader's Digest* of recent years. Medical knowledge of the effects of tobacco was even more limited in the 1860's than now, and the article contained a great deal of moralizing on the "barbarity" of the nicotine habit. The disparate but interested opinions of Doctor Holmes and Bayard Taylor were typical of the attitudes of the reading public toward the subject. Annie Fields recorded their comments in her diary:

Thursday morning, November 19, 1868.—Mr. Parton came to breakfast and Dr. Holmes came in before we had quite done. O. W. H. was delighted to see Mr. P., because of his papers on "Smoking and Drinking." He believes smoking paralyzes the will. Taylor, on the contrary, feels himself better for smoking; it subdues his physical energy so he can write; otherwise he is nervous to be up and away and his mind will not work.[11]

In spite of interruptions, Parton had not given up the idea of an article upon the Catholics. "I am hunting down the Catholics still," he wrote on December 22, after the tobacco article had been sent to Fields. "It is an enormous subject. I hope well of it, but it is a great and long job."[12] He revealed his personal attitude toward the Catholics when he wrote a few days later that he was "really alarmed at their power, their progress, their confidence."[13] Most

---

[10] Part printed in Flower, p. 94, with part of Fields's reply. An impersonal article on Grant, "The Next President," by Howells, appeared in the May 1868 *Atlantic*.

[11] Howe, *Memories of a Hostess*, p. 110.

[12] Quoted, but misdated, in Flower, p. 99.

[13] Parton to Fields, December 27, 1867. Part printed, but misdated, in Flower, p. 100.

of his information he gathered from Father Isaac T. Hecker of New York, founder and editor of the *Catholic World*. "Heavens!" Parton continued in the same letter, "how can you explain such a phenomenon as Father Hecker?" In January the writer had collected enough information for two articles, and he wrote to Fields, outlining the material:

N. Y. 303 E. 18th St. Jan. 21, 1868

Now, Mr. Fields, I must put to you the solemn question:
Will you have these Catholic Brethren in one article or in two? I have enough matter for two of 15 pages each.

If you say, one,—as I suppose you will—then say the greatest number of pages you can allow. To enable you to judge, I tell you how it goes.

First, I skirt round the subject. I go to the 6 A. M. mass on a very cold, dark morning. I go to Sunday School. I explain the financial system. The Charity system. The Propaganda, the revivals, the orders.

Then I come to Father Hecker—his life and career—how he is running the Catholic church on American principles, and letting up a little on the understanding—and what is to be the result. Are we going to be all Catholics, or are we not?

Father Hecker says we are and gives some truly portentous reasons. Two, or one, which? Speak! Two lines will do.

I thank Mrs. Fields for her benevolence in being about to lend me the book, and for the agreeable manner in which she communicates her intention. When the book arrives, I will announce the event to her.

Very truly yours,
Jas. Parton

The plan of arranging the article in two parts was adopted, and Parton sent the first part on the twenty-sixth. He thought of writing similar articles on the Protestant sects, but was afraid his point of view would be unacceptable to the public. Although he could not believe in Catholicism, he could speak of it with sympathy and admiration, but this he could not do with Protestantism:

N. Y. Jan. 26, 1868.

My dear Mr. Fields,
I put the Roman Catholics into the P. O. yesterday. As you read, you will perhaps think that I am too favorable to them, but at the end the apple-cart is upset. My next will be more interesting.

If these articles are approved, what do you say to "Our Israelitish Brethren"?

The notion is, to review these bodies from the point of view of the man of the world. I would like to go on with "Our Methodist Brethren," "Our Episcopal Brethren," etc. only I am afraid I dislike them too much. Perhaps, some one else could.

Mr. Dickens' last instalment, not so good as the first. The [February] number excellent as far as I have gone in it.

With my regards to the lady at 124 Charles St.

Yours very truly,
Jas. Parton

As soon as he had finished the first installment, Parton went to work on the second, which he sent about a month later. Actually the paper is not at all antagonistic, and the author maintained a tone of calm disinterestedness throughout, though he emphasized the rapid growth of the Catholic church in the United States and suggested that its power might reach tremendous proportions in the future. In his letter of submittal he mentioned that he had had a difficult time in trying to complete the paper "without giving the bigots a handle":

N. Y. 303 E. 18th St. Feb. 29, 1868.

My dear Mr. Fields,

Herewith I send the second Catholic article. I have been working upon the two, as my chief or morning work, ever since Dec. 2. The result seems small; yet so it is. I have had a severe struggle in winding up, to get out part of my idea without giving the bigots a handle. I hope it is safe as it is now. No exercise of the mind is so pleasing as to make the religious papers howl; but this luxury must be indulged in moderately.

I continue to hear about my smoking article, and get letters about it. I never had so much rebound before. People seem to expect that I will be published as a tract, and a lady writes for 100 copies. But I do not think she would have many imitators. I am strongly inclined to try my hand, some day, at the other subject: "Will the Coming man drink wine?" The trouble is, I don't know whether he will or not, and am not sure I could find out. If I should do this, and have some success with it, then the two might make a tract.

Of all the subjects we have lately mentioned, which do you most incline to? What shall I meditate first?

I have not heard of the verdict upon the Horse article.
I hope Mrs. Fields is in the enjoyment of perfect happiness. As for man, he never is, but always *to* be, blest.
Ever yours,
Jas. Parton

There ought to be *ladies* at the Press dinner to Dickens.[14]

Parton's foresight frequently proved to be quite accurate in editorial matters, particularly when he recommended to Fields an up-and-coming new writer, Mark Twain. His suggestion was made when he was visiting the Fieldses in November 1868 and is recorded in Annie Fields's diary: "Parton thinks it would be possible to make the 'Atlantic Monthly' far more popular. He suggests a writer named Mark Twain be engaged, and more articles connected with life than with literature."[15] But nothing by Twain appeared in the magazine until after Fields's editorship had terminated.

Within a year after the publication of "Our Catholic Brethren" Fields departed for Europe, and Parton's correspondence was with Howells. Parton continued to contribute articles during the rest of Fields's editorship. In January 1869 was a sketch of New England, "The Mean Yankees at Home," in the same vein as the articles on the western cities. In March appeared "Popularizing Art," in which the author gave vent to his belief in democratization. In May was "The Clothing Mania," upon which subject Parton was a Carlylean crank. Then followed several articles on political failures and corruption, such as "The 'Strikers' of the Washington Lobby" and "The Small Sins of Congress." In "The Correspondence of Napoleon Bonaparte" Parton exercised his biographical talent. And with "Our Israelitish Brethren" he returned to the religious study. For a year after Fields's retirement he contributed nothing, then he began again as regularly as ever. In all he contributed twenty-four articles while Fields was editor, or six per year—a considerable number, especially considering the diligent research that went into them.

[14]Part printed in Flower, p. 96.
[15]Howe, *Memories of a Hostess*, p. 111.

James Parton

Although not well known now, Parton had considerable reputation in his own time. So worthy a critic as William Dean Howells spoke very highly of him: "I cannot say how much his books, once so worthily popular, are now known, but I have an abiding sense of their excellence.... He was never of the fine world of literature," Howells continued, "the world that sniffs and sneers, and abashes the simpler-hearted reader. But he was a true artist, and English born as he was, he divined American character as few Americans have done."[16] As a writer of popular articles on timely subjects and as a reporter of the American scene, Parton filled, almost unrivaled, an important place among the contributors to the *Atlantic*.

---

[16] William Dean Howells, *Literary Friends and Acquaintance* (New York, 1901), p. 143.

Chapter XX:
New York to San Francisco

Of all the contributors to the *Atlantic* from outside New England, the great majority was from New York. In fact, except for Bayard Taylor, whose residence ranged from Russia to Pennsylvania during the sixties, and Rebecca Harding Davis of Wheeling, there was no writer from the rest of the country who contributed more than eight times. But the New Yorkers displayed a remarkable heterogeneity.

The list begins with Bryant, the grand old man of American poetry, who contributed ten poems, almost two a year, between 1864 and 1870. One of the first of these was "The Return of the Birds," published in the July 1864 *Atlantic*. Perhaps because it was a war poem, Bryant asked nothing for it.

Dear Mr. Fields.   Roslyn Long Island May 9th 1864.
 I send you what you ask—a poem for your July number. The matter for the June number, I dare say is already in hand. The one I now send, you remember is not to be paid for.
                                    Very truly yours
                                    W. C. Bryant
P.S. Please retain the date in printing the poem.
                                    W. C. B.[1]

The "matter for the June number" never appeared.

"My Autumn Walk" (January 1865) is one of Bryant's best contributions. Typically, it begins with musings upon the landscape which evolve into a message, in this case the sadness of the war:

> On woodlands ruddy with autumn
> The amber sunshine lies;
> I look on the beauty round me,
> And tears come into my eyes.

[1] MS in the Henry W. and Albert A. Berg Collection, New York Public Library.

> For the wind that sweeps the meadows
> Blows out of the far South-west,
> Where our gallant men are fighting,
> And the gallant dead are at rest.

Besides poems of this sort he contributed four selections from his translation of the *Iliad*, not published in full until 1870. His part in the *Atlantic* was not great, but it served to connect his revered name with the magazine that strove to represent the best in American literature.

A contemporary of Bryant was John Neal, the novelist, who wrote biographical reminiscences for the *Atlantic*. He was seventy-two when he contributed his first sketch, that of Jeremy Bentham in the November 1865 issue; and his importance to the magazine lay in his acquaintance with men of a past generation. For this reason the strongly personal reminiscences of Bentham, William Blackwood, and John Pierpont are of some small biographical value. He made six contributions, including the descriptive "London Forty Years Ago" (August 1866) and a long essay, "Our Painters" (December 1868 and March 1869).

Theodore Winthrop, a New Yorker thirty-five years younger than Neal, owed his fame largely to George William Curtis, who championed his works, and to Fields, who published them, mostly after Winthrop's death in June 1861. When Winthrop died a hero on the battlefield of Great Bethel, he was virtually unknown, except for an article "New York Seventh Regiment" (June 1861) that had appeared in the *Atlantic* three weeks before. He was to have written a full series of these reports of his army service. A second appeared in July, and a third, in the form of rough notes which brought the account up to the time of his death, was printed along with an essay on the writer by Curtis in August. Winthrop's articles were witty entertainment as well as good journalism. The rest of his writings were collected, with the encouragement of Curtis;[2] and Ticknor and Fields published the three novels in 1862, while two short stories, a poem, and a travel sketch went to the

---

[2] See George William Curtis to Fields, November 4, 1861.

Atlantic. "Saccharissa Mellasys" (September 1861) was the first and perhaps the best of the stories, being a wild and witty satire on New York "aristocracy" and Southern "hospitality." Winthrop's work was unpolished and lacked concentration, but it contained real humor and skill with language, and sometimes showed a very modern choice of subjects—as the labor-capital problem in "Love and Skates." Fields's interest in the author was justified by the tremendous popularity accorded his books.

A New Yorker who deserved better treatment than she got from Fields was Alice Cary, the Cincinnati-born poetess whose fame was greater for her social grace and hospitality than for her writing. Though she published eleven poems and two short stories in the *Atlantic* during Fields's time, the editor relentlessly rejected and corrected her work whenever he wished. She chafed under this treatment but continued to contribute. One of her letters, undated, illustrates her attitude:

My dear Censor. See what pains I have taken to please you, and try to be pleased, if you can. I have changed my title for one, in a sort, explanatory, but have at your suggestion, omitted the *buckles*, but fear you will not like the *Cap* & the *clasps* any better. But my shepherdess only sings about them, so I pray you put the responsibility where it belongs. I have pretty nearly re-written, as you see, and have, I think worked out my idea more clearly as I alter[?] it, there was some room you see, and I hope have profited.

For the suggestion of *Lochmarlie* see a note in Modern Painters, third volume, page 293, Wiley & Halstead's edition.

Of the Lover's May Song I have only to say that I selected my flowers with strict reference to truth as to season, colors & qualities. I mention this because I see you distrust my judgment.

But now, my dear Censor, I await your pleasure—hoping one of my ventures may find favor in your eyes.

If not, however, please let me have them back at your early convenience, and believe me

Very truly yours
Alice Cary.

53 East 90th St.
I send my ventures by the same mail with this.[3] [FI 597]

[3] The poem concerning buckles, caps, and clasps did not appear in the *Atlantic*. The other could have been any of several poems involving May flowers.

At another time, when Fields had accepted her story "The Great Doctor" but had not printed it immediately, she wrote: "Only tell me once for all whether I am to be a welcome visitor at your house, or a beggar to be kept waiting at the door."[4] The story appeared three and a half months later in the July 1867 *Atlantic* and was continued in the August number.

Her poetry was among the most lyrical—the least forced—in the magazine. Her love poems, such as "Presence" (February 1864), have grace and melody besides honest feeling. Her short narrative poems are often clever as well as graceful; for instance, "Worldly-Wise" (February 1868) tells the story of Ronsalee, who was faced with the choice of marrying a poor girl or a rich:

> Long time the balance even stood
> With our Ronsalee that day;
> But what was a little house in
>   the wood
> To a palace grand and gay?
> So he gave his heart to Jenny,
>   the good,
> And his hand he gave to May.

Her best story was "The Rose Rollins" (October and November 1867). Its representation of low class dialect is artificial and imitative of Dickens, but the humorous characterizations, though also imitative of Dickens, are delightful. After Parton, Miss Cary was the most frequent contributor to the magazine among the New Yorkers.

Another of the New York poets was Edmund Clarence Stedman. Of his six contributions, only the first was prose, and that was written reluctantly upon the request of Fields. It was an article on "Nature's sweet interpreter," the actor Edwin Booth, and appeared in the May 1866 *Atlantic*. Stedman had protested against writing it, but suggested that he send poems to the *Atlantic*.

My dear Sir: 184 East Tenth St. New York. Jan. 17th '66

    Mrs. Stedman has informed me of her pleasant meeting with you at Taylor's, & of your very kind request that I would prepare an

---

[4] Alice Cary to Fields, March 7, 1866.

article on Edwin Booth for *The Atlantic*. It would give me real pleasure, for many reasons, to furnish such a paper; but I am sure I shd. not do it so well as Mr. Hurlbut, Mr. Winter, Mr. House, or others, who have made the drama a specialty & are more closely acquainted with Booth's qualities and career. And my engagements are such that if you can think of some such substitute, I wd. *prefer* it. If not, however, I will make my acquaintance with Mr. B. available for such an article as I can write—and in such case would be obliged for a hint as to its nature & length.

At the suggestion of Mr. Taylor, I enclose for your acceptance or rejection a revised copy of a poem, of which he says he read you the unfinished draft. Having had considerable editorial experience, I know how editors are embarrassed by the pre-judgments of "mutual friends," and therefore hope that you will put Bayard's existence entirely out of the question, and send the Mss. back, if it is not *suited to the wants of your magazine.*

Being at last freed from business I am returning to active literary work, & would willingly be on your list for an occasional poem or article.

Let me ask you to excuse this too long letter, and exceed my right that as yet I have failed to meet you on your visits to New York. When you next come over, pray remember among the homes where you will be more than welcome that of

Yours very sincerely
Edmund C. Stedman[5]

Nevertheless, on February 27, he sent the article.

Probably the most famous of all the poems Stedman wrote is "Pan in Wall Street," which first appeared in the January 1867 *Atlantic*. Here he successfully contrasted the commercialism of the world with his dream of ideal beauty in art. The poem was submitted September 30, 1866, and a revised version sent to Fields in October.

New York. Oct. 8th 1866

My dear Sir:

Your hearty estimate of "Pan in Wall St." pleases me exceedingly—for I'll own that it is a pet poem & I shd. have been disappointed if it hadn't found you in a sympathetic mood. Thanks, both for your plaudits & your criticism—which latter seems to me well put. "Pants" *is* an American vulgarism, & no mistake—but you are a poet yourself, & if you'll just try to alter that stanza into anything else, & to preserve

---

[5]See Stedman to Fields, February 27, 1866.

the effect, you'll appreciate the exigencies of the case. The best I can do is to substitute the enclosed, for the entire stanza, if you deem it, on the whole, an improvement. As I use "concealed" in the last line, I change that word to "hidden thus" in the 2d. The new verse is also faulty in having the same structure in the 5th & 7th lines, but I can't better it. "Pants" may be blurted, when you recollect that Pan is in a Yankee street & guise, & observed by a Yankee—but choose according to your judgment (which I most sincerely respect) & believe me,

Very truly yours'
Edmund C. Stedman.[6]

"Trousers" was the word finally used in the fifth stanza. Stedman's critical power and influence soon surpassed his creative ability, but the occurrence of his poems in the *Atlantic* symbolized the new tendencies of genteel literature.

As an exponent of the later genteelism, there were few men more outstanding than Henry Mills Alden, managing editor of *Harper's Weekly* from 1863 to 1869 and editor of *Harper's Monthly* from 1869 to 1919. Through the intermediacy of Mrs. Stowe, he published his first paper, "The Eleusinia" (September 1859 and August 1860), in the *Atlantic* under Lowell, while he was still an undergraduate at Andover Theological Seminary. Fields aided him considerably with both money and encouragement when he most needed it, and he was exceedingly grateful.[7] For example, it was through Fields's aid that he received the Lowell Institute lectureship in 1863. In token of his esteem he named two of his daughters after Annie, one having died in infancy.

Alden's contributions to the magazine consisted of five reviews and two articles. "Pericles and President Lincoln" in the March 1863 number is an erudite comparison of the Civil War with the Peloponnesian. In spite of superior strength, said the author, both Athens and the North flounder against their enemies because "neither ourselves nor the ancient Athenians appear to have the remotest idea of the importance of the cause for which we are

---

[6]See also Stedman to Fields, September 30, 1866.

[7]Alden to Fields, February 21, 1862; February 25, 1862; February 27, 1862; September 11, 1863; November 5, 1862; and November 12, 1862.

contending." The most extensive of Alden's contributions is "Thomas De Quincey" (September 1863), in which he denounced the tendency to neglect De Quincey and developed the thesis that he "was the prince of heirophants, or of pontifical hierarchs, as regards all those profound mysteries which from the beginning have swayed the human heart." In writing the article Alden was aided by both James and Annie Fields, whose letters and reminiscences were copious.

The case of Henry Alden was one in which Fields proved to be right in his judgment of the potentialities of young writers. Not so with Walt Whitman. Only one of Whitman's poems appeared in the *Atlantic* during Fields's time. But it was not from malice that Fields neglected him, for as E. C. Stedman later pointed out[8] Whitman was a bad investment for an editor. Lowell had accepted one of his poems, "Bardic Symbols," which was printed in the April 1860 number, and in October 1861 the now-retired editor sent Fields three more contributions from Whitman.[9] Fields did not print them. Nor did he accept any of John Burroughs' essays on the poet. The Whitman poem that did appear was "Proud Music of the Sea-Storm" (February 1869), later called "Proud Music of the Storm," a good poem but lacking the "objectionable qualities" of sensuousness by reason of which Whitman was generally taboo among the genteel.

Whitman was neglected, but Herman Melville was almost completely ignored. He was the only one of the major writers of the North (excluding Emily Dickinson, who did not publish, and Mark Twain, who came in later) who was not represented in the *Atlantic*. Nevertheless he was once invited to contribute and consented. The invitation was extended by Francis Underwood in 1857 before the magazine had begun publication, and Melville replied on August 19: "I shall be very happy to contribute, though I cannot now name the day when I shall have any article ready."[10]

[8] Edmund Clarence Stedman, *Poets of America* (Boston, 1896), p. 361.
[9] Lowell to Fields, October 8, 1861.
[10] Bliss Perry, "The Editor Who Was Never the Editor," *Atlantic Monthly*, C (November 1907), 667.

New York to San Francisco

The day never arrived, and the present writer finds no evidence that Melville was ever asked to contribute again. The only mention of him during the first twenty-five years of the *Atlantic* was a review of his *Battle-Pieces and Aspects of the War* by Howells (February 1867), in which the reviewer fears, indeed, that Melville "has not often felt the things of which he writes, since with all his skill he fails to move us."

From Philadelphia, the third largest literary center in the North, the *Atlantic* received the contributions of George Henry Boker and Silas Weir Mitchell, each of whom had five pieces in the magazine under Fields. Though Boker had contributed one poem to Lowell in 1860, he sent no more until Fields requested them. It was in 1864, while Boker was in the process of publishing his *Poems of the War* with Ticknor and Fields, that he replied to the request with a list of poems Fields could use:

Philadelphia, August 1st 1864.
My dear Fields,
   I am glad to know that you like "Captain Semmes." My friends here—who are not the best judges in the world—thought below my mark, *infra viz.* &c. I often think of sending you a poem for the "Atlantic"; but when I have finished one of my war-poems, I am at once possessed with the idea that it will not keep,—that in order to do any good it must be printed at once, so away it goes to the press. If you wish a poem of mine in the "Atlantic," why not take one from the volume for your September number? I append you a list of those that have not been published:—
   "The Ride to Camp," "The Ballad of New Orleans," "Eric the Minstrel," "Before Vicksburg," "The Battle of Lookout Mountain," "Abou's Charity," "Idleness," "Dirge" at page 200.
   I think either "Eric" or "Idleness" would suit your purpose, the latter particularly; but you are welcome to take any you like.
                                         Yours sincerely,
                                         Geo: H. Boker[11]

The best thing of Boker's to appear in the *Atlantic* was "Countess Laura," a long narrative poem in the August 1865 number, concerning love renounced for duty's sake.

---

[11] Two of the poems Boker named, "Before Vicksburg" and "The Ride to Camp," were printed in the 1864 *Atlantic*.

Mitchell, whose first contribution, "George Dedlow" (July 1866), was sent in by Hale, was one of the earliest writers of psychiatric fiction. He related the circumstances of his initiation into the magazine thus:

I lent the manuscript to my friend Mrs. Casper Wister, who gave it to her father, the Rev. Dr. William Henry Furness. Then I forgot all about it. I was a busy practicing doctor, and it had been but the amusement of one or two evenings. Dr. Furness sent it to the Rev. Edward Everett Hale, then editor[sic] of the Atlantic, and to my surprise and amusement I received a check, I think about eighty dollars [actually fifty], and the proof of my story. So important was it considered that it was made the leading article in the next number but one. It attracted immense attention.... For a long while no one knew who had written this marvelous history![12]

"George Dedlow" is the story of a man who loses his arms and legs in the war, and whose personality and consciousness of self disintegrate as his limbs are amputated. It is told so convincingly that it appears to be true autobiography. The popularity of the story is evidenced by the fact that for his next story, "The Autobiography of a Quack" (October and November 1867), Mitchell asked and received the exceptional price of twelve dollars a page.[13] The letter of submittal for "The Autobiography of a Quack" indicates that Mitchell had disapproved of some unauthorized editorial tampering with "George Dedlow."

May 8 1867—

Dear sir. I have received your reply to my note of a recent date & will forward at once by express the Autobiography of Elias Sandcraft, Quack. If you want to use this as a title I would be quite willing— but I fancy the simple one I have used is better. I have looked the paper over carefully as to style etc. so that I do not think I shall need to read the proofs. It needs a good deal of—paragraphing etc.— which I can safely leave to your reader. I object very decidedly to your making any such omissions as were made in my last paper without consulting me. I have the honour to be very respecty. yours—

S. Weir Mitchell
1332. Walnut St. Phila.

I desire the present paper to be considered anonymous. S. W. M.

[12]Anna Robeson Burr, *Weir Mitchell* (New York, 1930), pp. 125-26.
[13]Letters from Mitchell to Fields, no date (FI 3213 and FI 3214).

The new story did have to be cut because of "certain offensive parts," as the memoranda of Howells and Fields on Mitchell's letter of May 12, 1867, indicate. What parts were actually deleted is not shown by the letters. Mitchell, a prominent physician, was eminently qualified to apprise the public of the malpractices of his less exemplary colleagues. He contributed another short story as well as two articles on poisons, which because of the recent discoveries of their functions and beneficial uses made popular reading.

Besides the Philadelphians, there were two other writers from the eastern United States, John Hay and John Burroughs, both of Washington, D. C. Hay had two articles in Fields's *Atlantic*: "Ellsworth" (July 1861), in memory of Ephraim Elmer Ellsworth, the Civil War hero who was killed at Alexandria, and "The Mormon Prophet's Tragedy" (December 1869), a vituperative denunciation of Joseph Smith with an account of his murder. Hay wrote to Fields concerning the former article, which Fields had asked him to submit:

Executive Mansion June 2. 1861

My Dear Sir;

Immediately on receiving your kind note of the 29th I wrote the enclosed paper. Additional labor bestowed upon it for August would not have compensated for the loss of timeliness.

I have written two titles at the head of the article. You can choose between them.

In the limits you mentioned, but little general discussion of military affairs could be introduced.

Will you have the kindness to inform me *at once* whether you can use the paper or not, and if not, to return it to my address as soon as convenient.

I am yours very truly

John Hay

Burroughs, the naturalist and protégé of Whitman, contributed seven of his nature essays to Fields. The first of these was "With the Birds" (May 1865), which became the first chapter of his *Wake Robin*, 1871. His opening words show his attitude, which he later reversed, toward laboratory science as opposed to appreciative observation in the field: "Not in the spirit of exact science, but rather with the freedom of love and old acquaintance, would I celebrate some of the minstrels of the field and forest,—these accredited and authenticated poets of Nature." "With the Birds" was one of the early landmarks in the long tradition of the nature essay, which still thrives. A letter from Burroughs to Ticknor and Fields, written three and a half years after his first publication in the magazine, shows that the author was asking ten dollars per page for his work. All three essays submitted at this time were accepted and published.

>   Treasury Dept. Washington D. C. Nov. 28th 1868
> Messrs.
> Since I wrote to you a few days ago I have thought more about your proposition to publish some of the new papers of "Feet & Wings" in the Atlantic Monthly.
> The pieces called "Birds-Nests" "Spring at the Capital," and "Birch Browsings" are the ones I should designate.
> I do not like to name any price for them, but I suggest, that all things considered, *ten dollars* per printed page, would not be unreasonable.
> In such a case I should postpone indefinitely the publication of them in book form.
>   Respectfully
>   John Burroughs
> P. S. I forgot to say that you may return me the balance of the package, or the whole of it if you do not keep the articles, by express.
>   J. B.

Twelve days later, December 10, Burroughs asked to be paid in advance.

If the *Atlantic* contributors from New York, Philadelphia, and Washington showed considerable variety, even more so did the few who represented the West: a romantic short story writer from San Francisco, a pedestrian poet from Cincinnati, a shrewd observer of American affairs from St. Louis, and a realistic novelist from Wheeling. Susan Francis, a secretary in the *Atlantic* offices, claimed the distinction of having introduced Bret Harte to the magazine,[14] but in reality it was Jessie Frémont, wife of General Frémont, who brought him to Fields's attention in a letter of October 3, 1862. Mrs. Frémont also advised Harte on his first contribution, after Fields had consented to consider it. On February 20, 1863, she told the editor: "He has some thing flaming in preparation for you."[15] It was "The Legend of Monte Del Diablo," a humorous story of the old Spanish missionaries in California, which appeared in the October 1863 issue. A well-told tale, it excited considerable interest in the young writer and was partly responsible for his decision to come to Boston. Upon his arrival in 1871 he was given a contract for a thousand dollars in return for twelve poems or sketches to be written during the year beginning with March[16]—a generous allowance for a young writer. But this was after Fields had officially retired, and was the doubtfully pleasant responsibility of Howells.

The poet from Ohio was John James Piatt, who lived in North Bend, near Cincinnati, at the time of his publications in the *Atlantic*. His first poem was printed by Lowell in 1859, but his later efforts to publish in the magazine were largely futile, even after his friend Howells had become assistant editor. His only poem during the sixties was "The Lost Genius" (August 1867), an allegory of wisdom and age. In 1868, Lowell pled with Howells to print some of the poet's work,[17] and this may have been the reason that two reviews by Piatt appeared in the magazine in 1870.

Another brief contributor in the sixties was Carl Schurz, the German-born critic of American politics and society, temporarily residing in St. Louis. His one article, "The True Problem" (September 1867), concerned the proposed Thirteenth Amendment to the Constitution: "A new constitutional basis had to be found

---

[14]Susan M. Francis, "The Atlantic's Pleasant Days in Tremont Street," *Atlantic Monthly*, C (November 1907), 719.

[15]See also the rest of Mrs. Frémont's letters to Fields written in 1862 and 1863.

[16]See Francis Bret Harte, *The Letters of Bret Harte*, ed. Geoffrey Bret Harte (Boston, 1926), p. 12.

[17]Robert Ernest Butler, "William Dean Howells as Editor of The Atlantic Monthly" (unpublished doctoral dissertation, Rutgers University, 1950), pp. 92-94.

for the development of the Republic, broad enough for whatever increase of population and diversity of interests the future might bring us, and strong enough to stand above the danger of being subverted by local hostility or any combination of perverse aspirations."

Nearly as acute in her observations of lower-class Midwestern society as Schurz was in politics, Rebecca Blaine Harding presented the sordid side of mid-century America as no one else in the *Atlantic* dared to do. Her first story, "Life in the Iron Mills," attracted considerable attention in the April 1861 issue for its stubborn realism, but she found her second contribution too strong for Fields to take without alterations. Her letter to Fields shows the editor's stand:

Wheeling, May 10

Mr. Fields

I am sorry. I thank you for the kindness with which you veil the disappointment. Whatever holier meaning life or music has for me, has reached me through the "pathetic minor"—I fear that I only have power to echo the pathos without the meaning. When I began the story, I meant to make it end in full sunshine—to show how even "Lois" was not dumb, how even the meanest things in life, were "voices in The World, and none of them without its signification." Her life and death were to be the only dark thread. But "Stephen Holmes" was drawn from life and in my eagerness to show the effects of a creed like his, I "assembled the gloom" you complain of. I tell you this in order to ask you if you think I could alter the story so as to make it acceptable by returning to my original idea. Let her character and death (I cannot give up all, you see) remain, and the rest of the picture be steeped in warm healthy light. A "perfect day in June." Will you tell me if that is your only objection—the one you assign? Would the character of Holmes be distasteful to your readers? I mean—the development in common vulgar life of the Fechtéan philosophy and its effect upon a self made man, as I view it? Let me thank you again for your candor and kindness. Will you return the story, directed to the address below. If you do not think I could alter the story, shall I try again, or do you care to have me as a contributor? I assume, you perceive that you agree with Carlyle that "sincerity is the chief merit of a book"-publisher and hope that you will always be sincere with me. If I write for you again, would it be any difference if the story was longer than the last? I felt cramped, and we of the West like room—you know—

> Very respectfully
> Rebecca B. Harding

H. Wilson Harding
Wheeling Va. [FI 1167]

The October *Atlantic* carried the first installment of the novel—or long short story, since it took six installments—*A Story of To-Day*. Regardless of Fields's criticism, it still did not end very happily. The opening paragraphs contain Miss Harding's apology:

> Let me tell you a story To-Day,—very homely and narrow in its scope and aim. Not of the To-Day whose significance in the history of humanity only those shall read who will live when you and I are dead. Let us bear the pain in silence, if our hearts are strong enough, while the nations of the earth stand far off pitying. I have no word of this To-Day to speak. I write from the border of the battle-field, and I find in it no theme for shallow argument or flimsy rhymes. The shadow of death has fallen on us; it chills the very heaven. No child laughs in my face as I pass down the street. Men have forgotten to hope, forgotten to pray; only in the bitterness of endurance they say "in the morning, 'Would God it were even!' and in the evening, 'Would God it were morning!' " Neither I nor you have the prophet's vision to see the age as its meaning stands written before God.... You want something, in fact, to lift you out of this crowded, tobacco-stained commonplace, to kindle and chafe and glow in you. I want you to dig into this commonplace, this vulgar American life, and see what is in it. Sometimes I think it has a new and awful significance that we do not see.

Not all of Miss Harding's stories are as gloomy as *A Story of To-Day*, which depicts Margaret Howth, a bookkeeper in a Midwestern factory and the fruitless efforts of idealists to ameliorate the factory conditions. But in all of the author's sixteen contributions to the *Atlantic*—for she became an important contributor—she remained loyal to her aims.

Her plots are usually laid near Wheeling (formerly in Virginia), where she lived until her marriage in 1863. The popular "David Gaunt" (September and October 1862), for example, concerns the daughter of a rebel farmer in northwestern West Virginia, and

"George Bedillion's Knight" (February and March 1867) pictures village life in southwestern Pennsylvania. "George Bedillion's Knight" was the last of her contributions and the only one contributed under her married name of Davis. It exhibits greater unity and more condensed expression than her earlier works, which are marred by a style that is ponderous and over-insistent. Nevertheless it was her early contributions to the *Atlantic* that made her famous, and as one of the earliest portrayers of the workingman in American fiction, she was a credit to the magazine.

The Westerner of importance whom Fields did not publish in the *Atlantic* was Mark Twain; it was not until 1872 that the humorist began writing for the magazine. He became, however, a welcome friend of the Fieldses in the seventies.

But if the West was scantily represented in the *Atlantic*, the South was not represented at all. Before the war, Lowell had published a half-dozen contributions of Paul Hayne, John Pendleton Kennedy, G. W. Bagby, Osmond Tiffany, and Francis Lieber, but during Fields's time not a single piece from any Southern writer of permanent reputation appeared.[18] The reason, of course, lay not only in the shortage of Southern literature after the war but also in the magazine's strong anti-Confederate policy. Almost from the beginning, the publishers of the *Atlantic* had ignored the Southern market and the editors had spurned the Southern culture. It was not surprising then that the *Atlantic* was not popular in the South.[19]

---

[18] I base this statement upon a comparison of the *Atlantic* Index with the list of authors in William T. Wynn, *Southern Literature* (New York, 1932).

[19] Moncure Daniel Conway (1832-1907), who contributed seven times to Fields, was a Virginian by birth, though he was a strong sympathizer with the North during the war. While he wrote for the *Atlantic*, he lived in Cincinnati (to 1862), Concord, Massachusetts (1862-1863), and England (from 1863). He contributed a wide variety of articles and one book notice. John B. Minor's *A Virginian in New England Thirty-five Years Ago* was published with the recommendation and the editing of Lowell in the 1870 *Atlantic*. Minor was a Virginian who had died long before his journal turned up and was printed.

PART FIVE

FROM OUR OLD HOME

FOREWORD TO PART FIVE

Hawthorne spoke of Fields as an Anglophile, because the publisher had a passionate fondness for English literature and writers. Here Fields again epitomized his times, for most of the respectable American writers, Yankee as they were, looked back with a certain reverence upon "our old home." The truth is, their very refinement of style and tone had a Victorian cast, and it was partly this that occasionally made them blind to the merits of a Whitman or a Twain.[1]

The foremost delight to Fields and his wife in their trips abroad was the chance to become intimate with great English authors. Fields wrote long, exultant letters to his friends about his sojourns at Gad's Hill and Farringford; he produced glowing essays about his correspondence with Mary Russell Mitford and Barry Cornwall; he told over and over the anecdotes of his visits with Wordsworth and Leigh Hunt. When Trollope and Thackeray and Dickens visited America, Fields aided in business arrangements and entertained them with dinners and visits.

Actually, although he loved it, this was part of his job. Lowell had not called him a "dining editor" for nothing, for he was responsible for the friendly relations between the firm and its British writers. William D. Ticknor's edition of Tennyson's poems in 1842 had been one of the first American publications of an English work for which a royalty was paid to the author;[2] and it had marked the beginning of a trend in which the Ticknor firm

---

[1] Frank Luther Mott in *A History of American Magazines*, II, 508, says of the *Atlantic*: "It may be noted in passing ... that the magazine was held rather firmly in the European literary tradition. If, as may well be contended, non-conformity and even iconoclasm are marks of a distinctively American literature, the *Atlantic*, which refused to countenance Whitman and Lanier and neglected Melville, was, in that respect at least, less American than its contemporary, the *Galaxy*, for example. But when American magazines were printing serial fiction by English writers, the *Atlantic* remained faithful to the American novel, except for her one flirtation with the seductive Charles Reade."

[2] Tryon and Charvat, p. 52.

took the lead in supplementing the inadequate laws with "trade-courtesy," a gentlemen's agreement whereby the American publisher that made the most acceptable offer to an English writer should be free from piracy by reputable competitors. The remittance made friends of the British writers, who were only too happy to receive any compensation under the existing laws. The following letter from Tennyson illustrates the good feeling that was generated. Although he had to modify his words in the postscript, he remained a loyal client and published a great many books with Ticknor and Fields in the following years:

Gentlemen,   Farringford March 18/56
From you alone among all American publishers have I ever received any remuneration for my books & I would wish therefore that with you alone should rest the right of publishing them in future.
   I have the honour to be Gentlemen Your obedt. Servt.
                                                              A. Tennyson
   i. e. American editors. Since writing the above I find that Moxon has promised the exclusive sale of the illustrated edition to Messrs. Appleton & Co. of New York. I regret that this letter has not been forwarded sooner; it got mislaid & forgotten.
   April 17th[3]

Besides Tennyson, several other English writers published with the firm. Browning was for many years as enthusiastic a client as Tennyson. Charles Reade haggled over terms, but usually remained loyal. Landor's business relations with the firm were friendly and profitable until he became too quarrelsome even for Fields. Fields went to a great deal of trouble to bring out the first collected edition of De Quincey's works, and though poor De Quincey gave him no cooperation, Fields paid him generously from mere kindness. And there were also Leigh Hunt, Bryan W. Procter (Barry Cornwall), and Mary Russell Mitford, among the older writers, and Harriet Martineau, Douglas Jerrold, and Thackeray, among the younger, who were published by Ticknor and Fields.

   When the *Atlantic Monthly* was started by Phillips and Samp-

[3]MS in possession of Mrs. Z. B. Adams.

son, some thought had been given to procuring English contributors on a large scale, though it never amounted to a great deal. F. H. Underwood had gone to England for the purpose,[4] and Lowell had kept on the lookout for contributions from across the ocean. In 1859, for example, he wrote a long letter to John Ruskin outlining the advantages of the new magazine and desiring Ruskin's participation.[5]

It was expected that Fields could do more because of his large acquaintance, but this was hardly the case. There were never a great many contributions to the *Atlantic* from England. As a rule the successful writers—and these were the only ones the *Atlantic* was much interested in—had no trouble publishing their works in English magazines, and it seemed an unnecessary bother to send the manuscripts overseas, especially when the risks of shipping were considered. Then, too, the English magazines could be bought in the United States, and readers who were not reached by this means read English works in the eclectic magazines of the period. Some articles were published simultaneously in English and American periodicals, and attempts were made to publish serials in this way. But the serials were mostly left to the weeklies, like *Harper's Weekly* and *Ticknor and Fields's Every Saturday*, which were avowedly eclectic, and which paid or pirated as they chose. The *Atlantic* did work out a few such interchanges: Harriet Beecher Stowe's *Agnes of Sorrento* appeared simultaneously in the *Cornhill Magazine*, and Charles Reade's *Griffith Gaunt* appeared in the *Argosy*, but they proved to be a great deal of trouble. Furthermore, Ticknor and Fields and the *Atlantic* had done so much for the prestige of American letters that it was no longer necessary to rely upon English names as feature attractions, for there were ultimately enough American names of equal luster.

A few British writers sent exclusive contributions to Fields;

[4] Charles Eliot Norton tells how Underwood collected several English manuscripts on this journey but that they were all lost in shipping, so that the magazine had to be made up of American contributions almost exclusively. Charles Eliot Norton, "Launching the Magazine," *Atlantic Monthly*, C (November 1907), 580.
[5] James Russell Lowell, *New Letters of James Russell Lowell*, ed. M. A. De Wolfe Howe (New York, 1932), pp. 98-99.

such was the case with Harriet Martineau. And a few others successfully managed simultaneous publication, as did the Scotsman Reverend Andrew Kennedy Hutchison Boyd, who published his essays in both *Fraser's* and the *Atlantic*.[6] Eight essays appeared in the *Atlantic* between 1861 and 1863—a large number for a transatlantic contributor. The author of the popular *Recreations of a Country Parson* (1859 and 1861), Boyd wrote what amounted to sermons in the style of the personal essay, applying commonplace Victorian ethics to such subjects as "Concerning Future Years," "Concerning People of Whom More Might Have Been Made," "Concerning Disagreeable People," and "Resignation." His style is simple and good-natured but extremely loquacious. He admitted it himself in "Concerning Things Slowly Learnt" (June 1861):

The author takes his stand upon this,—that there are few people who can beat out thought so thin, or say so little in such a great number of words. But I remember how a very great prelate (who could compress all I have said into a page and a half) once comforted me by telling me that for the consumption of many minds it was desirable that thought should be very greatly diluted; that quantity as well as quality is needful in the dietetics both of the body and the mind.

Most of his essays approached the maximum of sixteen pages that he was allowed. They show strikingly the amount of moralizing that the readers of the *Atlantic* were able to absorb.

Among the English writers who contributed to the magazine, the most important (from the point of view of their reputation, not the amount they contributed) were Dickens and Reade as fiction writers, and Tennyson and Browning as poets. Harriet Martineau and George Eliot were the most important women writers. The novelist Elizabeth Sheppard did not contribute during her lifetime, but a few of her shorter writings were posthumously published in the *Atlantic*. Charles Cowden Clarke and Joseph Severn each wrote a memoir of their friend Keats. Others who contributed one or two articles were Fanny Kemble, George Henry Lewes, Mary Cowden Clarke, W. M. Rossetti, William Morris, and Justin McCarthy.

[6] Letters from Andrew K. H. Boyd to Fields.

Chapter XXI:
Charles Dickens and Charles Reade

CHARLES DICKENS was one of the British writers whom Fields most idolized. He assiduously cultivated Dickens' friendship and tried hard, though with only limited success, to get him to contribute to the *Atlantic Monthly*.

As early as 1842 when the great Boz made his first trip to America, Fields was among the youthful admirers lucky enough to attend the magnificent Dickens dinner that all Boston talked about for years.[1] He did not meet Dickens then; he only gazed upon him from a distance. In 1846 he asked Dickens' friend Cornelius Felton for an autograph of the great man, and was rewarded with the perusal of a whole series of letters to Felton, letters which appeared many years later in Fields's own *Yesterdays with Authors*.[2] Fields's friendship with Dickens really began in 1859 in England. He attempted to persuade the author to make another American tour; but Dickens, after seriously considering it, deferred it temporarily, fearing a disappointment after the extravagant success of his first tour.

In the sixties Dickens was editing the weekly magazine *All the Year Round*, and it occurred to him and Fields to print articles simultaneously in both their magazines. Several attempts were made to do this, a few of them successful. In 1860 the two editors tried to work out plans with Charles Reade for the simultaneous publication of one of his novels, but failed. They succeeded, however, in printing one of Rebecca Harding's short stories, though because of the difference in publication dates of the magazines, it

---

[1]Fields, *Yesterdays*, pp. 127-30.

[2]Cornelius C. Felton to Fields, December 5, 1846, MS in possession of Mrs. Z. B. Adams.

had to appear two days later in the *Atlantic* than in *All the Year Round*. Fields offered Dickens the story, "Blind Tom," in the fall of 1862, and Dickens was "most glad and ready to avail myself of your permission to print it."[3] The story was printed in *All the Year Round* under the title "Blind Black Tom." It differed from the *Atlantic* version only in the omission of two lines of poetry that introduced the story. Instead, there appeared in the English version the following bracketed explanation:

We have received the following remarkable account from a valued friend in Boston, Massachusetts. It will be published in that city, within a few days after its present publication in these pages.

It was not until 1865 that anything by Dickens actually appeared in the *Atlantic*. The December number carried a memorial essay by him, "Adelaide Anne Procter," on the poetess and daughter of Barry Cornwall. Fields's interest in the subject, apart from his friendship with the Procter family, was due to the fact that the firm was publishing Miss Procter's *Legends and Lyrics* at this time.

In 1866 Fields tried to get a serial by Dickens for the *Atlantic*, but he did not succeed. In October the author wrote that he was far too busy to do anything of the kind at the moment, though his plans for the ensuing summer were indefinite:

Dear Fields.   Tuesday Sixteenth October 1866

Although I perpetually see in the papers that I am coming out with a new serial, I assure you I know no more of it at present. I am *not* writing (except for Christmas No. of all the Year Round), and am going to begin, in the middle of January, a series of 42 Readings. Those will probably occupy me until Easter. Early in the summer, I hope to get to work upon a story that I have in my mind. But in what form it will appear, I do not yet know, because when the time comes I shall have to take many circumstances into consideration. Regarding the choice of an American house, of course my personal feelings are with you. But I have no reason to complain of Harpers, and I have by me another proposal from Philadelphia. When I shall have decided on my mode of publication (having got to work as aforesaid), I will

---

[3] Dickens to Fields, October 2, 1862, in Charles Dickens, *The Letters of Charles Dickens*, ed. Walter Dexter (Bloomsbury, 1938), III, 305.

describe it to you, and to Harpers, and to the Philadelphian proposer, and my business decision shall be made according to the three replies.

A faint outline of a castle in the Air always dimly hovers between me and Rochester, in the great Hall of which I see myself reading to American audiences. But my domestic surroundings must change, before the castle takes tangible form. And perhaps *I* may change first, and establish a castle in the other world. So no more at present.

Believe me ever Faithfully yours
Charles Dickens[4]

A story by Dickens was finally printed in the *Atlantic* for 1868. Meanwhile, through Fields's urging, Dickens was persuaded to make a second lecture tour of America. In June 1867, the plans began to take shape. Dolby, Dickens' business manager, was to make a preliminary trip to view the financial potentialities of a lecture tour and to talk over business arrangements with Fields.

When Dolby came over in August, he brought the manuscript of Dickens' *Holiday Romance* for Ticknor and Fields's *Our Young Folks*. It is a series of stories supposedly narrated by children, who tell what they would do if they could rule the adults. Dickens wrote from the office of *All the Year Round*:

Dear Fields   Friday Twelfth July 1867

Our letters will be crossing one another rarely! I have received your cordial answer to my first notion of coming out; but there has not yet been time for me to hear again—except from Mr. Osgood.

As I told you in my last, Mr. Dolby (who sails on Saturday the 3d of August), will bring you out the children's paper. Of course he will bring the original MS, but, to ensure correct printing on your side, I am having it set up in type, to the end that I may send you, with the MS, a clear proof to set up again from. I do not know how they may humour the delicate little joke, on your side, but I am convinced that it would be a great success here. It is full of subjects for illustration.

In case you should desire to advertize, I send you on the other side the little Bill of Fare. You know best what will serve your magazine. Let me merely hint that it might be expedient to illustrate it very slightly, or not at all, there; and to republish in a little book with as

[4]Part printed in Dickens, *Letters*, III, 487-88.

much illustration as you please, if you can find (*I* can't!) a fanciful man.

With kindest regard to "both your houses"—public and private, Ever

                                Faithfully yours
                                Charles Dickens[5]

He spoke of the juvenile story in his next letter on July 25. In regard to his proposed tour, he was apprehensive about how the Americans would receive him, and his anxiety was reflected in his comments on the story: "I hope the Americans will see the joke of 'Holiday Romance.' The writing seems to me so like children's, that dull folks (on *any* side of *any* water) might perhaps rate it accordingly!"[6] *Holiday Romance* was printed in the January, April, and May issues of *Our Young Folks*. At the same time Dickens had it put in *All the Year Round,* from January through March.

Along with the story for *Our Young Folks,* Dolby brought over another manuscript, *George Silverman's Explanation,* directed to a certain Congressman who had promised a thousand pounds in gold for it for a New York paper. Dolby waited for the Congressman in New York for several days. The man called on Dolby's last day in the United States, and, in the presence of everyone who had come to see Dickens' manager off, tossed him a bag supposed to contain a thousand gold sovereigns. Having previously investigated the man's reputation and finding it none too pure, Dolby refused the money, saying that he did not have time to count it and that Ticknor and Fields would handle the business in his absence. For a moment it appeared that there would be a scene, but the irate Congressman promised to send a banker's order to the office of Ticknor and Fields in a few days. This he never did. Thus it was largely by accident that the *Atlantic* got its second contribution from Dickens. *George Silverman's Explanation* appeared in three installments from January to March 1868, the only serial Fields ever obtained from the author for the *Atlantic*. Ac-

[5]Part printed in Dickens, *Letters,* III, 537.
[6]Dickens, *Letters,* III, 539.

cording to Frank Luther Mott, Dickens received a thousand dollars for it,[7] only about one seventh of what he had hoped for, but still a handsome price.

Dolby's report on America was encouraging; so the plans for the tour were completed, and Dickens arrived in America on November 19, 1867. Fields was at hand upon his arrival to receive him, and immediately took charge of his entertainment and all the business arrangements that Dolby was not caring for. Mrs. Fields saw to the decoration of his rooms, and she and her husband arranged parties and dinners for him throughout his days in Boston. Fields was his companion on his regular morning walks, and together they arranged the celebrated International Walking Match, a race of twelve miles, between their unathletic associates Dolby and Osgood. Osgood, not yet a junior partner in the publishing firm, was appointed treasurer for the Dickens tour, and he accompanied the author and his manager in their travels, always looking out for the Ticknor and Fields interests, of course. For their aid in arranging the Boston readings, the firm received five per cent of the gross receipts from these.[8]

Besides helping to make the tour the tremendous financial success that it was, Fields and his wife achieved a personal success in the friendship of Dickens: "While Dickens had many friends in Boston and Cambridge, Cornelius C. Felton in 1842 and Mr. and Mrs. Fields in 1867-68 were the three who seemed nearest and dearest to his heart."[9] Though he had steadfastly declined staying at the Fields home when he arrived in the United States, Dickens was finally persuaded to accept the invitation upon his return from New York in January 1868, and he spent the rest of his time in Boston there. The friendship that grew between them is told without exaggeration in Fields's *Yesterdays with Authors*. From aboard the *Russia* on his trip homeward, Dickens wrote, April 26, 1868: "You will never know how I love you both; or what you have

---

[7]Mott, II, 509. See George Dolby, *Charles Dickens as I Knew Him* (Philadelphia, 1885), pp. 118-19, 128-29.

[8]Edward F. Payne, *Dickens Days in Boston* (Boston, 1927), p. 250, passim.

[9]Ibid., p. 222.

been to me in America, and will always be to me everywhere; or how fervently I thank you."[10]

In 1869 the Fieldses and Mabel Lowell visited Dickens in England. Fields related that long before they arrived Dickens had planned "such a protracted list of things we were to do together, that, had I followed out the prescribed programme, it would have taken many more months of absence from home than I had proposed to myself."[11] Annie Fields described some of their doings in her letters to her mother and sister:

Mr. Dickens came up to London and took rooms at the St. James for a few weeks that he and his family might the better devote themselves to us. The day after our arrival he drove us in the Park and carried us back to his hotel to a beautiful dinner afterward and the first day he called 4 times at this place, and the last time with Miss Hogarth and Miss Dickens. It is arranged that we should go to Gad's Hill the 2d of June until which time we all remain in town together.

And the following day, she wrote:

Of course you will understand that our opportunity of seeing London itself is a very exceptional one. Mr. Dickens knows it far better than any one else, that is more universally I should say than any one man, and he intends to show us what we are interested to see. He has already carried us to look at "The Small Star in the East," that touching little hospital of which he wrote last winter in his magazine and also the Foundling Hospital. We went too into one of the wretched houses such as he has so feelingly described but I will not make you sad by telling you the particulars or certainly not on this sheet.

This week we go to see the letters sorted in the Post Office and Jamie goes (a privilege Mabel and I envy him much) with the aid of one of the most distinguished detective officers in the world to pay a visit to the worst Thieves in London. Besides which Mr. Dickens has driven us in the Park and given us glimpses of fashionable London in this season.[12]

After the Fieldses had toured the Continent and were preparing to depart for America, they stopped again at Gad's Hill, where

[10] Fields, *Yesterdays*, p. 186.
[11] Ibid., p. 201.
[12] MSS, May 15 and May 16, 1869, in the Massachusetts Historical Society.

Dickens was beginning a new novel. He wrote the following note to Fields requesting him to come to the study, where the author read the opening chapters of *Edwin Drood*:

Sunday Tenth October, 1869

Mr. Charles Dickens presents his respectful compliments to the Hon. James T. Fields (of Boston, Mass. U. S.) and will be happy to receive a visit from the Hon. J. T. F. in the small library as above, at the Hon. J. T. F.'s leisure.[13]

A note written in Fields's hand and appended to Dickens' invitation explains the circumstances:

> The above invitation was handed into my room while we were on a visit to Gad's hill one lovely autumn morning, and I forthwith descended to Dickens's study where he proceeded at once to read what he had just written—viz.—the initial chapters of a new story—"The Mystery of Edwin Drood." In his own marvellous manner he acted, as he read to me, the peculiarities of his new characters, and gave the very tones of an old opium Eating woman we had seen together in London on a memorable night in the spring of this year. He has introduced her as the first figure in his new story.
>
> J. T. F.

Fields wanted to print a part of *Edwin Drood* in the *Atlantic* as a sort of preview of the book before its appearance in England. He wrote his wish to Dickens after he had returned home, but Dickens declined, because "it would entail upon me," he wrote on May 14, 1870, "the loss of copyright in England *of any parts of the book, first published in America.* . . . Imagine a copyright in Pickwick, with no copyright in the 'Trial!' . . . a Nickleby copyright excluding the Yorkshire School or the country actors; or a Dombey copyright, excluding the child's death; or a Copperfield copyright without the young married couple or the storm."[14]

One other article by Dickens did appear in the *Atlantic*, however. It was "On Mr. Fechter's Acting," printed in the August 1869 number. A close friend of Dickens, the renowned Fechter had

---

[13]MS in possession of Mrs. Z. B. Adams.
[14]Dickens, *Letters*, III, 777.

produced the Dickens and Wilkie Collins play *No Thoroughfare* in Paris a short time before, and it was natural that the author should be delighted to write about him. The occasion for the article was Fechter's proposed tour of America. The article was to serve as advance publicity, and, the better to accomplish this purpose, Dickens signed his name to it, contrary to the customary practice in the *Atlantic*.

Dickens' sudden death the following year shocked the reading public of England and America, and not the least among the mourners were James and Annie Fields. The pages of the *Atlantic* paid tribute to him with Fields's own "Some Memories of Charles Dickens" in the August issue and George W. Putnam's "Four Months with Charles Dickens" in October and November. Fields's article, supplemented by a series he wrote for the *Atlantic* the following year, was later made a part of *Yesterdays with Authors*.

Dickens' friend and fellow novelist Charles Reade had been a Ticknor and Fields client longer than Dickens, since 1855, in fact. In 1859, when the firm bought the *Atlantic,* Reade heard of it and offered Fields a contribution:

6 Bolton Row. Mayfair Nov. 3

Dear Mr. Fields,

Mrs. Fields is a duck—for making the extracts, and you are another for sending me them. The ladies for ever. She has just cut the things out I should have taken myself.

I hope you both enjoy Paris. When you return here you must see Oxford in term time when it is filled with the youth of the country; you only saw it in its solitude. As to the question in your note I can only say at present that I should be very glad if it could be managed. Can you suggest any way of dealing with the following materials?

My next work is to be a mixture of argument, scientific criticism not worded in jargon but telling English, and *personal narrative*. But, to make a book of this kind repay me one half what it costs me in research and labor, I must sell it in the first instance to some weekly, or monthly. I have a couple of weeklies nibbling at me now.

I myself see no way of dealing with America but in serial form. *But you may perhaps suggest some way, and I will hold it open till I hear from you.* Lowe's circular hints you are likely to become proprietors of the Atlantic monthly. These reports are as often false as true. If however you are *balancing* this, let me throw any little weight

I possess into the affirmative scale. I could do *great things* for you, if you had such a vent.

I confide to your honorable discretion, the opening passage of the work I am on. Mum as to the *title*, please. The first chapter is the *keynote* but of course those few lines can give you no idea of the work.

Perhaps the expression Spiced beef may give you some notion what I mean to try for.

I can only say that if you are going into the Atlantic M., and would like to have it, you can have it, and that it will be of service—*and* at all events you need fear no competition fr. any living *Englishman* in the line it will take. If the matter seems important write to me without delay.

I am Yours sincerely
Charles Reade

I hope Mrs. Fields will put by some extracts for me and bring me them and you to Bolton Row. At present no Publisher in E. or A. has seen the accompany[ing] paper. [FI 3656]

Nothing by Reade was published in the *Atlantic* immediately; but when the Fieldses, who were touring the Continent, returned to England, Reade promised Fields the right of serial publication of his next novel.

In 1859 and 1860, he was working on *A Good Fight*, which he had begun to publish serially in the English magazine *Once a Week*. When he had found that the editor of *Once a Week* insisted upon tampering with the story, he had ended it cursorily in the October 1, 1859, issue, but had not given it up. Instead he began rewriting, expanding, and improving *A Good Fight* until he eventually produced his masterpiece, *The Cloister and the Hearth*. He offered Fields the chance to print the American edition of the book simultaneously with the English, but Fields declined,[15] desiring the exclusive magazine rights on the next work instead. As it happened, the next work was a long time in coming out, because of the industry Reade expended upon the *Cloister*, and Fields did not actually print anything by the author until 1865.

When the editor returned home in 1860, the plans for the Amer-

---

[15]Reade to Fields, May 30, 1862. See Charles L. Reade and Compton Reade, *Charles Reade* (New York, 1887), pp. 277-80; Albert Morton Turner, *The Making of The Cloister and the Hearth* (Chicago, 1938).

ican publication of the future novel were settled, although no time limit had been set. Meanwhile, Dickens approached Reade with an offer to print his next story in *All the Year Round*; and, finding that it was already promised to Fields, Dickens suggested that it might be published simultaneously in his magazine and in Fields's. Reade wrote to Fields about Dickens' proposal:

Private & confident   6 Bolton Row Mayfair Sept. 25.
Dear Fields,

   Mr. Dickens has done me the honor to press me to write a serial for "All the year round" should terms suit. I have declined to entertain terms—because I think it impossible to do it without compromising *our* agreement, for Atlantic Monthly. Mr. Dickens however appears to think otherwise and finding that you are Master of the Situation proposes to talk to you about it. I hope he will think better of it. But in any case, to avoid misconstruction I have thought well to send you this line. Our agreement is mutually binding, and boná fide early sheets of my next serial are your *property*, as much as any chair or table in yr. home. On that basis I leave you to meet Mr. Dickens should he treat with you.

                              I am dear Fields Yrs. sincerely
                                    Charles Reade

N. B. Should you not hear fr. Mr. D. do not let it transpire that he is making overtures to me.[16]   [FI 3634]

Two weeks later Dickens himself broached the subject to Fields, but as Reade had foreseen, Fields felt that it would be impossible to work out a scheme for the weekly publication in England in conjunction with the monthly appearance in America without great inconvenience to the editors and without giving one magazine an advantage over the other. Also, with proofsheets being sent to both editors and with the complicated arrangement of publication dates, Fields feared that the pirates might find an opening.

Reade assured him that he would not consider Dickens' offer. He added, however, in his letter of November 20, 1860, that his new work would not be ready as soon as he had planned because of his slow progress on *The Cloister and the Hearth*, which he felt he must finish first. "In fact without this how should I be able

---

[16] See Dickens to Fields, October 9, 1860, in Dickens, *Letters*, III, 185-86.

to produce at my own cost a serial tale." His finances were low at the moment because of one of his numerous lawsuits over publishing rights, and having heard that "Ticknor was not exempt fr. mortal weaknesses and would at times draw cheques," he ventured to ask for "some of the far famed dollars": "they will arrive at a period of some tribulation and much indignation; and if in surplus of account be payed to your credit in future transaction."

Six months later the new story was still not ready. The Civil War had broken out in the United States, and Ticknor and Fields suddenly became less interested in literature from England. The firm wrote to Reade that his novel was no longer desired. The author replied good-naturedly but defensively:

Dear Sirs,   6 Bolton Row Mayfair London May 31 X 61

I beg to acknowledge your favor in which you tell me the story I promised you for Atlantic Monthly would now come too late, on account of the troubles in the U. S. A revolution so terrible and unexpected must always liberate the parties, who are the principal sufferers, from prospective arrangements of that nature. Permit me however to object to a line in your note. You seem to think "I have decided not to write the story in question." There is no ground for such a notion. I engaged that my next story *after* the mediaeval tale should be at your service. And the mediaeval tale is not yet finished. I have never for a moment contemplated receding from my engagement; and I have refused Mr. Dickens for your sake. I make this remark merely that the matter may rest on its true footing, and that in happier times you may come to me with undiminished confidence in one, who is lamentably slow; but sure.

I am dear Sirs Yrs. faithfully
Charles Reade

My mediaeval story has been interrupted by cruel lawsuits in defence of my copyrights, which have laid me on a sick bed, as well as hindered my work.

But that was not the end of the matter. By 1862 Reade had completed *The Cloister and the Hearth* and was beginning his new novel *Very Hard Cash*. He turned again to Dickens for the magazine publication and accepted a plan to publish in *All the Year Round* with the American serial rights going to *Harper's Weekly*.

Fields, unaware of the new developments, wrote again about the long-planned novel, and Reade had to tell him he could not have it. "I am sorry Ticknor & Co. had not more patience," Reade commented in his letter written May 30,

> Que Diable. Great works of Fiction cannot be produced *quickly* like little shoes. I cannot help thinking the story "All the year Round" is going to publish would have done considerable good to the Atlantic. But it is not my fault. If you want anything from my pen, you have only to tell me so, and speak in time. *I will always give you the preference.* [FI 3681]

Very Hard Cash, later called merely *Hard Cash*, began in *Harper's Weekly* on April 4, 1863, one week after it started in *All the Year Round*. Fields did not even receive permission to print the story as a book in America; Harper and Brothers offered a higher remuneration and Reade accepted. He wrote to Fields:

> 6 Bolton Row Mayfair. Sept. 25.
> Dear Sir,
> Many thanks for your offer, "Hard Cash." I think it a very fair one of the kind. But I wish to sell this one copyright, and the labor and research have been so great that I cannot, unfortunately put a moderate figure. Frankly I am not surprised that any publisher should demur to the figure. I think and hope however that the result will show there was a good profit left for the Pub. even at that sum.
> I am Yrs. very sincerely
> Charles Reade
> The offer you have made me will not be communicated to any one. This is a rule I have lain down in consequence of what I have observed in literary business. [FI 6001]

Finally, after the Civil War was over, Reade managed to publish a serial in the *Atlantic*. In June 1865 he was negotiating with Fields, though it was six months before the first installment of *Griffith Gaunt* was to appear. The plan was to publish the new novel in London in the *Argosy* at approximately the same time it appeared in the *Atlantic*. On June 15 Reade wrote that his London publisher had agreed to send revised proofsheets of each installment six weeks before it was to be published in the *Argosy*, although Fields had requested a two-month period. "I feel sure you need be under no anxiety whatever," wrote the author. "It is quite understood that the percentage you were to have paid for *the book* under an earlier agreement is remitted on account of the unfavourable exchange. This is not to govern future contracts, when American paper shall recover its European value, which I hope it soon will" (FI 3654). It was arranged to print the first installment of *Griffith Gaunt* in the December *Atlantic*, appearing on November 20, 1865. The *Argosy* would come out eleven days later, on December 1. Reade wrote on October 13, the day after he had sent the first sheets to Fields:

> Mr. Strahan undertook to let you know whether the "Argosy" is to appear on Dec. 1. I am sorry to learn by yours just received that he has neglected to do so. It does come out Dec. 1. However I hope you will ere this have seen his advertisement or Sampson Low's who is his agent on the matter. Yesterday I sent you out a duplicate of the first number. I promise faithfully to send duplicates of each succeeding number; and in good time. So be under no anxiety on that score. As to the payment, I do not expect it until the number is sold. Shall be quite content if on the 15th Dec. you will ship me the amount in sterling due on the December number; and so on. I think you will be satisfied with the story. It is a tale of the heart, and does not straggle into any eccentric topics. Need I say I shall make it as exciting and interesting as I can.

But Fields was still worried about the possibility of the *Argosy*'s being sold in America and so hindering the sale of the *Atlantic*. Reade wrote again to reassure him:

> 92. St. George's Road S. Belgravia Oct. 20.
>
> Dear Fields,
>
> I beg to acknowledge your favor of the 4th. I agree with you about the title. Your suggestion that Strahan must not offer the Argosy for sale in the U. S. is a very serious one. How can I hinder him? I hope however you mean that he must not ship his copies from these shores in time to interfere with your Priority. I have called on him, and read him your line, and told him that your early sheets forming part of my contract with him, it would be contrary to the spirit of that contract were he to offer the Argosy to the American public until a reasonable time after you have published the A. M. Strahan, who

is the most honorable and liberal man in our trade immediately acquiesced in this. I then reminded him that Harpers' agent is his agent, & not particularly friendly to you; and said that as your friend in the matter I trusted to him, and not to Sampson Low. He then undertook it should be all right, and accepted my further suggestion that you should correspond directly with him and arrange all things justly and amicably. N. B. He hinted further that if you could not be reconciled to the limited sale of the Argosy in U. S. he would rather pay me what you have agreed to pay me and have the whole affair in his hands than cause a difference of opinion between you and me. So I understood him. Now I must tell you something I did not mean to trouble you with. Messrs. Low wrote me an officious letter suggesting that the Atlantic Monthly ought not be sold in England with my story in it. I wrote back a very bitter reply, & sent the correspondence to Strahan. He sided at once with me and said he would not for the world be guilty of so illiberal an act as to oppose your English sale. Pray take this into account. To conclude—it is too late to introduce new stipulations into an agreement that has gone so far as ours. If you really *fear* the competition of the Argosy, you might I think easily sell the Magazine sheets to Harpers, reserving the book: for the fact is that although the pages of the A. M. are made the measure of value what I sell to you is not Magazine sheets only; but also book sheets, and there you have no English competitor. I dare say I am saying a great many useless things. But this is the curse of distance & slow communication. I have thought it wise to look at the matter in every light. No. 2. has gone to Press.

 With kindest regards to Mrs. Fields

Yrs. very truly
Charles Reade

Between the time the first installment appeared in the *Atlantic* on November 20, and the time it appeared in the *Argosy*, December 1, Reade wrote again; for Fields was still uneasy about the *Argosy* competition. The writer offered his assurances, and "Du reste should this honourable understanding be violated at any future time you will remonstrate, and I will take vigorous measures to give your remonstrance effect."[17]

 Upon its appearance, *Griffith Gaunt* was immediately attacked. The American press was especially vindictive, naming it "an

[17] Reade to Fields, November 24, 1865.

unpardonable insult to morality." Reade replied in an article in the *New York Times*, and instituted a libel suit against the *Round Table*, his chief detractor—all of which created a great deal of publicity. When he sent the July 1866 number of the novel, Reade asked Fields to send him all the American notices of it, the better to defend himself in the controversy.[18]

With the sending of the August number of the novel, Reade looked forward to the completion of the twelfth and last installment for November. Plans were progressing for the publication in book form, and Ticknor and Fields were to get the American rights. Reade wrote on June 6:

> I shall ask Strahan to let me come out in 3 Vols. 15 October: and, if he consents, you can publish the book 24 hours afterwards, so as just not to imperil my English Copyright. In any case we will be ahead of your pirates. Of course when you do publish some of the vagabonds will print on you: that I can not help.

Though Reade was paid three pounds sterling per page, the serial did not benefit the *Atlantic* nearly so much as had been hoped, in spite of the storm of publicity about it.[19] Yet as soon as the last pages of *Griffith Gaunt* were in his hands, Fields begged for more contributions. Reade was very popular in America despite the press attacks, and his dealings with Fields had been quite satisfactory. The writer planned another serial for Fields on approximately the same terms, but the plan never materialized. Nor was anything else by Reade printed in the magazine during Fields's editorship.

Dear Fields,   5 Albert Terrace   Knightsbridge Oct. 13.

Many thanks for yours just received. It is truly gratifying to find my publisher satisfied with my work: and desirous to have more from my pen. To tell you the truth I thought of the American public in writing it. I know they like a compact and ardent tale: and, having almost enticed you into dealing with me, I was determined you should not regret taking my advice.

[18] Reade to Fields, May 4, 1866. See Mott, II, 509.
[19] Mott, II, 509.

Now as to future operations, have you not received a letter in which I told you I meditated some extraordinary true narratives with illustrations designed by myself, and asked you whether this sort of thing done in a style as yet unattempted would come within the compass of your Monthly. If my letter has miscarried, tell me. As for the next monthly serial fiction I write, I am at your service, on the same terms, plus 5 per cent on the gross receipts of the *book*. Please to say whether these terms are acceptable. I assume that by the time I am ready, the exchange will no longer be seriously unfavorable to the U. S. Should this be otherwise, shall again remit the percentage. I thought it was quite understood that you were to publish G. G. in advance and defy the Pirates. I have been afraid to *say* too much lest I should compromise my English copyright by formally assenting to your publication preceding mine. I hope however you have comprehended the matter, and taken a devilish good start. Will you be kind enough to settle the balance, & send me the calculation of the pp. that I may verify it. I have a favor to ask you, which is to procure me two copies of a play in which Mrs. Wood has achieved a reputation. It is an adaptation of "La petite Fadette" by George Sand. I think the principal female character is called Fanchon. Shall be much obliged if you will send it me with speed. Will watch the catalogues for a letter of Goldsmith. My kindest regards to Mrs. Fields. I will write her a long letter—as I ought.

            Yrs. very truly
            Ch. Reade   [FI 3633]

  Ticknor and Fields continued to publish Reade's books, and Reade continued to pester Fields with conditions and requests. He became irritated when his nephew was permitted to draw money on his account with the firm in Boston. He expressed displeasure at Osgood's becoming a partner in the publishing business, because he thought he had been insulted by Osgood. He asked Fields to collect examples of the pirating of *Griffith Gaunt* in America.[20] But none of these vagaries dented Fields's complaisance, and the relationship proceeded as smoothly as possible. And like Dickens, Reade continued an enthusiastic client of the firm.

---

 [20]Reade to Fields, July 23 (? year) (FI 3627); December 14, 1868; and February 18, 1869.

Chapter XXII:

Tennyson and Browning, and Shades of Keats

AMONG the writers who influenced America, the guiding star beaming across the Atlantic from England was the poet laureate. Fields looked upon Tennyson with reverence as the sublimest of the living poets. Tennyson contributed only once to the *Atlantic* during the sixties, but the effect of his popularity upon the tone of the magazine was immeasurable. At the height of his fame he represented Victorian respectability and craving for culture, and these ideals his genteel American contemporaries were disposed to emulate.

Fields's business relations with Tennyson had begun very early and had become widely appreciated because of the publisher's talent for publicity. When Browning decided to publish *Men and Women* with Ticknor in 1855, he found it natural to refer to the good job Fields had done for Tennyson: "I am glad you have gained enough by Tennyson's Poems to be able to give *him* something: & you will remember me in like pleasant manner when you conscientiously can, I make no doubt."[1] Besides Fields's business interest, he and Annie had a genuine love for Tennyson's poetry. In 1857 a friend, C. B. Fairbanks, knowing their interest, sent them some unpublished stanzas of "Locksley Hall." And the same year Annie Fields wrote a poem on receiving a lock of hair from the laureate.[2]

In England in 1859 the Fieldses were invited to Tennyson's estate, Farringford, on the Isle of Wight. Fields described the visit in awed tones to Longfellow:

[1] Robert Browning to Fields, September 6, 1855.
[2] Charles B. Fairbanks to Fields, May 7, 1857, and Annie Fields to Bayard Taylor, July 27, 1857.

Bonchurch. Isle of Wight July 18. 1859.

My dear Longfellow.

It is Sunday morning in England, and we have just arrived here, in one of the most charming English rural spots, direct from Tennyson's house at Farringford where we staid two days. Mrs. Tennyson sent to us in London saying we must come to her place when we arrived in the Island, but we drove to a hotel from which both the bard & his wife insisted upon bringing us. A most hearty welcome greeted us and we found we were several days behind the time they had looked for us. I had already met Alfred the Great in London where he had gone to read the proofs of his new volume. We sat down together over the sheets one day in the Temple and talked over certain passages about which he seemed doubtful. The title then was "The True and The False" which he afterwards altered as it now stands. As you have never seen him I will try to make him out on paper for your inspection. A tall stooping figure clad in sober grey, beard full and flowing, moustache, long stringy hair, and spectacles. His voice is shaggy-rough, and his gait moves with his voice. His "rear sight" does not improve his general appearance, as you may imagine. In his own house and grounds (he owns some hundred and fifty acres) he stumbles about in a kind of Tennyson fix which he does not seem to be trying to move away from. One morning he read to us the whole of "Maud" in a style I cannot soon forget & on another occasion he read "Guinevere" from the new volume. "Come into the garden, Maud" he gave in a kind of chaunt, most impressive. I shall have much to say to you of him when we meet which I cannot write, but I will note down here that he strikes me constantly as the greatest man I have ever met in England. His Knowledge is most wonderful, and when he talks he says things that are apt to send a thrill with the words. His usual tone is a low unmelodious thunder-growl, but when he chooses he can melt as well as rasp with his Lincolnshire tongue. When he appears at the table in the morning with his old slouched sombrero hat, reading his letters while he takes his breakfast, he is apt to stick dagger-words up and down the present Emperor of France whom he variously designates as a beggar and a scoundrel. But I will not *write* of him any more. He has treated us both with marked kindness, and his lovely wife has made us feel the warmest friendship for the whole household. His two boys, Lionel & Hallam, are dream-picture-children, fair like their mother and as gentle too.

We have enjoyed every day of our sojourn here in dear Old England. All tongues ask for you, and every body loves you. "Give my *love* to Longfellow" said Tennyson when we parted last night. The

"Golden Legend" is his favorite I think. My wife thanks you again for the flowers you brought her that morning she sailed away from home.
Ever yours.
J. T. F.

Annie established a friendship with the Baroness Tennyson; a correspondence ensued; and after Lady Tennyson's death, Mrs. Fields included a sketch of her along with one of Lord Tennyson in her *Authors and Friends*.

Fields showed his esteem by writing for the *Atlantic* a biographical article on Arthur Hallam, the subject of Tennyson's *In Memoriam*. A factual though laudatory sketch, interspersed with quotations from the poetry of Hallam and Tennyson, it was inspired by a visit to the young man's grave. It was published in the December 1860 issue, and showed Fields's belief that anything Tennysonian would be of interest to *Atlantic* readers.

The one Tennyson poem printed in the magazine was "The Victim," in February 1868. Hallam Tennyson says it was first printed at the Guest Printing Press, Wimborne, in 1867, but he incorrectly places the date of its first publication as 1869.[3] A narrative poem covering two pages in the *Atlantic*, it was representative of the majority of poems in the magazine—having a setting in the indefinite past, a moral point of view, and a theme of motherly love and wifely devotion.

In 1869, Fields took a conciliatory part in a small squabble between Tennyson and Bayard Taylor. The incident is worth recording because it illustrates Tennyson's extreme touchiness in matters the least bit personal, and because it explains why Fields never published any reminiscences of Tennyson. What happened was that Taylor, after visiting the poet at Farringford, wrote an account of the visit in a letter to E. C. Stedman in the United States. Stedman permitted the letter to be printed, and Tennyson was furious, considering it a violation of his hospitality. He wrote Fields what he thought of Taylor, and Fields passed the word on —tactfully, of course:

[3] Hallam, Lord Tennyson (ed.), *The Works of Tennyson* (New York, 1928), p. 923.

Fields of the Atlantic Monthly

February 23, 1869.

My dear Taylor:

I have lately received a letter from Tennyson which I should like to answer as soon as possible, and I shall be glad to send him some explanation which shall come from you. He charges you, referring, I suppose, to something he has seen copied from an American newspaper, with having published an account of your visit to the household of Farringford. Now I shall be very glad to tell Tennyson that you have not violated any rules of hospitality, if such be the fact. Perhaps I am not doing right in quoting from his letter to me, this phrase, but I wish very much to set you right with him. Of course I should not like for him to know that I quoted his precise words about you. He says that you, "who being received with open arms (for he called himself a friend of Thackeray) saw in me, not a man but a paragraph, and even out of that made a parody." He evidently feels very sore about the matter. I have an indistinct recollection of having read, in American newspapers, a letter, or an extract from a letter, said to have been written by you; and I suppose it is to this passage he refers. I daresay I shall be able to say to him, after hearing from you, that you are in no way connected with the offense. With kindest regards to all,

Ever yours,
J. T. F.

When Taylor replied, asking what to do about it, Fields advised him to print an apology in the *New York Tribune*:

Boston, March 1, 1869.

My dear Taylor:

I think if I were you, I should print in the Tribune, over my own name, an explanation of the appearance in print of the offensive Tennyson paragraphs. It will show precisely your feeling about the common newspaper practise of unroofing the houses of English celebrities, for the public eye. If you do not do this, you will suffer the imputation of having committed a breach of good manners, and a tacit intention of going and doing likewise, whenever you please. Conway is doing more to close the doors of English households on American travellers, than we all unitedly can perform in opening them; therefore I advise that you speak a word in the Tribune. I shall of course, in writing to Tennyson, exonerate you, personally, from his charge against you. Tennyson is the most sensitive man in England, and in all my twenty years' experience with literary men, I have never met one who suffered so keenly as he from letter-writers. I have heard him say things, unequalled in severity, about people who had been visiting him, and had gone away and merely, in a few lines, mentioned the fact. He seems to have an undying hatred for reports about himself and family. But you knew all this before, and it remains for you now to tell him so. In writing to him, let there be no misunderstanding as to the person, to whom you had written, and who violated your confidence. 'Tis indeed, a most unfortunate affair, and as an American, I deeply regret Stedman's indiscretion. Curses on the woman [whom Stedman had permitted to see the letter and who was actually guilty of sending it to the press], too.

Ever sincerely yours
J. T. F.

Tennyson did not forgive Taylor. When the Fieldses and Mabel Lowell visited Farringford again in April 1869, his anger had not cooled. Upon being introduced to Miss Lowell, "He asked her if her father was a letter writer referring to Bayard Taylor's unfortunate half private epistle which leaked unhappily, most unhappily into print. He cannot get that out of his head and harps bitterly upon it continuously."[4]

In 1872 when Fields was planning a lecture on Tennyson, he wrote for permission to mention the poet's readings—probably the private readings of his own poems. Tennyson replied with customary dignity that Fields could speak as he pleased as long as he avoided reference to his domestic life:

Ap. 21/72

Dear Mr. Fields

The enthusiasm you express is hard to reconcile with business facts.

Be this as it may, since you do express it, I am bound to believe it, & grant that there may be some sufficient explanation of those facts, however difficult to conjecture.

I can have no objection to your mentioning my readings & that these were grateful to yourself & Mrs. Fields (to whom pray present our best remembrances)—but further than this—well—I trust that you will, as you say, respect the sanctity of home.

Yours very truly
A. Tennyson

When Henry Alden asked him in 1878 to write an article on Tennyson for *Harper's Monthly*, Fields hesitated, remembering

---

[4] Annie Fields's diary, April 25, 1869, MS in the Massachusetts Historical Society. See Richmond Croom Beatty, *Bayard Taylor: Laureate of the Gilded Age* (Norman, Okla., 1936), pp. 259-62.

the poet's idiosyncrasy. Alden assured him that it was perfectly proper: "I think Tennyson would not take unkindly a friendly paper (such as you would write) in an American Magazine—even if it is full of pleasant personal matter concerning his home life, etc. Besides your treatment of the subject will be a bar to less reverent attempts in that direction."[5] Nevertheless Fields declined. Finally Alden suggested that Fields send him the article along with one on Longfellow so that it could be kept on hand for publication after the death of the poet: "How would it do to write your memorials of Tennyson & Longfellow now, & place them in our hands so that we could have the illustrations engraved—it being understood that they are not to be published while these poets are living?"[6] The reminiscences were never published; however Annie Fields wrote in the January 1893 issue of *Harper's Monthly* a memorial article on Tennyson which she later used in her *Authors and Friends*.

Tennyson's reputation in America in the sixties did not undergo the slump that it did in England.[7] One reason for its decline in England was the burst of rival popularity afforded to Browning, but if James and Annie Fields's opinion was representative (and it usually was), Browning was hardly in the running in the United States, until later in the century.

Although as early as 1849 Ticknor, Reed, and Fields, the predecessor of Ticknor and Fields, had published a book of Browning's without his consent, as was the common practice, the firm's relationship with the poet really began in 1855 with the authorized publication of *Men and Women*. Browning had expressed the highest gratitude for Fields's fairness: "I take advantage of the opportunity of the publishing in the United States of my 'Men and Women'—for printing which, you, through being more righteous than the Law, have liberally remunerated me,—to express my earnest desire that the power of publishing in America this and every subsequent work of mine may rest exclusively with you

[5] Henry Alden to Fields, November 11, 1878.
[6] Alden to Fields, February 3, 1879.
[7] John Olin Eidson, *Tennyson in America* (Athens, Ga., 1943), pp. 147-49.

and your house."[8] Thanks mostly to Fields, Browning's reputation in the United States was better than in England at the beginning of the sixties,[9] though it did not so remain.

Browning published three poems in the *Atlantic*, all in 1864. Though the number is small, it is significant in view of Browning's known aversion to magazine publication. Fields had offered a hundred pounds for the early proofs of Browning's new book, *Dramatis Personae*, plus the right to print a few of the poems from the book in the *Atlantic*. Browning replied in October 1863:

London, 19. Warwick Crescent Upper Westbourne Terrace,
Oct. 16. '63.

Dear Mr. Fields,

I have been in France for the last two months and, only on returning, find your note.

With respect to your offer of "£60 for the sheets of my new volume, one month in advance of publication; or £100 for the additional right of printing one or two of the pieces (not printed elsewhere) in your magazine"—I accept it, provided you consider that by the arrival of the sheets six weeks before publication in England, "ample time for the magazine" will be allowed—I should peril my copyright here by suffering any earlier appearance in America. The poems will be in two volumes, most probably—and, with the exception of a single little thing, *none* have ever been printed. Will you have the kindness to let me know at once if this arrangement suits?

To tell you the truth, I hardly cared to take the trouble of sending the new Edition—having never got anything for the old, you know, "stereotyped" or otherwise—always excepting "Men & Women" which are fairly your own. I don't mind for myself, who have been paid and overpaid by the sympathy... [The remainder of the letter has been lost.]

[Written in at head of letter:] Many thanks to Mr. Higginson for his great kindness in sending his book—if it be to *him*, and not *you*, that I am indebted.[10]

"Gold Hair," the first of the poems, appeared for the first time in the May 1864 *Atlantic*. It is there in its original form; in later

---

[8]M. A. De Wolfe Howe, "James Thomas Fields," *Early Years of the Saturday Club, 1855-1870*, ed. Edward Waldo Emerson (Boston, 1918), p. 380.

[9]Letter from Elizabeth Barrett Browning in Mrs. Sutherland Orr, *Life and Letters of Robert Browning* (Boston, 1891), pp. 339-40.

[10]MS in Harvard University Library.

versions it underwent considerable change, the detached message at the end being afterward incorporated into the poem to achieve a more unified effect.[11] In the June number of the magazine were "Prospice" and "Under the Cliff." The first six of the sixteen stanzas of the latter had been printed in 1836 in the *Monthly Repository*. The new part, however, was a retraction of the gay optimism of the original. "Under the Cliff" was afterward entitled "Reading a Book, Under the Cliff," and became Part VI of *James Lee's Wife*. "Prospice" made its first appearance in the *Atlantic*. All three of the *Atlantic* poems appeared a few days later, May 28, in Browning's *Dramatis Personae*.

With the publication of Browning's next important work, *The Ring and the Book*, there developed a rupture in the friendship of the publisher and the poet, never fully reconciled. In July 1867 Browning agreed to let Fields publish the poem in America the following year. The firm (now Fields, Osgood, and Company) became dissatisfied with the plan of Browning and his English publisher, Smith, Elder, and Company, to publish in four volumes appearing at four different times, and wrote Browning to this effect in August 1868. This and the price offered for the work irritated Browning, and he wrote that he would be glad to dissolve the contract and look for another American publisher if the firm was not content. On September 19, 1868, Fields, who had not written earlier because of a lame hand, attempted to soothe him: "I hope our firm has set itself all right with you now, and that the terms submitted to you in Mr. Osgood's letter, by this mail, will be agreeable to you. We all regret that four volumes, coming out at different periods, will be the mode for the publication of the new poem. Four bites at such a masterly cherry as we are anticipating, I am afraid will puzzle greatly the American appetite."[12] But Browning was only partially appeased. He replied:

[11] William Clyde De Vane, *A Browning Handbook* (New York, 1940), p. 274. De Vane discusses the various changes in the successive printings of all three of these poems.

[12] MS in the Henry W. and Albert A. Berg Collection, New York Public Library. See William Clyde De Vane and Kenneth Leslie Knickerbocker (eds.), *New Letters of Robert Browning* (New Haven, 1950), pp. 183-84.

(19. Warwick Crescent, Upper Westbourne Terrace. W.)
Dear Mr. Fields, Oct: 23d '68

It was very good of you to write under such inconveniency as you describe: I hope very sincerely you are your old self again—hard to associate with lameness in any shape!

The Publisher will have done the business-part of our affair. I only mean to reply to a word or two kindly put in your note. I should never dream of objecting to your Firm's refusal to hold by the bargain on the intelligible ground that, by waiting till after publishing began here, you might be forestalled in America: but you proposed the new bargain, subject to the condition that you should *not* be so forestalled: in that case, wherein would you be the loser? It seemed to me a refusal to run risk and yet a mulcting me as if risk were to be run. Let it pass for a misunderstanding and then an end!

I can be no judge of what is expedient or otherwise with you in the four-volume plan. Only, when you call it "four bites of a cherry," I submit that this is an apple, which you will eat, unchoked, if you decently quarter it.

I have had only a few hours to look over the sheets; and see that there are some minute errors, and three or four lines to be inserted: but, to save time, I let them go: I may depend on you, I am sure, to correct them by the corrected Revises which you will certainly receive this day week,—or, I should say, which I will at least despatch on that day.

Pray thank Mrs. Fields for her kind remembrance of me & believe me
Yours faithfully ever
Robert Browning

Despite Browning's arguments, the American edition of *The Ring and the Book* was published in two volumes.

To make matters worse, Fields, baffled by the poem when he saw it, decided it was bad. Annie Fields, who always shared her husband's opinion, wrote disparagingly of it in her diary:

Dec. 2. Have read Browning's new poem—the longest single poem, I believe, from a noted hand, in the English language. [The next sentence reproduced here is crossed out and almost unreadable.] It is obscure, dirty, unpoetic [illegible word] like him himself. As for his publishers I fear the poem will be a dead loss of several thousand dollars to them. I see no help for this. I am sure the world is too wise to read such twaddle. Yet it is the work of a great *Brain*.[13]

[13] MS in the Massachusetts Historical Society.

Mrs. Fields was in this case a very poor prophet, for the poem was received with "almost universal acclaim,"[14] and there was no reason why Fields should have lost money on it.

The rift between Browning and the Fieldses widened, and the situation was aggravated when they met in England under the most unfortunate circumstances. It was at a dinner given by the smart set in London, where James and Annie were beyond their social depth, while Browning was quite at home. Annie transparently described her discomfiture in her diary for April 19, 1869:

Browning was like polished steel, receiving on his surface keen reflections of persons and giving back sharp points of light. He is scornful unsympathetic, powerful and swift. Ah! It seems as if a demon held him. Words forsook me and I was a stupid companion I know, mais, que faire? How could words come before such a nature? ... They were all entirely at home but did not succeed in making us feel so. There is an ignorance of, and a subtle contempt of outsiders in such a company which is little calculated to bring out the best from others.[15]

She never forgave Browning, and while writing the article, "Emily, Lady Tennyson" for *Authors and Friends* some twenty years later, she recalled this scene when she wrote the line: "I remembered the fatuous talk at dinner-tables where I had sometimes met Browning, and thought of Tennyson's great talk and the lofty serenity of his lady's presence."

With respect to Browning, the Fieldses' discrimination was distinctly at fault. They could be hoodwinked by the proper loftiness of Tennyson, but were only irritated by Browning's sharp loquacity. And while Tennyson held firmly to the principles of clearness of style and respectability in subject matter, Browning continually wandered in the shadows of psychological inquiry. Not understanding him, James and Annie suspected him, and eventually came to dislike him.

The interest of the *Atlantic* readers and the *Atlantic* editor in the English poets was great, and this was further demonstrated

---

[14] Samuel C. Chew, "The Brownings," *A Literary History of England*, ed. Albert C. Baugh (New York, 1948), p. 1396.

[15] MS in the Massachusetts Historical Society.

by the publication of two articles on Keats. The magazine frequently carried articles on English writers both past and present, but those on Keats deserve special mention since they are still important items in Keatsian scholarship. They are the reminiscences of the poet by Charles Cowden Clarke, Keats's tutor and friend, and Joseph Severn, the friend who attended Keats at his death and who painted some of the best portraits of him. Both were acquaintances of Fields and his wife, and were persuaded by the editor to record these invaluable notes. Clarke's article "Recollections of John Keats," came in the January 1861 *Atlantic*.[16] Cantankerous in regard to the poet's detractors, Clarke talked about Keats's school days, his reception of the criticism from *Blackwood's Magazine*, and his early acquaintance with Spenser's works. In describing the poet, he asserted that the color of his eyes was "light hazel," not blue—and the argument is still unsettled. Severn's paper "On the Vicissitudes of Keats's Fame," in the April 1863 number,[17] was shorter, but contained important information on Keats's last days, his love affair, and his fame.

---

[16] Charles Cowden Clarke to Fields, October 13, 1860.

[17] See Joseph Severn to Fields, July 23 (? year), and June 21 (? year) (FI 3803 and FI 3802).

Chapter XXIII:
Elizabeth Sheppard, Harriet Martineau, George Eliot

THE STORY of Elizabeth Sara Sheppard is indeed a sad one. Having shown tremendous promise when a child, she had written some half-dozen books and was on the verge of an established reputation when she died in 1862 at the age of thirty-two. By the time she met Fields, who visited her in England in 1859, it was already too late for him to advance her literary reputation while she lived, though this was not apparent at the time.

Her work was of the "gushy" kind, notable chiefly for its extravagance of feeling, which was, however, well expressed. She was an avid lover of music, and her first and most popular novel, *Charles Auchester*, a romanticized life of Mendelssohn, was good enough to receive the following exaggerated praise from Benjamin Disraeli: "No greater book will ever be written upon music, and it will one day be recognized as the imaginative classic of that divine art."[1] Disraeli's statement is ridiculous now, but Miss Sheppard did achieve a certain popularity in both England and America at a time when feminist literature was in demand.

She was delighted with Fields's interest in her work in 1859, and set about to prepare for him a novel, *Grey Magic*. Almost immediately, however, she was attacked by illness, and wrote to Fields—per amanuensis—that she would have to postpone it:

28 Cannon Place Brighton August 28th/59

Dear Sir
It is with inexpressible regret I have to address you, & from day to day, ever since my reception of your letter of the 10th August,

---

[1] Susannah Conyers, "Elizabeth Sara Sheppard," *Atlantic Monthly*, X (October 1862), 499.

I have delayed writing, hoping I might not finally be obliged to write as I now do. I had scarcely left Town a week, before I was seized with a very violent & serious attack of illness, I believe brought on by exposure to great heat. However this may have been, the attack, though slowly abating, has left me excessively weak, & I cannot conceal from myself nor from you that it is physically impossible I should complete my book by the 10th November. A physician & surgeon who both attended me, have peremptorily ordered me not to write at present—but if I *could* write, *I should*: unhappily I cannot yet even get through a letter. I have never had such a disappointment, & this is all I can say, except that the instant I am able (& I have no fear of not attaining the power sooner or later) nothing shall occupy my head or my hands until my little book is finished. You will perceive that I have employed a friend as my amanuensis & have only signed my name, as yours dear Sir

Very truly,
Elizabeth Sheppard

As Miss Sheppard had to depend for a living upon what she earned by teaching in her mother's school in Brighton, she was not very prosperous. Though her novels were not unpopular, they did not afford her much income, and her sickness aggravated the situation. Realizing all this, Fields offered to pay her an advance on the promised novel, but her pride prevented her from accepting:

28 Cannon Place Brighton Sept. 10th

Dear Sir

Your letter of the 4th is before me, & I wish I had it in my power to express to you as I could wish, my thanks for your generous & truly considerate offer. I am not at this moment in want of money—if I *were* so, I could not accept it *unearned*; but this fact does not interfere with my real appreciation of your kindness, which I shall never forget; & I hope to be able at length to write what will meet with your full approval.

I hope Mrs. Fields has gained much health in the vitalising air of Switzerland. May I beg to offer her my best regards.

Yours
Yours dear Sir
Very sincerely & gratefully,
Elizabeth Sheppard[2]

[2]MS in Harvard University Library.

The rest of Miss Sheppard's correspondence was carried on for her by her friend Susannah Conyers (afterwards Mrs. Da Costa), who stayed with her throughout her last illness. In November Miss Conyers wrote that Miss Sheppard would try to send the first installment of *Grey Magic* for the January 1860 *Atlantic*.

28 Cannon Place Brighton Nov. 14/59

Dear Sir

As Miss Sheppard's most intimate friend, (not having been separated from her for six years) I take the liberty of answering your letter to her, by her desire, & also by my own that I may explain all. My dear friend is quite unable at present to write to you herself although most anxious to do so, & chafing sadly at her enforced illness.

You will perhaps understand why the smallest exertion is impossible to her at present, when I tell you that she is suffering from the consequences of a sunstroke; this her physician pronounces the illness of July to proceed from, complicated with gastric fever—from the effects of this seizure she has as yet very partially rallied. Her physician gives us every hope of an ultimate recovery, *if* she can obtain perfect repose for some time, but prohibits anything like effort until her system (which is greatly shaken by the severity of her suffering) shall recover its usual tone. I cannot express to you how ardently my friend desires to set to work; the prospect of writing for those across the water is most enticing to her, & she begs me to ask (in case she should be able to write in the course of a few weeks) what is the outside time you can give her for two chapters of the proposed story to be published in your magazine, supposing you intend it to appear with the new year—at the same time she dares not *promise* nor would she choose to send anything short of her best. Nor will any one have a word from my friend's pen till she has fulfilled her promise to yourself. My great dread is lest her intense anxiety should keep her back, she is so energetic the moment she can work & so earnest in all her undertakings. But I am certain your kind consideration will comprehend how the slightest *pushing* is destructive to such nerves as hers which can only regain their equilibrium by perfect rest. My friend has not seen all I write though she helped[?] the message I have sent, & I mention our physician's opinion because though it orders quiet, gives hopes of recovery & future work. Miss Sheppard desires her kind regards to Mrs. Fields & yourself. I am dear Sir

Yours truly
Susannah Conyers

Ticknor and Fields had just bought the *Atlantic,* and Elizabeth Sheppard had been one of the first to be asked to write for the new owners. Since Fields was her personal friend, he handled the transaction even though Lowell was still the magazine's editor. On December 5, 1859, Miss Conyers wrote that Miss Sheppard was still unable to write: "Although out of danger she is still painfully weak & the slightest exertion brings on a recurrence of fever & the suffering in her head. She is constantly yearning to begin what she has not yet strength to undertake & is most anxious you should be aware that it is this weakness alone which keeps her quiet." Toward the end of the month she was not much better and her doctor forbade her to use her pen. "Miss S. informed him of her anxieties & of her wishes as far as it was necessary," wrote Miss Conyers, "& he gave it as his opinion that if my dear friend will keep perfectly quiet till he gives her permission to use her pen, he will enable her to do so in time, though he cannot say *certainly* exactly."[3] But in spite of the doctor's promises she become worse and worse, and the novel could not be written.

In March 1862 Elizabeth Sheppard died at Brighton. Her friend wrote distractedly to Fields:

Dear Mr. Fields   9 Park Cottages Loghborough Parks Brixton

I am in too deep sorrow to say more than that I have lost my only dearest friend Miss Sheppard. I may have further communication to make some time hence, but can say no more now.

Should there be any notice of her in any American paper pray let me have it.   Yours truly

Susannah Conyers   [FI 3757]

Fields had Harriet Prescott write a memoir of Miss Sheppard in the June 1862 number of the magazine. Flowery though this tribute is, it is one of the two most important sources for the biography of the writer. The other is Miss Conyers' article which appeared in the October *Atlantic.*[4]

[3]Susannah Conyers to Fields, December 28, 1859.

[4]See Elizabeth Lee, "Elizabeth Sara Sheppard," *Dictionary of National Biography.* The sources for the *DNB* article are these two articles and S. Austin Allibone's notice in *A Critical Dictionary of English Literature and British and American Authors,* II (Philadelphia, 1899), 2075. See also Harriet Prescott Spofford's introduction to Elizabeth Sheppard, *Rumour* (Chicago, 1893).

Miss Conyers' article was taken from her reply to Fields upon receiving Miss Prescott's article. She was pleased with what Miss Prescott had to say, but had a few additions and an alteration to make:

9 Park Cottages Brixton 4th June /62

My dear Mr. Fields

Thank you for everything—above all for your kind considerateness in sending me the advance sheets of the "Atlantic."...

Will you allow me to say that the notice of the "author of Charles Auchester" considered merely as a composition is perfection—as a criticism it is most subtle & powerful & could only come from the pen of an accomplished writer.... There is only one trifling mistake which I am sure you will forgive me for rectifying. I allude to the surmise that Miss Sheppard was not a great reader. It is indeed a perfectly harmless error, as it proves how perfect her taste must have been—& shows she had that charm as an author, which is alike the test of good writing & good breeding—an absence of all mannerism. But she was indeed & truly a book worm. She read everything or rather *devoured* everything, from the most abstruse works....

Yet again you are right in saying she could not be called a student, for (setting aside all partial views which I might be supposed to entertain) she made all information her own, as if by magic, & her memory was wonderful. As a child of 8 years old she learned "Childe Harold" through in twice reading it, during play hours; Shelley's "Prometheus Unbound" as quickly, and every thing by the same kind of intuition she mastered in the spirit while others were hammering away at the letter. Goethe & Schiller she translated from with ease at 15 & amused her teacher by writing long German critiques to imaginary magazines as an exercise....

She often talked of you & your gentle wife—& never forgot those flowers which came to her when we were very miserable—her constant expression being "I have seen them too late, 4 years ago I could have written for them as I could desire. I shall never write again." Yet she laid out 2 romances from which you were to have chosen; one called "Grey Magic" the other "An Old Story"—In "Grey Magic" the hero is once more "Bernard" under another name. There are a few pages copied out which you shall have; but her fearful sufferings made all reading & writing impossible for some time before her death. I also enclose a little sketch, evidently written by her for a magazine, *in her own handwriting*; which you may like to keep for her sake, whether you insert it or not in the "Atlantic Monthly." For the poems—I have quantities, of which I enclose a few, & will copy the others & send you in a box, through your agent Mr. Trübner....

I enclose the little notice for which you asked in your letter, I trust it is the kind of thing required—if it is too long, or too short pray tell me. What I have written is bare fact—& I have not allowed myself to indulge in expressions which might have rushed from my lips in conversation with one who loved her....

Mrs. Da Costa's article (for she was married by the time it appeared in October) was as eulogistic as Miss Prescott's. It was printed along with Elizabeth Sheppard's "A Niche in the Heart." Though Miss Sheppard's writings were widely ignored by the press at the time of her death, they continued to be read.[5]

Through arrangements with Mrs. Da Costa, three previously unpublished works of Elizabeth Sheppard appeared in the *Atlantic Monthly*. The first was a juvenile story, "The Children's Cities," printed in the July 1862 issue. It is a prettily written tale, very simple, but with the inevitable moral, taking the form of allegory. "A Niche in the Heart," the essay that appeared with Mrs. Da Costa's article in October 1862, is a saccharine meditation on charity, fame, and death, but in a prose style pleasingly imitative of De Quincey. Finally, a poem, "Threnody," was published in the February 1863 issue. It is typical of the highly stilted obituary poetry of the period. It was most unfortunate that Fields did not meet Miss Sheppard earlier, or that she did not live longer. With his financial encouragement, she might have written, instead of these feeble pieces and her girlish novels, something mature and valuable.

Representing a viewpoint directly opposite to the passionate sentimentality of Miss Sheppard was Harriet Martineau, who contributed five articles to the *Atlantic*. Fifty-five years old when the magazine was founded in 1857, she was already known as the foremost exponent of intellectual freedom for women in England. Most of her important works, which concern religion, morals, philosophy, political economy, and mesmerism, had already been published. It was therefore to an established writer that Fields appealed in 1860 and 1861 when he asked Miss Martineau

---

[5]Editions of *Charles Auchester*, *Cecilia*, and *Rumour* were published as late as the 1890's by A. C. McClurg and Company in Chicago. Thus Elizabeth Sheppard's almost complete obscurity came about in the twentieth century.

to contribute. Within the limits of respectability, he wished to make the *Atlantic* a forum for free thought, as Lowell had done before him. In Miss Martineau he knew that he would have a writer whose attitudes were fresh and intelligent, though sometimes controversial.

Her first article for the magazine was a memorial notice of Lady Byron. Though laudatory, as all such notices were at the time, it was succinct and restrained. Miss Martineau submitted it, in her characteristically willful way, in spite of objections from Lady Byron's granddaughter. She sent it to Fields in November 1860:

Ambleside November 29/60

Messrs. Ticknor & Fields
Gentlemen.

I received my friend, Charles Follen's note just in time to enable me to send you the Memoir of Lady Byron by the mail of tomorrow.

It occurs to me to put in a portrait of her, as she was at the time of her marriage. I have got it photographed from an engraving that I have. I don't know whether you insert illustrations in the "Atlantic Monthly"; but I thought you might like to have the portrait.

I think you will agree with me that what follows had better be between you & me, unless you see some particular occasion for speaking of it.

Within a few days, strong attempts have been made by Lady Byron's only granddaughter, Lady Annabella King, to stop this memoir; & she has engaged in the attempt several friends of Lady B's & her own, who were delighted, two or three weeks ago, at my doing it, & eager to help me with materials, in the form of reports of her benefactions &c. I think the women weak, & their alleged reasons weaker. Indeed, I have not,—nor has my best friend,—the niece who lives with me,—the slightest doubt in the world about my duty in the case. But it makes me extremely careful *how* I state the case; & I believe it is so done as to leave not an atom of ground for complaint of you or myself. I will explain this.

Immediately after her death, a short Memoir of Ly. B., by me, appeared in the London "Daily News." It is to the same effect as the one I send, in small compass. From that day to this we have heard of the good it has done. There is even an enthusiasm kindled by this appeal for tardy justice. Miss Carpenter, the depository of Ly. Byron's papers, wrote to tell me how gratified the family & friends were; & the only fault I have heard found is with my having called "a blighted life" that of a woman *so* separated from her husband at four & twenty! I took care, in writing that sketch, to disclose nothing new about the married life of Lady B. I know the facts; but I have never needlessly spoken of them; & in that sketch, there is nothing told that has not already been published from Lady Byron's own hand, or by her husband's very partial biographer.—What I want particularly to command to your attention is that I have, in the Memoir, referred to the sources of information throughout. By doing this, I trust I have precluded all attack from any quarter; &, if it should be made, our answer is easy. We have simply to point to Moore's Life of Byron (2d edition) containing Lady Byron's own published statement, in the Appendix; & to the statement issued by Campbell in the New Monthly Magazine, in 1836.—This last I hope will not be fished up; & I have not used it: but still, it *is* an existing publication, derived from Lady Byron herself.—I dare say you will hear nothing of the matter;—nor I either, perhaps. The ground of objection (*assigned*) is Lady B's own reserve & the feelings of Lady Annabella.—Now, I need not show you the pass society would come to if modest merit were to be suppressed, *after death*, & only braggarts celebrated, or held forth as examples. You will see my doctrine, however, in the Memoir; & I have no doubt whatever of your agreeing with me.—It must be said for Lady Annabella that she can have no idea how widely Lady Byron's affairs have been discussed, nor how unfavourable are the associations wh. still hang about her name. For my part, *I* owed her a duty before Ly. Annabella was born; & I shall not let her good name go down the wind at last, to spare the vanity, or even a better feeling, of the grandchild of Lord Byron. I am *most* scrupulous never to bring before the public the name of any person in private life, but Lady Byron *has been* the most notorious woman of her day; & the reparation due to her character must not be withheld because it was, in deference to her feelings, long deferred.

I will add that I have been her occasional correspondent, & I think she would have let me say a friend of hers for seven & twenty years. She preserved my letters, & endorsed them herself, to be returned at her death. I had her confidence as to her views on many subjects; & *some* in regard to her private (domestic) affairs. I feel unable, under these circumstances, to refuse the opportunity you offer me of procuring justice for her, & enriching the world with another example of an eminently good woman, of a very rare kind of goodness. It would have been easier to have sent you an excuse by this mail, & have burned the M. S. S., but I feel bound to do my duty to my old friend,—putting you in full possession of the circumstances.

My niece & I shall keep quiet about the matter: & we are disposed to think we shall hear no more in the way of objection, when it is once found to be too late. If there should be, we are on safe ground; & any attack will be a misfortune for those who make it.

We form this judgment from the effect of the existing Memoir, which, slight as it is, is more broad in its condemnation of Lord B. than the one I send. Thanks & "admiration" &c. flow in still, after 6 months.

I do not apologize for the length of this letter, as I could not be satisfied to keep back any part of the case from you.—As for the Memoir, I believe you will find it considerably within the limit (as to length) which you prescribed.

I have written my name in pencil, because I don't know whether you wish for my signature or not. Do as you like about it.

I am very ill myself; but I doubt whether the Memoir is the worse for that. Possibly it may be the better, except for my inability to revise it myself. My editors here kindly excuse me from that labour; & my niece is so good as to do it for me.

I am, dear Sirs, with much respect yours

Harriet Martineau.

"Lady Byron" was published in the February 1861 *Atlantic*. It naturally invites comparison with the Harriet Beecher Stowe article, "The True Story of Lady Byron's Life," published eight years later, which is an incoherent tirade in defense of what Mrs. Stowe considered a martyred reputation. Unlike the American writer, Miss Martineau wrote calmly and omitted to mention Lord Byron's incest, though she agreed that he had been the guilty cause of the break-up of the marriage.

The article was highly successful; Miss Martineau testified that the February *Atlantic* was sold out in London because of it. Fields was greatly pleased and requested more contributions from the authoress. She replied with "Lights of the Lake District" (in the May 1861 *Atlantic*), an anecdotal reminiscence of Wordsworth, Coleridge, and others who frequented the Lake District of Cumberland and Westmoreland, where Miss Martineau's own house stood at Ambleside. Because most of the matter of the article is first hand, it can claim a certain importance in the study of the writers it discusses. Such is also the case of the letter of submittal that accompanied Miss Martineau's manuscript:

Elizabeth Sheppard, Harriet Martineau, George Eliot

Janry. 26/61

Messrs. Ticknor & Fields
Dear Sirs:

By this mail I send you the article on the "Lights of the Lake District." I am glad you asked me to do this piece of work. I have done it with true, though a somewhat sad, pleasure. I believe you may rely on the statements throughout with entire confidence. Mrs. Arnold & her daughters are delighted at my doing this; & I feel sure that I should have the same sympathy from others, equally interested in my subject, if they also were beside me here.

The worst of it is, I have forestalled some few things which are,—not only written, but printed, in my Autobiography, which is ready for publication as soon as I am gone. I felt that it would be an injury, not only to this article but to the subject of it, if I omitted those very things that I could best speak to. I have no doubt of this article being read all over England, & reproduced in periodicals here; & then, when the Autobiography appears people will find they have read some small portions of it in 1861.—Very small portions, however.

I hope the length will not frighten you. It is longer than the Byron Memoir, but not, I believe, longer than the maximum of space you assigned for that Memoir. If you *should* find it desirable to omit some minor parts, do so; but I guess you won't.

You may like to know privately that Hartley Coleridge's saying[6] was about me. I thought it too characteristic to be lost because it was about me. He was desperately afraid of me, (his friends told me) & curious about me,—simply because I did not cultivate his acquaintance. A single woman, always busy & with no gentleman in the house, can't invite a man who might come, 6 days a week, at breakfast time, tipsy, & wear out the day & the carpet with pacing the room, maundering & quoting poetry, & swilling beer, till sunset. In families it cd. be, (& was) borne with, for his gentle nature's sake; but I have seen old friends quite worn out with him.—Another private light:—poor Miss Wordsworth was a remarkable instance of the inversion of moral qualities wh. some times appears in insanity. When in health, she was a worshipper of her brother & his works, & herself most humble & retiring. Latterly she complained of the world "making so much of William. Every thing that is really good in his poetry is mine," said she. When strangers walked on, in pity, & left us talking with her, she

---

[6] Miss Martineau refers to the following passage in "Lights of the Lake District": "Such a cast of character [the determination characteristic of Dr. Thomas Arnold] was an inexplicable puzzle to poor Hartley. He showed this by giving his impression of another person of the same general mode of life,—that A. B. [that is, Harriet Martineau] was 'a monomaniac about everything.'"

wanted them to come back. "But we have no time today," we used to plead. "Our friends have to see the curiosities of the District." "Then, *bring them to me*," said she peremptorily. "*I* am the greatest curiosity of the District." You can conceive the painfulness of the change!—I have tried to get for you vignettes of all the houses mentioned: but there is no sale at this season, & I fear I shall not succeed. I send you the cottage in wh. Hartley Coleridge lived & died. The Lake (Rydal) is just in front,—only the road & a bit of grass between. I send you my house. You see the oak copses where Wordsworth used to lie, before the house was built. My niece is trying to get two or three more,—Rydal Mount, Fac How[?] &c. We shall be very glad if you are pleased with what I have done. I need not say that your public affairs are in all minds & on all lips at present. The only wonder about the explosion is that it did not happen (or get prevented) long ago.

With best wishes, I am yours truly

H. Martineau

I can't get the other vignettes.[7]

The *Autobiography* Miss Martineau was writing was published as planned in 1877, the year after her death. Though this work was taking much of her time, she was still able to write for the *Atlantic*, upon Fields's invitation. She replied in March to his letter in which he had requested more contributions:

Messrs. Ticknor & Fields   Ambleside March 19/61
Dear Sirs.

I have much pleasure in acknowledging the arrival of your letter of March 4th, & in enclosing my receipt for your Bill of Exchange for £34. I must also thank you for a copy of the "Atlantic Monthly" for February, which gave me the opportunity of seeing the Byron Memoir in print.—That Memoir seems to have been most pleasantly received here,—judging by what I have heard, & some notices in print. The feeling is of surprise that Lady Byron was so unlike the common impression of her, & satisfaction that justice has been done at last. I have heard of no objections in any quarter.

I am glad the article on the Lakes pleases you. Your two suggestions of subjects have been so fortunate that it might be well if you would try again. You know, better than I, what wd. suit your readers. As I have more time before May than I am likely to have after, I think I will venture a short article without waiting for your reply.—I quite

[7]MS in possession of Mrs. Z. B. Adams.

forgot, in writing my Autobiography, an interesting incident,—the pathetic story of a young Irish Repealer, who died soon after I knew him. He had not a relation in the world, if I remember right: so there can be no scruple about telling his story,—which is highly honourable to him. There is so much delusion in your neighbourhood,—among some friends of mine, at least,—about that Irish claim, that the story may be useful: & I think it will be interesting. I shall change his name, & alter nothing else. It occurs to me as possible that an article containing sketches of the four seasons in rural England might possibly be interesting: but I am far from sure. You see, your countrymen come to *London*; & when there, they see a certain set,—a very good set, well born & bred, literary & political,—but no fair specimens of the general run of us. By all I heard in U. S., & all I see of Americans here, it appears to me that they have no conception of ordinary English life in the country,—of Ladies doing anything useful at home, of domestic economy, practices, & manners. Again, Irving's pictures of English country life are traditional & bookish & not in the least like the life of today. I shd. like to hear your opinion of this; & shall be thankful for suggestions from you, if you can think of any topics which will suit at once your readers & me. . . .

I have just seen an announcement that there is not a copy of "the Atlantic Monthly" for February unsold. I am applied to for a sight of my copy. I don't know whether you send many over; but I know there is much interest about the Byron Memoir.

I am, dear Sirs, truly yours   Harriet Martineau.

The articles that followed, all of them that same year, were "The Young Repealer," "Health in the Camp," and "Health in the Hospital." The first, appearing in the September *Atlantic*, was the true story of a young Irishman who found out for himself that independence was not the cure for Ireland's troubles. Perhaps it was intended as an object lesson for the Confederate States of America, the moral being that secession was not the cure for the South's troubles. At any rate, the other two articles, published in the November and December numbers, were definitely for the benefit of the North. They were concrete, detailed accounts of the British sanitation reforms in the camps and hospitals of the Crimean War. Their aim was to encourage similar action in the United States during the Civil War.

Here Miss Martineau's contributions ceased. The Trent Affair, late in 1861, had brought English diplomatic relations with the North to a crisis, and the ill feelings it aroused did not subside until the Emancipation Proclamation in January 1863 justified the Union cause in the eyes of most Britishers. Many Englishmen, previously friendly to the North, were repelled by the Trent Affair. Contributions to the *Atlantic* from overseas were all but discontinued. One reason, of course, was that Fields did not solicit such contributions, realizing that they would not be popular with the American public.

If Harriet Martineau was the leading woman of intellect in her generation, George Eliot succeeded to the position in the later nineteenth century. While Fields was abroad in 1869, he managed to get two poems from George Eliot. He wrote back to the firm on May 17 that he had offered George Henry Lewes, who took care of George Eliot's financial dealings, the tremendous sum of three hundred pounds for one of the poems:

I have seen her twice and they were most satisfactory interviews. Yesterday we spent an hour with her. All business arrangements are made with Lewes for she, on account of her nervous disinclination for affairs, never speaks of money. I have found Lewes a capital fellow and every way inclined towards us. He promises that his wife shall write for the uniform edition a few lines of authorization. He also says she is at work now upon a novel of English life but when it will be ready for publication no one can tell. It may be this year and it may be five years from now, but she will never again print another story in serial form. He has allowed me (without her knowledge) to read the two poems of which he spoke to Trübner some time ago and I thought it wise to offer for one of them 300 pounds. It will occupy several pages in the Atlantic. Whether I shall get it or no will be decided in a few days. The relation already established between the Lewes and ourselves is most satisfactory.[8]

The poem which brought the large offer from Fields was "Agatha," a Swiss idyl on the theme of doing good for others. It covered eight and a half pages of the August 1869 *Atlantic*. The other poem, "A Legend of Jubal," appeared in the May 1870 issue. George Eliot made only one more contribution to the magazine, and that was in 1871, after Fields had retired.

[8]MS in the Henry W. and Albert A. Berg Collection, New York Public Library.

PART SIX

AWAY FROM THE DESK

FOREWORD TO PART SIX

Fields's retirement from the firm of Fields, Osgood and Company was anything but sudden. He had for some years been suffering from neuralgia and wishing for some escape from his enervating routine. He had run off to Manchester, Massachusetts, for relaxation whenever he could get away, and his trip to Europe had been some diversion, though exhausting in itself. He had been grooming Howells since 1866 to fill his place as *Atlantic* editor, and Osgood since 1858 to handle the publishing. He had talked of doing some writing, and lecturing was also in the back of his mind, but his opportunities had been severely limited by more pressing duties. Retirement offered the chance to satisfy his long-cherished desire for public renown as a man of letters.

Furthermore, he had clearly been treading water for the last several years. The publishing business had become so large and profitable that it was no longer necessary or even desirable to attract many new writers; the old favorites served well enough. The *Atlantic*, Fields realized, must keep abreast of the times in order to survive, but he had left most of the recruiting of new writers to Howells. Howells was more sensitive to the literary trends of the time, being himself one of the youthful experimenters, while Fields was a mid-century Bostonian as long as he lived. A change in the editorship was almost as needed now as it had been a decade earlier.

Fields retired at an opportune moment. The country's economy was running smoothly in the North, and the firm's business was at its peak. The *Atlantic* had gained the largest circulation it was to have during its first half-century—although subscriptions had already begun to fall off since the publication of Holmes's *The Guardian Angel* and Mrs. Stowe's "The True Story of Lady Byron's Life." Fields had accumulated enough wealth to retire very comfortably, and even to buy a summer cottage a few years later in his beloved Manchester, and his affairs were so arranged that his wife would never be in need of money for the remainder of her long life. Osgood was not so fortunate. Encouraged by prosperous times, he enlarged the business beyond his ability to handle it. The great Boston fire of 1872 caused him considerable loss, and the Panic of 1873 nearly finished him. He was forced to sell the firm's periodicals, the *Atlantic* going into the hands of H. O. Houghton and Company, but he managed to remain in business until 1878, when he merged with Houghton to form Houghton, Osgood and Company, which lasted until Houghton bought him out in 1880.

Though the firm's name was officially changed on January 2, 1871, to James R. Osgood and Company, Fields remained to advise Howells with the *Atlantic* until September. He continued to correspond with the old contributors, who were frequently suspicious of the change to younger hands. But the final acceptance or rejection of manuscripts was in Howells' hands from the first of the year, and the way was gently prepared for Fields's final complete withdrawal. He had maintained the magazine's unique and enviable standing and kept it alive to the best in modern literature, and now he had insured its safe continuance for at least another decade.

Chapter XXIV:

Latter Days

A LIFE of retirement was pleasant, but for Fields it was not a life of ease. He certainly did not need to work for financial reasons, but his life had been one of such feverish activity that it was impossible for him to relax now that he had the chance. There is no doubt that he drove himself to an early death.

He began writing intensively even before the date of his retirement, and while he helped Howells with the editing of the *Atlantic* in 1871, he also had fifteen pieces of his own in it, more than he had contributed during the entire nine and a half years while he was full-time editor. The first of a series of his inimitable reminiscences marked the January number; and each month thereafter throughout 1871 appeared essays on Pope, Thackeray, Hawthorne, Dickens, Wordsworth, and Mary Russell Mitford under the title of *Our Whispering Gallery*. While this series was in progress, he also contributed a serious poem, and two brief bouquets of doggerel under the general title *Bubbles from an Ancient Pipe*. Most of these works later appeared in his books.

Besides contributions to other magazines—such as "The Owl-Critic," a poem, and "A Free Lecture Experience," a story, both in the 1879 *Harper's Monthly*—he wrote, edited, and re-edited so many books and parts of books during the seventies that their description here would be cumbersome. *Yesterdays with Authors* (1872), *Underbrush* (1877), and *Ballads and Other Verses* (1881) represent his best work as a reminiscent, a miscellaneous essayist, and a poet. The prose was immensely and deservedly popular; *Yesterdays* went through dozens of editions, being reprinted at least as late as 1901, and receiving the praise of critics and friends in both the United States and England.

With the conclusion of his work on the *Atlantic*, Fields began lecturing. His talks were soon popular and by March 1, 1872, George Putnam wrote him: "I hear a great deal more of your lecture than any other that is going. It must be the success of the season." The following fall he made a tour of the West, and the succeeding years took him as far west as Omaha, as far south as Washington, and as far north as Maine. He visited Chicago several times, New York saw him often, and he became familiar all over New England. But it was strenuous work. Train travel was unsafe, unhealthy, and uncomfortable; hotel food was bad; and faulty transportation facilities made for undue exposure and periods of unrelieved boredom. Even the healthiest of lecturers found the experience fatiguing, and Fields could not stand the strain forever. In 1874 he recorded the following memorandum in his notebook:

I will lecture for $100 in any place so near Boston that I can return the same evening. I decline lecturing for less. I will go to any place not farther off than 4 hours by Rail for $100, and I decline to have any arrangements made farther off than 4 hours, without first consulting me, or I intend to go on no long journeys without special terms are entered into. Western applications I must look over with the Bureau before a decision is made. Feb. 1874[1]

But as late as 1880 he was still traveling as far away as Utica and Philadelphia.

The American lyceum movement, of which Fields's lectures were a part, needs no explanation in these pages. Fields's lectures were much like those of many another, except that Fields had the advantage of a tremendously broad acquaintance with the living writers and their books. A typical repertoire was that delivered at Exeter, New Hampshire, in May 1874. In writing his letter of acceptance to Charles Marseilles of Exeter, who had asked for the lectures, Fields broke his rule of a hundred dollars a performance, but this was the month before he recorded his resolution:

[1] Uncatalogued Annie Fields MSS, Envelope 36, Huntington Library.

Latter Days

Boston. 148 Charles St. Jany. 17, 1874

Dear Sir.

I will then according to your request take the dates May 4, 6, 13, 18, 20, 27 and give my 6 Lectures in Exeter for 300$. I enclose all the documents I have by me, and don't care to have them returned.

Please not mention the terms as I go nowhere less than 100$ a night, but as Exeter is near my native town (Portsmouth), I feel like doing it for home.

Truly Yrs.
James T. Fields.

PROGRAMME.

I. May 4, Charles Lamb, and his Friends.
II. May 6, Sydney Smith, and his Work in Life.
III. May 13, "Christopher North," with Personal Recollections.
IV. May 18, Alfred Tennyson, the Man and the Poet.
V. May 20, Literary and Artistic Society in London Twenty-five Years Ago.
VI. May 27, Fiction, and its Eminent Authors.[2]

Besides his literary lectures, Fields delivered a few on morals and success, like "Masters of the Situation," a very popular speech given at Exeter just one year later.

As if his writing and speaking were not enough to keep him busy, he aided and took part in a great many public and private charities, and was constantly giving aid and advice to friends who asked for it. He frequently helped raise funds and donated money of his own for the aid of needy writers. In 1872 it was for George MacDonald, the Scotch writer and minister, who was in the United States. In 1875 he helped pay the funeral expenses of John J. Babson, a young historian of Gloucester, Massachusetts, whom he had aided before. In 1877 he sent money for the Christmas of an impoverished poet in New York, who was none other than Walt Whitman. And the following year it was D. G.

---

[2]MS in Harvard University Library. The "Programme" is a printed clipping which Fields corrected as above in ink; it is quoted here with the omission of unnecessary words.

Mitchell whom Fields helped save from eviction from his home.[3] Besides this and besides managing the Emerson lectures of 1872, he advised such people as Harriet Hosmer, E. P. Whipple, and Longfellow on matters of writing and publication.

It was little wonder that he relished his vacations. He and Annie went at least once a year during the summer to Manchester, Massachusetts, where he could breathe the fresh salt air and have no more company than he chose. In 1874 he began building there his "Gambrel Cottage" on "Thunderbolt Hill." He wrote of it to Bayard Taylor jubilantly the following summer:

My Dear Bayard.   July 8. 1875.

Now let us know when you and wife and daughter can come to us for a week. We are fast getting squarely in, and the hut is rapidly coming into order under the direction of A. F. the wise and good. Your suggestions as to African marble and porphyry have all been carried out, and the money borrowed for payment. The shops were aout of Leopard skins for the couches, but we got a couple of Tigers in the jungle and used them instead. The colossal bronze cats are up and squawking.

    With love to you all from both of us.

                                              Ever Yours
                                              James T. Fields

Sorry we were away when you called in B.

The cottage was his refuge for several months each summer for the rest of his life. After his death Annie made it her permanent home, where she lived for the rest of her life. The house still stands, in one of the wealthiest suburban residential districts in the state.

In spite of vacations, Fields's health became progressively worse. As early as 1867 his hand had become so lame as to prevent his writing with it. He was frequently bothered by colds. In the fall of 1873 a knee became lame; it bothered him for about three years, and part of the time he was on crutches. Much of

---

[3]Adeline Whitney to Annie Fields, letters from November 1872 to January 1873. George MacDonald to Fields, April 12, 1873, Harvard University Library. Hiram Rich to Fields, April 27 and May 1, 1875. John Burroughs to Fields, December 26, 1879. Whittier to Fields, March 17, May 11, June 17, and no date, 1880.

Latter Days

his correspondence after 1878 was done by Annie, for he was frequently too ill to write. He suffered from angina pectoris during the last five years of his life, and also at this time he developed frequent nosebleeds. While lecturing at Wellesley College in May 1879, he suffered a violent "hemorrhage from the head," from which he never fully recovered. He recuperated sufficiently, however, to continue lecturing in the winter of 1880-81, until a short time before his death. He died at home on Sunday evening, April 24, 1881, following an attack caused by coronary disease.[4] He was buried at Mount Auburn Cemetery in Boston. His minister, C. A. Bartol, conducted the funeral rites.

Immediately letters of sympathy began pouring in upon Annie. Besides those from Holmes, Lowell, Longfellow, and the other Bostonians and Cantabridgians, there were messages of condolence from Henry Alden, Joaquin Miller, E. P. Whipple, R. H. Dana, John D. Long (Governor of Massachusetts), and from Edward Lear, Mrs. Bryan Procter, and many others. The memorial notice in the *Atlantic* (August 1881) was written by Whipple, and Longfellow and Whittier wrote memorial poems. Other notices of the death appeared in many magazines and newspapers. As for public honors, Fields had already received in 1874 an honorary degree of Master of Arts from Dartmouth. In 1882 some trees were planted in a park in distant Cincinnati in memory of the publisher.[5]

The public sympathy seemed to call for the preparing of a biography of Fields, and soon after his death, Annie set about arranging his letters and notes, together with her own diary, for publication. It was exactly what she needed to relieve her sorrow. She undertook the work with the aid and advice of Holmes, who

---

[4]Annie Fields, *James T. Fields*, p. 273. M. A. De Wolfe Howe in *Early Years of the Saturday Club* agrees with this date. As Mrs. Fields does have the right weekday, Sunday, according to the calendar of 1881, and as she recalls particular circumstances in her biography, I have accepted April 24 as the correct date. However, Fields's death certificate in the Division of Vital Statistics, The Commonwealth of Massachusetts, gives April 23, 1881, age sixty-three years.

[5]Annie Fields to John Peaslee, April 25, 1882, MS in Dartmouth College Library. See Annie Fields, *James T. Fields*, pp. 259-68.

counseled her particularly on the delicate question of how much to leave out, and read proof for her.[6] Unfortunately her distracted state of mind was not conducive to effective organization of a book, and this was her first venture in sustained composition. Furthermore she was hypersensitive about the feelings of living people, and the omissions and lack of detail in the book are among its most outstanding characteristics. But despite its faults, *James T. Fields, Biographical Notes and Personal Sketches* was received with almost universal praise when it appeared at the end of 1881. Friends and acquaintances from all over the United States and the British Isles wrote letters of congratulation to the author, and once again complimentary notices—this time of the book as well as its subject—appeared in the press.

Thus ended the life of a man who in several vital ways had advanced the literary profession in the United States. He had played a major part in the revolution in book publishing which made it possible for American writers to earn a respectable living by their pens; he had fostered and stabilized the foremost literary magazine in the country, to bring forth the first and the finest works of many an author; and he had brought American writers to the people, not only as publisher and editor, but as one of the more popular lecturers in the far-flung lyceum movement. His writings are of secondary importance, but in his reminiscences, at least, he gave the world some of the most valuable personal sketches that exist of nineteenth-century literary figures.

---

[6]Letters from Holmes to Annie Fields, August 24, 1881, to March 3, 1882. Also September 15, 1881, in Harvard University Library.

Chapter XXV:

Yesterdays

IF WE ACCEPT the fact at the outset that Fields was not a real poet and that his lectures were not intended as literature, then we can come quickly to his true value as a nineteenth-century American writer. In a copy of the 1879 edition of *Verses for a Few Friends*, now in the Longfellow House, Fields wrote: "J. T. F. to H. W. L. With the Versifier's love to the Poet. 1879." Such was his own opinion of his poetic talent less than two years before he died, and it was a just estimate. He was a skillful metrist, he possessed a respectable vocabulary, and he developed in his later years a nice taste in diction and tone, all of which characteristics were adequately demonstrated in his editing. His early poetry was hopeless—sentimental, bombastic, moralistic, often meaningless. A stanza from the 1838 *Anniversary Poem*, read befort the Boston Mercantile Library Association, will serve to illustrate:

> There are, thank Heaven, beneath this fitful dome,
> Some leaflets floating near affection's home;
> Some cloudless skies that smile on scenes below,
> Some changeless hues in life's wide spanning bow.
> So let us live, that if misfortune's blast
> Comes like a whirlwind to our hearths at last,
> Sunbeams may break from one small spot of Blue,
> To guide us safe life's dreary desert through.

Yet his later verse has merits worth attending. The bombast and sentimentality were discarded during the days of the *Atlantic* editorship. Nor did the matured writer attempt anything of such magnitude as the *Anniversary Poem*.

Ballads and Other Verses (1881), his last collection of verses, contains several meritorious performances. He was at his best in humorous doggerel: "The Owl-Critic" is perhaps the best he ever did and one of his most famous poems. It tells of a "critic" who finds fault with what he considers the preposterous taxidermy displayed in an owl in a barber shop:

> Just then, with a wink and a sly normal lurch,
> The owl, very gravely, got down from his perch;
> Walked round, and regarded his fault-finding critic
> (Who thought he was stuffed) with a glance analytic,
> And then fairly hooted, as if he should say:
> "Your learning's at fault *this* time, any way;
> Don't waste it again on a live bird, I pray.
> I'm an owl; you're another. Sir Critic, good-day!
> And the barber kept on shaving.

"The Turtle and the Flamingo" is an equally pleasant bit of nonsense about the love affair of a turtle:

> Spake the turtle in tones like a delicate wheeze:
> "To the water I've oft seen you in go,
> And your form has impressed itself deep on my shell,
>   You perfectly modelled flamingo!
>   You uncommonly brilliant flamingo!
>   You tremendously scorching flamingo!
>   You inexpres-*si*-ble flamingo!"

The spurned turtle ends his days in Agassiz's soup.

But *Ballads and Other Verses* also contains a great many dull verses. There are memorial verses, such as "The Memory of Moore," "On Receiving a Lock of Keats's Hair," "With Wordsworth at Rydal," "Agassiz," and "To T[homas] S[tarr] K[ing]." There are moralistic poems on nature: "Spring, among the Hills," "Midnight Song by the Shore," "A Summer Retreat," and "Eventide in the Country." And there are several poems on the transiency of life. "But give the Past—'tis all thou canst—thy tears!" reads the final line of the closing poem, "The Old Year."

As popular verse, Fields's poetry was successful. It was frequently accepted for publication in magazines, and it appeared in anthologies of the period. A few lines are still quoted. The 1938 edition of John Bartlett's *Familiar Quotations* contains ten excerpts from his verses.

His familiar essays are much better. A collection of his magazine contributions, *Underbrush*, published in 1877 and enlarged in 1881, contains virtually all of them. Besides "My Friend's Library," "How to Rough It," and "The Pettibone Lineage," which have already been discussed, the book contains such delightful bagatelles as "Familiar Letter to House-Breakers," "A Watch that 'Wanted Cleaning,'" "Bothersome People," and "Abijah Dole's Free Lecture Experience." "A Watch that 'Wanted Cleaning,'" the story of a "gaunt individual I encountered a few weeks ago in Omaha" who was taken in by a sharper in "*She*-cargo," is funny enough to warrant its appearance in E. B. and K. S. White's *A Subtreasury of American Humor* (1941). "A Free Lecture Experience" (so the title read in the June 1879 issue of *Harper's New Monthly Magazine*, where it first appeared) is obviously a humorous recitation of Fields's own experience. The setting is in a small New England town in midwinter, and the inhospitable air of the place is well described. Most of Fields's humor derives from stating in a bookish manner things that are not ordinarily bookish—using fine language to describe trivial or commonplace situations. "Our Village Dogmatist," for example, begins:

> If "to be wise were to be obstinate," Underhill has lately lost its incarnation of wisdom. A few months ago we followed to his corner-lot in the windy graveyard all that was mortal (and there was considerable of it) of "old Cap'n Barker Brine," as he was familiarly called by man, woman, and child in our little community. Born with protruded lips and elevated eyebrows, he was for many years our village doubter, oracle, and critic,—our tyrannical master of opinion in all public and private matters; and even now the prelude to any wise commonplace is, "*Old Cap'n Brine used to say*."

Fields's literary aim was to soothe the miseries of humanity. In the essay "Pleasant Ghosts," he wrote of a neighbor who played Bach and Beethoven on the piano. "Such a neighbor," he said, "has the power not only to gladden our waking hours, but to bring us the blessed boon of pleasant dreams." His attitude was characteristic of that of many of his contemporary writers and readers; they wanted literature that would lull them rather than bring them face to face with life. Charles Lamb—"the gentle Lamb," who with Leigh Hunt was one of Fields's chief literary idols—said something of the kind in his essay "The Genteel Style of Writing." He was quoting Sir William Temple: "When all is done ... human life is at the greatest and the best but like a froward child, that must be played with, and humoured a little, to keep it quiet till it falls asleep, and then the care is over." Fields excelled at humoring his readers, but beyond that his art did not go.

The idea carried over into his lectures, one of which was entitled "Cheerfulness." The newspaper reviews of his lectures often mentioned the "pleasantness" of his delivery.[1] But he was also concerned with instructing his audience, both morally and intellectually. A folder of his notes written at this period contains a list of some length made up of sayings he intended to use in lectures; for example, "There are two things in this life that are never worth crying about: what *can* be cured and what *cannot* be cured."[2] One of his most popular talks was "Masters of the Situation," which he summarized thus in a newspaper advertisement:

> How to do it and how not to do it. True mastery never the result of accident. Illustrations of failures and successes in various walks of life. Nothing accomplished without preparation and earnest study. Triumphs in art, in literature, on the stage, at the bar, the result of enthusiastic endeavor. Edmund Kean, Napoleon, Charles Dickens, and other masters. The demand in America for thoroughbred men and women.[3]

Fields's lectures were prepared, not for scholarly audiences, but for the semi-literate crowds that gathered in lyceums and public halls for almost the only non-local entertainment they could find. If his moral complacency cannot be excused because of this, at least it can be explained. He spoke to the masses, and he felt it

---

[1] See Annie Fields, *James T. Fields*, p. 218.
[2] Uncatalogued Fields material, Huntington Library.
[3] Clipping in the uncatalogued Fields material, Huntington Library.

his duty to instruct them so that they, like him, could rise above their lot. He liked to recall those writers who had made good in spite of poverty or low station. In the lecture on Burns he paid tribute to the Scottish poet's triumphant ascent to greatness, and in "Keats and Shelley, with the Story of Their Lives" he remarked:

> Genius and Fame have nothing whatever to do with ancestry; but I am inclined to think Keats's father, from all we hear of him was a much more respectable person with his stall frock on, than hard old Timothy Shelley, lord of many lands, and never lord of himself.[4]

In his lectures on literary figures Fields's object was to inspire appreciation and respect for literature. This he effectively did, if the newspaper accounts speak the truth. From Exeter, New Hampshire, came the report: "Mr. Fields has done more than any other American to familiarize us with the men of letters of the old world [not to mention the new] and their works; and the nation owes him a debt of gratitude which will become greater as the ranks of our scholars increase!"[5] Lasting about an hour and a half, a lecture usually included a summary of the life of the writer being discussed, followed by quotations from his works, and interspersed with personal anecdotes, all bound together with instructive conclusions. For instance, in "Alfred Tennyson, the Man and the Poet" the lecturer concluded his comments on the *Idylls of the King* with praise of the poet's aim: "to teach this toiling, struggling world that no one can be doing the work of life well and lawfully unless he or she is setting up some high ideal, some lofty standard of right, which, amid all discomfitures, is ever to be kept in sight, and never for a moment to be cast aside for baser guidance."[6]

Fields seldom had anything bad to say of his subject. Believing

---

[4]MS notes for the lectures on Burns, and Shelley and Keats, uncatalogued Fields material, Huntington Library.

[5]Annie Fields, *James T. Fields*, p. 219.

[6]Clipping, "England's Great Poet," a review of Fields's lecture in the *Washington National Republican*, November 21, 1874, in the uncatalogued Fields material, Huntington Library.

that "A cheerful heart was our best introduction to the Deity,"[7] he continually attacked the sour critics "who cannot praise easily": "Habitual fault-finding is an immoral trait in any character, and a lesson we all should learn is to find out good things in what we see."[8]

As an editor of books Fields did not rank with the first-rate scholarly editors of his age, such as the Duyckincks, Allibone, or Roorbach, but his edition of De Quincey's works beginning in 1850 was a credit to American book publishing. It was the first collected edition, and involved a great deal of digging among old periodicals without much assistance from the author. A somewhat similar job on a smaller scale was the editing of the *Early and Late Papers hitherto Uncollected* of Thackeray (1867). This was a posthumous edition, collected by Fields from the pages of *Fraser's Magazine* and *Punch*, where the papers were written under pseudonyms. Besides the writings of De Quincey and Thackeray, and an edition in 1862 of Sir Thomas Browne's *Religio Medici* with a biographical introduction, Fields compiled the popular anthologies, *The Boston Book, Being Specimens of Metropolitan Literature* (1850), *Favorite Authors* (1861), and, with E. P. Whipple, *The Family Library of British Poetry from Chaucer to the Present Time* (1878). Here again he successfully strove to bring literature to the masses.

Fields's one book which lives as a whole is *Yesterdays with Authors* (1872). No biography of Thackeray, Hawthorne, Dickens, Wordsworth, Mary Russell Mitford, or Barry Cornwall—who are the authors sketched in the book—would be complete without reference to it. Its value lies first in the otherwise unpublished letters of these people, secondly in the first-hand accounts of their character, and thirdly in the simple and trustworthy manner of telling. The letters, of course, are edited according to the nineteenth-century manner. Names of living persons are usually omitted, excisions are made without acknowledgment, two letters

[7] Clipping, "Sidney Smith...Lecture by James T. Fields," *Philadelphia Press* (date missing), in the uncatalogued Fields material, Huntington Library.

[8] James T. Fields, "The Poet Longfellow," *Tribune Popular Science* (Boston, 1874), pp. 23-25, in Harvard University Library.

are combined under one date, punctuation is standardized, but the sins are not as bad as they sound. Actually they occur very rarely in Fields's book. When names are omitted, they can often be easily supplied by an alert reader. The excisions are nearly always marked except at the end of a letter, and the omitted portions consist merely of greetings or personal salutations. The present study has revealed only two or three instances in which the combining of parts of letters has occurred. And the corrections of punctuation are never made at the expense of meaning. Above all, Fields never distorted his quotations; the changes are stylistic. Then, too, the reader can trust his dating of the letters, and the dates are never missing when needed in either quotations or text; nor are the letters arranged in such an order that their connections are lost, but the organization is simple and systematic.[9]

Fields realized that details illustrate character better than generalities, and his sketches abound in the former. Besides important anecdotes like that of his discovery of *The Scarlet Letter* in Hawthorne's drawer, or Thackeray's sudden and unannounced departure from America because of homesickness, there are ones like the Great International Walking Match between George Dolby, managed by Dickens, and James Osgood, managed by Fields, and the talk with Landor at Barry Cornwall's table. Fields obviously relished his association with great men, and even the most minor incidents are significant when he describes them with enthusiasm and meticulous care. He apologized for the enthusiasm in his introduction: "My friends have often heard me in my 'garrulous old age' discourse of things past and gone, and know what they bring down on their heads when they request me 'to run over,' as they call it, the faces looking out upon us from these plain unvarnished frames."

Here, not as in his lectures, Fields's enthusiasm is illustrated by facts and bounded by limitations of space. In fact the very brevity of his remarks is admirable. Whenever possible he lets the subjects speak for themselves, and his own words often serve

---

[9]My criticism of Fields's editing is based upon an examination of much of the manuscript material he used for his book.

only to connect their diverse utterances. The connections are smooth and logical and in a language that had gained in simplicity as Fields's writing matured.

As the writer of *Yesterdays with Authors*, Fields could claim another noteworthy achievement, and the present age must credit him with being not only the foremost publisher of good literature in mid-nineteenth-century America, and one of the greatest magazine editors of the period, but also one who belongs in the first rank as a writer of reminiscences.

WORKS OF FIELDS

"Agassiz," *Scribner's Monthly*, VII (March 1874), 570.

Anniversary Poem, Delivered before the Mercantile Library Association of Boston, September 13, 1838. Boston: William D. Ticknor, 1838.

"Arthur Hallam," *Atlantic Monthly*, VI (December 1860), 694.

"At Rydal," *Atlantic Monthly*, XXIV (October 1869), 506.

Ballads and Other Verses. Boston: Houghton, Mifflin and Company, 1881.

"The Bells of Bethlehem. On Hearing Them in the Hill Country of New Hampshire September 1880." Broadside in the Huntington Library [1880?].

The Boston Book. Edited by James T. Fields. Boston: Ticknor, Reed and Fields, 1850.

"Bubbles from an Ancient Pipe," *Atlantic Monthly*, XXVII (May, June 1871), 590, 743.

Charles Dickens, Barry Cornwall and Some of His Friends. James T. Fields. *A Christmas Carol.* Charles Dickens. Boston: Houghton Mifflin Company [1881].

A Conversational Pitcher. Boston: R. Briggs, 1877.

"Diamonds and Pearls," *Atlantic Monthly*, VII (March 1861), 361.

Early and Late Papers Hitherto Uncollected. William M. Thackeray. Edited with prefatory note by James T. Fields. Boston: Ticknor and Fields, 1867.

Family Library of British Poetry from Chaucer to the Present Time. Edited by James T. Fields and Edwin P. Whipple. Boston: Houghton, Osgood and Company, 1878.

Favorite Authors. Edited by James T. Fields. Boston: Ticknor and Fields, 1861.

Favorite Authors: A Companion Book of Prose and Poetry. Edited by James T. Fields. Boston: Fields, Osgood and Company, 1869.

Favorite Authors in Prose and Poetry. Edited by James T. Fields. Boston: J. R. Osgood and Company, 1885.

A Few Verses for a Few Friends. [Cambridge: Privately printed, 1858?]

"A Free Lecture Experience," *Harper's New Monthly Magazine*, LIX (June 1879), 76.

"Getting Home Again," *Atlantic Monthly*, VII (February 1861), 196.

A Gift for You of Prose and Poetic Gems. Selections by James T. Fields. Edited by Eugene Sinclair. Boston: G. W. Cottrell, 1859.

Good Company for Every Day in the Year. Boston: Ticknor and Fields, 1866.

Hawthorne. Boston: J. R. Osgood and Company, 1876.

Household Friends for Every Season. Boston: Ticknor and Fields, 1864.

"How to Rough It," *Atlantic Monthly*, VIII (December 1861), 757.

"Impromptu Verses. Read at the Bookseller's Dinner, Given by Mr. G. P. Putnam, the Publisher at the Astor House." Broadside in Massachusetts Historical Society collection, n. d.

In and Out of Doors with Charles Dickens. Boston: J. R. Osgood and Company, 1876.

"Looking for Pearls," *Atlantic Monthly*, XXVII (March 1871), 287.

"Masters of the Situation." [Exeter, 1875?]

"The Memory of Moore." May 28, 1879. Broadside in the Huntington Library [1879].

"My Absent Friend." Attributed to James T. Fields. Broadside in the Huntington Library [1871].

"My Friend's Library," *Atlantic Monthly*, VIII (October 1861), 440.

"A New and True Ghost Story." [Manchester by the Sea, 1879.]

Old Acquaintance. Barry Cornwall and Some of His Friends. Boston: J. R. Osgood and Company, 1876.

"Our Whispering Gallery," *Atlantic Monthly*, XXVII (January to June 1871), 122, 246, 380, 504, 639, 763; XXVIII (July to December 1871), 106, 222, 358, 501, 624, 750.

"The Owl-Critic," *Harper's New Monthly Magazine*, LIX (July 1879), 177.

"A Peculiar Case," *Scribner's Monthly*, XIII (December 1876), 197.

"The Perpetuity of Song," *Atlantic Monthly*, XLVI (September 1880), 328.

"The Pettibone Lineage," *Atlantic Monthly*, XV (April 1865), 419.

Works of Fields

Poems. Boston: W. D. Ticknor and Company, 1849.

"The Poet Longfellow," *Tribune Popular Science.* Boston: H. L. Shepard and Co., 1874.

Poets and Poetry of America. Selections by James T. Fields. Edited by Rufus W. Griswold. Philadelphia: Abraham Hart, 1851.

Religio Medici. Sir Thomas Browne. Edited with biographical note on the author by James T. Fields. Boston: Roberts Bros., 1878.

Review of J. Cordy Jeaffreson's *A Book About Doctors, Atlantic Monthly,* IX (April 1862), 519.

Review of Alexander Carlyle's *Autobiography of Dr. Alexander Carlyle, Minister of Inveresk, Atlantic Monthly,* VII (February 1861), 249.

"The Sleeping Sentinel," *Atlantic Monthly,* XI (January 1863), 84.

"A Soldier's Ancestry," *Atlantic Monthly,* VIII (August 1861), 159.

"Some Memories of Charles Dickens," *Atlantic Monthly,* XXVI (August 1870), 235.

Some Noted Princes, Authors, and Statesmen of Our Time. James T. Fields et al. Edited by James Parton. New York: Thomas Y. Crowell and Co., 1885.

"The Stormy Petrel," *Atlantic Monthly,* VIII (November 1861), 581.

"Three Mile Cross," *Atlantic Monthly,* VI (September 1860), 355.

Underbrush. Boston: J. R. Osgood and Company, 1877.

Verses for a Few Friends. Cambridge: University Press [1879].

"A Watch that 'Wanted Cleaning,'" *A Subtreasury of American Humor.* Edited by E. B. White and Katherine S. White. New York: Coward-McCann, Inc., 1941.

"The White Throated Sparrow," *Atlantic Monthly,* XII (August 1863), 224.

Yesterdays with Authors. Boston: J. R. Osgood and Company, 1872.

INDEX

Agassiz, Louis, 164-166
Alcott, Amos Bronson, 304
Alcott, Louisa May, 315-317
Alden, Henry Mills, 363-364, 399-400
Aldrich, Thomas Bailey, 38, 148, 177, 207, 325
All the Year Round, 379-380, 382, 388-390
Allen and Ticknor, 8
Allen, Georgina Stowe, 282-284
Allibone, S. Austin, 11-12
Argosy, 390-392
Atlantic Almanac, 38, 62-63, 79-80, 94, 126-127, 198-200, 289
Atlantic Club, 26
Atlantic Monthly, founding, 26-28; purchase by Ticknor and Fields, 29; Fields's editorship, 29-34; contributions from Boston, 43-44; Lowell's editorship, 45-52; Howells as assistant editor, 143-161; Howells becomes editor, 160-161; contributions from New England, 183-184; contributions from outside New England, 325-326; contributions from England, 375-378

Babson, John J., 425
Bagby, G. W., 372
Bartol, Cyrus A., 38, 168-169
Beecher, Henry Ward, 167, 342-344
Bennoch, Francis, 228
Benson, Eugene, 172
Bigelow, Jacob, 74-75
Blackwood's Magazine, 291-292, 405
Boker, George Henry, 23, 24, 365-366
Boston Daily Advertiser, 123, 142
Boyd, Andrew Kennedy Hutchison, 378
Browne, Sir Thomas, 434
Brownell, Henry Howard, 76-77, 322
Browning, Robert, 395, 400-404; *Dramatis Personae*, 401-402; *The Ring and the Book*, 402-404
Bryant, William Cullen, 358-359
Buckle, Henry Thomas, 256-258
Burroughs, John, 367-368
Byron, Anna Isabella Milbanke, 290-295, 412-414

Carter and Hendee, 8
Cary, Alice, 360-361
Chapman and Hall, 209
Child, Lydia Maria Francis, 309-311
Christian Examiner, 250, 262
Christian Union, 298, 299
Clark, John S., 38
Clarke, Charles Cowden, 405
Clarke, James Freeman, 169-170
Clemens, Samuel Langhorne (Mark Twain), 148, 154, 356, 372
Cobbe, Mrs. Frances Power, 274
Coleridge, Hartley, 415
Continental Monthly, 105, 187-188, 334
Conway, Moncure Daniel, 372
Cooke, Rose Terry, 317-319
Cornhill Magazine, 268, 276-277, 334
Cranch, Christopher Pearse, 306-307
Crowe, Eyre Evans, 20-21
Curtis, George William, 22, 89, 238, 277-278, 307-308, 359

Da Costa, Susannah Conyers, 408-411
Darwin, Charles, 164-166
Davis, Jefferson, 32
Davis, Rebecca Blaine Harding, 370-372, 379-380
De Forest, John W., 154, 321-322
Demorest, Madam, 278-279
De Quincey, Thomas, 376, 434
The Dial, 306
Diaz, Abby Morton, 155-156, 305-306
Dickens, Charles, 94-95, 294, 379-386, 388-389, 434-435; *Edwin Drood*, 385; *George Silverman's Explanation*, 382-383; *Holiday Romance*, 381-382
Disraeli, Benjamin, 406
Dodge, Mary Abigail (Gail Hamilton), 3-4, 38, 240, 312-314
Dolby, George, 381-383
Draper, William, 260-261

Elderkin, John, 351-352
Eliot, Charles W., 166-167
Emerson, Ralph Waldo, 153, 231, 300-302, 426

Evans, Mary Anne (George Eliot), 418
Every Saturday, 38, 377

Fairbanks, C. B., 395
Felton, Cornelius, 379
Field, Margaret Beck, 7
Field, Michael, 7
Fields, Annie Adams, 3, 14-15, 22, 37, 62, 76, 83, 95, 106, 114, 120, 149, 155, 162-163, 200-201, 202-204, 206-207, 237, 242-243, 261-262, 278, 297, 309, 316, 319, 320, 353, 356, 363, 364, 383-384, 395, 397, 400, 403-404, 426, 427-428
Fields, Eliza Willard, 12-14
Fields, George A., 7
Fields, James T. LIFE: description, 3-5; birth, 7; Boston Mercantile Library Association, 8-9; to Boston, 9; marriages, 12-15; publishing, 16-18; in England, 18-20, 22-23; as publisher and editor of *Atlantic*, 29-34; publishing duties, 37-38; retirement, 39; relieves Lowell of editorship, 49-52; retirement, 421-422; lecturing, 424-425; death, 427

LETTERS: 12, 14-15, 18-19, 22-23, 25, 71, 85-98, 140, 142, 144, 149-150, 161-162, 186, 193, 194, 196-197, 197-198, 199, 201-202, 209, 212, 213, 218-219, 220, 221, 222-223, 225, 226, 230-234, 237-238, 239, 240, 304, 330, 332-339, 385, 396-397, 398-399, 402, 424, 425, 426

WORKS AND UNPUBLISHED LECTURES: 437-439; "Alfred Tennyson, the Man and the Poet," 425, 433; *Anniversary Poem*, 9, 429; "Arthur Hallam," 397; *Ballads and Other Verses*, 423, 429-430; "Barry Cornwall and His Friends," 161; *The Boston Book*, 11, 434; Browne's *Religio Medici*, 434; "Bubbles from an Ancient Pipe," 205, 423; "Charles Lamb, and his Friends," 425; "Cheerfulness," 432; "'Christopher North,' with Personal Recollections," 425; "Commerce," 10; De Quincey's *Writings*, 11, 434; "Fame," 205-206; *The Family Library of British Poetry*, 434; *Favorite Authors*, 11, 434; "Fiction, and Its Eminent Authors," 425; "A Free Lecture Experience," 431; "How to Rough It," 36-37; "Keats and Shelley, with the Story of Their Lives," 433; "Literary and Artistic Society in London Twenty-five Years Ago," 425; "Masters of the Situation," 425, 432; "My Friend's Library," 36; "Our Village Dogmatist," 431; "Our Whispering Gallery," 81, 423; "The Owl-Critic," 430; "The Pettibone Lineage," 37; "Pleasant Ghosts," 431; *Poems* (1849), 10; *Poems* (1854), 10; "The Post of Honor," 10; "The Sleeping Sentinel," 34; "A Soldier's Ancestry," 34; "Some Memories of Charles Dickens," 37, 386; "The Stormy Petrel," 34; "Sydney Smith, and his Work and Life," 425; Thackeray's *Early and Late Papers Hitherto Uncollected*, 434; "The Turtle and the Flamingo," 430; *Underbrush*, 423, 431; "A Watch that 'Wanted Cleaning,'" 431; "The White Throated Sparrow," 35; *Yesterdays with Authors*, 37, 81, 379, 383, 423, 434-436.

Fields, Osgood and Company, 38
Forten, Charlotte, 191-192
Francis, Susan, 368
Frank Leslie's Illustrated Weekly, 123
Frémont, Jesse, 369

Galaxy, 123
Giles, Henry, 212
Gilmore, James Roberts (Edmund Kirke), 32, 187-188
Godkin, Edwin Lawrence, 144
Godwin, Parke, 38-39
Goethe, Johann Wolfgang von, 263-264
Grant, Ulysses S., 33
Gray, Asa, 164-165
Greene, George W., 92-94
Griswold, Rufus Wilmot, 9, 11, 18-19
Guiccioli, Countess Teresa, 291-293

Hale, Edward Everett, 115-127; "The London Workingman's College," 115-116; "The Man without a Country," 118-120; "My Double; and How He Undid Me," 115; Sybarian sketches, 124-127
Hallam, Arthur, 397
Harper's New Monthly Magazine, 27-28; 161-162, 278, 363, 400, 423

Index

Harper's Weekly, 363, 377, 389-390
Harte, Francis Bret, 31, 148, 154, 368-369
Hawthorne, Nathaniel, 18, 22, 90-91, 208-243, 434-435; *American Note-Books*, 239-240; *The Blithedale Romance*, 209; "Chiefly about War Matters," 218-219; *Doctor Grimshaw's Secret*, 216; *The Dolliver Romance*, 231-235, 237, 238-239; *The Marble Faun*, 210-211, 212; *Our Old Home*, 210, 215-216, 220-231; *The Scarlet Letter*, 208; *Septimius Felton*, 216-217
Hawthorne, Sophia, 211, 237, 238-243
Hawthorne, Una, 236
Hay, John, 367
Hayne, Paul, 372
Hazewell, C. C., 176
Hearth and Home, 287
Hecker, Isaac T., 354
Hedge, Frederick, 108
Higginson, Thomas Wentworth, 29-30, 44, 46, 47, 48-49, 152, 172-173, 244-248, 250, 312, 314; "Americanism in Literature," 246-247; "Leaves from an Officer's Journal," 246; "Letter to a Young Contributor," 247-248
Hill, Thomas, 145
Holmes, Oliver Wendell, 38, 46, 70-83, 236-237, 293-295, 353, 427-428; *The Autocrat of the Breakfast-Table*, 70-71; "Dorothy Q," 81; *Elsie Venner (The Professor's Story)*, 71-72; *The Guardian Angel*, 75-78; *The Poet at the Breakfast-Table*, 81; *The Professor at the Breakfast-Table*, 71
H. O. Houghton and Company, 422
Houghton, H. O., 83
Houghton, Osgood and Company, 422
Howard, Mrs. John T., 271
Howe, Elias, 347-348
Howe, Julia Ward, 99-114; "Battle Hymn of the Republic," 104-105; *Lyrics of the Street*, 106-113; "The Manuscript," 99-101; *Passion Flowers*, 101
Howells, William Dean, 4-5, 67, 80, 81, 95-96, 139-163, 172-173, 293-294, 339, 356, 357, 365, 367, 369, 421; "Louis Lebeau's Conversion," 141; "The Pilot's Story," 139; *Venetian Life*, 142-143
Hunt, Leigh, 226

International Copyright Society, 38, 350
Irving, P. M., 89
Irving, Washington, 89

Jackson, Helen Maria Hunt, 314-315
James, Henry, 148-149, 178-179
Jaquess, James F., 32
Jeaffreson, J. Cordy, 35
Jewett, Sarah Orne, 320-321
Johnson, Andrew, 32-33

Keats, John, 405
Kennedy, John Pendleton, 372
King, Thomas Starr, 31
Kingsley, Charles, 261
Knickerbocker Magazine, 187

Lamb, Charles, 432
Landor, Walter Savage, 15, 376, 435
Larcom, Lucy, 38, 177
Leigh, Augusta, 292
Leland, Charles Godfrey, 54-55, 187-188
Lewes, George Henry, 418
Lieber, Francis, 372
Lincoln, Abraham, 32, 218-219, 271-273
Lippincott, Sara Jane Clarke (Grace Greenwood), 13-14
Lockhart, John Gibson, *Life of Scott*, 213-214
Longfellow, Henry Wadsworth, 9, 34, 84-98, 153, 237-238, 239-240, 396, 400, 429; "The Children's Hour," 85; "The Cumberland," 88; Dante sonnets, 91-92; *The Divine Comedy*, 88; "Morituri Salutamus," 96-97; "Paul Revere's Ride," 85-87; *Tales of a Wayside Inn*, 89
Longfellow, Samuel, 261
Lowell, James Russell, 26-27, 28-30, 38, 45-69, 72, 83, 84, 85, 115, 119, 128-129, 139, 143, 144, 153, 172-173, 210, 217, 239-240, 244, 249-250, 293-294, 302, 377; *Biglow Papers*, Second Series, 48, 53-54; *The Cathedral*, 68-69; "Two Scenes from the Life of Blondel," 56-58
Lowell, Mabel, 66-67, 399

443

McCarthy, Justin, 294
MacDonald, George, 425
Marseilles, Charles, 424-425
Martineau, Harriet, 291, 411-417; "Lady Byron," 412-414; "Lights of the Lake District," 414-416
Melville, Herman, 154, 364
Minor, John B., 61-62, 372
Mirror of Fashions, 278-279
Mitchell, Donald Grant (Ik Marvel), 38, 147, 206, 322, 425-426
Mitchell, Silas Weir, 121-123, 366-367
Mitford, Mary Russell, 19-20, 208-209, 434
Motley, John Lothrop, 71
Murdoch, James Edward, 74

Nation, 144
Neal, John, 359
New York Independent, 189, 269-270
New York Ledger, 340
New York Times, 393
New York Tribune, 398
Newman, Francis William, 261
Nichols, George, 116-117
North American Review, 38, 58, 59, 64, 340
Norton, Charles Eliot, 38, 151

Old and New, 127
Oliver, Marshal, 349-351
Once a Week, 387
Osgood, James R., 38, 293, 295, 383, 394, 421-422
Osgood (James R.) and Company, 38
Our Young Folks, 38, 60, 94, 131-132, 133, 138, 282, 381-382

Palfrey, Sara Hammond, 147-148
Parker, Theodore, 167-168
Parsons, Thomas W., 176
Parton, James, 340-357; "Chicago," 344-347; "Does It Pay to Smoke?" 352-353; "Henry Ward Beecher's Church," 342-344; "History of the Sewing Machine," 340, 347-348; "Our Roman Catholic Brethren," 349, 353-355
Parton, Sara Payson Willis (Fanny Fern), 340-344
Peabody, Elizabeth, 240-242

Peirce, Charles, 57-58
Phillips, Sampson and Company, 26-28
Piatt, John James, 57-58, 369
Piatt, Sarah Morgan, 58
Pierce, Franklin, 227-231, 236-237
Procter, Adelaide Anne, 380
Procter, Bryan Waller (Barry Cornwall), 434-435
Putnam, George W., 386

Reade, Charles, 386-394; *The Cloister and the Hearth*, 387-389; *A Good Fight*, 387; *Griffith Gaunt*, 390-394; *Hard Cash*, 389-390
Renan, Ernest, 260-261
Rossetti, Dante Gabriel, 153-154
Round Table, 393
Ruskin, John, 377

Sand, George, 103
Saturday Club, 26, 39
Schurz, Carl, 369-370
Severn, Joseph, 405
Sheppard, Elizabeth Sara, 406-411; *Grey Magic*, 406-408.
Smith, Elder, and Company, 228-229, 402
Spofford, Harriet Elizabeth Prescott, 147, 311-312, 409-410
Stebbins, L., 133
Stedman, Edmund Clarence, 361-363, 397-399
Stillé, Charles Janeway, 124-125
Story, William Wetmore, 55
Stowe, Calvin, 286-287, 289-290
Stowe, Charles, 299
Stowe, Fred, 270-271
Stowe, Harriet Beecher, 80, 158-160, 177, 231, 266-299, 414; *Agnes of Sorrento*, 267-271; *The Chimney-Corner (Little Foxes)*, 279-285; *The Chimney-Corner for 1866*, 286-287; *House and Home Papers*, 266-267, 275-280; *Lady Byron Vindicated*, 291-292, 295; *Men of Our Times*, 287; *Oldtown Fireside Stories*, 295-299; *Oldtown Folks*, 288; "Our Martyrs," 282-284; "Reply to the Address of the Women of England," 271-274; "The True Story of Lady Byron's Life," 290-295
Sumner, Charles, 32, 39, 170-172, 189

Index

Taylor, Bayard, 152, 161, 192-193, 237, 325-326, 327-339, 353, 397-399, 426; "The Bath," 328-329; *By-Ways of Europe*, 332-333, 336; "A Cruise on Lake Ladoga," 331-332; *Joseph and His Friend*, 336; "Notus Ignoto," 337-339; "The Sunshine of the Gods," 337-339; "Travel in the United States," 332
Tennyson, Alfred, 375-376, 395-400, 404; "The Victim," 397
Tennyson, Emily, 404
Thackeray, William Makepeace, 20-22, 329-330, 434-435
Thaxter, Celia, 319-320
Thoreau, Henry David, 46-47, 232-233, 245, 302-304
Ticknor and Fields, 16, 29, 37-38, 312-313, 350
Ticknor, Howard M., 38
Ticknor, Reed and Fields, 16
Ticknor, William D., 8, 235-236
Ticknor (William D.) and Company, 10, 16
Tiffany, Osmond, 372
Tilton and Company, 134-136
Trollope, Anthony, 212, 214-215
Trowbridge, John Townsend, 38, 128-138; *Coupon Bonds*, 132; Jack Hazard novels, 131-132; "The Jaguar Hunt," 130-131; *The South*, 133-136; "The Vagabonds," 129
Trübner, Nicholas, 31

Underwood, Francis H., 26-27, 128-129, 364, 377
United States Sanitary Commission, 124-125

Vallandigham, Clement L., 118

Wasson, David Atwood, 249-265; "Mr. Buckle as a Thinker," 256-258; "Ease in Work," 251-252; "Ice and Esquimaux," 262-263; "Individuality," 253-255; "Light Literature," 251-252; "The New World and the New Man," 250; "Time's Household," 250; "Whittier," 259-260
Watchman and Reflector, 276-277, 285
Weiss, John, 176
Welch, Bigelow and Company, 37
Winthrop, Theodore, 359-360
Whipple, Edwin Percy, 8-9, 146-147, 172-177
White, Andrew D., 39
Whitman, Walt, 45-46, 52, 364, 425
Whitney, Mrs. A. D. T., 176
Whittier, John Greenleaf, 71, 89-90, 185-207, 259-260; "Abraham Davenport," 194; "Among the Hills," 200-201; "Andrew Rykman's Prayer," 189-190; "Barbara Frietchie," 191; "The Countess," 190-191; "Freedom in Brazil," 197-198; "G. L. S.," 196-197; "Marguerite," 204; "Mountain Pictures," 186-187; "Peace Autumn," 193; *Snow-Bound*, 193-194; *The Tent on the Beach*, 194-197; "The Two Rabbis," 202
Willard, Mary, 12
Willis, Richard Storrs, 12
Wister, Annis Lee, 122
Wordsworth, William, 434

Youth's Companion, 97

B FIELDS, J. T.
Austin, James C ed.
Fields of the Atlantic monthly: letters to an editor, 1861-1870.